Exchange Rates, Capital Flows and Policy

T0361184

As globalisation progresses, exchange rate and international capital movements matter more and more. The choice of exchange rate, capital mobility and monetary policies cannot be mutually independent. Among the themes explored here are four important and interrelated questions:

- Which of the many different approaches to modelling exchange rates works best in practice?
- How much emphasis should be placed on the exchange rate when setting monetary policy?
- What determines and explains capital flows and their impact?
- What should policy makers do about monetary policy and capital flows?

This book combines thorough scholarship with illuminating real-world examples to shed light on these key issues. It is the culmination of two international research workshops held at the Centre for Central Banking Studies in the Bank of England. Using contributions by leading academics and policy makers, the editors have produced a book that will be of great value to both academics and practitioners.

Rebecca Driver is research adviser to the external members of the Monetary Policy Committee of the Bank of England. **Peter Sinclair** is Professor of Economics at the University of Birmingham, and was Director of the Centre for Central Banking Studies at the Bank of England from 2000 to 2002. **Christoph Thoenissen** is a former Bank of England economist who now teaches at the University of St Andrews.

Routledge international studies in money and banking

Exchange Rates, Capital Flows and Policy

Edited by Rebecca Driver, Peter Sinclair and Christoph Thoenissen

Routledge
Taylor & Francis Group

LONDON AND NEW YORK

First published 2005
by Routledge
2 Park Square, Milton Park, Abingdon, Oxon OX14 4RN

Simultaneously published in the USA and Canada
by Routledge
711 Third Avenue, New York, NY 10017

Routledge is an imprint of the Taylor & Francis Group

First issued in paperback 2012

Transferred to Digital Printing 2005

© 2005 The Bank of England

Typeset in Times by Wearset Ltd, Boldon, Tyne and Wear

British Library Cataloguing in Publication Data
A catalogue record for this book is available from the British Library

Library of Congress Cataloging in Publication Data
A catalog record for this book has been requested

ISBN 978-0-415-35263-5 (Hardback)
      978-0-415-64768-7 (Paperback)

Contents

Contributors

Rodrigo Caputo, Cambridge University, UK and Central Bank of Chile
Rebecca Driver, Bank of England, UK
Barry Eichengreen, University of California, Berkeley, USA
Charles Engel, University of Wisconsin, USA
Paul De Grauwe, University of Leuven, Belgium
Marianna Grimaldi, Sveriges Riksbank, Sweden
Paul Hallwood, University of Connecticut, USA
Douglas Hostland, Bank of Canada, Canada
Kalin Hristov, Bulgarian National Bank, Bulgaria
Dan Huynh, Bank of England, UK (at time of writing)
Mervyn King, Governor of the Bank of England, UK
Philip Lane, Trinity College Dublin, Republic of Ireland
Ian Marsh, Sir John Cass Business School, City University, UK
John H. Rogers, Board of Governors of the Federal Reserve System, USA
Jörg Scheibe, University of Oxford, UK
Lawrence Schembri, Bank of Canada, Canada
Ozge Senay, Middle East Technical University, Ankara, Turkey
Byung Han Seo, Bank of Korea, Korea
Peter Sinclair, University of Birmingham, UK
Peter N. Smith, University of York, UK
Steffen Sorensen, University of York, UK
Alan Sutherland, University of St Andrews, UK
Izumi Takagawa, Bank of Japan, Japan
Christoph Thoenissen, University of St Andrews, UK
Shing-Yi Wang, Yale University, USA
Peter Westaway, Bank of England, UK
Mike Wickens, University of York, UK

Foreword

Few subjects in macroeconomics arouse more controversy among both academics and policy makers alike than the exchange rate. And despite many intellectual breakthroughs, economists are still grappling with fundamental questions: What determines the rate of exchange of one currency against another? What impact do movements in exchange rates have on key economic variables? How should monetary policy respond to movements in the exchange rate?

This book brings together a collection of new research and insights which, I am sure, will contribute richly to the debate on the role of exchange rate in monetary policy design. The chapters are a diverse set that illustrate the wide range of empirical and theoretical approaches used to improve our understanding of the links between the exchange rate, capital flows and monetary policy.

The genesis of this book was two research workshops held at the Bank of England under the auspices of the Bank's Centre for Central Banking Studies. One was on Exchange Rates, which ran between 10 September 2001 and 26 November 2001. The other was on Capital Movements which ran from 10 June 2002 until 30 August 2002. I am very grateful to all the authors who contributed to the book and to all those who helped to make the workshops such a success.

Mervyn King
Governor of the Bank of England

1 Introduction

Rebecca Driver, Peter Sinclair and Christoph Thoenissen

Setting the scene

Exchange rates and capital flows are inseparable. Beyond the confines of barter, foreign trade requires either a loan or immediate cash settlement, in a currency that is foreign to the importer or the exporter (and sometimes to both). So trade frequently triggers capital flows. The time dimension of trade is richer still. Just as trades do not have to be balanced, they do not need to be synchronised either. This year's exports may be spent on future imports, or alternatively may be paying for previous imports. Intertemporal trade implies capital flows must take place, as agents are trading claims on future income. International capital flows do not just allow agents to restructure the time-profiles of their expected purchases and production: they can provide insurance, too. Capital flows permit trade across states as well as trade across dates. Capital flows may therefore also trigger trade. The price mechanism that triggers adjustment in trade flows will be linked to the exchange rate.

As claims are almost always denominated in currencies alien to at least one party, the exchange rate system – both now, and in the future – is central in allowing agents to understand how the value of these are likely to change over time. In a fixed exchange rate regime that is perfectly credible it is easy to calculate the expected local currency value of a claim denominated in the linked currency. If the exchange rate is floating then this will be harder. If the fixed exchange rate regime is less than perfectly credible, capital flows may themselves trigger a change in the regime.

This is particularly true as foreign exchange markets are now dominated by international flows of capital. These dwarf current transactions many times over, at least for advanced countries. International financial trade has grown very rapidly, and raises a fascinating set of questions that researchers have only recently started to get to grips with. Models of exchange rates limited to current account flows have ceased to be appropriate simplifications of reality. What is more, sudden revisions to expectations of the future values of exchange rates are a prime generator of capital flows. Despite this, a growing number of countries retain few if any controls on the international migration of capital, for either domestic or foreign residents.

Countries with obligations to non-residents expressed in foreign currencies are frequently worried about the effects of their own currency depreciation, because this will directly raise the home-money value of the costs of servicing them. The "fear of floating" literature (e.g. Calvo and Reinhart 2002) emphasises this point; its implications for inflation targeting by emerging countries are particularly important. More generally, a floating exchange rate regime introduces a new element of uncertainty about these costs, which ought to disappear under an enduring and fully sustainable peg to the currency in which these obligations are denominated. But a fixed-but-adjustable regime also carries risks, because the parity can be changed. In the experiences of many East Asian countries in 1997–1998, and of Argentina in 2001–2002, the role of foreign currency denominated obligations was all too plain. They helped to trigger large depreciations, and, at the same time, ensured that these depreciations were considerably more painful than they otherwise would have been – and more problematic from a financial stability viewpoint, as well.

What the fear-of-floating issue illustrates vividly is the fact that a country with a sufficiently high degree of exchange rate fixity on the one side, and international capital mobility on the other, cannot expect to be able to exercise a completely free monetary policy. If foreign currency denominated debt concerns incline you to reject a floating exchange rate, then you either have to subordinate monetary policy to exchange rate defence, or else be prepared, like Malaysia after the Asian crisis, to apply capital controls. This testifies to the "impossible trinity", or the claim that a country can, if it wishes, combine any pair of three policy frameworks (a fixed exchange rate, open capital markets and monetary independence), but never all three. Many of the contributions to this book may be seen as explorations of this theme – concentrating, for example, on the relationship between one of these three possible pairs of policy frameworks.

Among the key questions confronting policy makers and academics concerned with international economics today – questions on which several of the contributions to this book throw light – are the following:

1 What bearing do inflation targeting regimes have on exchange rate policy? Do they – and should they – imply that clean floating is best? Or should inflation targeters keep track of exchange rates too, and countenance changes to monetary policy decisions in the light of them? And do exchange rate considerations in fact make inflation targeting inappropriate for emerging countries?

2 Does floating the exchange rate increase or reduce welfare in comparison with holding to a fixed peg?

3 What are the special challenges to countries that adopt hard pegs,

such as currency boards, and what does evidence tell us about them and the factors that govern their sustainability?

4 What are the various meanings we can attach to *equilibrium* exchange rates, and how are they defined and measured? What does evidence tell us about the Law of One Price?

5 What influence does risk have on exchange rates?

6 What determines the dynamics of the current and capital accounts of a country's balance of payments, and how are these related to nominal and real exchange rate movements? When capital can move across international boundaries, what determines the evolution of different countries' net asset positions, and how is this related to paths for other important variables like real exchange rates and output?

7 What determines the sustainability of different net foreign asset positions? How important is the role of external debt in this? Do exchange rate regimes have a role to play?

8 Why do some countries open their capital accounts to free movement, and others not?

9 How effective is government intervention in the foreign exchange market? What particular difficulties does sterilisation pose?

10 How much noise is there in the foreign exchange market? How do exchange rates respond to news? Why are real exchange rates sometimes subject to big lurches, at first in one direction and then in the other?

This is not the place to probe all ten of these important questions: the book itself does that. But it is instructive to ponder one aspect of the last one. Two spectacular examples of exchange rate lurches are provided by the behaviour of the US dollar in the mid 1980s, and the euro immediately following its introduction. The US dollar climbed by over 35 per cent against a weighted average of other OECD currencies from 1982 to January 1985, and at an accelerating rate; then it suddenly reversed direction, falling back by almost as much in the following two years. The euro fell by over a quarter against the US dollar from its introduction in 1999 until late 2000. In early 2002 the euro then started to rise against the dollar, so that by end-2003 it was above its initial level. The experience of the euro against many other currencies was very similar.

Two sets of explanations can be offered for both episodes. One is that they are classic instances of bubbles that first grow, and then burst. Behind this account often lies the view that many foreign exchange market participants are chartists, inclined to extrapolative expectations based on recent short-term movements; but eventually the pressure from resulting real exchange rate disequilibria snaps, and fundamentals reassert themselves. Those who hold this view would look askance at a "news" interpretation of events, dismissing it, perhaps, as an ex post rationalisation.

That alternative story is based on the more optimistic hypothesis that foreign exchange markets should process information rapidly and efficiently. It would emphasise the significance of news leading to sharp re-evaluations of fundamentals. News could relate to President Reagan's fiscal policies and budget deficit projections, and the conflict between their immediate and longer run effects. Traditional (Mundell-Fleming) theory teaches that unilateral fiscal expansion, under full international capital mobility, should lead at once to exchange rate appreciation, to terms of trade improvement, to transfer resources from the current account of the balance of payments to the government. But with foreigners buying many of the newly minted government bonds, long-term equilibrium requires these to be serviced by trade *surpluses*, which only real exchange rate *depreciation* can engender. Some recent theories (like the Obstfeld and Rogoff "Redux" model (1995)) show that unilateral fiscal expansion should lead to immediate depreciation, not appreciation. But they might account for the events of the mid 1980s with the idea that there were large changes in people's beliefs about the future path of US fiscal (and monetary) policy.

The dollar-euro puzzle of 2000–2003 might be explained on not dissimilar lines. Bearish attitudes to the euro made much of the contrast between much of the euro area and the United States in output, employment and productivity growth patterns, observed and projected. These differences could have led market participants from say 1999 to late 2001 to anticipate higher policy interest rates for the US and lower ones for the euro area. But from late 2001 onwards, concerns about America's false profit accounting scandals, exaggerations in the expectations of trend productivity, and the long run need to generate trade surpluses to service her overseas debts, and mounting evidence of the euro area's abnormally large external competitiveness, could have prompted the euro's rapid recovery against the dollar.

Competing explanations for phenomena are widespread in international economics – better that there should be two or more accounts that appear to fit the facts, than none! So a crucial concept underlying many models is either what the exchange rate *ought* to be, or *ought to be eventually*. Some would follow the "new school" line, arguing that the current values of nominal and real exchange rates embody all relevant information, and therefore that they are what they ought to be anyway, if freely floating in a mature market. But even if today's (real) exchange rate between a pair of economies were what it "ought to be", that does not mean that it would be at what it "ought to be eventually". There are, in fact, many different possible meanings to this latter term. Such uncertainty often makes it hard for policy makers to know how to respond to exchange rate changes and what role to give the exchange rate when formulating policy.

The plan of the book

One of the big questions facing any country is what to do about exchange rate policy. It is probably unsurprising therefore that roughly half of the chapters in this book deal directly with different aspects of the theory and practice of exchange rate policy, particularly (although by no means exclusively) in the context of emerging market economies.

The book starts with a discussion by Barry Eichengreen about whether movements in the exchange rate will limit the ability of policy makers in emerging markets to pursue an inflation target. In any open economy, movements in exchange rates will affect inflation both through their impact on import prices and on the profits of domestic firms. The more open an economy is, the more important this channel will be. In addition, however, in emerging markets factors such as the existence of foreign currency liabilities which are difficult to hedge may mean that exchange rate movements could also have adverse repercussions for financial and fiscal stability. This in turn could force policy makers to choose between different objectives, potentially undermining their monetary policy credibility.

One implication of this is that in practice countries may choose to attempt to limit the size of exchange rate fluctuations – Calvo and Reinhart's (2002) famous fear of floating argument. This is confirmed, at least in the context of Chile, in the chapter by Rodrigo Caputo. The analysis in this chapter suggests that policy makers in Chile have used interest rates to react to exchange rate changes by more than they would have done, had they simply reacted to their inflationary implications. In addition the strength of this reaction has been greater for large exchange rate deviations than for small changes. Furthermore, if anything the response of policy rates to exchange rate changes increased following the decision in September 1999 to abandon an explicit exchange rate target zone (in addition to the inflation target).

Of course simply because inflation targeting is hard in open economies, does not necessarily make the alternatives any easier. The chapter by Ozge Senay and Alan Sutherland examines the welfare implications of the choice between fixed and floating exchange rate regimes. One of the roles of the exchange rate is to act as a shock absorber, enabling relative prices to change and so acting as a trigger for expenditure switching. However, there are certain factors which act to limit the degree to which expenditure switching takes place. One of these is the extent to which the pricing policies of firms act to limit the degree of relative prices adjustment. When prices are set in local currency, firms will not adjust their prices following exchange rate changes (at least in the short term), implying that there will be no shift in relative prices to trigger expenditure switching. However, another factor which limits the extent of expenditure switching is whether or not domestic and foreign goods are close substitutes. Low substitutability implies that expenditure switching will be limited. Senay and Sutherland show that the volatility of consumption is unambiguously lower in a floating rather than a fixed exchange rate regime. However the volatility of output is only lower in a floating exchange rate regime when the degree of substitutability between domestic and foreign goods is low. Welfare is therefore higher in a fixed exchange rate regime when the expenditure switching effects following an exchange rate change are strong.

Another aspect of fixed exchange rate regimes is the choice of which currency to fix to. There is a rich literature on the so-called optimum currency areas (or OCAs), which starts with the work of Mundell (1961) and McKinnon (1963). European Monetary Union has led to many recent advances in our knowledge of this issue. One of the implications of the literature is that the degree of symmetry of the economies involved, and particularly the symmetry of supply shocks, matters for the success of any fixed exchange rate regime. Paul Hallwood, Ian Marsh and Jörg Scheibe use this insight to examine one potential cause of the collapse of Argentina's currency board arrangement, namely the symmetry of the shocks hitting Argentina and the US. In general they find that the shocks hitting these two economies, particularly supply shocks, tended to be highly asymmetric. Given this, moving to an even harder peg, for example by dollarising, probably would not have helped. Argentina's decision to abandon its currency board did not arise because of a lack of credibility inherent in currency board arrangements relative to other fixed exchange rate regimes. Instead the issue was the compatibility of the two economies.

In addition to the symmetry of the shocks facing the economies within a fixed exchange rate arrangement, another issue that will determine a regime's survival chances is the extent of misalignment implied by the difference between the actual exchange rate and its equilibrium level. The difficulty is that exactly what is meant by equilibrium in this, and any other, context is potentially controversial. This controversy provides the motivation for the assessment by Rebecca Driver and Peter Westaway of exactly what is meant by the term equilibrium exchange rate. Driver and Westaway emphasise that there is no one correct measure of equilibrium and instead it is important to decide on the appropriate measure based on the question of interest. At any point in time there will be a set of short-, medium- and long-term factors which affect the exchange rate and the measure of the equilibrium exchange rate will therefore vary depending on the time horizon of interest.

In the context of fixing exchange rates, medium-term considerations are likely to be important for the durability of the peg. One well known method of estimating medium-term equilibrium exchange rates, discussed in Driver and Westaway, is the so-called FEER or Fundamental Equilibrium Exchange Rate approach. FEERs are therefore used by Kalin Hristov to investigate the degree of exchange rate misalignment for two currency board countries, Argentina and Estonia, over the 1990s. Hristov finds that the degree of exchange rate misalignment experienced by Argentina was not large. Although the Argentine peso was overvalued over the second half of the currency board arrangement, the size of this misalignment was estimated to be around 6 per cent at most. This suggests that other factors, such as fiscal policy, may bear the greater share of blame for the collapse of the Argentine currency board. If fiscal policy remains inconsistent with the monetary policy framework, whatever form it takes, that framework is ultimately doomed.

Possibly the best known theory of equilibrium exchange rates is that of purchasing power parity (PPP). One of the theories closely associated with PPP is that of the law of one price whereby the prices charged in different locations will be equal when adjusted into the same currency. Charles Engel, John Rogers and Shing-Yi Wang are able to use data on specific prices to examine whether long-term deviations from the law of one price exist for US and Canadian cities. They find that these can be greater than 7 per cent.

Peter Smith, Steffen Sorensen and Mike Wickens look at a very different set of factors which underlie exchange rate movements, namely those related to the risk premium. In particular, they look at how risk premia in different financial markets are linked. The chapter concentrates on risk in two financial markets, namely the FOREX and equity markets and models excess returns from the perspective of a UK investor. They find that the risk premium in the equity market is generally much more variable than that in the FOREX market. In addition they find further clear evidence against consumption-based capital asset pricing models (CCAPM), both from the perspective of individual asset returns and across assets.

Christoph Thoenissen's chapter analyses the relationship between the real exchange rate and the current account and looks at whether a country's existing net foreign asset position may be important. Thoenissen uses a model which allows for failures in the law of one price and finds that there is no unique structural link between the real exchange rate and the current account. Real exchange rate appreciations are as likely to be associated with capital inflows as they are with capital outflows. One of the key determinants of the sign of the correlation between the real exchange rate and the current account balance is the net foreign asset position.

The evolution and determinants of net foreign asset positions are the focus of Philip Lane's chapter. He provides an overview of the recent research that seeks to explain the spectacular growth of international financial trade and its macroeconomic implications. The chapter considers the determinants of net foreign asset positions, as well as their implications for a range of key macroeconomic variables, including the trade balance, the real exchange rate and the risk premium.

The links between exchange rate flexibility, openness, capital flows and the sustainability of external debt is the subject of the chapter by Douglas Hostland and Lawrence Schembri. The hypothesis of this chapter is that emerging market economies that have flexible exchange rates and are relatively open to trade can sustain higher levels of external debt. This is because such economies can more easily sustain shocks to capital flows. In particular, the necessary adjustment to external shocks takes place both through import compression and expenditure switching. The effectiveness of these channels is in turn determined by the degree of nominal exchange rate flexibility, as well as the degree of pass-through.

One of the ways in which countries have attempted to shield themselves from sharp swings in the resources available is through capital controls. The chapter by Dan Huynh and Peter Sinclair examines empirically which type of country typically does this. It examines whether the likelihood of imposing capital controls is non-linear in income, as well as looking at the impact of inflation volatility on this decision.

The final three chapters of this book return to the issue of exchange rate policy looking at different aspects of countries' ability to intervene in the foreign exchange market.

Izumi Takagawa's chapter examines whether a set of seven East Asian countries have been able to conduct simultaneously an independent monetary policy, maintain a degree of control over the exchange rate, as well as allow the free movement of capital across borders. The findings of this chapter suggest that Mundell and Fleming's impossible trinity had indeed been violated, but only temporarily, up until the onset of the Asian financial crisis in 1998.

Byung Han Seo's chapter analyses the effects of foreign exchange market interventions on the central bank's ability to control monetary aggregates. Focusing on the Korean experience, the author finds that the effects of foreign exchange market interventions on the monetary base can be successfully sterilised in the short term, but not however in the long-term. In the long term, even sterilised foreign exchange market interventions have had a significant effect on the growth of Korea's monetary base.

Paul De Grauwe and Marianna Grimaldi also focus on the effectiveness of sterilised interventions in the foreign exchange market. De Grauwe and Grimaldi use a model in which chartists and fundamentalists interact. Such a model produces speculative noise, which leads to systematic deviations of the exchange rate from its fundamentals. This causes exchange rates to be subject to the type of lurches discussed in the context of question 10 above. In such an environment, sterilised interventions can reduce the level of speculative noise thereby reducing the profitability of noise trading.

The purpose of this introduction has been to raise the main issues explored in this book and to give the reader some foretaste of its contributions. The main findings are gathered and assessed at the end of the book.

References

Calvo, G. and Reinhart, C. (2002), "Fear of floating", *Quarterly Journal of Economics*, 177: 379–408.

McKinnon, R.I. (1963), "Optimum currency areas", *American Economic Review*, 53: 717–725.

Mundell, R.A. (1961), "A theory of optimum currency areas", *American Economic Review*, 51: 657–665.

Obstfeld, M. and Rogoff, K. (1995), "Exchange rate dynamics redux", *Journal of Political Economy*, 103: 624–660.

2 Can emerging markets float? Should they inflation target?[1]

Barry Eichengreen

1 Introduction

The hot debate over the best monetary-cum-exchange-rate regime for developing countries shows no signs of cooling down. The Asian crisis and its fallout in Latin America and Eastern Europe have convinced many observers that soft currency pegs are crisis prone and that emerging markets should embrace greater exchange rate flexibility. The Turkish crisis reinforced that view. But worries that greater flexibility will impede market access, hinder financial development, and undermine rather than underpin financial stability have led others to advocate moving in the opposite direction – that is, hardening the peg by installing a currency board or dollarizing.[2] While there are prominent examples of countries that have moved both ways – Ecuador and El Salvador have dollarized while Brazil has embraced greater flexibility – many developing countries continue to occupy the middle ground in the sense of making extensive use of their reserves so as to limit the variability of their exchange rates.[3]

The one thing all of these regimes have in common is that none is an entirely comfortable solution to the monetary dilemma. Flexible rates tend to fluctuate erratically, especially if abandonment of a peg leaves a country without a nominal anchor, a clear and coherent monetary policy operating strategy, and credibility in the eyes of the markets. Unilateral dollarization limits policy flexibility, gives the country resorting to it no voice in the monetary policy it runs, and sacrifices seigniorage revenues. And ad hoc intervention to limit the variability of the exchange rate in the absence of a credible commitment to a transparent, coherent, and defensible monetary strategy is unlikely to inspire confidence; attempting to prevent the exchange rate from moving beyond set limits under these circumstances can render the central bank and its reserves sitting ducks for speculators. That none of these options is particularly appealing is, of course, the dilemma of a world in which markets are international but governments are national. It is why authors like Mundell (2000) and Cooper (1999) see a global currency and a global central bank as logical consequences of the globalization of markets.

Notwithstanding this vision for the future, countries opening their economies to capital flows will be forced, for the present, to choose from this limited menu of hard pegs (currency boards, dollarization), implicit target zones (de jure floating but de facto intervention to limit the variability of the exchange rate), and greater flexibility.[4] Other authors have made the case for the first two options, what can be called hard and soft or loud and quiet pegs.[5] In this chapter I consider the viability of the third.

Calling for emerging markets to abandon the exchange rate as an anchor for policy compels those issuing the call to offer an alternative.[6] The leading candidate is inflation targeting.[7] The task I take on in this chapter is to assess whether inflation targeting offers a viable alternative to an exchange-rate based monetary policy regime.

There has been some analysis of inflation targeting in emerging markets, most of it recent (the pioneering work is Masson *et al.* 1997; see also Eichengreen *et al.* 1999; Eichengreen 2000; Christoffersen and Wescott 1999; Mishkin 2000a; Mishkin and Savastano 2000; Bogdanski *et al.* 2000; Devereux and Lane 2000; Jonas 2000; Morande 2000; Schaechter *et al.* 2000). But none of these studies has considered the entire range of issues. And most have failed to distinguish between open-economy and developing-country aspects of inflation targeting.

I organize my discussion as follows. Section 2 defines inflation targeting and reviews some conceptual issues relating to its implementation. (Readers familiar with this literature may want to skip or skim this material.) Section 3 then asks what is distinctive about inflation targeting in open economies. Issues that arise in this section include susceptibility to external shocks and the sensitivity of output and inflation to the exchange rate. Section 4 then asks what is distinctive about inflation targeting in emerging markets. Topics in this section include passthrough, the difficulty of forecasting inflation, liability dollarization, and credibility issues.

The conclusion then returns to the question of whether inflation targeting is an option for emerging markets.

2 General Considerations[8]

I define inflation targeting as a monetary policy operating strategy with four elements: an institutionalized commitment to price stability as the primary goal of monetary policy; mechanisms rendering the central bank accountable for attaining its monetary policy goals; the public announcement of targets for inflation; and a policy of communicating to the public and the markets the rationale for the decisions taken by the central bank.[9] Institutionalizing the commitment to price stability lends credibility to that objective and gives the central bank the independence needed to pursue it. Mechanisms for accountability make this pursuit politically acceptable and impose costs on central banks that are incompetent or behave opportunistically. Announcing a target for inflation and articulating the basis for the central bank's decisions allows these mechanisms to operate.

The multi-dimensional nature of this definition explains why there is no consensus about which emerging markets are inflation targeters. Brazil, Chile, the Czech Republic, Israel, South Africa, Poland, Colombia, Thailand, Mexico, the Philippines, and South Korea are all cited in this connection.[10] But while all of these countries have announced numerical targets for inflation, not all of them have put in place the other elements of inflation targeting as defined above. At the time of writing, most observers would probably draw the line between the first five and last six countries, classifying only the former as full-fledged inflation targeters.

One can further distinguish "strict" inflation targeting from "flexible" inflation targeting. Strict inflation targeting is when only inflation enters the central bank's objective function, flexible inflation targeting is when there is also a positive weight on other variables, output for example (Svensson 1999). (Even with strict inflation targeting there is still a positive weight on output in the policy reaction function insofar as the information content of the output gap is useful for forecasting inflation.[11]) Since few central banks and polities are prepared to disregard all other variables under all circumstances, flexible inflation targeting is the policy-relevant case.[12]

This has a number of implications. Most obviously, whereas a central bank that targets inflation strictly will attempt to hit that target as quickly as possible under all circumstances (where the feasible speed depends on the control lag from its policy instruments to inflation), a central bank that pursues flexible inflation targeting will tend to push inflation toward its target more gradually. It will balance the benefits of minimizing the variability of inflation against the costs of creating additional variability in the other variables that enter its objective function.

So defined, inflation targeting is a "target rule," where policy is formulated to hit an appropriately weighted set of ex ante specified policy objectives. The question is how to move from a target rule to an "instrument rule" – that is, settings for the policy instrument or instruments as a function of the information available to policy makers.[13] This is not straightforward in a complex economy.[14] Three imperfect solutions are to fly by the seat of the central bank's pants, inflation-forecast targeting, and the Taylor rule. I consider these alternatives in turn.

Seat-of-the-pants inflation targeting (using everything from in-house econometric models to central banker's intuition to guide the setting of policy instruments) is what many central banks do – some with considerable success. But it is unlikely to be efficient insofar as it is not systematized. And to the extent that the rationale for the central bank's decision cannot be articulated and defended, it will lack credibility.[15]

Targeting the central bank's inflation forecast (conditional on the information available at the time of the forecast) is an example of an "intermediate targeting rule" that specifies a vector of intermediate targets that are correlated with the ultimate policy goal but easier to control and observe than the ultimate goal (Svensson 1999). Inflation forecast targeting should be more efficient than formulating policy on the basis of an ad hoc reaction function insofar as the policy instruments respond to all the information that is relevant to the forecast. It will have more credibility than the alternatives if the central bank has a track record of accurate forecasting.[16]

That seat-of-the-pants inflation targeting is arbitrary and that inflation-forecast targeting is no more reliable than the forecast have motivated the search for simple rules. The Taylor rule is the leading example. Taylor (1993) specifies a reaction function for a closed economy with positive weights on deviations from target inflation and from the natural rate of unemployment that closely tracks the actual policies followed by many central banks that target low inflation. Contributors to the closed-economy literature have shown how a Taylor rule can be derived as the optimal reaction function for a strictly inflation-targeting central bank. Let the economy be represented as:

$$\pi_{\tau+1} = \pi_{\tau} + \alpha(y_t - y^*) + \epsilon_{t+1} \tag{1}$$
$$y_{t+1} - y^* = \lambda(y_t - y^*) - \beta(r_t - r^*) + n_{t+1} \tag{2}$$

Equation (1) is an accelerationist Phillips Curve, where the change in inflation (π) between this period and next is a function of this period's gap between actual output (y) and its natural level (y*) and of a disturbance (denoted ϵ_{t+1}). Equation (2) is aggregate demand, where next period's output gap is a function of this period's output gap, the deviation of the interest rate (r) from normal (r*), and a disturbance (n_{t+1}). The key assumption is that the control lag until inflation responds to the central bank's instrument (r) is longer than the control lag for aggregate demand (equivalently in the present context, that policy affects inflation only through the aggregate-demand channel).

Under strict inflation targeting, the optimal policy is to target inflation two periods ahead, setting $\pi_{t+2} = \pi^*$, where π^* denotes target inflation. (Inflation one period ahead is given by output in the current period, which is predetermined; hence inflation one period ahead cannot be controlled.) To solve for the optimal reaction function, shift equation (1) forward, substitute in (2), and set π_{t+2} (the two-year inflation forecast) equal to π^* (thus adopting a version of inflation-forecast targeting). This yields:

$$r_t = r^* + \phi(\pi_t - \pi^*) + \chi(y_t - y^*) \tag{3}$$

This is a Taylor rule with positive weights on deviations of inflation from target and of output from its natural rate, where the weights ϕ and χ

depend on the parameters α, λ, and β. We see the point mentioned above, that even under strict inflation targeting there is still a positive weight on output in the reaction function because of its information content for future inflation.

However, equation (3) is a peculiar Taylor rule. Strict inflation targeting implies sharp changes in the interest rate in response to deviations of inflation from target and output from its natural level, since $\phi = 1/(\alpha\beta)$ and $\chi = (1 + \lambda)/\beta$.[17] For example, if $\lambda = 0.8$, $\alpha = 0.4$, and $\beta = 0.6$, values that approximate realistic conditions, then we would observe changes in the interest rate in response deviations to both variables of several times the magnitude suggested by Taylor as matching the actual behavior of central banks.[18] This in turn implies very considerable output fluctuations. It is worth emphasizing that we obtain this solution only because we are assuming that the central bank cares exclusively about inflation to the total disregard of output. This is a further indication, if one was needed, that central banks are not strict inflation targeters; they care also about the behavior of other variables.

If it cares about the deviations of output from the natural rate as well as deviations of inflation from target, then an optimizing central bank, instead of adjusting two-year-ahead expected inflation all the way to the inflation target, will adjust it part way:

$$E(\pi_{\tau+2}) = \kappa\pi^* + (1 - \kappa)E(\pi_{\tau+1}) \tag{4}$$

where κ is a constant between zero and one, and E denotes an expectation. Svensson (1996) derives this relationship in the present model and shows that κ will be a decreasing function of the weight on output stabilization in the central bank's objective function.[19]

Life is more complicated if the structure of the economy is more complex – for example, if the economy is open. It is to the complications that arise in the case of open-economy inflation targeting that I now turn.

3 What's different about open economies?

The openness of emerging markets raises obvious questions about the relevance of the simple closed-economy inflation targeting framework. Openness exposes the economy to foreign shocks to both commodity and financial markets and introduces additional channels for policy. For example, the central bank's policy instrument (r) will now affect output not just directly, as in equation (2), but also indirectly through its impact on the exchange rate. While the direct interest-rate channel will dampen investment, as in a closed economy, the indirect channel will reduce net export demand by appreciating the exchange rate. This is easiest to see by starting from the interest parity condition that will hold in a financially open economy:

$$e_t - E(e_{t+1}) = r_t - r' + \nu_t \tag{5}$$

where the exchange rate e is defined as the foreign price of domestic currency (an increase is an appreciation), r' is the foreign interest rate, and ν is a financial market (or "pure portfolio") disturbance.[20] Ball (1999) and Mishkin and Savastano (2000) consider a simplified version of this relationship where the expected future exchange rate is constant (so that $e_t = r_t - r' + \nu_t$).[21] For convenience, I adopt this simplification in what follows. The additional impact of the interest rate on output, operating through the exchange rate, then implies nothing more than a larger coefficient on the domestic interest rate in equation (2). Since it is assumed (for the time being) that the exchange rate and the interest rate affect the change in output with the same lag, equation (2) can be written as:

$$y_{t+1} - y^* = \lambda(y_t - y^*) - \beta(r_t - r^*) - \delta e_t + n_{t+1} \tag{2'}$$

Note that $\beta(r_t - r^*) + \delta e_t = (\beta + \delta)r_t - \beta r^*$. In open economies where the output response is larger, adjustments in the policy instruments will be smaller. But the reaction function is otherwise unchanged.

The implications are more complex if exchange rate movements also affect inflation directly with the same one-period lag as it is affected by the output gap.[22] In other words, we rewrite equation (1) as:

$$\pi_{\tau+1} = \pi_\tau + \alpha(y_t - y^*) - \gamma(e_t - e_{t-1}) + \epsilon_t \tag{1'}$$

Strict inflation targeting is the simple case as always. Now a central bank that wishes to hit its inflation target in $t+1$ can do so. It does this by using its instrument (the interest rate) to alter the exchange rate and hence import prices. But output is more variable than before, since the interest rate is no longer adjusted to push output back toward its natural level (that having been the only channel, in the closed economy, through which policy could affect inflation in the event of an aggregate demand shock). Thus, strict inflation targeting that puts a high weight on inflation stability will result in more output instability in an open economy.[23]

Intuition suggests that when the central bank values the stability of both inflation and output, the ratio of the two reaction function coefficients (the response to inflation deviations relative to the response to output deviations, that is, the ratio ϕ to χ in equation (3) above) will be smaller in more open economies.[24] In terms of equation (4), the central bank will move more slowly to restore inflation to its target level (κ will be smaller). Because the policy instrument, operating through the exchange rate, has a more powerful first-period effect on inflation, tending to destabilize output as well as stabilizing inflation, policy is used more moderately in response to a given ratio of deviations of inflation to deviations in output.

An open economy is susceptible to shocks emanating from international commodity and financial markets. Although both types of shocks will affect the exchange rate, the appropriate policy response by an inflation-targeting central bank will depend on the source. Consider first a shock emanating from financial markets – a change in the direction or availability of capital flows due to, say, a rise in world interest rates (or a deterioration in foreign investor sentiment toward the country). I refer to this in what follows as "Calvo shock."[25] This can be modeled as an increase in r' (or as a low realization of *v*). A higher foreign interest rate implies less capital inflow for a given domestic interest rate and therefore a weaker currency, ceteris paribus. As the exchange rate weakens, higher import prices are passed through into inflation.[26] The optimal response is then to raise interest rates.

Note that this encourages "fear-of-floating" type behavior by an inflation targeting central bank (although the exchange rate may still be considerably more flexible than if it is pegged). If a Calvo shock displaces the exchange rate, then the interest rate adjustments that offset the inflationary consequences have the effect of moderating the change in the value of the currency (of bringing the exchange rate back toward its previous level). If the currency weakens, the central bank raises interest rates, which strengthens it, ceteris paribus. If it strengthens, the central bank reduces rates, which weakens it, other things equal. This is not because the central bank cares about the exchange rate in and of itself but because it cares about inflation.

However, while a central bank confronted by a Calvo shock will raise interest rates in order to moderate the depreciation of the currency, it will not prevent the exchange rate from moving, as the strong "fear-of-floating" view would suggest. Higher interest rates imply weaker domestic demand in the new long-term equilibrium, and that decline in domestic demand will have to be offset by additional export demand created by a weaker exchange rate. Thus, while the degree of exchange rate flexibility will be limited by central bank policy, such flexibility will not be eliminated entirely. The currency will still exhibit greater flexibility than when it is pegged.

The intuition that central banks concerned about future inflation should adjust the interest rate to counter fluctuations in the exchange rate has been formalized as the idea of a "monetary conditions index." The MCI, which indicates the overall stance of policy, is a weighted average of the interest rate and the exchange rate (since these two variables are linked by equation (5)) where the former is adjusted to offset finance-induced fluctuations in the latter.[27] Using a simulation model of the New Zealand economy, Hunt (1999) shows that when the main source of shocks is from international financial markets to the exchange rate, it will be desirable to target an MCI which includes both the interest rate and the exchange rate (raising interest rates when the exchange rate weakens, other things equal).

What if the shock is temporary? A transitory shock to ν that depreciates the exchange rate will still dictate a limited rise in interest rates to damp down future demand-induced inflation.[28] But because the direct impact on inflation through higher import prices is transitory, responding to it with sharply higher interest rates will only amplify the volatility of output and inflation, since ν, and with it underlying inflationary pressures, will have returned to normal in the next period. Interest rates should be hiked to damp down only the domestic component of inflation (which derives from the persistent increase in aggregate demand), but not also the contribution of imported inflation (which is temporary). Responding this period to a problem that will have disappeared by next period, using an instrument that takes one period to work, will only produce cycles of output and inflation.

In Ball's (1999) model, the implication is that the monetary conditions indicator (the weighted average of the interest rate and the exchange rate) should be adjusted not to movements in π_t but to movements in $\pi_t + \gamma(e_t - e_{t-1})$, where γ is the response of inflation to a change in the exchange rate. In other words, the authorities should target domestic inflation and not CPI inflation. Bharucha and Kent (1998) use a simulation model of Australia to show that responding only to the domestic component of inflation (and not also to imported inflation) delivers better results when shocks to the exchange rate are temporary.[29] Since the interest rate response to movements in the exchange rate will be less, "fear-of-floating" type behavior will be less when capital market shocks are temporary.[30]

All this rests on the assumption that the source of disturbances is international financial markets. Assume instead that the disturbance is to the foreign component of aggregate demand (to the terms of trade or to export demand). I refer to this as a "Prebisch shock." The exchange rate will again weaken, since export revenues will have declined while nothing else affecting the foreign exchange market will have changed in the first instance. In addition, aggregate demand will weaken, since foreigners are demanding fewer of the country's exports.[31] Now there are two offsetting effects on inflation: while higher import prices will be passed through into inflation, weaker aggregate demand will be deflationary.

In the real world the first effect is likely to dominate.[32] If the central bank attaches a high weight to output variability, it may still hesitate to raise interest rates, knowing that inflation will decline subsequently due to the weakness of output. If, as is more typically the case, it attaches a high weight to deviations of inflation from target, it will raise interest rates to limit currency depreciation in the short term, while still allowing the exchange rate to adjust eventually to its new long-term equilibrium level. While it will lean against the wind, it will not prevent the exchange rate from moving. It will not display fear of floating in this strong sense.

Note that the monetary conditions indicator now sends the wrong signal in response to this shock. It suggests raising interest rates to counter the weakness of the exchange rate, where the appropriate response is to allow the exchange rate to move down to a lower long-term equilibrium level to offset the negative real shock. Mishkin (2000b) cites cases (such as New Zealand in 1997 and Chile in 1998) where the central bank either utilized a monetary conditions indicator or attempted to limit the variability of the exchange rate as part of its inflation targeting regime, inducing precisely the wrong response to a shock to external demand (tightening when the economy was weakening).

To summarize, inflation targeting is more complicated in open economies, reflecting the additional shocks to which such economies are exposed and the additional channels linking policy instruments and outcomes. Insofar as policy has more powerful effects when it operates through the exchange rate as well as the interest rate, this implies, other things equal, that policy instruments should be adjusted less in response to the same shocks. Insofar as the additional exchange rate channel linking interest rates to inflation changes the structure of policy lags, openness also requires rethinking the relative weights on inflation and output in the reaction function. In general, the central bank of an open economy will respond less to inflation deviations relative to output deviations, since monetary policy, which also operates through the exchange rate, now has a more powerful, immediate effect on inflation.

Will open-economy inflation targeters exhibit "fear of floating?" In general, an inflation targeting central bank will let the exchange rate adjust, although it may wish to smooth its movement. It will lean against the exchange rate change in response to shocks. If the exchange rate depreciates, it will raise the interest rate. But it will not prevent the exchange rate from adjusting to a new long-term equilibrium level. It will not display fear of floating in this strong sense.

4 What is different about emerging markets?

What is different about emerging markets is the speed of passthrough, the difficulty of forecasting inflation, liability dollarization, and credibility issues.

4.1 Higher passthrough

Calvo and Reinhart provide evidence that changes in import prices due to movements in the exchange rate are passed through into domestic prices faster in emerging markets than industrial countries. A history of inflation may have raised agents' awareness of and sensitivity to imported inflation and led to formal indexation. The commitment to price stability may lack credibility; hence, it may be feared that transitory shocks leading to depreciation of the exchange rate will be validated by policy and hence become permanent.[33]

Faster passthrough can be formalized as a larger γ and a smaller (absolute value of) δ in equation (1'). With high passthrough, a change in the exchange rate has a large short-term impact on inflation and a small short-term impact on output. If there is a shock to the foreign exchange market (a negative Prebisch shock, for example, that causes the rate to depreciate and output to fall), the authorities will have less reluctance to tighten than in the case of slower passthrough, since they gain more in terms of disinflation as the currency stabilizes and strengthens, while losing less as output falls due to declining competitiveness.

But the preceding paragraph makes clear that passthrough is not an exogenous parameter that can be regarded as independent of the monetary regime. If the credibility of the commitment to low inflation is enhanced by an institutionalized commitment to price stability, central bank independence and accountability, and policies of communicating the rationale for monetary-policy decisions, then agents will revise downward the likelihood they attach to the prospect that transitory shocks will be validated by policy and hence become permanent, and therefore how quickly they adjust prices in response to a weaker exchange rate.[34]

Under full (instantaneous, 100 percent) indexation, monetary policy has no capacity to stabilize – or, for that matter, destabilize – output.[35] It can simply be used to target inflation. With full indexation, that target can be hit immediately.[36] Full indexation thus simplifies the inflation targeting problem since it reduces the central bank's objective function to the one variable that it can now influence and allows the authorities to hit that target immediately.[37]

The implications for exchange rate management depend on the source of shocks. If domestic monetary policy is the source of the instability, then stabilizing the exchange rate will force the central bank to undo such shocks immediately. If shocks are external, then the exchange rate should be adjusted to offset them. Foreign deflation will induce an inflation-targeting central bank to expand the money supply and allow the currency to depreciate, while an inflationary shock will induce the opposite reaction.[38] Thus, while rapid passthrough will modify the implementation of monetary policy by an inflation targeting central bank, it is not a fundamental challenge to the viability of that approach to its formulation.

4.2 Difficulty of forecasting inflation

Disturbances make it difficult for observers to evaluate the central bank's commitment to inflation targeting, since it is often hard to determine the extent to which divergences between actual inflation and the target are due to the monetary policy implemented several quarters ago as opposed to shocks occurring during the control lag. This uncertainty may reduce credibility – it will not be clear whether the central bank is in fact following the announced policy.[39] This is where the conditional inflation forecast comes in.[40] The central bank announces a point or range forecast for inflation and explains how its instrument settings are consistent with its forecast. If it misses the target, it must then be able to point to unanticipated disturbances occurring during the control lag that can account for the discrepancy or risk losing credibility.

If reliable forecasting is not possible, then the markets may be unable to determine the intent of the authorities. A brutally-honest central bank might surround its point forecast with a wide confidence interval. But a wide range of outcomes will be consistent with a wide range of policies, complicating efforts to determine the authorities' intent. Nor will specifying a narrow forecast range and missing it repeatedly build confidence in the central bank's commitment to its target.

Forecasts based on historical relationships can be invalidated when there is a change in the policy process – that is to say, a change in the monetary regime. And what is the adoption of formal inflation targeting but a change in regime? Thus, the problem of forecasting inflation in the early phases of the new regime is general, not specific to emerging markets. But there are reasons to worry that it is especially difficult there. Emerging markets attracted to inflation targeting will typically be bringing down inflation from high levels. Thus, the change in regime is likely to be particularly sharp and inflation volatility particularly pronounced during the transition. Passthrough may change. De-indexation will be proceeding with uncertain consequences. The shift from an alternative monetary policy operating strategy to inflation targeting will be part of a package of stabilization measures, typically including structural reforms of the public and private sectors that transform the inflation process in unpredictable ways. If the country is emerging from a period of strict central planning, price controls may be in the process of elimination, and there may be the prospect of sharp changes in excise taxes to augment public sector revenues and enhance the efficiency of tax collection.

While these are reasons why inflation forecasting may be especially difficult during the transition, they do not obviously challenge its feasibility once the aforementioned structural and policy reforms have been put in place. Revealingly, those emerging markets that have adopted full-fledged inflation targeting have not generally started from a position of high inflation; rather, they have first brought inflation down to moderate levels and pursued other reforms before installing the new regime.[41]

But are there also structural features of emerging markets that complicate the forecasting exercise even once these reforms are complete? Emerging economies are more commodity-price sensitive than their advanced-industrial counterparts, and commodity-price fluctuations can wreak havoc with the forecastability of consumer price inflation. There is the fact that foodstuffs, whose prices are affected by the weather, have a heavy weight in the CPI in low-income countries. The obvious solution to both problems is to target "core" (or underlying) inflation net of commodity prices, as is the practice of some industrial countries.[42]

Then there is such countries' disproportionate dependence on capital flows. Sensitivity of domestic financial conditions to international capital flows is, in a sense, the defining feature of an emerging market. The literature on asymmetric information suggests that unpredictable volatility is especially pronounced in the financial sphere, and nowhere more than in international financial markets. Because information is costly to acquire and process, investors are imperfectly informed. They therefore herd in and out of markets in response to the movements of other investors, amplifying volatility. Because asymmetric information reduces the liquidity of financial assets in periods of distress (reflecting fears that assets liquidated in fire sales are damaged goods), illiquidity and balance-sheet problems may transmit financial difficulties across borders, with destabilizing repercussions for innocent bystanders.[43] These phenomena will be most pronounced in international markets, where information must travel geographical and cultural distance, and in emerging markets, where the information environment is least developed.

The univariate forecastability of inflation, ultimately, is an empirical issue. Hoffmaister (1999) has analyzed it in South Korea, finding that inflation is roughly as forecastable there as in Sweden. Univariate models of inflation perform similarly in Korea and in the high-income inflation targeters in the period immediately preceding their adoption of the strategy, although there is some evidence of positive kurtosis, as if inflation is subject more frequently to larger shocks than would be expected given its standard deviation. Christoffersen and Wescott (1999) and Rivas (2001) similarly find evidence of kurtosis and skewness for Poland in 1992–98 and Nicaragua in 1988–98, respectively. But upon eliminating some of the largest and smallest price changes each month among the 33 main categories in Poland's CPI to derive a measure of core inflation, Christoffersen and Wescott find that a limited set of economic variables forecast one-period-ahead core inflation reasonably well by international standards.[44] Rivas similarly has considerable success in forecasting core inflation in Nicaragua so long as he focuses on the period of moderate inflation starting around 1993.

Thus, the difficulty of forecasting inflation may be an obstacle to effective inflation targeting in an economy in economic and financial disequilibrium. It is not realistic to hope to forecast inflation with the requisite reliability if the country is still bringing inflation down from high levels, comprehensively reforming the tax and public-spending systems, and radically restructuring the private sector. But where such reforms have been underway for some time and are proceeding at a measured pace – as in Poland, South Korea, and Brazil – forecasting difficulties would not appear to be an insurmountable obstacle to inflation targeting.

4.3 Liability dollarization

In many emerging markets, the obligations of banks, corporations, and governments – their foreign obligations in particular – are denominated in foreign currency, while their revenues are domestic-currency denominated to a considerable extent. Insofar as banks and other intermediaries close their open foreign-currency positions by issuing dollar-denominated loans, they will simply pass on that problem of liability dollarization to their customers. When the exchange rate depreciates, their balance sheets will still suffer, and this "financial accelerator" will depress output and employment.

The simplest way of thinking about liability dollarization is as reducing δ, the positive response of output to currency depreciation in equation (2'). While depreciation renders domestic goods more competitive, as before, it now also weakens the balance sheets of banks, firms, households, and governments, depressing consumption and investment. The second effect partially offsets the first.[45]

Consider the response to a Calvo shock, compared to the benchmark case analyzed in section 2. Weaker consumption and investment due to adverse balance-sheet effects now imply less inflation in the intermediate run than before. An inflation-targeting central bank will therefore feel *less* compelled to raise interest rates in order to push up the exchange rate and damp down the increase in import prices.[46] If the shock to the exchange rate instead emanates from commodity markets (a negative Prebisch shock), higher import prices will still be passed through into inflation, but now aggregate demand will be weaker than before because of the adverse balance-sheet effects. Since output is lower and inflation is no higher than in the absence of liability dollarization, again there will be *less* pressure to hike interest rates in order to stabilize the currency and damp down inflation, and more incentive to cut interest rates to stimulate production (compared to the situation where balance-sheet effects are absent). This suggests that, regardless of the source of shocks, "fear of floating" will be *less* in the presence of liability dollarization.[47]

While this may seem counterintuitive, it is simply an illustration of the general point that when the central bank worries more about variables other than inflation, either because of a heavier weight on those variables in its objective function, or because the parameters of the model cause those other variables to be displaced further from their equilibrium levels (where the latter is the case presently under discussion), it will move more gradually to eliminate discrepancies between actual and target inflation. Because the exchange rate must move more to increase output and employment, and because measures which would limit its fluctuation and thereby reduce imported inflation tend to destabilize the real economy, the now weaker tendency for depreciation to stimulate activity means that the central bank will do even less to limit depreciation.

The same is true when the problem in the financial system is maturity mismatches rather than currency mismatches. (This can be modeled as an increase in the coefficient β in the aggregate demand equation.) Again, the more the central bank fears that an interest rate hike designed to damp down inflation will cause financial distress (because the maturity of banks' liabilities is shorter than their assets, or because higher interest rates will increase default rates among bank borrowers), the less it will raise interest rates in the intermediate term to strengthen the exchange rate and limit inflation.

Clearly, those who argue that liability dollarization creates fear of floating have something else in mind, presumably that the balance-sheet effects of currency depreciation are so strong that they turn δ negative. Let $-\delta > \beta$, so that a cut in the interest rate which weakens the exchange rate depresses output on balance. This constellation of parameter values is extreme (and it has some peculiar implications, as we will see momentarily), but it would appear to be what the Cassandras of liability dollarization have in mind.

As before, a negative Calvo shock fuels inflation through higher import prices. It also now lowers output through the adverse balance-sheet effect. The appropriate response, which damps down inflation *and* stabilizes output by limiting balance-sheet damage, is to raise interest rates and push the exchange rate back up to its pre-shock level.[48] "Fear-of-floating" type behavior results. If the disturbance is instead a Prebisch shock, the weaker exchange rate again means more imported inflation and lower levels of output. (The decline in output is even larger than in the comparable thought experiment in section 2 because the direct effect of the decline in foreign demand is reinforced by the indirect effect of exchange rate depreciation via its adverse impact on balance sheets.) Again, interest rate hikes are the appropriate response to both problems, since a higher interest rate which strengthens the exchange rate not only damps down inflation but also strengthens balance sheets. Again, the central bank will not hesitate to raise interest rates. Again, its response will resemble fear of floating.

This formulation has some peculiar implications, as already noted. For one, a negative shock that reduces export demand and depresses output must be offset in the new long-term equilibrium by an appreciated exchange rate, not a depreciated one.[49] In this peculiar world, overvaluation is good for output because its favorable financial effects dominate its adverse competitiveness effects. It can be reasonably objected that this is unrealistic – that it is implausible to assume that $-\delta > \beta$. But relaxing this assumption means we are back in a world not just where the authorities allow the exchange rate to adjust to a new lower level following an adverse Prebisch shock but also where they do not jack up interest rates to significantly slow its movement. In other words, we are back in the world where they display "fear of fixing" rather than "fear of floating."

A possible reconciliation is that when the exchange rate depreciates by a large amount, the adverse balance-sheet effects dominate, but when it depreciates by a small amount, the favorable competitiveness effects dominate. Large depreciations cause severe financial distress because they confront banks and firms with asset prices for which they are unprepared, while doing little to enhance competitiveness because of the speed with which they are passed through into inflation. For small depreciations, the balance of effects is the opposite; small depreciations are more likely therefore to satisfy the conditions for an expansionary devaluation. There is a range of exchange rates far from prior levels for which $-\delta > \beta$, in other words, and another range closer to prior levels where $-\delta < \beta$.[50] While this nonlinearity in the effect of the exchange rate on output might seem arbitrary, it is precisely the way authors like Aghion *et al.* (1999) and Krugman (2001) model the interplay of competitiveness and balance-sheet effects: the former dominates for small depreciations but the latter dominates for large ones, producing a nonlinear aggregate equation of precisely the sort being assumed here.

If the exchange rate then falls sufficiently to enter the first range, an inflation-targeting central bank will raise interest rates sharply and push the currency up quickly in order to minimize financial damage to banks, firms, and households. But if the depreciation is modest, so too will be the rise in interest rates; the central bank will allow the currency to fall to a new lower level so long as the competitiveness effects continue to dominate the balance-sheet effects. In fact, heavy intervention when the exchange rate drops precipitously but light intervention when it fluctuates around normal levels is not unlike the observed behavior of many central banks.

It is important to emphasize that liability dollarization, as analyzed here, in no sense precludes inflation targeting. The preceding propositions for how the central bank should respond flow directly from the standard inflation-targeting framework. But in the extreme case of liability dollarization where interest-rate cuts depress output as well as aggravating inflation (that is, where $-\delta > \beta$), that response will be such as to limit exchange rate variability. If the perceived advantage of inflation targeting is that it permits a greater exchange rate flexibility (compared to the alternative of a hard peg), then the advantages of inflation targeting are in practice correspondingly less in highly dollarized economies.

This discussion assumes that the output effects of liability dollarization are independent of the policy regime. This assumption may be no more appropriate here than it is for passthrough and indexation. The greater exchange rate variability that the shift from pegging to inflation targeting implies, even if it is slight, will encourage hedging by banks and corporates. Whereas a policy of pegging the currency is tantamount to providing implicit insurance against currency risk, which discourages private purchases of currency hedges (Why hedge when doing so is costly and the government avers its commitment to limiting currency fluctuations?), the knowledge that the exchange rate is allowed to move on a daily basis will strengthen the hand of a chief financial officer trying to convince his CEO of the importance of purchasing a hedge. Precisely those banks and corporates most vulnerable to financial distress because the liability side of their balance sheets is dollarized will have the greatest incentive to hedge. Even if banks and firms are unable to borrow abroad in their own currency in the aggregate, they will have an incentive to redistribute that foreign exposure in ways that limit the adverse output effects of depreciation. Thus, the adverse balance sheet effects that occur in a country that has traditionally oriented its monetary policy strategy around the level of the exchange rate may not be a good guide to the magnitude of these effects when the central bank shifts to an inflation targeting regime that implies even a modest increase in exchange rate flexibility. And even a modest increase in exchange rate flexibility that leads to a modest increase in hedging will make it optimal for an inflation-targeting central bank to allow a bit more exchange rate flexibility, which may encourage a bit more hedging, and so on. If the demand for unhedged dollar liabilities is endogenous, then behavior under the new regime – by the central bank as well as the private sector – may be quite different than behavior under the old one.

What if this response is not forthcoming, perhaps because the relevant hedging instruments are not available? If the authorities are concerned that inflation targeting still looks too much like a de facto soft peg, rendering the country vulnerable to a build-up of speculative pressure, then it may be possible to fulfill the desire for greater flexibility only through the imposition of limits on gross and net foreign currency exposures. The regulatory authorities will have to limit the gross foreign-currency exposures of the banking system (and strengthen corporate governance and prudential practices in the financial sector so as to encourage banks to better manage and limit those exposures on their own). The central government will have to limit its foreign-currency borrowing to the extent that its domestic-currency-denominated revenues are imperfectly indexed to the exchange rate, and it should similarly take steps to discourage excessive foreign-currency borrowing by states and municipalities.

Such measures are in fact integral to the agenda pursued by G-7 governments and the multilaterals under the umbrella of the "new international financial architecture." Greater exchange rate flexibility has also been an element of this agenda.[51] But if this ability to regulate markets (and for markets to regulate themselves) is beyond the capacity of an emerging economy, then evasion and regulatory laxity will result in destabilizing balance-sheet effects, undermining the viability of an inflation targeting regime that aspires to permit increased exchange rate flexibility. It is revealing that those emerging markets which have moved to inflation targeting and have succeeded in achieving greater de facto exchange rate flexibility have generally had relatively well-developed financial systems and regulatory capacity.

One can question whether the solution is worth the price. If the exchange rate movements implied by inflation targeting are compatible with financial instability only when foreign borrowing is curtailed, then the cost may be slow growth and underdevelopment. The severity of this risk depends on one's evaluation of the importance of foreign capital for domestic development and of the extent to which gross (as opposed to net) exposures must be curtailed to reconcile exchange rate flexibility with financial stability. Those fearful that curtailing capital flows will hinder growth logically prefer full dollarization.

4.4 Credibility problems

We have already seen how the difficulty of forecasting inflation can lessen the credibility of inflation targeting in emerging markets (although I have argued that the point should not be pushed too far). In addition, a history of arbitrary enforcement that lessens respect for constitutional and statutory law may limit the effective independence of the central bank, whose insulation from pressure to pump up activity before an election or to help meet the government's financial needs is a prerequisite for effective inflation targeting. Central bankers threatened with dismissal, notwithstanding laws ostensibly guaranteeing them long terms in office, will be more inclined to bow to pressure to purchase government securities on the primary market. And chronic budget deficits can convince even an independent central bank that it has no choice but to meet the government's fiscal needs if it wishes to preserve financial stability, sowing the seeds of time inconsistency.[52]

Historically, lack of effective central bank independence has been a major impediment to the pursuit of an independent monetary policy in developing countries. At the same time, emerging markets have come a long way in recent years in developing political support for low inflation and buttressing the independence of their central banks.[53] Although budget deficits have been chronic problems, there has also been considerable progress in strengthening fiscal institutions and bringing down budget deficits.[54] The dozen or so transition economies seeking membership in the EU and its monetary union, for example, have made very considerable progress in bringing their deficits and debts to within the Maastricht Treaty's 3 and 60 percent ceilings. To the extent that inflation targeting is less credible in emerging markets, its benefits will be less. Absent confidence that the central bank is committed to low inflation, interest rates will not fall to the levels of other low-inflation countries. Shocks will raise questions about whether the authorities are prepared to stay the course. Sharp changes in interest rates, exchange rates and international capital flows may feed upon themselves: financial variables will be volatile, with negative implications for the economy. If policy is not credible, then firms will not reduce price increases to meet the inflation target. Hitting it will require an increase in interest rates sufficient to deliver a substantial reduction in import prices (through a sharp appreciation of the exchange rate), with destabilizing output effects.[55]

A wide variety of models of monetary policy point to the fact that there is a tradeoff between flexibility and credibility. Central banks most lacking in credibility will have an incentive to move along the frontier of feasible credibility-flexibility combinations in order to obtain it. In particular, imperfect credibility may require the central bank to target inflation rigidly. Absent credibility problems, a central bank faced with inflation in excess of its target may want to raise interest rates and damp down inflation only gradually in order to avoid causing or compounding a recession. Faced with a weak banking system ill prepared to absorb interest rate increases, which raise the cost of servicing its short-term liabilities and increase default rates by borrowers, it may want to limit interest-rate volatility and administer its anti-inflationary medicine in small doses. But if the monetary authorities fail to respond quickly when inflation heats up, observers may begin to wonder whether they are optimally trading off objectives or they are in fact not really committed to price stability. Asset prices and the variables they affect will not respond as hoped. Similarly, if the central bank targets core rather than headline inflation, observers may wonder whether this is because monetary policy should not attempt to offset temporary commodity price fluctuations, or whether the authorities are really just seeking an excuse to disregard inflationary pressures.[56] Monetary policy will thus have to respond more sharply to exchange rate and commodity-price fluctuations than would be the case if it was being implemented by a highly credible central bank. The monetary authorities may not be able to afford even modest deviations from strict inflation targeting for fear of sending the wrong signal.

In addition, central banks in emerging markets will have an incentive to use transparency to further enhance their credibility. This will tend to push them in the direction of a fully-articulated inflation-targeting framework rather than the seat-of-the-pants approach preferred by, inter alia, the Federal Reserve. Its hard-won credibility allows the Federal Reserve Board to hint at its inflation forecast rather than announcing it. It allows the Fed to sketch the model used to link its policy instruments to that forecast rather than describing it in any great detail. Most emerging markets do not enjoy this luxury.[57] To convince investors that they mean what they say, their central banks will have to publish the forecast and the model. Chile, for one, has moved in this direction, while Mexico and Brazil, among others, publish an *Inflation Report*.

Another implication is that effective inflation targeting will require steps to eliminate fiscal dominance as a way of building credibility. In particular, inflation targeting must be supported by the reform and reinforcement of fiscal institutions as a way of delivering better fiscal outcomes. Fiscal-policy making processes and procedures should be centralized to reduce free riding. Vertical fiscal imbalances should be reduced. The budget constraints facing sub-central governments should be hardened.[58] An example of progress in this direction is Brazil's Fiscal Responsibility Law, which bans the federal government from bailing out debt-ridden states and municipalities and has produced visible improvements in state and municipal fiscal performance. The federal fiscal authorities, for their part, can invest in the monetary regime so as to intentionally incur costs if it fails, further limiting problems of time inconsistency. Thus, inflation targets in a number of emerging markets are announced not by the central bank but by the government (Chile, Poland) or by the central bank and government jointly (Brazil, Israel) precisely as a way for the government to commit to the fiscal discipline needed to achieve the target.

These implications are evident in the behavior of those emerging markets that have embraced inflation targeting. Such countries have generally moved toward the adoption of a formal framework. Their central banks have been reluctant to miss the inflation target even temporarily, or to slow the pace at which deviations between target inflation and actual inflation are eliminated, for fear of undermining their anti-inflationary credibility.[59] The credibility problem has tended to dictate that the change in the CPI must be the operational measure of inflation, because it is widely understood and therefore more credible, even when core inflation purged of import-price fluctuations would be more appropriate in principle.[60]

Credibility problems make inflation targeting less attractive. They imply more volatility and less flexible policy implementation. The question is then how quickly credibility can be gained, and whether or not inflation targeting can be part of that process.

5 Conclusion

Inflation targeting is the increasingly fashionable alternative for countries unable or unwilling to abolish the national currency.[61] It is seen as providing a coherent alternative to exchange-rate-based monetary policy strategies that are overly restrictive and crisis prone. But is it feasible for emerging markets?

Inflation targeting is difficult in emerging markets for three reasons: they are open, their liabilities are dollarized, and their policy makers lack credibility. Openness exposes their economies to external disturbances.[62] It makes inflation forecasting more difficult. And it opens additional, exchange-rate-related channels linking the central bank's instruments and targets that operate with very different control lags. Because an inflation-targeting central bank will want to respond differently to exchange-rate changes depending on their source and persistence, these problems cannot be solved simply by adding the exchange rate to the standard reaction function. None of this is to suggest that inflation targeting is infeasible in open economies, only that it is more complicated to operate.

Liability dollarization introduces more fundamental complications. Financial institutions and their customers will be saddled with currency mismatches, given the difficulty these countries have in borrowing abroad in their own currencies. Under these circumstances, an inflation targeting central bank will be reluctant to let the exchange rate move; it will be unable to partake of the greater flexibility ostensibly offered by that regime.

In practice, whether countries with partially dollarized economies reap any advantages from inflation targeting – whether the framework will provide even limited scope for policy autonomy, and in particular whether it will enable them to allow the exchange rate to fluctuate more freely – depends on the exact nature, extent, and effects of their liability dollarization. If even a small depreciation of the exchange rate threatens to desta-bilize balance sheets and output (in other words, if the country immediately enters the zone where depreciation and lower interest rates are recessionary), then the central bank will be unwilling to let the exchange rate move. In this case, inflation targeting and a hard peg are basically indistinguishable. If the perceived advantage of inflation target-ing is that it permits a greater flexibility, then the advantages of inflation targeting are correspondingly less in highly dollarized economies. Inflation targeting has no obvious advantages under these circumstances, while a hard peg has the advantages of simplicity, transparency and credibility.

For countries where the adverse balance-sheet effects dominate only when exchange rate movements reach a certain point, conventional infla-tion targeting will be viable so long as shocks and corresponding exchange rate movements are small, while the desire to intervene and stabilize the exchange rate will dominate when they grow large. The greater exchange rate flexibility promised by inflation targeting will be possible, although the central bank's appetite for indulging in it will have limits.

Such countries will wish to implement inflation targeting flexibly, by adjusting monetary policy in response to large exchange rate movements, for example, while treating small movements with benign neglect. Unfor-tunately, flexibility can be destabilizing when credibility is lacking. A central bank that temporarily disregards a surge in inflation in order to, say, stabilize the financial system may find its commitment to price stability questioned. Credibility problems will force precisely those emerg-ing markets where a flexible approach to inflation targeting is most valu-able to adopt a relatively rigid version.[63]

These observations suggest what countries should find inflation target-ing attractive. Inflation targeting will be less attractive the more open the economy, for the reasons detailed several paragraphs back. Note the con-sonance of this argument with a key implication of theory of optimum cur-rency areas. Inflation targeting will be less attractive the dimmer the prospects of the central bank acquiring policy credibility. Note this time the consonance of this argument with the idea that countries in crisis whose credibility has been shredded should rebuild their reputations by dollarizing. Finally, inflation targeting will be more attractive where liability dollarization is limited and banks and corporations have markets on which to hedge their exposures, so that limited exchange rate fluctuations will not irreparably damage their balance sheets. Note here the consonance of this observation with popular explanations for the success of inflation targeting in Brazil.

On the other hand, emerging markets that are less open, that have well regulated financial institutions and markets on which foreign exposures can be hedged, and whose central banks possess a reasonable degree of policy credibility may prefer inflation targeting. The question is how many emerging markets will soon fall under this heading.

Notes

1 An abbreviated version of this chapter appeared in *The Annals of the American Academy of Political and Social Science* (January 2002), and appears here with the permission of the Academy. For helpful comments I thank Lawrence Ball, Paul Masson, Rick Mishkin, Peter Sinclair, Lars Svensson, Ted Truman, and John Williamson, as well as seminar participants at the Bank of England, Bank of Mexico, and Central Bank of Brazil.
2 I use the term "dollarization" generically to denote the adoption of a major (international) currency, be it the dollar, the euro or another unit.
3 Calvo and Reinhart (2000) are leading exponents of the view that many emerging markets exhibit "fear of floating" – that, despite being reclassified by the IMF as embracing a greater degree of exchange rate flexibility, they continue to intervene heavily to limit the actual variability of the currency.
4 A further option, the adjustable peg, may be viable for countries with capital controls, as the experiences of China and Malaysia have shown. I disregard this option here on the grounds that trends in technology and policy (domestic financial liberalization, in particular) will lead additional countries to liberalize their international financial transactions, limiting those to which this option is relevant.
5 On dollarization, see Hausmann (1999) and Calvo (2000a). On bands and pegs for emerging markets, see Williamson (2000). In order to reduce effective options to three, I lump together under the heading of "intermediate regimes" pegs, bands, and crawls a la Williamson and implicit strategies to limit exchange rate flexibility a la Calvo and Reinhart (2000), since both are monetary policy strategies framed in terms of the level of the exchange rate, while neither hardens the peg to the extent of a currency board. This follows the policy literature on target zones, which encompasses both hard and soft zones (that is, with and without buffers and escape clauses) and loud and quiet zones (in other words, those that are announced and unannounced).
6 Not all of the advocates of greater flexibility take this additional step. Calvo (2000b) criticizes contributions to this literature, with no little justification, for failing to specify the alternative to an exchange-rate based policy regime.
7 Brazil, Chile, Colombia, Israel, the Czech Republic, and Poland all adopted inflation targeting in conjunction with a recognition of the need to widen or abandon an exchange rate band. Clearly, inflation targeting and flexible

exchange rates are not synonymous, although, as Calvo (2000b: 28) writes, there is a tendency to erroneously identify inflation targeting with flexible rates. Flexible rates can be backed by no coherent monetary policy operating strategy of any kind or by a number of alternatives to inflation targeting. The other options for policy are monetary targeting, which is impractical in emerging markets (and most other places) because of the instability of the relationship between monetary aggregates and policy targets, and nominal income targeting, which has formidable data requirements and has never been tried. Another option is the so-called Taylor rule for monetary policy, whose connection to inflation targeting I elaborate below.

8 There exist more complete and authoritative surveys of the literature on inflation targeting than I am able to provide here, for example, Bernanke *et al.* (1999).

9 Others would add following an information-inclusive strategy where the variables to which the central bank responds are not limited to, say, current inflation and the output gap, and/or using an inflation forecast as the intermediate guide for monetary policy.

10 Such lists are constantly changing. Thus, in June 2001 Hungary joined the inflation targeting club "implicitly," while Thailand, according to some, backed away from full-fledged inflation targeting by embracing a more exchange-rate oriented strategy (J.P. Morgan 2001: 11).

11 I show this below using a simple model. De Brouwer and O'Regan (1997) also show that using a simulation model that inflation targeting which ignores the information content of output deviations results in not just more variable output but more variable inflation as well.

12 Calvo (2000b: 28) asserts that "Inflation targeting is equivalent to pegging the currency to a basket of goods." This is true of strict inflation targeting but not of its flexible counterpart.

13 The language here is from Svensson (1999). Other authors refer to this as the distinction between policy objectives and policy rules.

14 And where outcomes are uncertain. There is a growing literature on inflation targeting under uncertainty (for example, Levin *et al.* 1999, Kumhof 2000), which I leave aside in this chapter.

15 Something that is likely to be particularly problematic in emerging markets, as I analyze below.

16 This is another big if, and it is something that is likely to be especially problematic in emerging markets (as I discuss below). In addition, simply targeting the inflation forecast does not solve the problem that additional information about the structure of the economy and its reaction to policy is needed to inform the central bank's decision of how quickly to eliminate any discrepancy between the inflation forecast and the inflation target.

17 In the general case where the central bank cares not just about inflation but also about other variables like output, the reaction coefficients will also depend on the parameters of its objective function (see below). But that is not the case here.

18 Taylor identifies $\phi = 1.5$ and $\chi = 0.5$ as replicating the actual behavior of inflation-targeting central banks. Here we get $\phi \approx 4$ and $\chi = 3$.

19 Similarly, the higher the central bank's discount rate (the more it cares about the present relative to the future) and the less responsive is inflation to output fluctuations (the smaller α), the less will be the weight on target inflation. If inflation two periods ahead is of less concern (because the discount rate is higher), then the central bank will be prepared to incur less output variability in order to stabilize it. And if output has to be pushed around a lot in order to hit the inflation target, then the weight on that target in the reaction function

will be less. These relationships are easy to show for shocks to ϵ_t when the control lag from the policy instrument to inflation is only one period – if we rewrite equation (2) as $y_t - y^* = -\beta(r_t - r^*) + n_t$ for example, so that the interest rate affects output immediately but inflation only with a one period lag – but harder to show in the model in the text (again, however, see Svensson 1996). In contrast to the response to shocks to ϵ, in the variant in this note the interest rate is adjusted immediately in response to shocks to aggregate demand (to n_t), so as to return both inflation to target and output instantaneously to the natural rate; equation (4) in the text is irrelevant.

20 This is a "pure portfolio disturbance" in the sense that it appears only in this condition for financial market equilibrium, not also in the aggregate demand equation. Later in the paper I introduce an international commodity market (or "export market") disturbance that affects financial and commodity markets simultaneously. The implications for policy turn out to be rather different.

21 One can attempt to justify this by arguing that since the expected values of the disturbances to equations (1) and (2) are zero, the exchange rate is expected to return to its (constant) level in the long run. But this ignores the distinction between temporary and permanent disturbances and between the long-term equilibrium level and the level one period out.

22 In the model of the previous section, the policy instrument could affect inflation only after two periods, since there was a one-period lag from policy to the output gap and a further one-period lag from the output gap to inflation. Ted Truman has raised the question (in private correspondence) of whether there is strong empirical support for this assumption that the impact of monetary policy on inflation is felt faster in open economies.

23 Note that it is current account openness as well as financial openness that matters for this conclusion.

24 While a closed-form solution demonstrating this result is not available, Ball (1999: 132–133) obtains it in a simulation of the present model. Gomez (2000) conducts analogous exercises using the more elaborate model in Svensson (2000). For flexible CPI inflation targeting (the case relevant to the present discussion), he obtains this result over most of the relevant range: as the share of imported goods in the CPI rises from, say, 10 to 50 percent, the reaction to innovations in domestic inflation declines relative to the reaction to output innovations. However, as openness begins to rise from very low levels, the reaction to inflation innovations falls relative to the reaction to output innovations. Since an increase in the share of imported goods affects several parameters of Svensson's model (notably the effects of both the exchange rate and the output gap on inflation and the effect of the exchange rate in the Phillips Curve) in interdependent nonlinear ways, it is not surprising that the change in the ratio of the two reaction function coefficients is not the same over the entire range of possible values for openness.

25 Guillermo Calvo having emphasized the impact of capital-flow-related shocks to emerging markets.

26 The weaker exchange rate also implies future inflation insofar as it boosts export demand, but this is a secondary effect. That a decline in capital inflows would raise aggregate demand seems peculiar; it is a figment of the present thought experiment because the domestic interest rate (the other main determinant of aggregate demand) is held constant. The paradox is dissolved by the next sentence in the text.

27 Freedman (1994) has suggested that the weights in the composite indicator made up of the interest rate and the exchange rate (the "monetary conditions indicator") should be proportional to the coefficients on e and r in the Phillips

Curve (equation (2′) above). That is, they should be proportional to the parameters β and δ above. For representative parameter values, this means that when the exchange rate depreciates by 1 percent, holding everything else constant, the interest rate has to be raised by some 30 basis points to damp down growth and the domestic inflation that it provokes. (In constructing this example I assume that it is the log exchange rate but the level of the interest rate that enter equation (2′).) In reality, the optimal response depends on more than simply these two parameters, as should now be clear, but Ball (1999) shows that Freedman's intuition is basically correct: that the weights coefficients are likely to be fairly close to the ratio of coefficients on the exchange rate and the interest rate in the Phillips curve.

28 Under the assumption that even temporary shocks to the foreign exchange market have persistent output effects, as will be the case given the structure of equation (2′).

29 Ryan and Thompson (2000) suggest that it may not be necessary to explicitly target the domestic price index if the CPI target is defined as an interval rather than a point. They argue that Australia's monetary policy framework deals with this problem by permitting relatively small divergences from the 2–3 percent target band over the cycle "provided inflation is forecast to be back within 2–3 percent in the medium term. The forward-looking nature of policy should also be sufficient to prevent the RBA from responding to exchange rate shocks which are only expected to have a temporary effect on inflation" (Ryan and Thompson 2000: 2).

30 It may seem peculiar that the central bank will intervene less to neutralize transitory shocks to the foreign exchange market (which standard efficiency arguments suggest it might want to obviate) than in response to long-lived shocks. The result reflects the existence of control lags between monetary policy on the one hand and inflation and output on the other; in this setup, responding as vigorously to a purely temporary shock as to a permanent shock just destabilizes the target variables.

31 We can model this by adding the commodity market disturbance μ to the exchange-rate and aggregate-demand relationships, equations (5) and (2′). The former becomes:

$$e_t - E(e_{t+1}) = r_t - r' + \nu_t + \mu_t \tag{5′}$$

while the latter becomes:

$$y_{t+1} - y^* = \lambda(y_t - y^*) - \beta(r_t - r^*) - \delta e_t + \xi\mu_t + n_{t+1} \tag{2″}$$

where ξ is a parameter linking the terms-of-trade shock to aggregate demand. (The export-demand shock is assumed to affect output with the same lag as movements in the exchange rate emanating from other sources.)

32 Otherwise, inflation will decline with the growth in the gap between potential and current output. The appropriate response for an inflation-targeting central bank is to cut interest rates, regardless of the weight it attaches to output variability. Now central bank behavior will not resemble fear of floating. To the contrary, the cut in interest rates will accentuate the change in the value of the currency. Because the decline in foreign demand requires a weaker exchange rate in order to stabilize output (and because the cut in demand also subdues inflation), the central bank does nothing to limit the adjustment of the exchange rate; to the contrary, it encourages it to adjust.

33 The sources and further implications of limited credibility are left to Subsection 4.4 below.

34 There is some anecdotal evidence of this for Brazil and Mexico (Mishkin and Savastano 2000) and Israel (Leiderman and Bufman 2001).
35 See Sachs (1980).
36 This is not to say that central bankers in fully indexed economies have necessarily had particular success in hitting that target, especially in those countries where fiscal deficits are chronic and central bank independence is limited.
37 This is just the limiting case of the thought experiment described at the beginning of the previous paragraph.
38 We are in what Calvo (2000b) refers to as the world of the traditional model.
39 See below.
40 As noted above, this can be interpreted as minimizing the loss function using all the relevant information. This should be the central bank's internal forecast and not a market forecast to avoid problems of multiple equilibria.
41 The point applies to Brazil, for example, which had considerable success in moderating inflation between 1994 and 1998.
42 There are likely to be credibility issues here as well. Again I defer these to a subsequent subsection.
43 The now extensive literature on contagion is concerned with this point.
44 Since their measure of core inflation is constructed transparently, this should be something that private agents are able to replicate.
45 It turns out that this is not precisely what those concerned with the perverse effect of exchange rate changes in the presence of liability dollarization have in mind, as I explain momentarily.
46 We can also see this from Freedman's formulation of the monetary conditions indicator and from Ball's model, where the weight on the exchange rate in the MEI declines with δ.
47 This is therefore what Cespedes *et al.* (2001), find in their simulation model of optimal monetary policies in the presence of liability dollarization.
48 Here it is important to interpret e as the *real* exchange rate and r as the *real* interest rate, since even temporary depreciation will lead to inflation and a higher price level, whose implications for the real exchange rate are otherwise suppressed in this simple model by omitting that price level from the aggregate demand equation.
49 The same is now true of a negative Calvo shock: the tendency for higher (domestic and world) interest rates to depress output is offset by policies that push the exchange rate up and strengthen balance sheets.
50 If, for example, default rates are not just proportional to the rate of currency depreciation but increase at an accelerating pace, this could plausibly be the case.
51 In either a rare instance of internal consistency or a fortuitous coincidence.
52 It is revealing that emerging markets have generally introduced full-fledged inflation targeting only after first attaining strong fiscal positions. See Schaechter *et al.* (2000). Then there is the argument of whether inflation targeting is part of the solution to the problem of "fiscal dominance," as the time inconsistency problem created by chronic deficits is known. This is, of course, the same argument made by some advocates of hard pegs and is open to the same objections. I return to this point below.
53 A comprehensive compendium of the relevant evidence is Mahadeva and Sterne (2000).
54 I say more on the reform of fiscal institutions below.
55 The same negative implications also follow, of course, for any other monetary regime if the financial system is fragile, the commitment to fiscal discipline is questionable, the monetary authorities lack autonomy and independence, and the economy is subject to foreign disturbances. I return to this point in the conclusion.

56 In countries where the authorities have manipulated price indices in the past, they may question whether an index specially constructed for use in inflation targeting can be taken at face value.

57 As Jonas (2000: 3) writes of the Czech case, "The 'just-do-it' approach to monetary policy probably would not be very effective in bringing inflation expectations and actual inflation down. Public announcements by the CNB about its expectations of future inflation would also probably not suffice to anchor inflation expectations and persuade economic agents that monetary policy would actually be conducted with the aim to achieve the announced inflation."

58 There is evidence that more centralized and hierarchical fiscal policy-making processes lead to better fiscal outcomes and that large vertical imbalances heighten bailout and inflation risk (von Hagen and Eichengreen 1996).

59 While the Czech Republic and South Africa have escape clauses spelling out in advance the circumstances in which targets may be missed and requiring the central bank to indicate the time frame over which it will attempt to return to the target inflation path, in practice neither country has been willing to utilize the provision.

60 Chile is thus said to have chosen "a clear and widely understood index like the headline CPI ... [in order] to enhance the communicational effectiveness of inflation targeting" (Morande 2000: 161). From this point of view it is no coincidence that emerging market inflation targeters typically target the CPI while industrial-country inflation targeters generally target core inflation (Schaechter *et al.* 2000).

61 Or, in the European case, by joining a monetary union in partnership with the issuers of a recognized international currency.

62 In this respect, it obviously complicates the execution and effects of *any* monetary policy operating strategy, and not just inflation targeting. I return to this momentarily.

63 Even if they do, questions about the central bank's intentions and independence mean that financial variables and the nonfinancial magnitudes they affect will be more volatile than in a country whose inflation-targeting central bank enjoys greater credibility. Under such circumstances, it is unrealistic to promise that volatility will fall to the levels enjoyed by advanced-industrial economies that target inflation. The same is true, of course, of any other monetary regime so long as the financial system is fragile, the commitment to fiscal discipline is questionable, and the economy is subject to foreign disturbances. A dollarized emerging market subject to these conditions will similarly be more volatile than the typical advanced-industrial country. Some may argue that the very act of dollarizing can solve all problems of financial fragility. Others will suggest that explicit inflation targeting can solve problems of fiscal indiscipline. If either argument is correct, then it creates a strong presumption in favor of one or the other of these regimes. But most readers presumably believe that financial problems have deeper roots than simply the monetary regime, and that fiscal problems are a function of more than just the availability of seignorage revenues. This is just another way of saying that a mere change in monetary regime is unlikely to solve all problems of economic development, miraculously transforming developing countries into G7 nations.

References

Aghion, Philippe, Bachetta, Philippe and Banerjee, Abijit (1999), "Capital markets and instability in open economies," unpublished manuscript, Study Center Gerzensee.

Ball, Lawrence (1999), "Policy rules for open economies," in Taylor, John (ed.), *Monetary Policy Rules,* Chicago: University of Chicago Press, pp. 127–156.

Bernanke, Ben, Lubach, Thomas, Mishkin, Frederic and Posen, Adam (1999), *Inflation Targeting: Lessons from the International Experience,* Princeton: Princeton University Press.

Bharucha, Nargis and Kent, Christopher (1998), "Inflation targeting in a small open economy," Discussion Paper no. 98-07, Reserve Bank of Australia (July).

Bogdanski, Joel, Tombini, Alexandre and Werlang, Sergio (2000), "Implementing inflation targeting in Brazil," Working Paper no. 1, Central Bank of Brazil (July).

Calvo, Guillermo (2000a), "The case for hard pegs," unpublished manuscript, University of Maryland at College Park.

Calvo, Guillermo (2000b), "Capital markets and the exchange rate, with special reference to the dollarization debate in Latin America," unpublished manuscript, University of Maryland at College Park.

Calvo, Guillermo and Reinhart, Carmen (2000), "Fear of floating," NBER Working Paper no. 7993 (November).

Cepedes, Luis Felipe, Chang, Roberto and Velasco, Andres (2001), "Dollarization of liabilities, net worth effects, and optimal monetary policy," unpublished manuscript, NYU, Rutgers and Harvard University.

Christoffersen, Peter and Wescott, Robert (1999), "Is Poland ready for inflation targeting?" IMF Working Paper no. 99/41 (March).

Cooper, Richard (1999), "Exchange rate choices," in Little, Jane Sneddon and Olivei, Giovanni (eds), *Rethinking the International Monetary System,* Boston: Federal Reserve Bank of Boston, pp. 99–123.

De Brouwer, G. and O'Regan, J. (1997), "Evaluating simple monetary-policy rules for Australia," in Lowe, Philip (ed.), *Monetary Policy and Inflation Targeting,* Sydney: Reserve Bank of Australia, pp. 244–276.

Devereux, Michael and Lane, Philip (2000), "Exchange rates and monetary policy in emerging market economies," unpublished manuscript, University of British Columbia and Hong Kong Monetary Authority.

Eichengreen, Barry (2000), "When to dollarize," *Journal of Money, Credit and Banking* (forthcoming).

Eichengreen, Barry, Masson, Paul, Savastano, Miguel and Sharma, Sunil (1999), "Transition strategies and nominal anchors on the road to greater exchange rate flexibility," *Essays in International Finance* no. 213, International Finance Section, Department of Economics, Princeton University (April).

Freedman, Charles (1994), "The use of indicators and of the Monetary Conditions Index in Canada," in Balino, Tomas J.T. and Cottarelli, Carlo (eds), *Frameworks for Monetary Stability,* Washington, DC: International Monetary Fund, pp. 458–477.

Gomez, Javier (2000), "Inflation targeting and openness," unpublished manuscript, Central Bank of Colombia.

Hausmann, Ricardo (1999), "Should there be 5 currencies or 105?," *Foreign Policy,* 122: 44–53.

Hoffmaister, Alexander (1999), "Inflation targeting in Korea: an empirical exploration," IMF Working Paper no. WP/99/7, Washington, DC: IMF (January).

Hunt, Ben (1999), "Inter-forecast monetary policy implementation: fixed-instrument versus MCI-based strategies," Discussion Paper no. G99/1, Reserve Bank of New Zealand (March).

Jonas, Jiri (2000), "Inflation targeting in transition economies: some issues and experience," in Coats, Warren (ed.), *Inflation Targeting in Transition Economies: The Case of the Czech Republic* (forthcoming).

Krugman, Paul (2001), "Crises: the next generation," unpublished manuscript, Princeton University.

Kumhof, Michael (2000), "Inflation targeting under imperfect credibility," unpublished manuscript, Department of Economics, Stanford University.

Leiderman, Leo and Bufman, Gil (2001), "Surprises on Israel's road to exchange rate flexibility," *Emerging Markets Research,* Deutsche Bank, 23 March.

Levin, Andrew, Wieland, Volker and Williams, John C. (1999), "Robustness of simple monetary policy rules under model uncertainty," in Taylor, John (ed.), *Monetary Policy Rules,* Chicago: University of Chicago Press, pp. 263–299.

Mahadeva, Lavan and Stern, Gabriel (eds) (2000), *Monetary Policy Frameworks in a Global Context,* London: Routledge.

Masson, Paul, Savastano, Miguel and Sharma, Sunil (1997), "The scope for inflation targeting in developing countries," IMF Working Paper no. 130 (October).

Mishkin, Frederic (2000a), "Inflation targeting for emerging-market economies," *American Economic Review Papers and Proceedings*, 90: 105–109.

Mishkin, Frederic (2000b), "Issues in inflation targeting," in Bank of Canada, *Price Stability and the Long-Run Target for Monetary Policy,* Ottawa: Bank of Canada (forthcoming).

Mishkin, Frederic and Savastano, Miguel (2000), "Monetary policy strategies for Latin America," NBER Working Paper no. 7617 (March).

Morande, Felipe G. (2000), "A decade of inflation targeting in Chile: main developments and lessons," in Joseph, Charles and Gunawan, Anton (eds), *Monetary Policy and Inflation Targeting in Emerging Economies,* Jakarta: Bank Indonesia, pp. 149–179.

Morgan, J.P. (2001), "Hungary Joins Inflation Targeting Club 'Implicitly,'" *Global Data Watch*, 15 (June): 11–12.

Mundell, Robert (2000), "The International monetary system in the 21st century," Latrobe, PA: St. Vincent's College.

Rivas, Luis A. (2001), "Underlying inflation measures as short-run inflation targets in developing economies: the case of Nicaragua," unpublished manuscript, Central Bank of Nicaragua.

Ryan, Chris and Thompson, Christopher (2000), "Inflation targeting and exchange rate fluctuations in Australia," Research Discussion Paper 2000-06, Reserve Bank of Australia (September).

Sachs, Jeffrey A. (1980), "Wages, flexible exchange rates, and macroeconomic policy," *Quarterly Journal of Economics*, 94: 737–747.

Schaechter, Andrea, Stone, Mark R. and Zelmer, Mark (2000), "Adopting inflation targeting: practical issues for emerging market countries," Occasional Paper no. 202, Washington, DC: IMF.

Svensson, Lars (1996), "Commentary," in Federal Reserve Bank of Kansas City, *Achieving Price Stability,* Kansas City: Federal Reserve Bank of Kansas City, pp. 209–228.

Svensson, Lars (1999), "Inflation targeting as a monetary policy rule," *Journal of Monetary Economics*, 43: 607–654.

Svensson, Lars (2000), "Open-economy inflation targeting," *Journal of International Economics*, 50: 155–183.

Taylor, John B. (1993), "Discretion versus policy rules in practice," *Carnegie Rochester Conference Series on Public Policy*, 39: 195–214.

von Hagen, Juergen and Eichengreen, Barry (1996), "Fiscal restraints, federalism and European Monetary Union: is the excessive deficit procedure counterproductive?," *American Economic Review Papers and Proceedings*, 86: 134–138.

3 Exchange rates, inflation and monetary policy objectives in open economies

The experience of Chile

Rodrigo Caputo[1]

1 Introduction

Inflation targeting was adopted by Chile in 1990. In practice, this means that every year the Chilean Central Bank (CCB) announced the inflation target,[2] and then it made use of the monetary instruments (interest rate) to fulfill this objective. Some other objectives, like controlling the real exchange rate or avoiding excessive fluctuations in the output level were not explicit objectives of the CCB.

There is some evidence, however, that central banks in emerging economies use the interest rate to avoid exchange rate fluctuations. In fact, Calvo and Reinhart (2002), concluded that in some countries interest rate and exchange rate move in the same direction; depreciations in the exchange rate (domestic price of foreign currency) generate an increase in the interest rate controlled by the central bank. Furthermore, they argue that interest rate policy is replacing foreign exchange intervention as the preferred means of smoothing exchange rate fluctuations. According to this view monetary authorities try to stabilize the exchange rate, even if they claim to have a flexible exchange rate system.

Another reason why a central bank may react to real exchange rate, independently of its impact on future inflation, is that in this way it can improve macroeconomic performance. In fact, some simulations reported by Cecchetti *et al.* (2000), suggest that responding to exchange rate shocks over and above the effect of such a shock on the central bank's inflation forecast appears to be welfare-improving.[3] In a different study, Batini *et al.* (2003), concluded that an inflation-forecast-based rule, i.e., one that reacts to deviations of expected inflation from target, performs well in a two-sector model calibrated on UK data. Adding a separate response to the level of the real exchange rate (contemporaneous and lagged) appears to reduce the difference in adjustment between output gaps in the two sectors of the economy.

Finally, on a different strand of literature, Vitale (2003) shows that monetary policy decisions and foreign exchange rate interventions may be correlated. In fact, if a central bank is in charge of both interest rate decisions and foreign exchange rate interventions – as it was the case in Chile until September, 1999 – it can intervene in the exchange market to signal the implicit target for the exchange rate. In particular, it buys (sells) the foreign currency to signal a greater (smaller) than expected target for the exchange rate. In this case, a reduction (increase) in the interest rate is a policy reaction that is consistent with this signal. In fact, if the uncovered interest parity condition (UIP) holds, a reduction (increase) in the domestic interest rate generates a depreciation (appreciation) consistent with the new target for exchange rate. Hence, when the central bank perceives a real exchange rate misalignment, it may use both foreign exchange rate interventions and monetary policy interest rate to correct it.

The objective of this chapter is to assess the importance of exchange rate and output fluctuations in the conduct of monetary policy in Chile. In doing so, we estimate the monetary policy reaction function of the CCB using monthly data from 1985.01 to 2002.04. In practice, we present estimations for two subsamples; first from 1985.01 to 1990.08 where the CCB did not have any explicit target, and then for the sub-sample 1990.09 to 2002.04 where inflation was the only explicitly-stated objective of monetary policy. Contrasting results from both periods allows us to compare the reaction functions under the two regimes.

Besides characterizing the CCB reaction function, we test for nonlinear responses to real exchange rate deviations. In particular, we test whether relatively large deviations generate a stronger policy response. On the other hand, we also assess the importance that future paths of inflation, beyond the specific targeting horizon, have in determining the policy interest rate.

The theoretical framework used here allows us to test whether inflation played an important role in the determination of the CCB interest rate. In this setup, suggested by Clarida *et al.* (1998) and Clarida (2001), we can also assess the importance of non-explicit objectives that the central bank may have, namely controlling exchange rate fluctuations or avoiding deviations of output from its potential level.

In previous studies for Chile, Parrado (2000) and Parrado and Velasco (2002), the basic findings were that neither the real exchange rate, nor output deviations play a significant role in determining the monetary policy in Chile. Those were the first attempts to identify, in a framework different than the VAR,[4] the CCB monetary policy reaction function. Although, we adopt a similar approach, Generalized Method of Moments (GMM), to identify the systematic components of the monetary policy, the questions we address, and to some extent the methodology itself, differ substantially from Parrado (2000) and Parrado and Velasco (2002).

The basic results are as follows:

1   As expected, in the targeting period, 1990.09 to 2002.04, the CCB reacted to anticipated inflation deviations from target. The CCB also reacted to output and exchange rate fluctuations above the predicted

inflation effects. Then, we conclude that in this period there were additional non-explicit objectives of the monetary authority. This result was robust to different specifications of the monetary policy reaction function.

2   In the pre-explicit inflation targeting period, 1985.01 to 1990.08, the CCB reacted to exchange rate and output fluctuations. The response to anticipated inflation was, however, with the opposite sign and significant. Therefore, monetary policy in this period was an accommodative one with respect to inflation, although it stabilized output and exchange rate.

This chapter is organized as follows; in section 2 we briefly describe the main objectives of the CCB and the instrument it has been using since 1985. In section 3, we specify a simple forward-looking model of policy interest rate. This is a modified version of Clarida *et al.* (1998, 2000) model. In particular, we introduce modifications to estimate a rule that is based on managing the real (ex-post) interest rate as opposed to the nominal one. This modification is of crucial importance, given the way in which the monetary policy is formulated in Chile. Section 4 describes the estimation procedure and the data that are used in this study. In section 5, we present the basic results from estimating by GMM the monetary policy reaction function. Finally, section 6 concludes.

2 Monetary and exchange rate policies in Chile

The 1980 Chilean Constitution empowers the CCB to "stabilize the value of the currency and provide normality in the functioning of internal and external payments." This statement has been interpreted as giving three main objectives to the CCB: to control inflation, to provide a sound regulation of the banking system, and to avoid situations that may lead to currency crisis.

From 1980 to 1990, the CCB did not have any explicit target for inflation. It is only from 1990 that the CCB adopted an explicit inflation targeting regime. The procedure works as follows: each September, in its Report to the Congress, the CCB announces the CPI inflation target for the end of the following year (December year-on-year CPI inflation). This means that the target is announced fifteen months in advance. In practice, the target was gradually adjusted so as to allow for a gradual reduction of inflation. In fact, in 1990 the target, for the following year, was set at 27 percent whereas from 2001 onwards the target was 3 percent (Figure 3.1).

As noted by Parrado (2001), the inflation targeting regime allows for flexibility; there is no legal mandate to achieve the target each year. This flexibility along with the gradual adjustment of the inflation target, has contributed to maintain high rates of real GDP growth; on average 6.7 percent a year between 1990 and 2000.

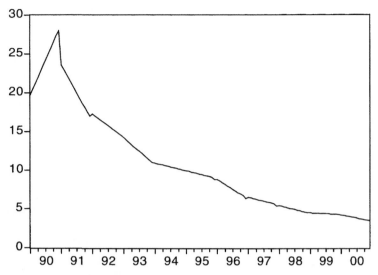

Figure 3.1 Chile. CPI inflation target (%).

Since 1985, the interest rate has been the main instrument of monetary policy. From 1985 to April 1995, the CCB used a short-term (three months) interest rate indexed to CPI inflation. In May 1995 the CCB changed its policy instrument to an overnight indexed interest rate which is controlled through open-market operations. Those operations are performed by issuing CCB papers and by conducting repos and anti-repos.

As pointed out by Valdes (1997), the use of indexed interest rates is equivalent to set ex-post real interest rates. There were, at least, three reasons for using real interest rates. First, the demand for money had been unstable over the period, therefore the use of interest rate, as a policy instrument, had more predictable effects over output and inflation than monetary aggregates. Second, the high degree of indexation of the Chilean economy (including financial contracts) made it difficult to use nominal interest rates. Finally, in an environment of high and unpredictable inflation, movements in the real interest rates were easy to understand and did not have double interpretations as in the case of nominal rates.[5]

The CCB has also the power to set the exchange rate policy. From August 1984 to September 1999, the CCB adopted a crawling exchange rate band, which was subject to several modifications (see Figure 3.2). Since September 2, 1999, the country has embraced a fully-flexible exchange rate regime, with the possibility of monetary authority interven-

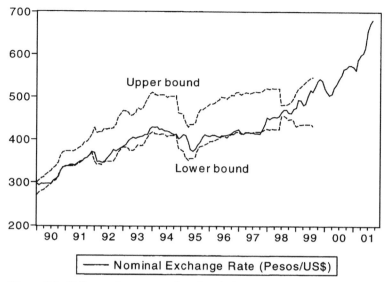

Figure 3.2 Chile: exchange rate band and observed exchange rate.

ing in the market only if the exchange rate does not reflect the "real" value of the foreign currency (Parrado 2001: 7).

The basic instruments the CCB used to stabilize the nominal exchange rate, within the band, were interventions in the foreign exchange market and, in some cases, modifications to the limits of the band. As noted by Parrado (2001), at the end of 1991, Chile's strong external accounts forced the CCB to lower the referential dollar exchange rate (central parity) by 5 percent and to widen the band to ±10 percent. Although this decision was taken to increase the market role in determining the exchange rate, in March of 1992 it was decided that the CCB should have a "dirty" floating option to intervene within the band. In this context, intra-marginal foreign-exchange rate interventions by the CCB were frequent and, at times, intense (Landerretche *et al.* 1999).

The elimination of the band in September 1999, did not imply the absence of foreign exchange interventions. In fact, "in response to large exchange rate depreciation and volatility, the CCB announced and carried out a temporary policy of sterilized interventions between July 2001 and January 2002.[6] The stated objectives of the interventions were to reduce excessive exchange rate volatility and provide a hedge against future devaluations, without affecting exchange rate trends." Schmidt-Hebbel and Werner (2002: 72).

3 A forward-looking model of interest rate

Following Clarida *et al.* (1998, 2000) and Clarida (2001), we specify a forward-looking model for the nominal interest rate. We introduce, however, some modifications in order to obtain the ex-post real interest rate that is, in practice, the instrument used by the CCB since 1985.

In a forward-looking environment, the nominal policy interest rate will be determined by current expectations of central bank's objectives. If we assume the central bank is concerned about deviations of future inflation, output, and exchange rate, we can express the reaction function as follows:

$$i_t^* = i + \beta(E_t[\pi_{t+n}] - \pi_{t+n}^*) + \gamma_1(E_t[y_t] - y_t^*) + \gamma_2(E_t[e_t] - e_t^*) \tag{1}$$

where i_t^* is the nominal interest rate set by the central bank, i is the equilibrium nominal interest rate and $(E_t[\pi_{t+n}] - \pi_{t+n}^*)$ is the deviation of expected inflation from a predetermined target π_{t+n}^*.[7] The central bank may also be concerned about deviations of output from the equilibrium level, $E_t[y_t] - y_t^*$, and deviations of the real exchange rate, $E_t[e_t] - e_t^*$. It is important to notice that the parameters γ_1 and γ_2 capture the non-inflationary components of output and exchange rate deviations. That is, both elements may be objectives of monetary policy even when expected inflation is on target; $(E_t[\pi_{t+n}] - \pi_{t+n}^*) = 0$. Therefore, the specification in equation (1) allows us to test whether output and exchange rate are *per se* objectives of the monetary authorities. In fact, under the null hypothesis that the central bank is not concerned with output and exchange rate, the coefficients γ_1 and γ_2 should be equal to zero.

We can re-express equation (1) in real terms by subtracting $E_t[\pi_{t+n}]$ from both sides of equation (1), and by adding and substracting π_{t+n}^* from the right hand side of equation (1). Hence, the ex-ante, n period, real interest rate is expressed as follows:

$$r_{ea,t}^* = \bar{r} + (\beta - 1)(E_t[\pi_{t+n}] - \pi_{t+n}^*) + \gamma_1(E_t[y_t] - y_t^*) + \gamma_2(E_t[e_t] - e_t^*) \tag{2}$$

where $r_{ea,t}^* = i_t^* - E_t[\pi_{t+n}]$ is the ex-ante real interest rate and $\bar{r}$ is the equilibrium real interest rate. In this specification, if β is greater than one, the real interest rate increases whenever expected inflation is above the target level. In this case, the central bank tries to stabilize inflation.

On the contrary, when β is less than one the central bank moves the interest rate in order to partially accommodate any increase in the expected level of inflation. As a result, the monetary authority is not stabilizing inflation.

Now, in order to obtain an expression for the ex-post real interest rate, we add and subtract the actual inflation over $t + n$ on the left hand side of equation (2). Then, the ex-post real interest rate is defined as:

$$r_t^* = \bar{r} + (\beta - 1)(E_t[\pi_{t+n}] - \pi_{t+n}^*) + \gamma_1(E_t[y_t] - y_t^*) + \gamma_2(E_t[e_t] - e_t^*) + \epsilon_t \tag{3}$$

where $r_t^* = i_t^* - \pi_{t+n}$ is the ex-post real interest rate and $\epsilon_t = E_t[\pi_{t+n}] - \pi_{t+n}$ is the inflation prediction error. Equation (3), however, does not capture the tendency that a central bank may have to smooth changes in interest rates. Introducing this tendency may be a difficult task so it is assumed, for simplicity, that the ex-post real interest rate, r_t, partially adjusts to its target level, r_t^*. This assumption can be expressed as:

$$r_t = (1 - \rho)r_t^* + \rho r_{t-1} + v_t \qquad (4)$$

where the parameter $\rho \in [0, 1]$ captures the degree of interest rate smoothing and v_t represents a zero mean real interest rate innovation.

Combining equations (3) and (4), gives an expression for the real interest rate that allows for inertial behavior:

$$r_t = (1 - \rho)\bar{r} + (1 - \rho)[(\beta - 1)(\pi_{t+n} - \pi_{t+n}^*) + \gamma_1(y_t - y_t^*) \\ + \gamma_2(e_t - e_t^*)] + \rho r_{t-1} + u_t \qquad (5)$$

equation (5) is expressed now as function of realizations of the relevant variables, plus an error term, u_t, which is a linear combination of prediction errors and the policy innovation, v_t. In particular, u_t is defined as:

$$u_t = \{v_t + (1 - \rho)[\beta(E_t[\pi_{t+n}] - \pi_{t+n}) + \gamma_1(E_t[y_t] - y_t) + \gamma_2(E_t[e_t] - e_t)]\}$$

Equation (5) is the expression to be estimated empirically. One advantage of this formulation is that all the dependent variables are future and current realizations of observable variables. Therefore, we avoid the problem of modeling, explicitly, agents' expectations.

4 Estimation

Equation (5) contains all the parameters of interest. In fact, it is straightforward to test whether exchange rate and output misalignments, are objectives of the central bank – independently of their impact on future inflation. In this case, a simple t-test on the significance of γ_1 and γ_2 can be performed. If γ_1 and γ_2 are statistically different from zero, then it is not possible to reject the hypothesis that the central bank has additional objectives.

Now, it is evident that the correlation between the error term, u_t, and future inflation in equation (5) is different from zero. In these circumstances, estimating this relationship with Ordinary Least Squares (OLS) will generate biased estimators. To overcome this problem, equation (5) is estimated using GMM, as in Clarida *et al.* (1998, 2000).

To apply GMM it is necessary to impose an orthogonality condition between the explanatory variables and the error term in equation (5). In particular, let Z_t be the set of instruments orthogonal to u_t; $E[Z_t u_t] = 0$. This set of instruments is known when the CB sets the real interest rate, r_t.

Then, it is possible to estimate the parameters in the following expression using GMM:

$$E_t\{(r_t - (1 - \rho)\bar{r} - (1 - \rho)[(\beta - 1)(\pi_{t+n} - \pi^*_{t+n}) + \gamma_1(y_t - y^*_t) + \gamma_2(e_t - e^*_t)])Z_t\} = 0$$

By construction, the residual series u_t features and $MA(n-1)$ structure and empirical moments cannot be considered as serially independent. In order to sort out this problem we follow the estimation procedure suggested by Favero (2001); when implementing GMM estimation we correct for heteroscedasticity and autocorrelation of unknown form with a lag truncation parameter of $n-1$. Furthermore, Barlett weights are chosen to ensure positive definiteness of the estimated variance-covariance matrix (see Favero 2001: 233).

In order to assess whether a particular set of instruments, Z_t, is valid a J-test of overidentifying restrictions is implemented. This test has a χ^2 distribution with $m - k$ degrees of freedom, where m is the number of instruments used and k is the number of variables to be instrumented.

4.1 Data

We use monthly time series from 1985.01 to 2002.04. The data are[8]:

y_t: log IMACEC[9] (source: Central Bank of Chile)

π_t: year on year CPI variation (source: Central Bank of Chile)

π^*_t: inflation target from 1990 to 2002 CCB data; from 1987 to 1990 private expectations (Valdes 1997)

e_t: log of the real exchange rate (source: Central Bank of Chile)

r_t: CCB's domestic real interest rate, this is an hybrid definition: from 1987 to 1995 is the indexed interest rate on the three months CCB instruments (PRBC 90); from 1995 to 2001 is the CCB's overnight indexed interest rate (source: Central Bank of Chile)

tot: terms of trade, this variable is used as one of the instruments (Valdes and Bennett (2001)).

4.1.1 Identifying the cyclical component in the series

The long-term equilibrium of the relevant variables, output and exchange rate, can be obtained by applying different filtering techniques. For instance, Parrado (2000) in a similar exercise for Chile used a quadratic detrending procedure to obtain the output gap, $(y_t - y^*_t)$. Alternatively, a Hodrick and Prescott (HP) filter can be used.

In this chapter we use an alternative methodology; in order to determine the output gap, $(y_t - y^*_t)$, and the exchange rate misalignment, $(e_t - e^*_t)$, a structural times series model for each series is fitted. Using this approach has the advantage of avoiding the creation of spurious cycles, that can be one of the consequences of using an HP *ad hoc* filtering procedure (Harvey and Jaeger 1993). Another advantage of this procedure is that the irregular movements of the series can be separated from the cycle.

Fitting a trend plus cycle model to the Chilean output,[10] y_t, results in an output gap series, *y_stam*, that is less volatile than the series obtained with the HP filter, *y_hp* (see Figure 3.3). In a similar way, the output gap obtained by using linear or quadratic detrending procedures is much

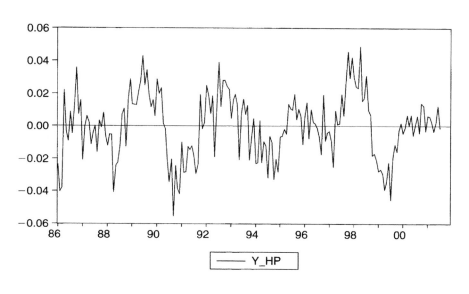

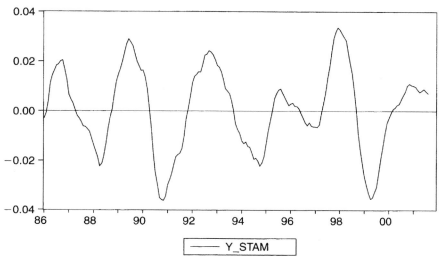

Figure 3.3 Chilean output: cyclical deviations.

noisier. The cyclical component obtained from the HP, linear and quadratic detrending procedures is much more volatile because it includes the irregular movements in output which appear to be substantial.[11] On the other hand, when a structural times series model is fitted, the irregular component is removed from the cycle. As a result, the output gap series, y_stam, is less volatile.

From an economic perspective, the cycle obtained with a structural times series model has a meaningful interpretation. In fact, it captures many of the stylized facts of the Chilean business cycle. In particular, the slowdown of the Chilean economy at the beginning of the 1990s and the subsequent recovery, between 1992 to 1994, are well reflected by this cycle. On the other hand, the rapid expansion of the economy between 1997 and mid 1998 and the subsequent crisis in 1999 are also captured. Finally, the slow recovery of the economy in 2000 and 2001 is reflected at the end of the period.

To obtain the cyclical component of the real exchange rate, e_t, the same procedure is applied; a structural time series model is fitted. As before, the cycle obtained by fitting a structural model, rer_stam, is less volatile than a cycle obtained using the HP filter, rer_hp (Figure 3.4). On the other hand, the rer_hp series presents a seasonal behavior; appreciations at the beginning of each year. This may reflect changes in seasonality that are not captured by the HP procedure. In fact, Harvey (2002) argues that changes in seasonality may not be captured by the non-model-based seasonal adjustment procedure such as the US Census Bureau's X-12 used when filtering by HP. Again, this problem is overcome when using a structural time series model.

The economic interpretation of real exchange rate deviations is more difficult. In fact, there is no consensus in Chile about the level of the equilibrium real exchange rate in the past decade. Many economists suggested that an important degree of real appreciation was present in the 1990s, but there is no a clear description of this appreciation path on a monthly basis. In any case, the pressure over the exchange rate market in 1998–1999 is well reflected by the real exchange rate misalignments presented in Figure 3.4.

Finally, for inflation we do not need to use any detrending procedure, instead we compute the inflation gap, $\pi_{t+n} - \pi_{t+n}^*$, as the difference between actual inflation and target inflation. The series is presented in Figure 3.5.

5 Results

In this section, we present the results of estimating the policy reaction function in equation (5) and three alternative specifications. We assume $n = 15$, which is consistent with the way in which the CCB sets its inflation targets. On the other hand, due to the lag in the availability of informa-

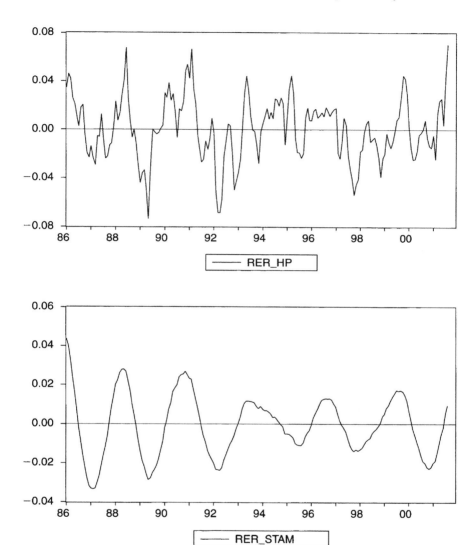

Figure 3.4 Chilean real exchange rate: cyclical deviations.

tion, the CCB cannot observe output in t nor in $t-1$. As a result, at time t the CCB forms expectations about y_{t-1}. In a similar way, the CCB cannot observe perfectly the contemporaneous level of real exchange rate misalignments, hence at time t, it forms expectations about e_t using past information.

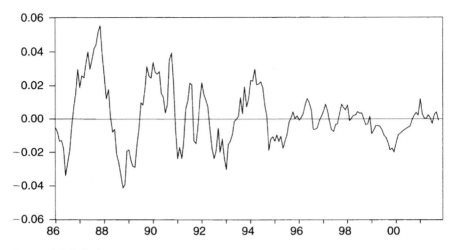

Figure 3.5 Inflation gap.

Now, the set of instruments, Z_t, included six lags in output gap (from $t-2$), three lags in policy interest rate, five lags in the inflation gap, three lags in the real exchange rate, and lags in the terms of trade variation. In all cases the *J*-test cannot reject the validity of this set of instruments.

5.1 Linear policy response to exchange rate

In Table 3.1, we present the result of estimating by GMM the monetary policy reaction function in equation (5). The implicit assumption in this formulation is that policy response to real exchange rate deviations is linear. This assumption will be removed later on.

For the period without an explicit inflation target, 1985.01 to 1990.08, we find a negative and significant response to expected inflation. On the contrary, the CCB's response to exchange rate and output deviations was positive and significant. The degree of inertia in the policy rule is high;

Table 3.1 Estimation of equation (5) by GMM

	$\bar{r}$	ρ	$(\beta-1)$	γ_1	γ_2	*J*-test
Non targeting period	0.069	0.900	−0.384	1.840	1.607	4.2
(1985.01–1990.08)	(0.00)	(0.01)	(0.03)	(0.06)	(0.10)	[0.99]
Targeting period	0.052	0.878	0.786	1.122	0.633	6.8
(1990.09–2002.04)	(0.00)	(0.02)	(0.18)	(0.31)	(0.18)	[0.99]

Notes
J-test is the test for overidentifying that has a distribution χ^2_{19}.
Standard errors in parentheses.
p values in square brackets.

$\rho = 0.90$ and the average real interest rate is 7.0 percent. The monetary policy in this period can be characterized as an accommodative one with respect to inflation. The main concerns of the central bank, according to the results, where exchange rate and output deviations.

As expected, the results for the targeting period, 1990.09 to 2002.04, show a positive and significant response to expected inflation. This is consistent with the widespread view that, since 1990, the CCB has responded aggressively to inflation deviations from target. On the other hand, CCB's responses to output and exchange rate are positive and significant. In particular, it is possible to reject the null that $\gamma_1 = 0$ and $\gamma_2 = 0$. This latter result indicates that the CCB had some concerns about output and real exchange rate deviations, even though they were not explicit targets. The average real interest rate in this period is 5.2 percent and the degree of inertia in the policy is, again, high; $\rho = 0.878$.

In both cases, the policy rule is quite inertial. However, on a monthly basis this means that the mean lag of a monetary shock is less than one year.[12] For the United States, Clarida *et al.* (2000) find that the implied smoothness parameter is of the same magnitude but the mean lag is larger because the data are on a quarterly basis.

5.1.1 *Structural break*

As discussed previously, Chile moved to a floating exchange rate in September 1999. This policy change may have affected the way in which the CCB set interest rate in response to various shocks. In particular, it is possible that the CCB used the interest rate to avoid exchange rate fluctuations in a more aggressive way after September 1999. In fact, if foreign exchange rate interventions are not as important as before, the only instrument left to the CCB, to stabilize the exchange rate, is the interest rate. In order to test the importance of this policy change, we include a multiplicative dummy variable in equation (5). In particular, the dummy variable is $DUM99 = 0$ after September 1999 and $DUM99 = 1$ before that date. As a result the alternative specification for the CCB's reaction function is given by:

$$
\begin{aligned}
r_t &= (1 - \rho)\bar{r} + (1 - \rho)[(\beta - 1)(\pi_{t+n} - \pi_{t+n}^*) + \gamma_1(y_t - y_t^*) \\
&+ \gamma_2(e_t - e_t^*) + DUM99(e_t - e_t^*)] + \rho r_{t-1} + u_t
\end{aligned} \tag{6}
$$

Equation (6) is estimated using the same set of instrumental variables as before. The results are presented in Table 3.2.

There is evidence that, after September 1999, the CCB's reaction to exchange rate misalignments was stronger. In fact, this response is $\gamma_1 = 0.693$ after that date and it is $\gamma_1 = 0.693 - 0.483 = 0.21$ before that. One interpretation of this result is that the abandonment of an explicit exchange rate band put additional pressure on the monetary policy when

Table 3.2 Estimation of equation (6) by GMM

	$\bar{r}$	ρ	$(\beta-1)$	γ_l	γ_2	$DUM99$	J-test
Targeting period	0.051	0.895	1.100	1.170	0.693	−0.483	6.8
(1990.09–2002.04)	(0.00)	(0.02)	(0.29)	(0.32)	(0.20)	(0.22)	[0.99]

Notes
J-test is the test for overidentifying that has a distribution χ^2_{19}.
Standard errors in parentheses.
p values in square brackets.

faced with exchange rate shocks. The second interpretation is that the shocks themselves were, on average, bigger. In fact, as it will be shown later, the response of the CCB is more aggressive when the level of misalignment is higher. However, the absolute size of the real exchange rate misalignments, after September 1999, does not differ substantially from the previous misalignments (see Figure 3.3).

5.1.2 Response to long-term inflation deviations

The formulation in equation (5) can be modified to allow for responses not only to a specific target in time, but to a path of future inflation gaps. As suggested by Wadhwani (2000), in the short term, policymakers may react to exchange rate fluctuations to stabilize the future path of inflation. In fact, if exchange rate misalignment affects the future path of inflation (relative to the horizon that is considered in the design of monetary policy), then it is may be the case that policymakers will react to exchange rate fluctuations, even if those fluctuations do not have any impact on short-term inflation (or, in this case, inflation in $t + 15$).

A way in which we can test the above hypothesis is by re-expressing equation (5) as:

$$r_t = (1 - \rho)\bar{r} + (1 - \rho)[(\beta - 1)\Sigma^{24}_{n=15}\frac{(\pi_{t+n} - \pi^*_{t+n})}{10} + \gamma_1(y_t - y^*_t) + \gamma_2(e_t - e^*_t)] + \rho r_{t-1} + u_t \tag{7}$$

Now, if the monetary authority wants to stabilize the future path of inflation gaps (from $n = 15$ to 24 for instance), then $\beta > 1$ and γ_1 and γ_2 will capture the degree to which CCB is concerned about output and exchange rate deviations that do not affect this path. In Table 3.3 we present the results of estimating equation (7) for the two sub-samples.

The results indicate that, even in the case where longer horizons for the inflation gap are considered, the CCB is still concerned about output and exchange rate deviations. This result is consistent for the two sub-samples and reinforce the idea that the CCB does have additional, non-explicit, objectives.

Table 3.3 Estimation of equation (7) by GMM

	$\bar{r}$	ρ	$(\beta-1)$	γ_1	γ_2	*J-test*
Non targeting period	0.075	0.927	−1.250	1.770	1.083	2.5
(1985.01–1990.08)	(0.00)	(0.00)	(0.04)	(0.07)	(0.06)	[0.99]
Targeting period	0.050	0.930	2.263	2.919	1.907	5.2
(1990.09–2002.04)	(0.00)	(0.01)	(0.63)	(0.62)	(0.40)	[0.99]

Notes
J-test is the test for overidentifying that has a distribution χ^2_{19}.
Standard errors in parentheses.
p values in square brackets.

5.2 Nonlinear policy response to exchange rate

It has been argued (Calvo and Reinhart 2002), that monetary policy can be determined by exchange rate considerations. In particular, developing economies may react to exchange rate misalignment because the abandonment of an exchange rate regime may cause important economic disruptions.

In Chile, the CB had an explicit band for the nominal exchange rate but, as we discuss in section 2, was not supposed to use the interest rate to fulfill this objective.

In practice, however, the CB may respond to real exchange rate fluctuations even if those fluctuations are consistent with the nominal exchange rate band. In fact, fluctuations in the exchange rate may signal a probability of devaluation. In this case, monetary authorities will try to avoid an exchange rate collapse by defending a non-explicit exchange rate target. This reaction corresponds to the "fear of floating" suggested by Calvo and Reinhart (2002). This argument is also consistent with Vitale's (2003) argument; a monetary authority that wants to signal a new level for the exchange rate may use both, foreign exchange rate interventions and the monetary policy instrument.

In some ways, the results in Tables 3.1, 3.2 and 3.3 confirm the fact that the CCB wanted to stabilize the exchange rate independently of its inflationary impacts. However, it is difficult to distinguish whether the CCB is reacting just to large real exchange rate misalignments. In fact, large misalignments may signal a high probability of real exchange rate collapse, and therefore they have to be avoided. On the contrary, relatively small deviations may be transitory events with no further implications for the exchange rate regime. As a consequence, the central bank may not intervene in this case.

In order to test whether CCB's response to real exchange rate is linear, we re-state equation (5). In particular, we allow for differentiated responses to different levels of misalignment. In doing so, we split real exchange rate deviations into "small" and "large" ones.[13] Equation (5), then can be expressed as follows:

$$r_t = (1 - \rho)\bar{r} + (1 - \rho)[(\beta - 1)(\pi_{t+n} - \pi^*_{t+n}) + \gamma_1(y_t - y^*_t)$$
$$+ \gamma^1_2(e_t - e^*_t)_L + \gamma^2_2(e_t - e^*_t)_S] + u_t \tag{8}$$

where γ^1_2 is associated with large deviations and γ^2_2 is associated with small ones. The results of estimating equation (8) are presented in Table 3.4.

According to the above results, there is a nonlinear response of the CCB to real exchange fluctuations; in both sub-periods responses to large deviations are more important. In particular, in the inflation targeting period the response to small real exchange rate deviations is not statistically different from zero.

On the other hand, responses to larger deviations, in the non-targeting period, are considerably higher than in the targeting period. This difference may signal different objectives in each period and is consistent with the view that the main concern of the CCB, in the late 1980s, was to avoid external imbalances generated by real exchange rate misalignments (Magendzo 1997).

6 Conclusions

This chapter provides empirical evidence on the way in which the CCB had implemented its monetary policy. We concluded that the CCB had been forward looking: it responded to anticipated inflation as opposed to lagged inflation. Furthermore, we find evidence that the CCB had some implicit objectives; avoiding output and exchange rate deviations from equilibrium. Therefore, even when inflation was under control, the CCB showed some concern about real activity and the evolution of the real exchange rate. In this respect, the CCB monetary policy can be characterized as a flexible approach to inflation targeting, as described in Svensson (1997).

On the other hand, the central bank's reaction to exchange rate deviations was nonlinear; it reacted more strongly to large deviations rather than to small ones. This is true in the two sub-samples considered. This

Table 3.4 Estimation of equation (8) by GMM

	$\bar{r}$	ρ	$(\beta - 1)$	γ_1	γ^1_2	γ^2_2	J-test
Non targeting period	0.070	0.888	−0.160	1.846	1.595	0.279	4.1
(1985.01–1990.08)	(0.00)	(0.00)	(0.04)	(0.06)	(0.06)	(0.17)	[0.99]
Targeting period	0.052	0.893	0.703	1.386	0.860	0.557	7.0
(1990.09–2002.04)	(0.00)	(0.02)	(0.19)	(0.32)	(0.20)	(0.54)	[0.99]

Notes
J-test is the test for overidentifying that has a distribution χ^2_{19}.
Standard errors in parentheses.
p values in square brackets.

provides evidence that the CCB either tried to avoid excessive exchange rate depreciations (fear of floating), or to control large appreciations.

In this chapter we use structural time series models to derive long-term deviations in the relevant variables. We believe this is a better alternative than other *ad hoc* detrending procedures, like the HP filter. However, one limitation, specially in the case of the real exchange rate, is that even if this is a better statistical procedure, it may not correspond to misalignments derived from a specific economic model of real exchange rate determination.

Finally, this is a descriptive study that characterizes the CCB reaction function in the last decade. The normative question of whether this policy is optimal cannot be answered in this framework. In this sense, future research should try to assess the property of this type of reaction function in an estimated or calibrated model of the Chilean economy.

Notes

1 This chapter is part of my PhD dissertation at Cambridge University. I am grateful to my supervisors Dr Petra Geraats and Dr Peter Tinsley for their constant support and orientation. I thank Stephen Millard for very helpful comments to a previous version of this work. I extend my gratitude to Professor Andrew Harvey, Carlos Lopes, Vasco Carvhalo an anonymous referee for helpful suggestions and advice. I thank participants in the Exchange Rate Workshop at the Bank of England (November 2001), the EEA/ESEM 2002 meeting and LACEA 2002 conference for comments and suggestions. Any remaining error or misinterpretation is my own.
2 From 2001 onwards the target was set at 3 percent.
3 The simulations reported in Cecchetti *et al.* (2000) are based on the Batini and Nelson model for the UK (Batini and Nelson 2001).
4 For a VAR approach to modeling the monetary transmission mechanism in Chile see Valdes (1997).
5 Given a more stable, and low, path for inflation, the CCB abandoned, in August 2001, the use of real interest rates as policy instrument. Since then, the policy instrument is an overnight nominal interest rate.
6 The Bank intervened by selling US$800 million (less than its preannounced ceiling of US$1.5 billion) and issuing the equivalent of US$3 billion (as announced) in dollar-denominated peso CCB debt (to provide a hedge against future exchange rate devaluation), Schmidt-Hebbel and Werner (2002: 72).
7 In general, the inflation target is assumed to be a fixed number. We adopt a more general approach that enables us to consider the case in which the target is changing over time. This case is of particular importance in economies where inflation is a non-stationary process, and where targets are converging gradually to the long-term inflation level.
8 Most data are available from the CCB's web page: www.bcentral.cl. Alternatively, the data are available, on request, from the author.
9 The IMACEC is a monthly indicator of economic activity, which covers over 90 percent of Chilean GDP.
10 The models have been estimated using STAMP 6.0 software.
11 Changing the smoothing parameter in the HP does not change the results; for alternative values of this parameter the HP cycle is always noisier than the cycle obtained using a structural time series model.

12 The mean lag of a monetary shock, in months, is defined as $(1/(1 - \rho))$.
13 We assume that large deviations are equal or greater than 1.5 percent (in absolute value) and small ones are smaller than 1.5 percent. Under this assumption, roughly half of the observations in the full sample correspond to "large deviations."

References

Batini, N., Harrison, R. and Millard, S. (2003), "Monetary policy rules for open economies," *Journal of Economics Dynamics and Control*, 27(11–12) (September): 2059–2094.

Batini, N. and Nelson, E. (2001), "Optimal horizons for inflation targeting," *Journal of Economic Dynamics and Control*, 25: 891–910.

Calvo, G. and Reinhart, C. (2002), "Fear of floating," *Quarterly Journal of Economics*, 177: 379–408.

Cecchetti, S., Genberg, H., Lipsky, H. and Wadhwani, S. (2000), *Asset Prices and Central Bank Policy*, ICMB (International Center for Monetary and Banking Studies) and CEPR.

Clarida, R. (2001), "The empirics of monetary policy rules in open economies," *International Journal of Finance and Economics*, 6(4): 315–323.

Clarida, R., Gali, J. and Gertler, M. (1998), "Monetary policy rules in practice: some international evidence," *European Economic Review*, (June): 1033–1067.

Clarida, R., Gali, J. and Gertler, M. (2000), "Monetary policy rules and macroeconomic stability: theory and evidence," *Quarterly Journal of Economics*, 115(1): 147–180.

Favero, C. (2001), *Applied Macroeconometrics*, Oxford: Oxford University Press.

Harvey, A. and Jaeger, A. (1993), "Detrending, stylized facts and the business cycle," *Journal of Applied Econometrics*, 8: 231–247.

Harvey, A. (2002), "Trends cycles and convergence," in Loayza, N. and R. Soto (eds), *Economic Growth: Sources, Trends and Cycles*, Santiago de Chile. On line, available at: www.bcentral.cl/eng/stdpub/conferences/annual/30112001.htm.

Landerretche, O., Morande, F. and Schmidt-Hebbel, K. (1999), "Inflation targets and stabilization in Chile," Central Bank of Chile Working Paper no. 55.

Magendzo, I. (1997), "Monetary policy in Chile: objectives, instruments and indicator," (in Spanish), Central Bank of Chile Economic Studies.

Parrado, E. (2000), "Inflation targeting and exchange rate rules in an open economy," New York University, Mimeographed.

Parrado, E. (2001), "Effects of foreign and domestic monetary policy in a small open economy: the case of Chile," Central Bank of Chile Working Paper no. 108.

Parrado, E. and Velasco, A. (2002), "Alternative monetary rules in the open economy: a welfare based approach," in Loayza, N. and Soto, R. (eds), *Inflation Targeting: Design, Performance, Challenges*.

Schmidt-Hebbel, K. and Werner, A. (2002), "Inflation targeting in Brazil, Chile and Mexico: performance, credibility, and the exchange rate," *Journal of the Latin American and Caribbean Economic Association*, 2(2): 31–79.

Svensson, L. (1997), "Inflation forecast targeting: implementing and monitoring inflation targets," *European Economic Review*, 41: 1111–1146.

Valdes, R. (1997), "The transmission of monetary policy in Chile," Central Bank of Chile Working Paper no. 16.

Valdes, R. and Bennett, H. (2001), "Terms of trade for Chile a monthly series," Central Bank of Chile Working Paper.

Vitale, P. (2003), "Foreign exchange rate intervention: how to signal policy objectives and stabilize the economy," *Journal of Monetary Economics*, 50(4): 841–870.

Wadhwani, S. (2000), "The exchange rate and the MPC: What can we do?," Bank of England.

4 The expenditure switching effect and the choice between fixed and floating exchange rates*

Ozge Senay and Alan Sutherland

1 Introduction

This chapter analyses the macroeconomic implications of fixed and floating exchange rate regimes and presents a welfare comparison of the two regimes in the presence of stochastic foreign monetary shocks. The main focus of analysis is the role played by the expenditure switching effect of exchange rate changes in the choice of exchange rate regime.

Early proponents of floating exchange rates, such as Friedman (1953), argued that floating exchange rates are desirable because they provide a degree of insulation against foreign shocks. A floating rate regime allows a country to set monetary policy independently from monetary policy in other countries. This prevents the transmission of foreign monetary policy shocks to the domestic economy. Furthermore, when goods prices are sticky, a floating rate regime allows relative prices to adjust in response to country specific real demand and supply shocks. Thus, it was argued, floating exchange rates act as a 'shock absorber' which helps stabilise the domestic economy in the face of both monetary and real shocks.

Recently there has been a growing literature on the choice of exchange rate regimes based on welfare comparisons in general equilibrium models with sticky-prices. This new literature has allowed a re-examination of the shock-absorber role of the exchange rate. A particularly important issue that has emerged in the recent literature (see Devereux and Engel (1998, 2003), Devereux (2000) and Bachetta and van Wincoop (2000)) is the distinction between 'producer currency pricing' (where prices are fixed in the currency of the producer) and 'local currency pricing' (where prices are fixed in the currency of the consumer). One implication of local currency pricing is that the expenditure switching effect of exchange rate changes is much reduced (or even eliminated). This tends to reduce the ability of the exchange rate to act as a shock absorber in response to real demand and supply shocks and thus alters the welfare case for floating exchange rates.

The present chapter also considers the implications of the expenditure switching effect for the choice of exchange rate regime, but here the important issue is the degree of substitutability between home and foreign goods (rather than the currency in which prices are set). Recent papers have focused on models where the elasticity of substitution between home and foreign goods is restricted to unity. They therefore implicitly restrict the strength of the expenditure switching effect. This issue is not relevant in the case of local currency pricing (because relative prices do not change) but it can be important in the case of producer currency pricing (as the results presented in this chapter show).

The chapter uses a two-country sticky-price general equilibrium model (where prices are fixed in the currency of the producer) to compare the welfare properties of exchange rate regimes. The foreign country is subject to stochastic money supply shocks and the focus of interest is on the stabilisation and welfare implications of regime choice for the home country. A comparison between the two exchange rate regimes shows that, while the volatility of consumption is unambiguously lower in the floating exchange rate regime, the volatility of home output is only lower in the floating rate regime when the elasticity of substitution between home and foreign goods is low. Thus the ability of floating rates to insulate the home country from foreign monetary shocks depends on the strength of the expenditure switching effect. A floating rate regime allows the home economy to set its money supply independently and thus foreign money shocks are not transmitted to the home economy via home monetary policy. But a floating rate regime implies that foreign monetary shocks cause movements in the exchange rate which, in turn, affect home output through the expenditure switching effect. The strength of the expenditure switching effect therefore determines the relative stabilising properties of the two regimes.

The strength of the expenditure switching effect is also found to be important for determining the relative welfare performance of the two regimes. A floating exchange rate regime yields higher welfare when the expenditure switching effect is relatively weak, but a fixed exchange rate regime is superior when the expenditure switching effect is strong.

The chapter proceeds as follows: section 2 presents the model; section 3 describes the solution method and approximation of the model; section 4 derives expressions for consumption and output in fixed and floating exchange rate regimes and compares their volatilities under the two regimes; section 5 presents the derivation of the welfare measure and a welfare comparison of different exchange rate regimes; and section 6 concludes the chapter.

2 The model

The model is a variation of the sticky-price general equilibrium structure which has become standard in the recent open economy macro literature (following the approach developed by Obstfeld and Rogoff (1995, 1998)).[1] The main point at which the model differs from many others in the recent literature is that the elasticity of substitution between home and foreign goods can differ from unity. The only source of stochastic shocks in the model is the foreign money supply. Two possible regimes for the home monetary authority are considered. In a fixed exchange rate regime the home money supply is used to achieve the desired target exchange rate. In a floating exchange rate regime the home money supply is fixed.[2]

2.1 Market structure

The world exists for a single period and consists of two countries, which will be referred to as the home country and the foreign country. There is a continuum of agents of unit mass in each country with home agents indexed $h \in [0, 1]$ and foreign agents indexed $f \in [0, 1]$. Agents consume a basket of goods containing all home and foreign produced goods. Each agent is a monopoly producer of a single differentiated product. All agents set prices in advance of the realisation of shocks and are contracted to meet demand at the pre-fixed prices. Prices are set in the currency of the producer.

The detailed structure of the home country is described below. The foreign country has an identical structure. Where appropriate, foreign real variables and foreign currency prices are indicated with an asterisk.

2.2 Preferences

All agents in the home economy have utility functions of the same form. The utility of agent h is given by

$$U(h) = E\left[\log C(h) + \chi\log \frac{M(h)}{P} - \frac{K}{2}y^2(h)\right] \tag{1}$$

where χ and K are positive constants, C is a consumption index defined across all home and foreign goods, M denotes end-of-period nominal money holdings, P is the consumer price index, $y(h)$ is the output of good h and E is the expectations operator.

The consumption index C for home agents is defined as

$$C = \left[\left(\frac{1}{2}\right)^{\frac{1}{\theta}}C_H^{\frac{\theta-1}{\theta}} + \left(\frac{1}{2}\right)^{\frac{1}{\theta}}C_F^{\frac{\theta-1}{\theta}}\right]^{\frac{\theta}{\theta-1}} \tag{2}$$

where C_H and C_F are indices of home and foreign produced goods defined as follows

$$C_H = \left[\int_0^1 c_H(i)^{\frac{\phi-1}{\phi}} di\right]^{\frac{\phi}{\phi-1}}, \quad C_F = \left[\int_0^1 c_F(j)^{\frac{\phi-1}{\phi}} dj\right]^{\frac{\phi}{\phi-1}} \tag{3}$$

where $\phi > 1$, $c_H(i)$ is consumption of home good i and $c_F(j)$ is consumption of foreign good j. The parameter θ is the elasticity of substitution between home and foreign goods. This is the key parameter which determines the strength of the expenditure switching effect.

The budget constraint of agent h is given by

$$M(h) = M_0 + p_H(h)y(h) - PC(h) - T + PR(h) \tag{4}$$

where M_0 and $M(h)$ are initial and final money holdings, T is a lump-sum government transfer, $p_H(h)$ is the price of home good h, P is the aggregate consumer price index and $R(h)$ is the income from a portfolio of state contingent assets (to be described in more detail below).

The government's budget constraint is

$$M - M_0 + T = 0 \tag{5}$$

Changes in the money supply are assumed to enter and leave the economy via changes in lump-sum transfers.

2.3 Price indices

The aggregate consumer price index for home agents is

$$P = \left[\frac{1}{2} P_H^{1-\theta} + \frac{1}{2} P_F^{1-\theta} \right]^{\frac{1}{1-\theta}} \tag{6}$$

where P_H and P_F are the price indices for home and foreign goods respectively defined as

$$P_H = \left[\int_0^1 p_H(i)^{1-\phi} di \right]^{\frac{1}{1-\phi}}, \ P_F = \left[\int_0^1 p_F(j)^{1-\phi} dj \right]^{\frac{1}{1-\phi}} \tag{7}$$

The law of one price is assumed to hold. This implies $p_H(i) = p_H^*(i)S$ and $p_F(j) = p_F^*(j)S$ for all i and j where an asterisk indicates a price measured in foreign currency and S is the exchange rate (defined as the domestic price of foreign currency). Purchasing power parity holds in terms of aggregate consumer price indices, $P = P^*S$.

2.4 Consumption choices

Individual home demand for representative home good, h, and foreign good, f, are given by

$$c_H(h) = C_H \left(\frac{p_H(h)}{P_H} \right)^{-\phi}, \ c_F(f) = C_F \left(\frac{p_F(f)}{P_F} \right)^{-\phi} \tag{8}$$

where

$$C_H = \frac{1}{2}C\left(\frac{P_H}{P}\right)^{-\theta}, C_F = \frac{1}{2}C\left(\frac{P_F}{P}\right)^{-\theta} \tag{9}$$

Foreign demands for home and foreign goods have an identical structure to the home demands. Individual foreign demand for representative home good, h, and foreign good, f, are given by

$$c_H^*(h) = C_H^*\left(\frac{p_H^*(h)}{P_H^*}\right)^{-\phi}, c_F^*(f) = C_F^*\left(\frac{p_F^*(f)}{P_F^*}\right)^{-\phi} \tag{10}$$

where

$$C_H^* = \frac{1}{2}C^*\left(\frac{P_H^*}{P^*}\right)^{-\theta}, C_F^* = \frac{1}{2}C^*\left(\frac{P_F^*}{P^*}\right)^{-\theta} \tag{11}$$

Each country has a population of unit mass so the total demands for goods are equivalent to individual demands. The total demand for home goods is therefore $Y = C_H + C_H^*$ and the total demand for foreign goods is $Y^* = C_F + C_F^*$.

2.5 Optimal price setting

The first-order condition for price setting for home agents is derived in Appendix 1 and implies the following

$$P_H = \frac{\phi}{\phi - 1} \frac{KE[Y^2]}{E[Y/(PC)]} \tag{12}$$

A similar expression can be derived for foreign agents, as follows:

$$P_F^* = \frac{\phi}{\phi - 1} \frac{KE[Y^{*2}]}{E[Y^*/(P^*C^*)]} \tag{13}$$

2.6 Financial markets and risk sharing

The asymmetric structure of shocks and monetary policy, coupled with a non-unit elasticity of substitution between home and foreign goods, makes it necessary to adopt a more explicit structure for international asset markets than is usual in the recent literature.[3] It is assumed that sufficient contingent financial instruments exist to allow efficient sharing of consumption risks. All consumption is financed out of real income so the only source of consumption risk is variability in real income. Efficient sharing of consumption risk can therefore be achieved by allowing trade in two state-contingent assets, one which has a payoff correlated with home aggregate real income and one with a payoff correlated with foreign real income. For simplicity it is assumed that each asset pays a return equal to the relevant country's real income, i.e. a unit of the home asset pays $y = YP_H/P$ and a unit of the foreign asset pays $y* = Y*P_F/P$.[4] The portfolio pay-offs for home and foreign agents are given by the following

$$R(h) = \zeta_H(h)(y - q_H) + \zeta_F(h)(y* - q_F) \tag{14}$$

$$R*(f) = \zeta^*_H(f)(y - q_H) + \zeta^*_F(f)(y* - q_F) \tag{15}$$

where $\zeta_H(h)$ and $\zeta_F(h)$ are holdings of home agent h of the home and foreign assets, $\zeta^*_H(f)$ and $\zeta^*_F(f)$ are the holdings of foreign agent f of home and foreign assets and q_H and q_F are the unit prices of the home and foreign assets.

It is important to specify the timing of asset trade. It is assumed that asset trade takes place after the choice of exchange rate regime. This implies that agents can insure themselves against the risk implied by a particular exchange rate regime but they cannot insure themselves against the choice of regime.[5]

Appendix 2 shows that risk sharing implies the following relationship between consumption, asset prices and expected output levels in the two countries

$$\frac{C}{C*} = \frac{q_H}{q_F} = \frac{E\left[\dfrac{y}{y + y*}\right]}{E\left[\dfrac{y*}{y + y*}\right]} \tag{16}$$

2.7 Money demand and supply

The first-order condition for the choice of money holdings is

$$\frac{M}{P} = \chi C \tag{17}$$

The money supply in each country is assumed to be determined by the relevant national monetary authority. The foreign money supply is subject to stochastic shocks such that log $M*$ is symmetrically distributed over the interval $[-\epsilon, \epsilon]$ with $E[\log M*] = 0$ and $Var[\log M*] = \sigma^2$. In the case of a floating exchange rate the home monetary authority is assumed to keep the home money supply constant at $\overline{M}$. In the case of a fixed exchange rate the home monetary authority is assumed to use the home money supply to maintain the exchange rate at the target level, $\overline{S}$. For simplicity $\overline{M} = \overline{S} = 1$.

3 Model approximation

It is not possible to derive an exact solution to the model described above.[6] The model is therefore approximated around a non-stochastic equilibrium.

Before proceeding it is necessary to define and explain some notation. The non-stochastic equilibrium of the model is defined as the solution which results when $M^* = 1$ with $\sigma^2 = 0$. For any variable X define $\hat{X} = \log (X/\overline{X})$ where $\overline{X}$ is the value of variable X in the non-stochastic equilibrium. $\hat{X}$ is therefore the log-deviation of X from its value in the non-stochastic equilibrium.

The only exogenous forcing variable in the model is the foreign money supply, M^*, so all log-deviations from the non-stochastic equilibrium are of the same order as the shocks to $\hat{M}^*$, which (by assumption) are of maximum size ϵ. When presenting an equation which is approximated up to order n it is therefore possible to gather all terms of order higher than n in a single term denoted $O(\epsilon^{n+1})$. Thus, when the term $O(\epsilon^2)$ appears in an equation the variables in that equation should be understood to be accurate up to order one. While an equation which includes the term $O(\epsilon^3)$ should be understood to contain variables which are accurate up to order two. And an equation which does not include any term of the form $O(\epsilon^n)$ should be understood to hold exactly.

The analysis of the model proceeds in two stages. The first stage considers the implications of fixed and floating exchange rates for the volatilities of macro variables. The second stage considers a welfare comparison between fixed and floating exchange rates.

Variances are, by definition, at least of second order so an analysis of volatilities requires the derivation of at least second-order accurate solutions for variances. But second-order accurate solutions for variances can be obtained from first-order accurate solutions for the relationships between endogenous variables and the shock variable. The analysis of volatility therefore involves working with a log-linearised (i.e. first-order approximated) version of the model.

The expressions for second moments obtained in the analysis of volatility also enter into the analysis of welfare. But a full second-order expression for welfare requires second-order accurate solutions for *both* the first and second moments of variables. So a full analysis of welfare involves working with a second-order approximation of the model.

4 Macroeconomic volatility

A first-order expansion of equation (16) shows that risk sharing implies the following relationship between consumption levels in the two countries

$$\hat{C} - \hat{C}^* = 0 + O(\epsilon^2)$$

where, as explained above, the term $O(\epsilon^2)$ indicates that the variables in this relationship should be understood to be accurate up to a first-order approximation. When combined with the purchasing power parity relationship (which implies $\hat{S} = \hat{P} - \hat{P}*$) and the expressions for home and foreign money demand (which imply $\hat{M} = \hat{P} + \hat{C}$ and $\hat{M}* = \hat{P}* + \hat{C}*$) the following expression for the exchange rate is obtained

$$\hat{S} = \hat{M} - \hat{M}* + O(\epsilon^2) \tag{18}$$

This expression immediately shows that a fixed exchange rate implies that the home money supply is set equal to the foreign money supply, i.e. $\hat{M} = \hat{M}*$, while a floating exchange rate implies that $\hat{S} = -\hat{M}* + O(\epsilon^2)$.

The assumption of fixed goods prices implies

$$\hat{P}_H = \hat{P}_F^* = 0 + O(\epsilon^2)$$

so consumer prices are given by

$$\hat{P} = \frac{1}{2}\hat{S} + O(\epsilon^2), \ \hat{P}* = -\frac{1}{2}\hat{S} + O(\epsilon^2)$$

These expressions, combined with the money demand relationships imply that consumption levels are

$$\hat{C} = \hat{C}* = \frac{1}{2}(\hat{M} + \hat{M}*) + O(\epsilon^2) \tag{19}$$

Thus consumption in the two countries responds equally (because of risk sharing) to aggregate world monetary policy.

First-order approximations for home and foreign aggregate output levels yield

$$\hat{Y} = \frac{1}{2}(\hat{C} + \hat{C}*) - \theta(\hat{P}_H - \hat{P}) + O(\epsilon^2) \tag{20}$$

$$\hat{Y}* = \frac{1}{2}(\hat{C} + \hat{C}*) - \theta(\hat{P}_F^* - \hat{P}*) + O(\epsilon^2) \tag{21}$$

Combining these expressions with the solutions for consumption and price levels implies

$$\hat{Y} = \frac{1+\theta}{2}\hat{M} + \frac{1-\theta}{2}\hat{M}* + O(\epsilon^2), \ \hat{Y}* = \frac{1+\theta}{2}\hat{M}* + \frac{1-\theta}{2}\hat{M} + O(\epsilon^2) \tag{22}$$

These expressions reveal the importance of the expenditure switching effect (as measured by the parameter θ) for determining the impact of monetary policy on output. If θ is greater than unity monetary policy has a beggar-thy-neighbour effect. An expansion in the foreign money supply increases foreign output but reduces home output (and vice versa for an expansion of the home money supply). The beggar-thy-neighbour effect arises because of the impact of monetary policy on relative prices. An expansion of the foreign money supply causes an appreciation of the nominal exchange rate (see equation (18)) which, for given values of $\hat{P}_H$ and $\hat{P}_F^*$, causes a reduction in the relative price of foreign goods. Equations (20) and (21) show that the change in relative prices has an expenditure switching effect, i.e. there is a shift of demand from home goods to foreign goods. The size of this expenditure switching effect depends on the substitutability of home and foreign goods, i.e. it depends on the value of θ. The negative impact of the exchange rate change on home output is partly offset by the positive impact of foreign money on total world consumption (see equation (19)). Thus the beggar-thy-neighbour effect only arises when θ is greater than unity.

It is now simple to derive expressions for consumption and output levels in fixed and floating exchange rate regimes. In a fixed exchange rate regime (i.e. where $\hat{M} = \hat{M}^*$) it follows that consumption levels are given by

$$\hat{C} = \hat{C}^* = \hat{M}^* + O(\epsilon^2)$$

and output levels are given by

$$\hat{Y} = \hat{M}^* + O(\epsilon^2), \ \hat{Y}^* = \hat{M}^* + O(\epsilon^2)$$

Therefore the variances of consumption and output in a fixed rate regime are given by

$$E[\hat{Y}^2] = E[\hat{Y}^{*2}] = E[\hat{C}^2] = E[\hat{C}^{*2}] = \sigma^2 + O(\epsilon^3) \tag{23}$$

In a floating rate regime (i.e. where $\hat{M} = 0$) consumption levels are

$$\hat{C} = \hat{C}^* = \frac{1}{2}\hat{M}^* + O(\epsilon^2)$$

and output levels are

$$\hat{Y} = \frac{1-\theta}{2}\hat{M}^* + O(\epsilon^2), \ \hat{Y}^* = \frac{1+\theta}{2}\hat{M}^* + O(\epsilon^2)$$

so the variances of consumption and output are

$$E[\hat{C}^2] = E[\hat{C}^{*2}] = \frac{1}{4}\sigma^2 + O(\epsilon^3) \tag{24}$$

$$E[\hat{Y}^2] = \left(\frac{1-\theta}{2}\right)^2 \sigma^2 + O(\epsilon^3) \tag{25}$$

$$E[\hat{Y}^{*2}] = \left(\frac{1+\theta}{2}\right)^2 \sigma^2 + O(\epsilon^3) \tag{26}$$

A comparison between the two exchange rate regimes shows that the volatility of consumption is unambiguously lower in the floating exchange rate regime but the volatility of home output can be higher or lower in the floating exchange rate regime depending on the value of θ. Equations (23) and (25) show that home output is less volatile in the fixed exchange rate regime when $\theta > 3$. Foreign output is more volatile in the floating rate regime for $\theta > 1$.

The explanation for these effects follows quite easily from consideration of the above equations. Equation (19) shows that consumption depends on aggregate world monetary policy. In a floating exchange rate regime home monetary policy is passive while a fixed exchange rate regime implies the home monetary authority must replicate foreign monetary developments exactly. World monetary policy must therefore be less active in the floating rate regime and hence consumption must be less volatile. The impact of the exchange rate regime on output volatility can be understood from equation (22) (which highlights the role of the expenditure switching effect of exchange rate changes). The expenditure switching effect becomes more powerful the higher the value of θ. This implies that foreign monetary shocks, which are partly transmitted to the home economy via the expenditure switching effect, have a larger impact on home output when θ is larger than 3. A fixed exchange rate neutralises the expenditure switching effect and can therefore stabilise home output when $\theta > 3$.

5 Welfare

This section compares the welfare implications of fixed and floating exchange rates. Following Obstfeld and Rogoff (1998, 2002) it is assumed that the utility of real balances is small enough to be neglected. It is therefore possible to measure aggregate welfare of home agents using the following

$$\Omega = E\left[\log C - \frac{K}{2} Y^2\right] \tag{27}$$

As stated above, it is not possible to derive exact analytical solutions to the model. In order to analyse welfare it is therefore necessary to consider a second-order approximation of the welfare measure. This is given by

$$\tilde{\Omega} = E\{\hat{C} - K\overline{Y}^2[\hat{Y} + \hat{Y}^2]\} + O(\epsilon^3) \tag{28}$$

where $\tilde{\Omega}$ is the deviation of the level of welfare from the non-stochastic equilibrium.[7] Notice that this expression includes the first moments of output and consumption and the second moment of output. Welfare is increasing in the expected level of consumption and decreasing in the expected level and variance of output. A second-order accurate expression for the second moment of output has already been derived in the previous section. But it is now necessary to derive second-order accurate solutions for the first moments of output and consumption. This requires second-order approximations of the equations of the model.

5.1 Solving for first moments

It is useful to start by considering the first-order conditions for price setting. Second-order expansions of equations (12) and (13) yield

$$\hat{P}_H = E[\hat{Y} + \hat{P} + \hat{C}] + \lambda_{PH} + O(\epsilon^3)$$

$$\hat{P}_F^* = E[\hat{Y}^* + \hat{P}^* + \hat{C}^*] + \lambda_{P_F^*} + O(\epsilon^3)$$

where

$$\lambda_{P_H} = \frac{1}{2}E\left[4\hat{Y}^2 - (\hat{Y} - \hat{C} - \hat{P})^2\right]$$

$$\lambda_{P_F^*} = \frac{1}{2}E\left[4\hat{Y}^{*2} - (\hat{Y}^* - \hat{C}^* - \hat{P}^*)^2\right]$$

Notice that these expressions both include terms (denoted λ_{P_H} and $\lambda_{P_F^*}$) which depend on the second moments of output, consumption and consumer prices. These terms represent a form of risk premium which is built into goods prices by risk-averse agents who have to set prices before shocks are realised. The risk premium depends on the variances and covariances of work effort, the marginal utility of consumption and the consumer prices.

The expected values of $\hat{M}$ and $\hat{M}^*$ are both zero by assumption so it follows from the money demand relationships that

$$E[\hat{P} + \hat{C}] = 0, \quad E[\hat{P}^* + \hat{C}^*] = 0$$

(Note that the money demand relationships are linear in logs so they do not require any approximation.) The expressions for home and foreign goods prices therefore simplify to

$$\hat{P}_H = E[\hat{Y}] + \lambda_{P_H} + O(\epsilon^3), \quad \hat{P}_F^* = E[\hat{Y}^*] + \lambda_{P_F^*} + O(\epsilon^3)$$

These expressions can be combined with second-order expansions of the definitions of consumer prices to yield

$$E\left[\hat{P}\right] = \frac{1}{2}\lambda_{P_H} + \frac{1}{2}\lambda_{P_F^*} + \frac{1}{2}E[\hat{Y} + \hat{Y}* + \hat{S}] + E[\lambda_{CPI}] + O(\epsilon^3)$$

$$E\left[\hat{P}*\right] = \frac{1}{2}\lambda_{P_H} + \frac{1}{2}\lambda_{P_F^*} + \frac{1}{2}E\left[\hat{Y} + \hat{Y}* - \hat{S}\right] + E[\lambda_{CPI}] + O(\epsilon^3)$$

where

$$\lambda_{CPI} = \frac{1}{8}(1 - \theta)\hat{S}^2$$

Notice that the non-log linearity of consumer prices gives rise to another second-order term (denoted λ_{CPI}). This term implies that the expected value of consumer prices is negatively affected by exchange rate volatility when $\theta > 1$. This effect can be understood by considering the definition of the consumer price index. The CPI is concave in the prices of home and foreign goods so any volatility in the relative price of home and foreign goods (which would result from exchange rate volatility) will reduce the expected level of aggregate consumer prices. (Another way to understand this effect is to note that, when home and foreign goods are substitutable, agents can reduce the average cost of their consumption basket by switching expenditure towards whichever set of goods are cheapest *ex post*. Relative price volatility therefore reduces the average price of the consumption basket.)

The expressions for consumer prices can be combined with the money market equations to yield the following expressions for consumption.

$$E\left[\hat{C}\right] = -E\left[\hat{P}\right] = -\frac{1}{2}\lambda_{P_H} - \frac{1}{2}\lambda_{P_F^*} - \frac{1}{2}E\left[\hat{Y} + \hat{Y}* + \hat{S}\right] - E[\lambda_{CPI}] + O(\epsilon^3) \quad (29)$$

$$E\left[\hat{C}*\right] = -E\left[\hat{P}*\right] = -\frac{1}{2}\lambda_{P_H} - \frac{1}{2}\lambda_{P_F^*} - \frac{1}{2}E\left[\hat{Y} + \hat{Y}* - \hat{S}\right] - E[\lambda_{CPI}] + O(\epsilon^3) \quad (30)$$

A second-order expansion of equation (16) shows that risk sharing implies that the first moments of consumption and output in the two countries are related as follows

$$E[\hat{C} - \hat{C}*] = E[(\hat{Y} - \hat{Y}*) + (\hat{P}_H - \hat{P}_F^*) - (\hat{P} - \hat{P}*)] + O(\epsilon^3) \quad (31)$$

while second-order expansions of the home and foreign output relationships yield.[8]

$$E[\hat{Y}] = E\left[\frac{1}{2}(\hat{C} + \hat{C}*) - \theta(\hat{P}_H - \hat{P})\right] + O(\epsilon^3) \tag{32}$$

$$E[\hat{Y}*] = E\left[\frac{1}{2}(\hat{C} + \hat{C}*) - \theta(\hat{P}_F^* - \hat{P}*)\right] + O(\epsilon^3) \tag{33}$$

Combining equations (31), (32) and (33) with the purchasing power parity condition yields the following expression for the expected level of the exchange rate

$$E\left[\hat{S}\right] = \frac{\theta - 1}{2\theta}(\lambda_{P_H} - \lambda_{P_F^*}) \tag{34}$$

Using the above equations it is possible to write consumption and output levels entirely in terms of λ_{P_H}, $\lambda_{P_F^*}$ and λ_{CPI} as follows

$$E[\hat{C}] = -\left(\frac{2\theta - 1}{4\theta}\right)\lambda_{PH} - \frac{1}{4\theta}\lambda_{P_F^*} - \left(\frac{1 + \theta}{2}\right)E[\lambda_{CPI}] + O(\epsilon^3) \tag{35}$$

$$E[\hat{C}*] = -\frac{1}{4\theta}\lambda_{PH} - \left(\frac{2\theta - 1}{4\theta}\right)\lambda_{P_F^*} - \left(\frac{1 + \theta}{2}\right)E[\lambda_{CPI}] + O(\epsilon^3) \tag{36}$$

$$E[\hat{Y}] = -\frac{1}{2}\lambda_{P_H} - \frac{(1 - \theta)}{2}E[\lambda_{CPI}] + O(\epsilon^3) \tag{37}$$

$$E[\hat{Y}*] = -\frac{1}{2}\lambda_{P_F^*} - \frac{(1 - \theta)}{2}E[\lambda_{CPI}] + O(\epsilon^3) \tag{38}$$

It is useful at this stage to consider what these expressions reveal about the determination of the expected levels of consumption and output. Equations (35), (36), (37) and (38) show that the risk premia, λ_{P_H} and $\lambda_{P_F^*}$, have a negative impact on expected output and consumption. Any factor which increases the risk faced by producers (such as an increase in the volatility of output) will discourage the supply of work effort and therefore depress output. By definition this also reduces the quantity of goods available for consumption and therefore reduces the expected level of consumption. Equations (35), (36), (37) and (38) also show that the λ_{CPI} term implies that, when $\theta > 1$, exchange rate volatility has a positive impact on the expected level of consumption and a negative impact on the expected level of output. As discussed above, exchange rate volatility tends to reduce the average cost of the consumption basket when $\theta > 1$. This allows agents to reduce work effort and consume more goods.[9]

The only remaining task is to derive expressions for the second-moment terms λ_{P_H}, $\lambda_{P_F^*}$ and λ_{CPI}. This can be done simply by using the expressions for realised output, consumption, prices and the exchange rate derived in section 4.

In the case of a fixed exchange rate, it follows that

$$\lambda_{P_H} = \lambda_{P_F^*} = 2\sigma^2$$

$$E[\lambda_{CPI}] = 0$$

so the expressions for the first moments of consumption and output in a fixed rate regime can be rewritten as

$$E[\hat{C}] = E[\hat{Y}] = -\sigma^2 + O(\epsilon^3) \tag{39}$$

In the case of a floating rate the following expressions for λ_{P_H}, $\lambda_{P_F^*}$ and λ_{CPI} are obtained

$$\lambda_{P_H} = \frac{3(1-\theta)^2\sigma^2}{8}$$

$$\lambda_{P_F^*} = \frac{(3+10\theta+3\theta^2)\sigma^2}{2}$$

$$E[\lambda_{CPI}] = \frac{1}{8}(1-\theta)\sigma^2$$

so the expressions for the first moments of consumption and output in a floating rate regime can be rewritten as

$$E[\hat{C}] = \left(\frac{-6+3\theta-\theta^2}{8}\right)\sigma^2 + O(\epsilon^3) \tag{40}$$

$$E[\hat{Y}] = -\left(\frac{1-\theta}{2}\right)^2\sigma^2 + O(\epsilon^3) \tag{41}$$

5.2 Welfare

It is now simple to combine the above expressions to obtain the final expressions for welfare. Combining equations (23) and (39) yields the following expressions for welfare in the fixed rate regime

$$\tilde{\Omega}_{Fix} = -\sigma^2 + O(\epsilon^3) \tag{42}$$

and combining equations (25), (40) and (41) shows that welfare in the floating rate regime is given by

$$\tilde{\Omega}_{Float} = -\left(\frac{6-3\theta+\theta^2}{8}\right)\sigma^2 + O(\epsilon^3) \tag{43}$$

It immediately follows from these expressions that the floating rate regime yields higher welfare than the fixed rate regime when $\theta(\theta-3)<2$ or when $\theta\lesssim3.56$. Thus a floating exchange rate regime yields higher welfare when the expenditure switching effect is relatively weak, but a fixed exchange rate regime is superior when the expenditure switching effect is strong.

This result can be understood by considering the impact of exchange rate volatility and the expenditure switching effect on the three components of the welfare measure (i.e. the expected levels of consumption and output and the variance of output). Equations (41) and (40) show that the expected levels of output and consumption in a floating rate regime decline as the expenditure switching effect becomes stronger (at least for high values of θ). The decline in the expected levels of output and consumption is a direct result of the rise in the volatility of output that occurs in the floating rate regime as the expenditure switching effect becomes stronger. Higher output volatility raises the risk premia in goods prices (λ_{P_H} and $\lambda_{P_F^*}$) and therefore lowers work effort and the supply of consumption goods.

In summary, therefore, a strong expenditure switching effect (i.e. a high value of θ) implies a high variance of output (which has a negative effect on welfare), a low expected level of output (which has a positive effect on welfare) and a low expected level of consumption (which has a negative effect on welfare). Furthermore, a comparison of equations (25) and (41) shows that the positive welfare effect of the expected level of output exactly offsets the negative welfare effect of the variance of output. The net result is that welfare in the floating rate regime declines as the expenditure switching effect becomes stronger because of the negative impact of output volatility on the expected level of consumption. And, for large values of θ, this effect can become so strong that it implies that a fixed rate regime is welfare superior to a floating rate regime.

6 Conclusions

This chapter has analysed the implications of the expenditure switching effect for the choice of exchange rate regime in the presence of foreign monetary shocks. A comparison between fixed and floating rate regimes shows that, while the volatility of consumption is unambiguously lower in the floating exchange rate regime, the volatility of home output can be higher or lower depending on the value of the elasticity of substitution between home and foreign goods. A welfare comparison of the two regimes concludes that a floating exchange rate regime yields higher welfare when the expenditure switching effect is relatively weak, but a fixed exchange rate regime is superior when the expenditure switching effect is strong.

It is necessary to conclude with some qualifying remarks. The results presented above are obviously derived in a restricted model. There are a number of highly relevant and feasible ways in which the model can be generalised. For instance, the preference function could be generalised to allow for variable degrees of risk aversion in consumption and labour supply. Given the trade-off between consumption and output volatility which arises when the expenditure switching effect is strong, the degree of risk aversion in consumption and labour supply will have important implications for the welfare comparison between regimes. It is also necessary to extend the analysis to consider other sources of shocks. The shock-absorbing role of floating exchange rates in the presence of real demand and supply shocks was an important element in Friedman's case for floating rates (and also in the analysis of Mundell (1960)). This is not addressed by the above model.

Finally, there is the issue of local currency pricing (or more generally the extent of exchange rate pass-through). Devereux and Engel (2003) argue that local currency pricing is so prevalent that relative prices are insensitive to exchange rate changes. This implies that the elasticity of substitution between home and foreign goods is less relevant than the model of this chapter implies. Indeed, when there is full local currency pricing, the elasticity of substitution becomes irrelevant. However, the assumption of full local currency pricing is an extreme case (just as our assumption of full producer currency pricing is an extreme case). A full analysis of this issue requires a more general model, which allows for a partial degree of pass-through (or partial local currency pricing)[10] and which also allows the elasticity of substitution to differ from unity. It would then be possible to analyse the welfare comparison between fixed and flexible exchange rates against the background of a realistic degree of pass-through coupled with empirically relevant values for the elasticity of substitution and risk aversion.

Appendix

Appendix 1: Optimal price setting

The price-setting problem facing representative home producer h is

$$MaxU(h) = E\left\{ \log C(h) + \chi\log\frac{M(h)}{P} - \frac{K}{2}y^2(h) \right\} \tag{44}$$

subject to

$$PC(h) = p_H(h)y(h) + M_0 - M(h) - T + pR(h) \tag{45}$$

$$y(h) = c_H(h) + c_H^*(h) = (C_H + C_H^*)\left(\frac{p_H(h)}{P_H}\right)^{-\phi} \tag{46}$$

The first order condition with respect to $p_H(h)$ is[11]

$$E\left\{\frac{y(h)}{PC(h)} - \phi\left[\frac{p_H(h)}{PC(h)} - Ky(h)\right]\frac{y(h)}{p_H(h)}\right\} = 0 \tag{47}$$

In equilibrium all agents choose the same price and consumption level so

$$E\left\{\frac{Y}{PC} - \phi\left[\frac{P_H}{PC} - KY\right]\frac{Y}{P_H}\right\} = 0 \tag{48}$$

where

$$Y = C_H + C_H^* \tag{49}$$

Rearranging yields the expression in the main text. The derivation of the first-order condition for the representative foreign producer follows identical steps (and is omitted).

Appendix 2: Portfolio allocation, asset prices and risk sharing

There are four first-order conditions for the choice of asset holdings. After some rearrangement they imply the following four equations

$$E[C^{-1}y] = E[C^{-1}]q_H, \quad E[C^{-1}y^*] = E[C^{-1}]q_F \tag{50}$$

$$E[C^{*-1}y] = E[C^{*-1}]q_H, \quad E[C^{*-1}y^*] = E[C^{*-1}]q_F \tag{51}$$

The combination of the private and government budget constraints and the portfolio payoff functions for each country imply that aggregate home and foreign consumption levels are given by

$$C = y + \zeta_H(y - q_H) + \zeta_F(y^* - q_F) \tag{52}$$

$$C^* = y^* + \zeta_H^*(y - q_H) + \zeta_F^*(y^* - q_F) \tag{53}$$

where in a symmetric equilibrium $\zeta_H(h) = \zeta_H$ and $\zeta_F(h) = \zeta_F$ for all h and $\zeta_H^*(f) = \zeta_H^*$ and $\zeta_F^*(f) = \zeta_F^*$ for all f. Equilibrium in asset markets implies $\zeta_H + \zeta_H^* = 0$ and $\zeta_F + \zeta_F^* = 0$. These equations can be used to solve for q_H, q_F, ζ_H, ζ_F, ζ_H^*, ζ_F^*, C and C^* in terms of y and y^*.

Using the solution procedure outlined in Obstfeld and Rogoff (1996: 302–303) it is possible to show that the two asset prices are given by

$$q_H = \frac{E\left[\dfrac{y}{y+y*}\right]}{E\left[\dfrac{1}{y+y*}\right]}, q_F = \frac{E\left[\dfrac{y*}{y+y*}\right]}{E\left[\dfrac{1}{y+y*}\right]} \qquad (54)$$

and consumption levels in the two countries are given by

$$C = \frac{q_H(y+y*)}{q_H+q_F}, C* = \frac{q_F(y+y*)}{q_H+q_F} \qquad (55)$$

Thus

$$\frac{C}{C*} = \frac{q_H}{q_F} = \frac{E\left[\dfrac{y}{y+y*}\right]}{E\left[\dfrac{y*}{y+y*}\right]} \qquad (56)$$

which is equation (16) in the main text.

Notes

* This research was supported by the ESRC Evolving Macroeconomy Programme grant number L138251046.
1 See Lane (2001) for a recent survey of this literature.
2 This is, of course, only one form of floating rate regime. There are many other options for the home monetary authority in a floating rate regime. In particular the home monetary authority could adopt a monetary rule which maximises home welfare. The fixed money assumption adopted here is, however, a natural benchmark which corresponds to the Friedman policy prescription (and also to the analysis of Devereux and Engel (1998)).
3 When θ is equal to unity the trade balance between the two countries automatically balances in all states of the world, in which case financial markets are irrelevant. When $\theta \neq 1$ it becomes necessary to consider the structure of financial markets. Additionally, when shocks are asymmetric and when the focus of interest is the policy choice and welfare of a single country, it becomes necessary explicitly to consider how policy choices affect asset prices and portfolio decisions.
4 Note that asset pay-offs are correlated with aggregate income. Individual agents therefore treat pay-offs as exogenous. This implies that the existence of contingent assets has no direct impact on optimal price setting.
5 If, alternatively, asset trade takes place before the exchange rate regime is chosen, it would be possible for agents to insure themselves against the choice of regime. This could have very significant implications for the optimal choice of regime. The home monetary authority would be tempted to choose a regime which implies high volatility of demand for home goods. The high volatility of demand would discourage home labour supply and reduce home work effort but the level of home consumption would be protected by the risk-sharing arrangement. This alternative risk-sharing structure raises some interesting

issues but it also involves some technical problems which go beyond the scope of this chapter.

6 The complication arising in this model is contained in equation (6). When θ is different from unity this equation is not linear in logs.

7 In the non-stochastic equilibrium individual budget constraints imply that $\bar{P}\,\bar{C} = \bar{Y}\,P_H$. Combining this expression with equation (12) shows that $\bar{Y} = [K\phi/(\theta - 1)]^{-1/2}$, thus $K\bar{Y}^2 = (\phi - 1)/\phi$. It will become apparent below that the main welfare results are independent of the value of $\bar{Y}$.

8 In general the following equations should include terms which depend on the second moments of home and foreign consumption. However, the perfect cross-country correlation of consumption levels implies that these terms are equal to zero. They are therefore omitted from equations (32) and (33).

9 Note that this last point only relates to the effect of exchange rate volatility operating through the λ_{CPI} term. Exchange rate volatility affects λ_{P_H}, $\lambda_{P_F^*}$ and λ_{CPI} simultaneously, so, in equilibrium, it will not be possible to increase world consumption and reduce world output simply by making the exchange rate more volatile.

10 For instance following the model of Corsetti and Pesenti (2001).

11 Notice that this first-order condition is unaffected by the existence of income contingent assets because the asset returns are assumed to be correlated with aggregate real income. Asset returns are therefore treated as exogenous from the point of view of individual agents.

References

Bachetta, Philippe and van Wincoop, Eric (2000), 'Does exchange rate stability increase trade and welfare?', *American Economic Review*, 90: 1093–1109.

Corsetti, Giancarlo and Pesenti, Paolo (2001), 'International dimensions of optimal monetary policy', NBER Working Paper no. 8230.

Devereux, Michael B. (2000), 'A simple dynamic general equilibrium model of the trade-off between fixed and floating exchange rates', CEPR Working Paper no. 2403.

Devereux, Michael B. and Engel, Charles (1998), 'Fixed vs. floating exchange rates: how price setting affects the optimal choice of exchange rate regime', NBER Working Paper no. 6867.

Devereux, Michael B. and Engel, Charles (2003), 'Monetary policy in an open economy revisited: price setting and exchange rate flexibility', *Review of Economic Studies*, 70: 765–783.

Friedman, Milton (1953), 'The case for flexible exchange rates', in Milton Friedman, (ed.), *Essays in Positive Economics*, Chicago, IL: University of Chicago Press.

Lane, Philip (2001), 'The new open economy macroeconomics: a survey', *Journal of International Economics*, 54: 235–266.

Mundell, Robert A. (1960), 'The monetary dynamics of international adjustment under fixed and floating exchange rates', *Quarterly Journal of Economics*, 74: 227–257.

Obstfeld, Maurice and Rogoff, Kenneth (1995), 'Exchange rate dynamics redux', *Journal of Political Economy*, 103: 624–660.

Obstfeld, Maurice and Rogoff, Kenneth (1996), *Foundations of International Macroeconomics*, Cambridge, MA: MIT Press.

Obstfeld, Maurice and Rogoff, Kenneth (1998), 'Risk and exchange rates', NBER Working Paper no. 6694.

Obstfeld, Maurice and Rogoff, Kenneth (2002), 'Global implications of self-oriented national monetary rules', *Quarterly Journal of Economics*, 117: 503–536.

5 Economic shocks and the choice of currency area

The case of Argentina, 1991–2002*

Paul Hallwood, Ian W. Marsh and Jörg Scheibe

1 Introduction

This chapter offers an economic explanation for the demise of Argentina's currency board system that tied the peso to the US dollar at parity, and operated over the period 1991–2002. It also comments on the suggestion that the official dollarization of the Argentine monetary system (i.e., replacing the peso with the US dollar) would have been an appropriate policy in Argentina's economic circumstances (e.g. Hanke and Schuler 1999). On the basis of the findings discussed below, we are reasonably confident that official dollarization sometime in the early 1990s would not have averted the macroeconomic wreckage that piled up under the currency board in the recession beginning in 1998.

It is fanciful to argue that official dollarization would have straightened out Argentina's economy to such a degree that the recession that led to the demise of the de la Rue government, and with it the currency board system, would not have occurred. Our argument is that monetary union with the US dollar is simply not a good monetary arrangement for Argentina.

Those in favor of dollarization generally argue that by taking monetary decisions out of the hands of local politicians monetary credibility will increase, so bringing down interest rates and stimulating the economy. Indeed, the finding that aggregate demand shocks to Argentina and the United States in the 1970s–1980s were highly asymmetric is supportive of this line of reasoning (Bayoumi and Eichengreen 1994b). It suggests that macroeconomic policy makers in Argentina were going their own way, with the outcome that they produced very high rates of inflation. However, failures in macroeconomic management do not make the whole case for a country to give up its currency. Just as pertinent is the behavior of aggregate supply shocks – for example to levels of productivity – that are much less under the command of macroeconomic decision makers.

Our finding that temporary, and more particularly, permanent shocks were highly asymmetric between Argentina and the United States through the 1990s is suggestive of the need for the maintenance of a system affording a high degree of flexibility in real exchange rates between the countries. As always, the choice is between systems that allow an exchange rate to adjust, and those that require adjustment in relative price levels. As it turned out, under the currency board, Argentina persisted with attempting real exchange rate adjustment through price deflation until the economic and social cost of it became too hard to bear. As we can think of no credible reason why dollarization would have quickly altered the asymmetry of permanent shocks we think this arrangement was and is just as unsuitable for Argentina.

We are not the first to make the point that a tight monetary arrangement between Argentina and the United States is a bad policy.[1] Nor are we the first to apply the Blanchard–Quah structural VAR methodology to analyze the asymmetry shocks hitting the Argentine and US economies.[2] However, we do claim to be the first, as far as we know, to investigate shock asymmetries for the entire period of Argentina's currency board. Moreover, having the whole period before us we are better positioned than predecessors were to discuss the robustness of our statistical findings.

The rest of this chapter proceeds as follows. In section 2 we briefly describe the behavior of some major macroeconomic variables in the United States and Argentina over the period of interest in order to set the scene for subsequent analysis. In section 3 we offer a theoretical discussion of some of the main implications of giving up monetary sovereignty on a spectrum from a pure float to full dollarization. In section 4 we briefly discuss the Blanchard–Quah structural VAR methodology and then offer our statistical findings. Section 5 summarizes our conclusions.

2 Descriptive data

We present a selection of data comparing Argentina and the United States in order to set the scene for subsequent theoretical and empirical analysis. More detailed discussion of the behavior of the Argentine economy can be found in Hausmann and Velasco (2002) and De la Torre *et al.* (2003).

Table 5.1 shows the trade pattern of the country. Argentina remained a rather closed economy throughout the 1990s, although the importance of international trade did grow after the economy stabilized in 1992. The USA ranks only third in importance as a trade partner after Europe and Brazil. The importance of Argentine trade with US-linked economies outside the USA is minor. Trade linkages point, if anything, toward a currency union with the Mercosur partners, Brazil, Paraguay and Uruguay. While we recognize that trade linkages may well be endogenous to a currency union, work by Besedes and Prusa (2003) suggests that these structural changes may be slow developing. In their comprehensive analysis of *Direction of Trade* data they find strong evidence of persistence in trade links with established trade partners in differentiated products. And, while persistence in standardized goods – such as agricultural products, is much

Table 5.1 Argentine trade (as a percentage of GDP)

Argentine	Exports					Imports				
	1980	1985	1990	1995	2000	1980	1985	1990	1995	2000
GDP										
total	**6.74**	**9.52**	**8.74**	**8.12**	**9.26**	**8.85**	**4.33**	**2.88**	**7.80**	**8.88**
Industrial countries	**2.90**	**4.00**	**4.35**	**2.57**	**3.06**	**6.03**	**2.61**	**1.70**	**4.10**	**4.33**
US	0.60	1.17	1.20	0.58	1.12	2.00	0.79	0.62	1.42	1.70
Canada	0.04	0.07	0.06	0.03	0.10	0.09	0.04	0.02	0.10	0.11
Australia	0.01	0.03	0.04	0.02	0.02	0.07	0.06	0.06	0.05	0.02
Japan	0.18	0.41	0.28	0.17	0.13	0.82	0.30	0.09	0.26	0.35
New Zealand	0.00	0.00	0.01	0.00	0.02	0.01	0.00	0.00	0.01	0.01
Europe	**2.08**	**2.32**	**2.76**	**1.77**	**1.67**	**3.04**	**1.43**	**0.91**	**2.27**	**2.14**
Spain	0.16	0.26	0.24	0.26	0.32	0.34	0.08	0.07	0.32	0.32
Western hemisphere	**1.61**	**1.78**	**2.30**	**3.77**	**4.44**	**1.89**	**1.50**	**1.00**	**2.33**	**3.06**
Mercosur	**0.96**	**0.76**	**1.30**	**2.53**	**2.96**	**1.10**	**0.79**	**0.62**	**1.70**	**2.53**
Brazil	0.64	0.56	1.01	2.07	2.46	0.90	0.69	0.51	1.56	2.28
Uruguay	0.16	0.11	0.19	0.23	0.29	0.12	0.07	0.08	0.10	0.15
Paraguay	0.16	0.08	0.10	0.22	0.21	0.07	0.02	0.03	0.04	0.10
Chile	0.18	0.13	0.33	0.54	0.94	0.21	0.10	0.08	0.19	0.21
USD countries	**0.19**	**0.42**	**0.38**	**0.46**	**0.51**	**0.17**	**0.02**	**0.08**	**0.39**	**0.68**
Hong Kong	0.02	0.01	0.04	0.11	0.03	0.09	0.00	0.00	0.04	0.02
China	0.16	0.35	0.17	0.11	0.28	0.03	0.00	0.01	0.22	0.41
Thailand	0.00	0.00	0.00	0.00	0.07	0.00	0.00	0.01	0.03	0.05
Malaysia	0.00	0.03	0.09	0.10	0.09	0.00	0.00	0.00	0.01	0.07
Indonesia	0.00	0.02	0.07	0.06	0.02	0.04	0.01	0.05	0.01	0.04
Taiwan	0.00	0.00	0.01	0.07	0.02	0.00	0.00	0.01	0.09	0.10

Source: IMF Direction of Trade Statistics.

less evident, this would seem not to be all that helpful to Argentina given that its agricultural sector is somewhat complementary to that of the USA, and that the USA continues to subsidize its domestic farm sector.

While not particularly open, Argentina satisfies the small country assumption. Argentine GDP at purchasing power parities was around 6.5 percent that of the USA during the period of the peg. Figure 5.1 compares the development of key variables in Argentina and the USA from 1991 to 2001. Panel a of Figure 5.1 shows the financial market's view on the credibility of the currency board arrangements. The Argentine money market rate was always greater than the US Federal Funds rate, indicating a lack of trust in the permanence of the dollar link. Panel b illustrates the sharp depreciation of the real effective exchange rate of Brazil, and the fall in 2002Q1 for Argentina when the currency board was abandoned. The devaluation of the Brazilian real on 13 January 1999 is widely credited with

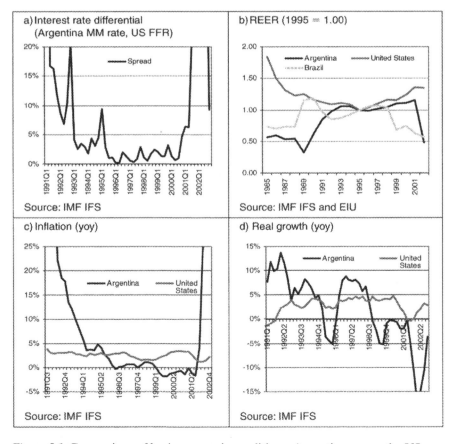

Figure 5.1 Comparison of basic economic conditions: Argentina versus the US.

contributing to the economic difficulties in Argentina, which was not given the option to ease the competitive pressures by devaluing the peso. Although the impact of the real's depreciation on the Argentine real effective exchange rate remained low in 1999, the competitive pressures abroad were large in agricultural products. Panels c and d show low inflation and robust growth in Argentina for most of the period under the currency board. Nevertheless, the country fell into recession in 2001, and subsequently found the cost of maintaining the exchange rate peg to be too high.

3 A monetary model of dollarization

Even before the end of the currency board there was wide discussion of the appropriate exchange rate regime for Argentina. In this section we offer a fairly simple conceptual framework capable of nesting the full range of exchange rate regimes from free float to full dollarization. For each regime we describe the policy tools the authorities retain to deal with economic shocks – which, in section 4, we show to be highly asymmetric between Argentina and the USA. We conclude that these were so large and so asymmetric that no fixed rate regime could have survived.

We will use the exchange market pressure (EMP) model of Girton and Roper (1977) to frame the issue.[3] Their paper, in effect, combined the monetary approaches to the balance of payments and to the exchange rate. Thus, if an exchange rate is allowed to move within a target zone (explicit or implicit), taken separately, neither the movement of the exchange rate nor the movement of foreign exchange reserves will necessarily give an accurate measure of exchange market pressure. For example, the exchange rate could be steady, or, even, appreciating, while foreign exchange reserves were falling heavily. However, taken together, movements in rates and reserves can be used to indicate exchange market pressure.

As in all the other monetary models, the central equations in the EMP model are a pair of money demand and supply equations – one pair for each country in a two-country world (with a small open economy assumption possible but not necessary). Since excess monetary balances have sooner or later to be adjusted through either changes in the balances of payments or in the exchange rate (and price level), variations in other assumptions do not make an awful lot of difference to the basic assertion that an excessive rate of domestic credit expansion will increase EMP. It is this very robustness of the EMP model that has made it such a popular model with researchers. For example, Tanner (2001) uses the EMP model to examine the coincidence of monetary policy and exchange market pressure in several Asian and Latin American countries. Kaminsky *et al.* (1998) use it to build currency crisis indicators, and Hallwood *et al.* (2000) use it in their analysis of the collapse of the gold standard.[4]

In this chapter the EMP framework is used to "nest" various exchange rate regimes and highlight exactly what degree of flexibility and policy tools are given up on the road from fully floating exchange rates, through a currency board and on to dollarization. We do not estimate an EMP model since our interest is not in what actually happened under the currency board, but on what might have happened in counterfactual regimes (dollarization or some form of floating regime). However, analysis of the assumed exogenous shocks that hit Argentina and the United States between 1991 and 2002 sheds light on the degree of exchange rate and policy flexibility that seems with hindsight appropriate for Argentina to have retained.

The Girton and Roper (1977) model of flow equilibrium can be expressed in logarithms as

$$\Delta m_t^s = \Delta d_t + \Delta f_t \qquad\qquad \Delta m_t^{*s} = \Delta d_t^* + \Delta f_t^* \tag{1}$$

$$\Delta m_t^d = \Delta p_t + \beta \Delta y_t - \alpha \Delta i_t \quad \Delta m_t^{*d} = \Delta p_t^* + \beta \Delta y_t^* - \alpha \Delta i_t^* \tag{2}$$

$$\Delta p_t = \Delta p_t^* - \Delta e_t + \theta_t \tag{3}$$

$$\Delta i_t = \Delta i_t^* + \delta_t \tag{4}$$

Variables with an asterisk signify foreign (US) variables, and those without an asterisk, domestic (Argentine) variables. Equation (1) sets the growth in the supply of base money equal to the sum of domestic credit expansion (Δd) and the growth of foreign exchange reserves (Δf).[5] Equation (2) describes the growth of demand for nominal domestic money balances in terms of growth in domestic prices (Δp), real income (Δy) and an appropriate index of nominal interest rates (Δi). Equivalent money supply and demand relationships hold for the foreign country and for notational convenience we assume both countries have identical income elasticities (β) and interest semi-elasticities (α) of demand for money. Equation (3) allows relative purchasing power parity to hold continuously if θ_t is forced equal to zero but the model is capable of handling deviations from PPP represented by a non-zero θ_t. Note that the exchange rate is defined such that positive values of Δe represent the rate of appreciation of the domestic currency (pesos) in terms of the foreign currency (dollars). Equation (4) simply denotes the change in the uncovered interest differential by δ_t. It does not impose uncovered interest parity although this could be handled in the model. Similarly, static exchange rate expectations would mean δ_t represents changes in the risk premium implicit in domestic interest rates.

It is clear from the description of the model that the Girton–Roper approach, in common with all highly reduced-form monetary models, suffers from a lack of rigorous analytical footings based on fully specified microfoundations. Our primary defense in continuing to use such a workhorse model is that its simplicity makes it easier to understand, particularly in policy discussions. Further, since they are still in their relative infancy, the implications of the new open-economy macroeconomic models are frequently dependent on the exact specification of the crucial microfoundations, over which there is little professional consensus and less empirical evidence pertaining to Argentina for the period we consider.[6] The Girton–Roper approach as used here is perhaps better thought of as a conceptual framework than a model.

Some manipulation of the basic equations yields:

$$\Delta f_t - \Delta f_t^* + \Delta e_t = -\Delta d_t + \Delta d_t^* + \beta(\Delta y_t - \Delta y_t^*) + \theta_t - \alpha\delta_t \tag{5}$$

The composite dependent variable in equation (5) is called "exchange market pressure." In particular, a decline in the rate of growth of either or both of f or e represents a weakening of a country's external position as, respectively, the increase in foreign exchange reserves or currency appreciation falls.

There are two exogenous foreign (US) shocks in this model that originate either from a policy induced change in the domestic assets of the Federal Reserve, or from a shock to US real GDP. Shocks to θ_t, Argentina's real exchange rate, may be either monetary or real in origin. The key point illustrated by equation (5) is that shocks exogenous to Argentina may be absorbed, at least temporarily, by either monetary or real variables depending on the monetary-exchange rate regime in force. If the exchange rate is floating, such that $\Delta f = \Delta f^* = 0$, shocks may initially be absorbed by variations in Δe. With an exchange rate pegged to a fluctuation band both foreign exchange reserves and the exchange rate can act as shock absorbers – though the exchange rate can only adjust to a limited extent owing to the narrowness of a typical fluctuation band. The same is also true of a "dirty float," where, presumably, the exchange rate has greater scope to vary. Critical in this is the degree of price flexibility in the system. If domestic and foreign prices are both perfectly sticky θ_t equals Δe. Foreign-sourced shocks cannot be absorbed by the exchange rate and all adjustment falls on foreign exchange reserves (or the other monetary variables or even income). However, since reality is somewhere between the two extremes of perfect price flexibility and perfect stickiness, the exchange rate will have some ability to absorb shocks in each of these regimes.

This ability is lost in a currency board arrangement such as the one run by Argentina between 1991 and 2002 since Δe must exactly equal zero. Thus, it is variations in Δf, with some sterilization, which acts as a limited shock absorber. This limit depends on the extent to which variation in the money base can be insulated from variation in foreign exchange reserves. Thus, it is reported that for much of the period 1991–2002 Argentina held foreign exchange reserves in excess of the level strictly required by law to back the money base. However, the insulation property of sterilization turned out to be more apparent than real as markets feared that the base could be excessively increased relative to reserves as a matter of policy choice. This fear may be the reason why the Argentine peso carried a risk premium relative to the US dollar ever since Argentina established its currency board in 1991.

With dollarization and the doing away with all vestiges of an independent monetary policy, the rule becomes $\Delta f = \Delta e = 0$, $\Delta d = \Delta b$, where Δb represents the rate of inflow (if positive) of dollars from the rest of the dollar area. Domestic credit expansion within the dollar zone as a whole is the sole prerogative of the US Federal Reserve. Equation (5) becomes:

$$0 = \Delta b_t + \Delta d_t^* + \beta(\Delta y_t - \Delta y_t^*) + \theta_t - \alpha \delta_t \tag{6}$$

Thus, with dollarization, the nominal shock absorbers largely become inoperative, except to the extent that other institutional arrangements can be made. A dollarized country might be able to negotiate some sort of direct or indirect influence over Federal Reserve policy. However this has so far not happened for extant dollarized countries such as Panama and it would anyway seem to be a distant possibility. Also, while access to the federal funds market is likely to be denied, use of international inter-bank arrangements such as negotiated by Argentina during the 1990s, would seem, because of their limited size, to be no more than short-term palliatives.

The fiscal deficit has a role to play in our discussion. In moving from a currency board to a dollarized economy the domestic component of domestic credit expansion is forced to zero. In a scenario where domestic credit expansion is driven by fiscal deficits untamed even by the discipline of a rigidly pegged exchange rate, control of the government balance might be achieved by dollarization. Thus the loss of shock absorbers under dollarization might be offset by better control of a key source of domestic shocks. However, we think this reasoning is fanciful. De la Torre *et al.* (2003) demonstrate that the Argentine government was willing to circumvent the supposed budget constraint imposed by the currency board by issuing central and provincial government paper only cosmetically different from currency.[7] What this indicates is that the political choices over monetary and fiscal balances are to some extent independent of each other. Politicians do not see that the choice of one may foreclose choices over the other. Alternatively, they may delink political choices in an effort to satisfy different political constituencies. In the case of Argentina central government support for provincial spending occurred because, for whatever reason, the provinces were a constituency thought to be worthy of central government support.[8] Indeed, the strong possibility that politicians will not allow the choice of monetary regime to foreclose choices over fiscal spending and deficits surely lies at the heart of the EU's "growth and stability pact" that limits fiscal deficits to 3 percent of a member's GDP. And within a short period of time of the pact coming into force several EU members are in distinct danger of breaking their own rules and there is even talk of having the rules changed.

In the absence of monetary shock absorbers, exogenous variations in the real exchange rate, θ, will have a destabilizing effect on the Argentine real economy. A real appreciation (a rise in θ) would, for a constant risk premium, require either a contraction of real income or an increase in b, the flow of dollars to Argentina. However, it is hard to see why the latter, preferable, adjustment would automatically occur given the contractionary affect of real exchange rate appreciation on Argentine real GDP and price level. The importance of real exchange rate shocks is exacerbated given the diversified geographic structure of Argentine foreign trade. Changes in bilateral dollar rates, say with the euro (dominated no doubt by US rather than Argentine monetary conditions), will impact Argentina's real exchange rate. This is another way of saying that if a country were to join a monetary union it would be beneficial to choose one that accounts for a high share of its foreign trade. However, the plain fact is that Argentine bilateral trade with the United States is not at all great (Table 5.1).

Shifts in δ_t, a (noisy) measure of movements in the risk premium on Argentine assets, can also play a prominent role in a dollarized system. The interest differential grew larger and larger during the last four or so years of Argentina's currency board, reaching some 2,000 basis points just before the end (Figure 5.1). Many commentators have implicated the risk premium in the demise of Argentina's currency board. For example, such large risk premiums almost certainly discouraged international bank lending to Argentina that would have helped in financing the troublesome central-plus-provincial government fiscal deficit. Of course, those same fiscal deficits were a major cause of δ_t in the first place.

Supposing counter-factually that the Argentine fiscal authorities managed the economy to achieve $\alpha\delta_t = 0$ (at a minimum a highly disciplined fiscal policy would have been necessary), then an increase in Δy^* may be balanced by an increase in Δy. An issue concerns how the latter is to be brought about given the combination of weak trade linkages between Argentina and the United States and an (assumed) tight fiscal policy in Argentina. Similarly, an increase in Δy^* could be balanced by a decrease in the flow of dollars to Argentina – so reducing b. However, such a monetary contraction may also not happen to suit the Argentine economy. Furthermore, if Argentina and the United States are subject to asymmetric shocks it is quite unlikely that changes in Δy^* will suit business conditions in Argentina. Such an asymmetry is precisely why a country should retain some monetary shock absorbers. An important issue therefore concerns the degree of symmetry between shocks in Argentina and the United States. This matter is the main focus of the rest of this chapter and we will turn to it in a moment.

A line of argument against the foregoing reasoning is that the history is no guide to the future. Thus, geographic patterns of trade, business cycle synchronization and asymmetry of shocks are irrelevant to a currency union since the formation of the union will alter these variables in a direction favorable to the union (Frankel and Rose 1997 and 1998). Linkages between a pair of economies, it has been argued, will increase in a currency union. For example, Argentine trade shares with the United States will increase with the use of a common currency and with this, business cycles will synchronize and shocks will become less asymmetric (Rose and Engel 2000; Corsetti and Pesenti 2002). In answering this it is hardly possible to resist Keynes' well-known dictum concerning the long term and being dead. The relevant long term here is the span of a democratically elected government. Ten years of currency board and four years of deepening recession was all the Argentine electorate were willing to wait for their currency board experiment to work. In other words, a currency regime has only a limited time to induce symmetry, and the political reality in Argentina was that their currency board had just ten years. As we are about to show this was not long enough to align supply shocks in Argentina to those in the United States. Indeed, in our econometric results, we find that the largest asymmetric supply shocks occurred at the end of the decade-long currency board experience. While a currency board is not the same as official dollarization – because it allows some degree of monetary independence – the persistence of asymmetric permanent shocks even after ten years, many of them of great economic sacrifice, can hardly be taken as a positive signal for the rapid endogenization of an optimal currency area.

4 Econometric analysis

No matter how dissimilar the profiles of Argentina and the United States may appear from these data, they merely show that the economies behaved differently over the decade. They do not show whether this was due to the enactment of different policies, for example, or due to different shocks impinging on the economies.

Our discussion in the previous section focused on the progressive reduction in monetary shock absorbers available as a country moves from some kind of floating regime through a currency board to dollarization. While we could examine the adjustment process followed by Argentina under the observed currency board regime through impulse response analysis, it is not straightforward to empirically determine the counterfactual policy adjustment mechanisms that Argentina would have employed had it, for example, floated or dollarized. We can, however, attempt to determine the shocks (presumed to be policy-invariant) that hit the economies during the period. A consideration of the nature of those shocks can, we argue, point to the approximate degree of shock absorption necessary.

To reveal these shocks, some econometric modeling is required. Using a methodology developed by (Blanchard and Quah 1989) and extended by Bayoumi (1991), Bayoumi and Eichengreen (1992, 1993, 1994a, 1994b) and Bayoumi and Taylor (1995) we identify aggregate shocks from a bivariate VAR system, defined across the price level (we use CPIs[9]) and output (real GDP). In vector notation, the evolution of log first differences of real output (Y) and prices (P) is represented by an infinite moving average system of structural innovations, which, as we discuss, can be interpreted as temporary and permanent shocks:

$$X_t = \begin{bmatrix} \Delta Y_t \\ \Delta P_t \end{bmatrix} = \sum_{m=0}^{\infty} L^m \begin{bmatrix} a_m^{11} & a_m^{21} \\ a_m^{12} & a_m^{22} \end{bmatrix} \begin{bmatrix} \epsilon_t^t \\ \epsilon_t^p \end{bmatrix} \tag{7}$$

L is the lag operator and the ϵ terms are unobservable structural shocks identified by superscripts as either temporary or permanent.[10] The afore-mentioned papers show in detail how the structural disturbances are recovered from the reduced form estimation. Essentially, two restrictions are necessary. First, the shocks are assumed to be orthogonal. Second, temporary shocks are so defined since they do not have permanent impacts on output. This implies the restriction that $\sum_{m=0}^{\infty} a_m^{11} = 0$.

The VAR methodology in general and the identification restrictions in particular come with caveats which are well documented in the literature. First, VARs with their limited number of variables are criticized for being overly simplistic. Although we agree with this point in general, we believe that the framework we use is well contained and warrants a bivariate analysis – and hence gives meaningful shock identifications. Lippi and Reichlin (1993) draw attention to the potential existence of non-standard moving-average representations.[11] Lütkepohl (1993) makes the more telling point that impulse response analyses based on VARs have to be used with caution because of the likely omitted variable effects. This is one technical reason why we concentrate in this chapter on looking at the nature of the shocks impinging on the economies rather than the adjustment process to those shocks.

We now move on to the estimation of the disturbances for Argentina and the US. The Argentine currency board arrangements lasted from 1 April 1991 to 6 January 2002. In effect, however, the exchange controls imposed on 1 December 2001 ended the currency board. In our econometric analysis we will primarily consider the period from 1991Q3 to 2001Q4. We use seasonally adjusted quarterly data for Argentina and the United States collected from the International Monetary Fund's International Financial Statistics database and Datastream.

The VAR specification is valid under the assumption that both season-ally adjusted GDP and the CPI are integrated of order one and that the two level series are not cointegrated. Dickey–Fuller tests suggest these assumptions are valid for both the USA and Argentina. The system is modeled as a bivariate VAR(4) process with the relevant identification conditions imposed, which provides time series estimates of the shocks ϵ^t and ϵ^p for both countries.

Table 5.2 provides the results of the reduced-form estimation.[12]

Our analysis focuses on the structural disturbances plotted in Figure 5.2 and statistically summarized in the first panel of Table 5.3. While the temporary shocks hitting the two countries were of approximately equal size, it is apparent from both the statistics and the graphs that the permanent shocks impinging on Argentina were of an order of magnitude greater than those affecting the United States. Further, and equally important, the permanent shocks hitting Argentina in any quarter were essentially uncorrelated with those hitting the United States at the same time. Whatever the true extent of the macroeconomic links between the two countries, they were not strong enough for the economies to be subjected to similar exogenous shocks. If asynchronous correlations are considered, US shocks seem to be transmitted to Argentina with a six to twelve month delay, although the degrees of correlation remain low.[13] There is also little evidence that as the pegged exchange rate regime approached its tenth anniversary that the shocks were becoming more similar.[14] Indeed, the correlation of permanent shocks was even lower during the latter half of the currency board era.

Focusing on the end of the currency board experiment, it is apparent that the final few quarters were characterized by large negative shocks to Argentina. The negative supply shock experienced in 2001Q3 was the largest single shock affecting Argentina (or, of course, the United States) during the entire pegged period, and was followed by another large negative supply

Table 5.2 Results of VAR modelling (1993Q1–2001Q4)

Independent variable	Argentina		USA	
	ΔY_t	ΔP_t	ΔY_t	ΔP_t
Constant	0.008	−0.028**	0.009**	−0.006
ΔY_{t-1}	0.776**	0.169**	0.194	0.335
ΔY_{t-2}	−0.148	−0.041	0.196	0.052*
ΔY_{t-3}	0.352*	0.002	−0.086	0.772**
ΔY_{t-4}	−0.268	0.054	−0.220	−0.587*
ΔP_{t-1}	−0.602	0.062	0.030	0.641**
ΔP_{t-2}	−1.093**	0.365**	−0.041	0.017
ΔP_{t-3}	0.623*	0.048	−0.332**	0.496**
ΔP_{t-4}	0.841**	0.094	0.083	−0.407*
R-squared	0.64	0.95	0.48	0.65

Note
* and ** denote significance at the 90 percent and 95 percent level respectively.

a) Temporary shocks

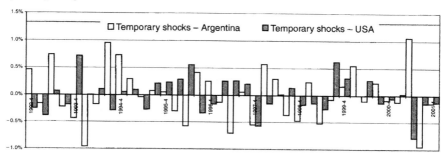

b) Permanent shocks

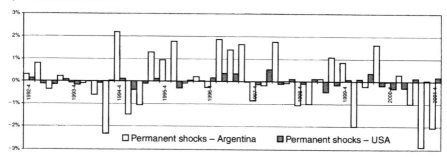

c) Accumulated relative permanent shocks

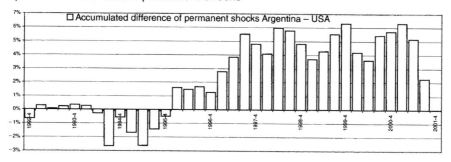

Figure 5.2 Temporary and permanent shocks in the USA and Argentina.

Table 5.3 Summary statistics of temporary and permanent shocks (1993Q1–2001Q4)

	Argentina	USA
Temporary shocks		
Median	−0.08%	0.01%
Standard deviation	0.49%	0.31%
Minimum	−0.96%	−0.78%
Maximum	1.06%	0.72%
Permanent shocks		
Median	0.10%	0.02%
Standard deviation	1.31%	0.21%
Minimum	−2.89%	−0.47%
Maximum	2.21%	0.53%
Cross-period correlation of US and Argentine...[16]	*...temporary shocks*	*...permanent shocks*
−4 quarters	0.00	0.16
−3 quarters	−0.12	0.38
−2 quarters	0.39	0.19
−1 quarter	−0.14	−0.28
0	−0.30	−0.01
+1 quarter	−0.11	0.25
+2 quarters	0.06	0.06
+3 quarters	0.27	0.26
+4 quarters	0.34	−0.10

shock in the following quarter.[15] Cumulating the relative permanent shocks (Argentina minus the United States) makes clear the deterioration of the economic situation at the end of 2001 (Panel c). From a highly positive cumulated relative supply shock position in 1990Q1, Argentina lost all of its gains in just two quarters (Panel c). The final shock took Argentina to the worst supply position it had faced relative to the United States since the end of 1995. The pegged regime had weathered the negative supply shocks in the early 1990s, helped in part by the offsetting positive demand shocks (Panel a). However, in late 2001 cumulated relative demand shocks were small. Ultimately the final two massive negative supply shocks proved too asymmetric for the regime to handle and the link with the dollar was broken.

Some sensitivity analysis is in order at this point. It is well known that the Bayoumi–Eichengreen method of extracting shocks is sensitive to the exact specification of the underlying VAR. To examine this issue, we compare the results of the Argentine VAR models estimated over different time periods:[17]

1   1991Q3–2001Q4
2   1990Q2–2002Q4
3   1995Q1–2001Q4.

Interval 1 is our preferred interval and the relevant results have already been discussed. The second interval maximizes the use of available data. The final interval excludes data from early in the currency board when the Argentine economy may have been transitioning from one regime to another. It also allows us to consider the role of Brazil since Brazilian inflation and growth data meet the statistical requirements of stationarity after this point. The correlation between identified disturbances across our three main estimation periods is displayed in Table 5.4. Figure 5.3 makes the point graphically.

We do find different results if alternative specifications are adopted. In particular, if we estimate the VAR over a longer period that includes data from before the pegged regime when inflation, in particular, was much higher, the magnitude of the extracted permanent and especially temporary shocks is greater. The correlation between permanent shocks is extracted from the VAR over 1991Q3–2001Q4 with those from 1990Q2–2002Q4 is 0.73, and that for temporary shocks just 0.32. This is perhaps not surprising since the decision to follow a strict peg probably invalidates the use of data from the two regimes to estimate a single VAR representation of the economy.

Reducing the estimation period to exclude the first few years following the peg also alters the exact patterns of the extracted shocks, but not nearly so much, and not enough to significantly change our interpretation of the results. The correlation with shocks extracted with our preferred

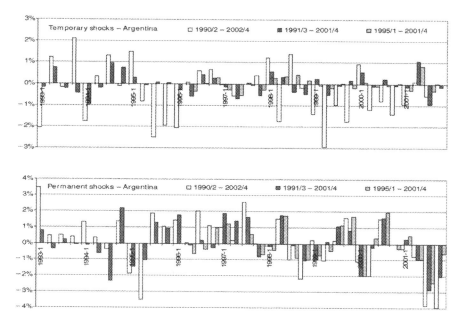

Figure 5.3 Sensitivity of VAR estimates to the estimation period.

Table 5.4 Correlation of temporary and permanent shocks

Temporary shocks

	ARG 90Q2–02Q4	ARG 91Q3–01Q4	ARG 95Q1–01Q4	BRA 95Q1–01Q4	US 90Q2–02Q4	US 91Q3–01Q4	US 95Q1–01Q4
ARG-90Q2–02Q4	1.00						
ARG-91Q3–01Q4	0.32	1.00					
ARG-95Q1–01Q4	0.33	0.69	1.00				
BRA-95Q1–01Q4	0.05	−0.22	−0.06	1.00			
US-90Q2–02Q4	**−0.06**	**−0.17**	**−0.37**	−0.20	1.00		
US-91Q3–01Q4	**−0.03**	**−0.30**	**−0.44**	−0.09	0.85	1.00	
US-95Q1–01Q4	**−0.22**	**−0.39**	**−0.43**	−0.07	0.71	0.92	1.00

Permanent shocks

	ARG 90Q2–02Q4	ARG 91Q3–01Q4	ARG 95Q1–01Q4	BRA 95Q1–01Q4	US 90Q2–02Q4	US 91Q3–01Q4	US 95Q1–01Q4
ARG-90Q2–02Q4	1.00						
ARG-91Q3–01Q4	0.73	1.00					
ARG-95Q1–01Q4	0.67	0.85	1.00				
BRA-95Q1–01Q4	0.35	0.36	0.40	1.00			
US-90Q2–02Q4	**−0.15**	**0.04**	**−0.08**	−0.41	1.00		
US-91Q3–01Q4	**−0.06**	**−0.01**	**−0.09**	−0.52	0.80	1.00	
US-95Q1–01Q4	**−0.10**	**−0.12**	**−0.07**	−0.54	0.87	0.97	1.00

VAR is 0.69 for temporary shocks and 0.85 for permanent shocks. Using the short data periods inevitably increases estimation error and risks over-fitting given the small number of observations available so we prefer to use results from data covering the entire pegged period.

Nevertheless, no matter how we alter the specification of the VAR, three critical empirical findings remain:

1   The permanent shocks hitting the Argentine economy were much greater than those affecting the United States
2   The shocks affecting Argentina and the United States were essentially uncorrelated (and demand shocks were possibly even significantly negatively correlated)
3   The final few quarters of the peg were characterized by a series of large, negative permanent shocks specific to Argentina.

A final finding, deserving of further exploration, is that the contemporaneous correlation between permanent shocks to Argentina and Brazil is substantially higher than between Argentina and the US (or any other country that we examined).[18] This suggests that the pressure brought to bear on Argentina after the real's devaluation in January 1999 was not just a case of unlucky spillovers from a third country. Instead, Argentina's main trading partner, neighbor and competitor in third markets was experiencing similar shocks, unlike Argentina's chosen partner. Although tying the peso to the Brazilian real would not have imported much anti-inflationary credibility, particularly at the start of the 1990s, this finding does indicate that Brazil might be a better partner in any future fixed exchange rate regime where avoidance of asymmetric shocks is of paramount importance.

5 Conclusions

In this chapter we have discussed a number of matters pertaining to the choice of a monetary-exchange rate system by Argentina. We suggest that pertinent to the choice of such a system is the asymmetry of shocks and especially the asymmetry of permanent shocks, between a pair of countries in a monetary union. On the basis of our finding that permanent shocks to Argentina and the United States remained highly asymmetric even in the later years of the currency board system, we draw the conclusion that close monetary union between Argentina and the United States is unsuitable for the former country. The problem is that the occurrence of asymmetric shocks requires real exchange rate flexibility if macroeconomic stability is to be maintained. This conclusion is entirely supportive of the prescient observation by Bayoumi and Eichengreen (1994b) that in the Americas, including Argentina, "countries in this region would have to undertake very major adjustments in policy and performance in laying the groundwork for monetary union" (34–35). Unfortunately, price deflation as a means of achieving this flexibility proved to be just too costly for Argentina. Economic and resulting political circumstances forced it to give up its currency board so allowing it to choose the other method of real exchange rate adjustment – through nominal exchange rate flexibility. How this will work out is yet to be determined. Managed properly with disciplined monetary and fiscal policies, increased exchange rate flexibility may achieve the degree of real exchange rate flexibility appropriate for the Argentine economy. Then again, the untethering of Argentine monetary and fiscal policy from the constraints of the currency board might reintroduce high inflation and nominal and real exchange rate instability to the Argentine economy. But to those that say that official dollarization would avert such problems we ask how such an arrangement would create the necessary real exchange rate flexibility without the need for prolonged price deflation.

Notes

* The authors would like to thank the editors and an anonymous referee for helpful comments on earlier drafts of this chapter.
1 See, for example, Alberola *et al.* (2003) and De la Torre *et al.* (2003).
2 Bayoumi and Eichengreen (1994b) did so before us.
3 To save space we do not discuss the background to the model. Weymark (1997, 1998) discusses EMP in considerable detail.
4 The original application by Girton and Roper (1977) was to the Canadian economy. Reconsiderations of the Canadian case using similar models include Burdekin and Burkett (1990) and Laidler *et al.* (1982). Other countries examined within the Girton–Roper framework include Brazil (Connolly and Da Silviera 1979), Ireland (Kenneally and Finn 1985), and several Caribbean economies (Pollard 1999).
5 It is worth remembering that domestic credit expansion will include private capital inflows from abroad.
6 In the words on Sarno and Taylor (2003) "new open-economy models are perhaps more analogous to finely tuned, thoroughbred racehorses than workhorses."
7 Prominent were lecop, small denomination federal bonds redeemable for federal tax payments, and the provincial version, patacon.
8 Jones *et al.* (2000) discuss the political drivers of provincial government spending. As under Argentine law this spending is financed by taxes raised by central government they model these taxes as a common pool resource – nonexcludable, but depletable in that provincial "over-spending" creates central government fiscal deficits. In their test of this model they find that a "party affiliation effect" (when the central and provincial governments are of the same party) helps to internalize the externality and reduce provincial spending. However, when provincial and central government are of different parties no such spending-reduction effect occurs.
9 Blanchard and Quah (1989) use first log-differences of real GDP and the level of the unemployment rate, Bayoumi and Eichengreen (1992) specify their model in terms of first log-differences of real GDP and the GDP deflator. Bayoumi and Taylor (1995) use real GDP and the CPI. We also use the CPI since data for the GDP deflator is not available for the entire period for the two

South American countries we analyze. Indeed, consumer prices, producer prices and the GDP deflator are highly correlated (>0.89) for the periods where available as the countries under examination are rather closed economies.

10 Blanchard and Quah, Bayoumi and Eichengreen in their various papers, and Bayoumi and Taylor interpret temporary and permanent shocks as demand and supply disturbances. There are potential caveats to this dichotomy – which Blanchard and Quah discuss in detail – as supply shocks could be temporary (e.g. a temporary shift in productivity) while demand shocks could have permanent effects (e.g. where there are hysteresis effects). We want to steer clear of potential interpretational and semantic ambiguities and so couch our analysis in terms of temporary and permanent shocks without making the additional step to demand and supply shocks. Nevertheless we note that the AD–AS interpretation does tend to find support in post-World War II data (Keating and Nye 1998).

11 See also the reply by Blanchard and Quah (1993).

12 In order to capture potentially remaining seasonal patterns in the data the regressions include a set of seasonal dummies.

13 What constitutes a high correlation is rather subjective. Bayoumi and Eichengreen (1992) suggest that the core EU countries could be defined as the group with contemporaneous permanent shock correlations in excess of 0.5 with respect to Germany. The same paper noted correlations in excess of 0.65 for the core regions of the US.

14 Indeed, Brazil would have been a better partner on that measure (see Table 5.4).

15 Argentina also faced a large negative temporary shock at the same time, although this was almost matched in magnitude by a negative temporary shock in the US.

16 For example, the +4 row indicates the correlation of US shocks at time t with Argentine shocks at time $t + 4$.

17 For completeness we also examine the robustness of the US estimates. As the correlations in Table 5.4 suggest, the critical supply shocks are highly correlated across the different estimation periods.

18 Over the period 1995Q1–2001Q4 but irrespective of the period used to identify Argentine shocks.

References

Alberola, E., Lopez, H. and Serven, L. (2003), "Tango with the gringo: the hard peg and real misalignment in Argentina", World Bank, Washington DC, Working Paper no. 3322.

Bayoumi, T. (1991), "A note on the decomposition of vector autoregressions," unpublished manuscript, Bank of England, London.

Bayoumi, T. and Eichengreen, B. (1992), "Shocking aspects of European monetary unification," NBER Working Paper no. 3949.

Bayoumi, T. and Eichengreen, B. (1993), "Exchange rate and monetary arrangements for NAFTA," IMF Working Paper no. WP/93/20.

Bayoumi, T. and Eichengreen, B. (1994a), "Macroeconomic adjustment under Bretton Woods and the post-Bretton-Woods float: an impulse-response analysis," *Economic Journal*, 104: 813–827.

Bayoumi, T. and Eichengreen, B. (1994b), "One money or many? Analyzing the prospects for monetary unification in various parts of the world," *Princeton Studies in International Finance*, 76 (September).

Bayoumi, T. and Taylor, M.P. (1995), "Macro-economic shocks, the ERM, and tri-polarity," *Review of Economics and Statistics*, 77: 321–331.

Besedes, T. and Prusa, T.J. (2003), "On the direction of trade," unpublished manuscript.

Blanchard, O.J. and Quah, D. (1989), "The dynamic effect of aggregate demand and supply disturbances," *American Economic Review*, 79: 655–673.

Blanchard, O.J. and Quah, D. (1993), "The dynamic effects of aggregate demand and supply disturbances: reply," *American Economic Review*, 83: 653–658.

Burdekin, R.C.K. and Burkett, P. (1990), "A re-examination of the monetary model of exchange market pressure: Canada 1963–88," *Review of Economics and Statistics*, 72: 677–681.

Connolly, M. and Da Silviera, J.D. (1979), "Exchange market pressure in postwar Brazil: an application of the Girton–Roper monetary model," *American Economic Review*, 69: 448–454.

Corsetti, G. and Pesenti, P. (2002), "Self-validating optimal currency areas," unpublished manuscript, Yale University.

De la Torre, A., Yeyati, E.L. and Schmukler, S.L. (2003), "Living and dying with hard pegs: the rise and fall of Argentina's currency board," unpublished manuscript, World Bank.

Frankel, J.A. and Rose, A.K. (1997), "The endogeneity of the optimum currency area criteria," *Swedish Economic Policy Review*, 4: 487–512.

Frankel, J.A. and Rose, A.K. (1998), "The endogeneity of the optimum currency area criteria," *Economic Journal*, 108: 1009–1025.

Girton, L. and Roper, D. (1977), "A monetary model of exchange market pressure applied to the postwar Canadian experience," *American Economic Review*, 67: 537–548.

Hallwood, C.P., MacDonald, R. and Marsh, I.W. (2000), "An assessment of the causes of the abandonment of the gold standard by the USA in 1933," *Southern Economic Journal*, 67: 448–459.

Hanke, S.H. and Schuler, K. (1999), "A monetary constitution for Argentina: rules for dollarization," *CATO Journal*, 18: 405–420.

Hausmann, R. and Velasco, A. (2002), "The Argentine collapse: hard money's soft underbelly," unpublished manuscript, Harvard University.

Jones, M.P., Sanguinetti, P. and Tommasi, M. (2000), "Politics, institutions, and fiscal performance in a federal system: an analysis of the Argentine case," *Journal of Development Economics*, 61: 305–333.

Kaminsky, G., Lizondo, S. and Reinhart, C. (1998), "Leading indicators of currency crises," *IMF Staff Papers*, 45: 1–48.

Keating, J.W. and Nye, J.V. (1998), "Permanent and transitory shocks in real output: estimates from nineteenth century and postwar economies," *Journal of Money, Credit, and Banking*, 30: 231–251.

Kenneally, M. and Finn, M. (1985), "The balance of payments as a monetary phenomenon: a review and consideration of the Irish evidence 1960–78," *Economic and Social Review*, 17: 39–72.

Laidler, D., Bentley, B., Johnson, D. and Johnson, S.T. (1982), "A small macroeconomic model of an open economy – the case of Canada," in Claassen, E.M. and Salin, P. (eds), *Recent Issues in the Theory of Flexible Exchange Rates*, Amsterdam: North-Holland.

Lippi, M. and Reichlin, L. (1993), "The dynamic effects of aggregate demand and supply disturbances: comment," *American Economic Review*, 83: 644–652.

Lütkepohl, H. (1993), *Introduction to Multiple Time Series Analysis*, Berlin: Springer-Verlag.

Pollard, S.K. (1999), "Foreign exchange market pressure and transmission of international disturbances: the case of Barbados, Guyana, Jamaica and Trinidad and Tobago," *Applied Economic Letters*, 6: 1–4.

Rose, A.K. and Engel, C. (2000), "Currency unions and international integration," NBER Working Paper no. 7872.

Sarno, L. and Taylor, M.P. (2003), *The Economics of Exchange Rates*, Cambridge: Cambridge University Press.

Tanner, E. (2001), "Exchange market pressure and monetary policy: Asia and Latin America in the 1990s," *IMF Staff Papers*, 47: 311–333.

Weymark, D.N. (1997), "Measuring the degree of market intervention in a small open economy," *Journal of International Money and Finance*, 16: 55–79.

Weymark, D.N. (1998), "A general approach to measuring exchange market pressure," *Oxford Economic Papers*, 50: 106–121.

6 Concepts of equilibrium exchange rates

Rebecca L. Driver and Peter F. Westaway

1 Introduction

This chapter sets out to examine the concept of equilibrium exchange rates. Empirical estimates of equilibrium exchange rates are frequently cited in policy-related discussions of the international conjuncture, not only by academics (see Williamson 1993; Wren-Lewis *et al.* 1991) but also by policy institutions. Such estimates are found to be useful for various closely related reasons:

- It is useful to know where current exchange rates stand relative to longer-term measures of equilibrium, as these may provide some information on likely future movements in exchange rates.
- In the context of fixed exchange rate arrangements, in particular monetary union, it is important to know whether a particular entry rate will be costly to sustain or whether subsequent adjustment of relative inflation rates will be necessary to justify any nominal exchange rate peg.
- When interpreting economic out turns, it is useful to know whether an observed change in the value of exchange rate is justified by perceived shocks to the macroeconomic environment. Different shocks can have very different implications for the outlook, especially so in open economies such as the UK where terms of trade effects can have significant implications for inflation outcomes. Therefore knowing which is the most likely shock to account for observed exchange rate movements may help to determine the best policy response.

One of the purposes of this chapter is to examine more carefully why concepts of equilibrium might be informative. To do this, the chapter begins in section 2 by drawing a distinction between short-, medium- and long-term concepts of equilibrium. All these forms of equilibrium will be present in the economic system at any point in time and there is no reason why they should be the same. It is worth emphasising that if the current exchange rate is not at the level predicted by medium- to long-term measures of equilibrium this does not necessarily mean that the exchange rate is misaligned. If the economy as a whole is in disequilibrium, then a different level of the exchange rate may well be warranted. We emphasise that what is important when it comes to choosing between different equilibrium concepts (and the models that have been used to represent them) is their relevance to the question in hand.

In section 3 we consider some of the practical issues that face researchers working on this topic, including which measures of the exchange rate are likely to be appropriate for different questions, different modelling strategies and some criteria which can be used to distinguish between rival models.

In section 4 we describe some of the different methods researchers have used to attempt to capture different measures of equilibrium empirically. This work has spawned a bemusing array of acronyms to describe different measures of equilibrium. In describing these we provide a taxonomy of the different approaches, attempting to explain the differences and similarities between them. We start by discussing three popular building blocks of international macroeconomics, given by uncovered interest parity, purchasing power parity and the Balassa–Samuelson model. We then discuss various approaches which have been used to try to model short-term movements in exchange rates. The next class of model we discuss are the underlying balance models, which represent a medium-term notion of equilibrium whereby the economy is in internal and external balance. This naturally leads to a discussion of different long-term measures of equilibrium. Finally we consider models which aim to shed light on the impact of different shocks, but which do not explicitly allow for an equilibrium level of the exchange rate to be calculated.

Section 5 concludes by emphasising that equilibrium exchange rate measures can provide useful tools in helping to interpret the macroeconomic outlook. But we draw attention to the dangers of drawing over simplistic policy conclusions from the existence of some measure of misalignment.

2 What do we mean by equilibrium?

When thinking about the meaning of equilibrium it quickly becomes apparent that it is a difficult concept to pin down. This is clearly illustrated by the discussion in Milgate (1998) which charts the development of the concept of equilibrium within economics. The debate over what constitutes equilibrium has ranged over issues as diverse as its existence, uniqueness, optimality, determination, evolution over time and indeed whether it is even valid to talk about disequilibrium. All of these points are important, as is the question of whether the concept of equilibrium can be separated from the models which are used to measure it. Clearly in theory this is desirable, but in practice it may be much harder to do. As most models tend to have an equilibrium associated with them, the question arises as to how to distinguish between these different equilibria? The work of von Neumann and Morgenstern (1944) suggests that without imposing a structure by which to judge different models it is not possible to choose between them as the solution to all models must enjoy equal analytical status. What is important therefore is their significance, which is determined by whether they are 'similar to reality in those respects which are essential in the investigation in hand' (von Neumann and Morgenstern 1944: 32).[1]

Equilibrium therefore means different things to different people and this is no less true in the context of exchange rates than it is for any other field in economics. The aim of this section is therefore to discuss how different concepts of equilibrium can inform our understanding of the exchange rate. In particular we emphasise how the time scale under consideration will affect the concept of equilibrium, since it will influence the questions of interest and hence the significance of a given equilibrium.[2] We do not claim to have provided a new theory of equilibrium. Instead we are trying to apply some of the existing insights in the context of exchange rates.

2.1 What do we mean by an equilibrium exchange rate?

One of the important points to clarify when discussing equilibrium is the time horizon over which the equilibrium might be achieved. In the context of exchange rates, at one level one might argue that since the exchange rate is determined continuously in foreign exchange markets by the supply and demand for currencies, the exchange rate will always be at its equilibrium value. This is clearly linked to what Williamson (1983) distinguishes as the *market equilibrium exchange rate*, which is the one which balances demand and supply of the currency in the absence of official intervention. However, in attempting to interpret movements in the real exchange rate it is necessary to go beyond this truism.

Drawing on the analysis of Clark and MacDonald (1997) the exchange rate can be characterised in terms of a dynamic reduced form relationship which relates it to a set of explanatory variables as follows:

$$e_t = \beta' Z_t + \theta' T_t + \epsilon_t \tag{1}$$

where e_t is the exchange rate in time t, Z is a vector of economic fundamentals that are expected to influence the exchange rate in the medium to long term, T is a vector of transitory factors (including current and lagged variables as well as dynamic effects from the fundamentals, Z) which have an impact on exchange rate in the short term, ϵ_t is a random disturbance and β and θ are vectors of coefficients. Within this framework therefore the choice of fundamentals will be determined by the theoretical framework, while the value of the fundamentals will be determined by the type of equilibrium of interest. In particular these fundamentals can take their actual values, or alternatively their medium- or long-term values.

We find it informative to define three different types of equilibrium exchange rate concepts which differ according to the time horizon to which they apply.

2.1.1 Short-term equilibrium

Short-term equilibrium is defined as the exchange rate which would pertain when its fundamental determinants are at their current settings after abstracting from the influence of random effects (for example from the effect of asset market bubbles). Hence, the short-term equilibrium exchange rate would be:

$$e_t^{ST} = \beta' Z_t + \theta' T \tag{2}$$

i.e. a measure which abstracts from the influence of unexpected shocks.[3]

If the whole economy is in disequilibrium, in the short term the exchange rate will need to move to help markets deal with this. This is why it relates to the actual value of fundamentals, rather than their equilibrium values, such as trend output for example.

The concept of short-term equilibrium is closely related to what Williamson (1983) calls the *current equilibrium exchange rate* which he argues will pertain if the market has full knowledge of the facts and reacts rationally. Of all the equilibrium concepts, this is perhaps the most difficult to define rigorously in economic terms but, as will be explained later, it clearly defines a particular empirical estimation approach.

2.1.2 Medium-term equilibrium

The definition of medium-term equilibrium is the exchange rate which is compatible with the economy being at internal and external balance. There are therefore two parts to this equilibrium. The first is *internal balance*, which occurs when demand is at the level of supply potential and the economy is running at normal capacity. By construction, this equilibrium can be defined as the point reached when nominal inertia (or factors which prevent prices adjusting fully) has washed out of the system so any output gap is zero and unemployment is at the non-accelerating inflation rate of unemployment, or NAIRU.

However, internal balance alone is not sufficient for this to be a valid equilibrium. Instead the rest of the world also needs to be at internal balance, which from the domestic point of view is equivalent to *external balance* being achieved. However, this does not mean that all current accounts will be equal to zero, as there is no reason why in the medium term savings has to equal investment in every economy. As such, for medium-term equilibrium, the current account of the balance of payments will be at a 'sustainable' level in the sense that it will be consistent with eventual convergence to the stock-flow equilibrium. This is often what is used to mean *external balance*.[4] Importantly, since the real exchange rate is still converging towards its long-term stock-flow equilibrium, domestic real interest rates will still be in the process of converging to world levels. This type of equilibrium will therefore be particularly important in models with real rigidities, where the adjustment to steady state asset stocks is consequently protracted.[5]

The assumption that at this time horizon any nominal inertia will have been washed out of the system also implies that the medium-term equilibrium can be thought of as a *flexible price equilibrium*. Finally, it is worth noting that typically this horizon is taken to imply that the real exchange rate will be independent of monetary policy.[6] This is because the equilibrium is defined in real terms by variables (such as potential output) that monetary policy cannot influence, at least assuming superneutrality holds.

If all economies are at internal balance then by definition the fundamental determinants of the exchange rate (e.g. fiscal policy, productivity growth) are at their medium-term setting. However, one important caveat is that, simply because cyclical factors have been eliminated, it does not necessarily follow that the associated settings are sustainable in a long-term sense. The conventional assumption that medium term implies sustainable may therefore sometimes be violated. For example, once cyclical influences have been eliminated then fiscal policy can be thought of as structural. Importantly, however, the fact that fiscal flows are structural (or unrelated to the cycle) does not imply anything about whether they are either normal, or optimal or even sustainable. Similarly, persistent expectational errors may also move the medium-term equilibrium away from its sustainable level.

In terms of the model given by equation (1), it is possible to define a measure of medium-term exchange rate equilibrium ($\hat{e}$):

$$\hat{e}_t = \beta' \hat{Z}_t \tag{3}$$

which is consistent with fundamentals being at their trend values (denoted by hats), but where these may still be adjusting towards some longer-term steady state.

2.1.3   Long-term equilibrium

A long-term equilibrium is defined as the point when stock-flow equilibrium is achieved for all agents in the economy. This may take many years or decades to achieve. The medium-term equilibrium concept is conditioned on prevailing levels of national wealth (once cyclical effects and bubble effects have washed out). Assets stocks may therefore still be adjusting over time. The long-term equilibrium pertains when net wealth is in full stock-flow equilibrium, so that changes to asset stocks (as a percentage of GDP) are zero. Long-term equilibrium, therefore, can be thought of as occurring when the economy has reached the 'point from which there is no endogenous tendency to change' (Milgate 1998: 179). This equilibrium is given by:

$$\overline{e}_t = \beta' \overline{Z}_t \tag{4}$$

where overbar denotes the long-term values of variables.

These different equilibrium exchange rate concepts have been specified in very general terms. No attempt has been made to specify the relevant fundamentals, as it is intended to encompass all the different approaches to be described. It has the advantage that it can also be used to clarify the extent to which exchange rate movements might be warranted over the short, medium and long term.

At any point in time all these different types of equilibrium will be present within the system and policy makers can make use of information on all these different measures. For example, consider the role of the random disturbance, which is what distinguishes e^{ST} from the actual exchange rate. If there is evidence that the behaviour of this random disturbance has changed then this might be an indication of the existence of a bubble, perhaps caused by misperceptions about fundamentals.[7] Many factors will determine the appropriate policy response to a speculative bubble in the exchange rate including, for example, how long the bubble is expected to last and on how quickly it will be reversed. For an extended discussion of the issues surrounding the appropriate policy response to asset price bubbles, see Bernanke and Gertler (1999) Cecchetti *et al.* (2000). A decision to act or not, will not undermine the usefulness of that information.

Monetary policy will not be able to influence the medium- and long-term values of fundamentals, however, it may well be able to influence the transition path back to equilibrium.[8] If fundamentals are not at their equilibrium levels (or in other words $(Z - \hat{Z})$ is not equal to zero) there is no reason why this exchange rate ($\hat{e}$) should be the observed rate.[9] Nonetheless information on this rate is still useful. Consider for example the situation where firms' pricing policy for either imports or exports is influenced by beliefs about whether observed changes in the exchange rate are temporary or permanent. Under these circumstances a medium- or long-term measure of equilibrium can be used to identify how an observed change in the exchange rate is likely to be passed through into import or export prices and hence on likely inflationary pressures.

In concluding this section, it is worth emphasising that, so far, the different equilibrium exchange rate concepts have been deliberately defined without referring to the array of acronyms that have been proposed in the economics literature or to the different empirical techniques that have been used to measure these equilibria. Such measures include FEERs, DEERs, BEERs, PEERs, NATREX, APEERs, ITMEERs and CHEERs. What is important for policy makers is to know how the different concepts of equilibrium are related to the myriad of different methods for calculating equilibrium exchange rates, as the policy implications and relevance for a given question of each of them may differ. These approaches will be defined and explained in section 4.

3   Choosing between equilibrium exchange rate measures

The previous section has emphasised how there is no one single definition of equilibrium in the context of exchange rates. The choice between approaches must therefore be judged relative to the question of interest. However, as section 4 demonstrates, there are many different ways to attempt to measure equilibrium exchange rates for any given time horizon or question. Before detailing these different approaches, therefore, it is useful to provide some guidelines for why different attempts at measuring equilibrium exchange rates for a given time horizon may give different answers, as well as some potential selection criteria for choosing between approaches. We start by discussing which definition of the exchange rate our concepts relate to and how different definitions may influence the question of interest. We also look at different modelling strategies and why this choice may influence the results. Finally, we go on to discuss ways in which the success of a particular approach to equilibrium exchange rates can be judged and how the question of interest may influence the choice of metric.

3.1   How is the exchange rate defined?

So far we have been deliberately vague about which measure of the exchange rate we are referring to: whether it is nominal or real and if real which price deflator is used; or even if it is a bilateral or effective measure. Knowing which measure is used and why it is important. For some the obvious measure of the exchange rate is a nominal bilateral exchange rate, as it is that which is determined directly in the financial markets. However, most theories of equilibrium exchange rates refer to real effective (whole economy) measures of the exchange rate, albeit using different definitions of the relevant price index.[10] Associated with any given real exchange rate equilibrium are an infinite number of combinations of nominal exchange rates and relative price levels. If the equilibrium exchange rate is a real rate, then it will not matter for the economy what the corresponding level of the nominal exchange rate is.[11] The factor that will determine the level of the nominal exchange rate will be monetary policy at home and abroad.

Real exchange rates can be defined in a variety of ways depending on the question at hand. A general expression for the effective real exchange rate of country i (E_i) is given by:[12]

$$E_{it} = \prod_{j=1}^{n} \left(\frac{P_{it}S_{ijt}}{P_{jt}^*} \right)^{\varpi_{ij}} \tag{5}$$

where P_i measures the domestic price level in country i; P_j^* the foreign price level in country j; S_{ij} is the relevant nominal exchange rate (defined as foreign currency per unit of domestic between countries i and j); and ϖ_{ij} is the weight of country j in country i's effective exchange rate index.[13] As such an increase in E_i implies that the currency has appreciated, or alternatively that it has become less competitive.

Although it can sometimes be useful to think about whether particular bilateral exchange rates represent an equilibrium, in general most concepts of equilibrium are likely to relate to the whole economy and hence effective rates. Of course this says nothing about how this effective rate should be measured: whether it should use simple trade shares as weights; allow for third party effects (the IMF's so-called MERM weights would do this); or whether weights should take into account the distribution of overseas investment holdings. At an n-country level there are $(n-1)$ independent exchange rates which can be expressed in bilateral or effective terms. It is therefore possible to calculate measures of the associated bilaterals from a set of effective exchange rate measures using information about ϖ_{ij} (see Alberola *et al.* 1999).

The domestic and foreign price levels themselves can be defined in a number of ways depending on which definition of the real exchange rate we are interested in. The choice of price index matters because real exchange rates defined using different price indices can move in very different ways (see, for example, Marsh and Tokarick (1994) and Chinn (2002), as well as the discussion in Benigno and Thoenissen (2002)). The most commonly used definitions of the real exchange rate include measures based on:

- *Consumer price indices.* This will be appropriate if we are concerned with a comparison of price levels for goods bought by consumers in different countries.
- *The prices of tradable goods or output prices.* This will be used if we are concerned with the price competitiveness of goods exported by an economy.
- *The price of an economy's exports compared to the price of its imports.* This gives a measure of a country's terms of trade, or the relative purchasing power of domestic agents.
- *Relative unit labour costs.* This will be appropriate if we are focussing on the cost competitiveness of an economy.

- *The ratio of tradable to nontradable prices.* This is appropriate for assessing the real exchange rate within an economy.

Since these different price indices do not move together in the short term or even necessarily in the longer term, there is no unique measure of the real exchange rate on which it is appropriate to focus. Of course for any horizon there will be an equilibrium configuration of these exchange rate measures. It is also perfectly possible for these exchange rate measures to be moving in different ways over time. These relative movements in different measures will shift resources between sectors as well as economies. Which of the measures is seen as being most important will depend on beliefs about the key adjustment mechanisms. For example, in Obstfeld and Rogoff (1995), real exchange rates measured using consumer prices remain constant, but the terms of trade shift in response to shocks because countries produce different goods. Therefore the real exchange rate defined using consumer prices provides little insight into what is happening within the model, as all the action is in the terms of trade. Of course in the real world nothing is quite that simple. However, for the sake of simplicity, in the rest of this chapter references will be made to *the* real exchange rate. Wherever the differences between these alternative measures are important, the distinction will be explained.

3.2 Modelling options

As section 4 makes clear, there is no single dominant approach to modelling equilibrium exchange rates. Different authors have used methods ranging from the purely statistical to the purely theoretical, with a myriad of options in between. The aim of this subsection is not to identify best practice.[14] Instead we aim to provide a very brief review of some of the issues which face researchers choosing between direct estimation methods and model-based approaches in the context of exchange rates. Of course it is possible to over-exaggerate the differences between them. In general both approaches share the simple principle that the real exchange rate can be characterised as one endogenous variable in a complete macroeconomic system.[15] Where they differ is for example in the treatment of dynamics and the time frame they concentrate on. By and large, model based simulation approaches tend to have much stronger predictions for medium- to long-term equilibrium measures.

3.2.1 Model-based approaches

One approach to capturing movements in equilibrium exchange rates is to use a model. How complicated the model needs to be will in turn be determined by the question of interest. It will also depend on whether the emphasis of the investigation is theoretical or empirical understanding.[16]

What will be important will be how the model articulates the role of the real exchange rate within the economy. Essentially real exchange rates are relative prices and therefore movements in real exchange rates help to shift resources in order to reconcile demand and supply. The emphasis on thinking about the real exchange rate as the relative price which reconciles supply and demand is given its most explicit formulation within the underlying balance models (see section 4.3). However, this type of mechanism is implicit within any macromodel. Section 3.1 discussed the fact that there are a large number of definitions of the real exchange rate and that it is perfectly possible for these exchange rate measures to be moving in different ways. Different assumptions about the transmission mechanism could therefore potentially have very different implications.

One of the most controversial aspects of the transmission mechanism is how firms respond to exchange rate changes (see, for example, Obstfeld (2002)). At one end of the spectrum it is assumed that firms set prices in their domestic currency (producer currency pricing) and fully pass through any changes in the exchange rate into the prices they charge in foreign markets. Under the alternative assumption of local currency pricing, it is assumed that prices are set in the buyer's currency and, in the short term at least, changes in exchange rates will have no impact on these prices. Local currency pricing may therefore be part of the explanation for the so-called 'exchange rate disconnect' puzzle: that is, that large movements in the exchange rate have not been associated with large movements in import and export prices and the consumer price index, as might be suggested by a standard model; see for example Devereux and Engel (2002). The two extremes of producer currency and local currency pricing therefore clearly suggest very different transmission mechanisms from the exchange rate to the rest of the economy as well as a very different relationship between real and nominal exchange rates.

In the long term firms may still choose to charge different prices in different markets regardless of how they deal with exchange rate pass-through. In other words firms may price-to-market, see Krugman (1987). If the elasticity of demand differs across markets, charging different prices will be optimal assuming that there are trade barriers (such as transport costs or tariffs) which prevent consumers from arbitraging across markets.[17] The extent to which pricing-to-market occurs will determine the degree to which firms' domestic and export prices move together over time when adjusted into the same currency. Of course if firms decide to set export prices to reflect their foreign competitors' prices rather than domestic prices this does not imply that the exchange rate will have no role in the transmission mechanism. Under these circumstances its impact will be via firms' profits.

Equilibrium exchange rates may therefore vary because of differences in consumer preferences, the existence of differentiated products, imperfectly competitive markets and the existence of nontradables (see section

4.1). These factors all call for a rich model of equilibrium and once some or all of them have been incorporated then the resulting equilibrium will also potentially depend on a variety of additional factors including: productivity differentials, both between economies and different sectors within a given economy; demographics; and fiscal policy. There are therefore many reasons why equilibrium exchange rates may vary over time and why the short-, medium- and long-term equilibrium for exchange rates may also differ. The advantage of model based approaches is that they potentially deal with variations across both these dimensions.

3.2.2 Estimation-based approaches

Direct estimation methods involve estimating a model for exchange rates explicitly. In principle, such approaches should yield the same estimate of equilibrium as measures based on the same fundamental determinants that take a more structural approach. But in practice the theoretical underpinnings to direct estimation methods tend to be slightly more *ad hoc*. Accordingly, for example it is possible to use this type of approach to estimate equilibrium bilateral exchange rates directly. In addition the treatment of dynamics tends to be based on criteria such as goodness of fit rather than theoretical priors. This therefore makes many estimation based methods better suited to tasks such as forecasting.

The issue which dominates how equilibrium exchange rates are estimated is that of the data properties of the real exchange rate and whether it is stationary or non-stationary. If real exchange rates are stationary this implies that they revert to a constant value at least in the long term, which is equivalent to finding purchasing power parity in the long term, and in one sense the search for a measure of medium- and long-term equilibrium can end there.[18] Section 4.1 discusses some of the evidence for PPP. However, even if real exchange rates are stationary there is still the issue of how quickly this equilibrium is approached. For example, Murray and Papell (2002), find that the estimated half lives associated with deviations in the real exchange rate are within the 3–5 years suggested in Rogoff (1996) for the countries in their sample.[19] However, Murray and Papell (2002) also find that, in most cases, the upper bound of the confidence intervals are infinite, suggesting that the estimated half lives provide little information about the speed of mean reversion.

In cases where this mean reversion is a medium- or a long-term phenomenon it might still be useful to investigate whether there are measures of equilibrium available which explain short-term movements in the real exchange rate. One issue here is whether adjustment to this long-term equilibrium will be a linear process. For example, Taylor *et al.* (2001), find evidence to suggest the adjustment towards a stationary long term may be non-linear and that this may account for why unit root tests often reject the stationarity of the real exchange rate.

If, however, the chosen measure of the real exchange rate is nonstationary then any estimate of the equilibrium must take account of this property. Essentially therefore the estimated equilibrium must also be nonstationary, but the difference between the equilibrium and the actual real exchange rate must itself be stationary. Some methodologies deal with this issue directly by using cointegration, which essentially estimates a stationary reduced form relationship between the real exchange rate and the variables which are thought to explain it.[20] The equilibrium exchange rate is then derived as the statistical long-term of the estimated relationship, for example by taking the predicted value from the relevant cointegrating vector.

3.3 Picking a measure

At any point in time there will be a set of equilibrium exchange rates which will depend in part on the time frame of interest. Simply because the actual exchange rate is not at its long-term equilibrium level does not mean that it is not in equilibrium in some other sense. There may be many reasons why the actual exchange rate should differ from long-term equilibrium in the short term, including the influence of both nominal and real inertia.

Deciding what type of equilibrium to model will depend on the question of interest. For example questions relating to the impact of the underlying structure of the economy will be best answered using a structural modelling framework which incorporates these features. An estimate of equilibrium derived using univariate statistical methods will have little to say about the impact of changes in the trend rate of productivity growth. It would therefore be inappropriate to use a univariate approach if the question of interest is what happens to equilibrium if trend productivity changes. Univariate methods may though be helpful in deriving estimates of short-term movements in exchange rates.

For a given question, identifying which of several competing models is the most appropriate will be based on several criteria, including the model's forecast performance; ability to match key moments as well as co-movements between different variables; and whether it has a sensible long-term path. The aim of this section is to provide a very brief review of these criteria. Which of these criteria is seen as most important will again depend on the question of interest.

3.3.1 Equilibrium exchange rates and the predictability of exchange rate movements

Probably the best known criteria for judging exchange rate models is the out-of-sample forecast test. The argument runs that a good model of the exchange rate should be able to out predict a forecast of no change, because it embeds within it information on the economic fundamentals that affect exchange rates. However, Meese and Rogoff (1983) found that although traditional (monetary) models might fit well in-sample, their out-of-sample forecasting performance was extremely poor. In short, it proved to be impossible to out forecast a random walk (or prediction of no change) when modelling the exchange rate.

The Meese and Rogoff (1983) finding has dominated the exchange rate literature ever since; see, for example, the discussion in Rogoff (2001). While exceptions have been found, these exceptions are not found to be particularly robust to changes in sample period or the currencies used. In general, however, it is thought that exchange rate models are better at predicting over longer horizons, see, for example, Mark (1995). Even using non-linear models it is often difficult to beat a random walk except at long horizons, see, for example, Kilian and Taylor (2003). One reason for this excess volatility (compared to other fundamentals) may be the existence of noise traders, see, for example, Jeanne and Rose (2002).[21] An important development in the exchange rate literature which we do not cover here is therefore the market microstructure literature which attempts to understand how trading behaviour influences exchange rates. Instead we confine ourselves to a discussion of the models linking macroeconomic fundamentals and exchange rates.

3.3.2 Evaluating co-movements

As well as (or indeed instead of) wanting an explicit forecast for the actual exchange rate, it is often hoped that models of equilibrium exchange rates will be able to throw some light on what is actually happening in the economy. For example, can the relative movements of variables such as the exchange rate, consumption, output and prices be explained by changes to productivity? For this type of analysis the crucial test of a model of equilibrium is whether it captures the relationship of interest. This means that not only must the model include the key variables of interest but its predictions for their impact on each other must also make sense empirically. Models can therefore be judged on whether they predict sensible co-movements in the variables of interest; see, for example, Finn (1999). What is important here will be the conditional as well as the unconditional co-movements. If a particular type of shock occurs only infrequently then the co-movements that it generates would not be expected to dominate the behaviour of the data in normal times. One way to extract information on the empirical impact of shocks is to use VAR analysis (see, for example, Kim (2001), as well as section 4.5.1).

3.3.3 The issue of the long term

As noted above, models of exchange rates based on economic fundamentals often struggle to explain short-term movements in exchange rates, although there is some indication that they may be better predictors at longer horizons. Clearly that is not good news if the aim of the exercise is to forecast exchange rate movements. However, not all models of exchange rate behaviour are intended to be used for forecasting. Instead many models, including for example underlying balance models, aim to capture medium- to long-term concepts of equilibrium where economic fundamentals themselves are also in equilibrium. As there will be many reasons why at any point in time an economy is away from equilibrium, judging this type of model based on their forecast performance is clearly undesirable. The question then is how best to judge their long-term performance. Two issues come to mind here. The first is whether or not they actually explain long-term trends in exchange rates and the second is whether the models on which the calculations are based embody a sensible long-term solution.

One way to judge whether a given technique provides a good model of long-term exchange rate behaviour is to think in terms of the consistency test proposed by Cheung and Chinn (1998). For the forecast or outcomes of the model to be consistent they must first have the same statistical properties as the actual exchange rate series being modelled. If the actual exchange rate is nonstationary, then the predicted equilibrium must also be nonstationary, otherwise it will be unable to capture its movements. Second, the actual and the model outcomes must combine to produce a stationary residual, so that the difference between the two series cannot increase without bounds (as would be the case if the residual were nonstationary). In other words the predicted exchange rate series must act as an attractor for the actual series. Finally the coefficients on the two series that combine to give this stationary residual must be unitary, so that if the predicted equilibrium moves the actual exchange rate will also move one-for-one (on average). This is essentially what Barisone *et al.* (2003) do in their test of the validity of the FEER model.

The second criteria is whether the model embodies a sensible long term. In the very long term it is usually assumed that all variables within the economy, including asset stocks, will reach their steady state growth path. This can be thought of as full stock-flow equilibrium.[22] If a given model does not have a stock equilibrium embedded in it, shocks will act to move the long-term equilibrium. This means that calculations of equilibrium will be subject to a starting point problem, whereby current conditions determine the eventual equilibrium, rather than equilibrium being given by the equilibrium out turns of economic fundamentals.

On this final point, it is worth noting that the mere fact that DSGE models are theoretically more rigorous than many macroeconometric models, does not mean that they cannot suffer from an undefined long term. This is particularly true of many small open economy models, where steady state holdings of net foreign assets are often undefined. As a result temporary shocks will shift the steady state through their affect on wealth.

Since log-linear approximations are taken around the initial steady state within DSGE models these approximations will become arbitrarily bad over time. One question is always whether the approximation errors are small enough to ignore for the experiments of interest. The problem of tying down the steady state level of net foreign assets can be addressed in a number of ways, see Schmitt-Grohe and Uribe (2003).

As was stated at the beginning of this section, the aim here has not been to provide a model of the exchange rate (equilibrium or otherwise). Instead it has been to provide a general framework which can be used to think about the assumptions that are implicit within both empirical and theoretical work on equilibrium exchange rates. The relevance of individual assumptions may well depend on exactly how equilibrium has been defined. The next section therefore discusses different approaches to measuring equilibrium exchange rates and how these relate to each other.

4 Measures of equilibrium exchange rates: theory and taxonomy

There is, sadly, no completely comprehensive and logical mapping from one equilibrium exchange rate methodology to another. However, in this section some of the more popular methods of estimating equilibrium exchange rates are discussed. The list includes BEERs, PEERs, CHEERs, ITMEERs, APEERs, FEERs, DEERs and NATREX. We also touch on how the Balassa–Samuelson hypothesis and monetary models are linked to equilibrium exchange rates. The list we consider is undoubtedly not exhaustive, as new methods and acronyms are being invented all the time.[23] However, it covers most of the main candidates. Having already explained what we mean by different concepts of equilibrium in section 2, we also attempt to place the different methodologies used to estimate equilibrium exchange rates (of which there are many) within this framework. Needless to say the mapping between the different time frames is often far from perfect. However, in general the monetary models, BEERs, ITMEERs and CHEERs are most closely related to short-term equilibrium concepts; FEERs and DEERs are all interested in medium-term equilibrium; while APEERs, PEERs, NATREX models aim to capture some concept of long-term equilibrium. Alternative methodologies such as SVARs and DSGE models do not provide any information on the level of the real exchange rate but can provide helpful information on the likely response of the exchange rates in the face of shocks and also on their short-, medium- and long-term response. However, this section starts with a discussion of the arbitrage conditions that theory should influence exchange rates. Table 6.1 provides an overview of these different methods and crucially spells out the acronyms.

4.1 The real exchange rate and the role of arbitrage

There are two main arbitrage conditions which dominate any discussion of exchange rates: uncovered interest parity (UIP) and purchasing power parity (PPP). The aim of this subsection is to discuss some of the main issues surrounding these two conditions. The background for the Balassa–Samuelson hypothesis is also discussed. The Balassa–Samuelson model assumes that the forces of arbitrage which underlie PPP will only affect traded goods and therefore that productivity differentials between traded and nontraded goods sectors will influence real exchange rates defined using the consumer price index (which therefore also incorporate nontraded goods).

4.1.1 Uncovered interest parity

A common place to start when considering movements in the exchange rate are arbitrage conditions, and in particular those given by the risk-adjusted uncovered UIP condition. This condition equalises the *ex ante* risk-adjusted nominal rate of return on domestic and foreign currency assets. As such the expected change in the nominal exchange rate is determined by the interest rate differential and any risk premium so that:

$$s_t = E_t s_{t+1} + i_t - i_t^* + \sigma_t \qquad (6)$$

where s_t is the (logged) nominal exchange rate (foreign currency per unit of home) at time t, i and i^* the nominal interest rates on one period bonds at home and abroad, σ the foreign currency risk premium (which is potentially time-varying) and E_t is the expectations operator denoting the expectation of a variable taken at time t. Assuming that the risk premium is zero therefore implies that if domestic interest rates are above foreign rates then the domestic exchange rate must be expected to depreciate against the foreign exchange rate in order for investors to be indifferent between holding domestic and foreign assets.

Since here we are more interested in the real exchange rate, it is straightforward to re-express this simple UIP condition in real terms (by subtracting the expected inflation differential from both sides of the equation)[24] so that:

$$e_t = E_t e_{t+1} + r_t - r_t^* + \sigma_t \qquad (7)$$

where e is the real exchange rate, and r and r^* are the respective domestic and foreign *ex ante* real interest rates. This expression thus equalises the *ex ante* risk-adjusted real rate of return on domestic and foreign currency assets. An alternative way of expressing equation (7) would be to use

Table 6.1 Summary of empirical approaches to estimating equilibrium exchange rates

	UIP	PPP	Balassa–Samuelson	Monetary models	CHEERs	ITMEERs
Name	Uncovered interest parity	Purchasing power parity	Balassa–Samuelson	Monetary and portfolio balance models	Capital-enhanced equilibrium exchange rates	Intermediate term model-based equilibrium exchange rates
Theoretical assumptions	The expected change in the exchange rate determined by interest differentials	Constant equilibrium exchange rate	PPP for tradable goods. Productivity differentials between traded and nontraded goods	PPP in long term (or short term) plus demand for money	PPP plus nominal UIP without risk premia	Nominal UIP including a risk premia plus expected future movements in real exchange rates determined by fundamentals
Relevant time horizon	Short term	Long term	Long term	Short term	Short term (forecast)	Short term (forecast)
Statistical assumptions	Stationarity (of change)	Stationary	Non-stationary	Non-stationary	Stationary, with emphasis on speed of convergence	None
Dependent variable	Expected change in the real or nominal	Real or nominal	Real	Nominal	Nominal	Future change in the nominal
Estimation method	Direct	Test for stationarity	Direct	Direct	Direct	Direct

forward substitution to replace successive values of the expected exchange rate so that: [25]

$$e_t = \sum_{j=0}^{n-1} E_t \delta_{t+j} + \sum_{j=0}^{n-1} E_t \sigma_{t+j} + E_t e_{t+n} \tag{8}$$

where $\delta_t = (r_t - r_t^*)$. In other words the real exchange rate depends on the expected path for interest rate differentials and risk premia, as well as the expected long-term value of the real exchange rate itself.

Perhaps the most important point to note in the context of this chapter is that the UIP arbitrage condition is only informative in explaining the adjustment path of the exchange rate back to its equilibrium. To simplify the UIP condition does not tie down the *level* of the real exchange rate, only the rate of change.[26] The level of the real exchange rate today will

BEERs	FEERs	DEERs	APEERs	PEERs	NATREX	SVARs	DSGE
Behavioural equilibrium exchange rates	Fundamental Equilibrium exchange rates	Desired equilibrium exchange rates	Atheoretical permanent equilibrium exchange rates	Permanent equilibrium exchange rates	Natural real exchange rates	Structural vector auto regression	Dynamic stochastic general equilibrium models
Real UIP with a risk premia and/ or expected future movements in real exchange rates determined by funda-mentals	Real exchange rate compatible with both internal and external balance. Flow not full stock equilibrium	As with FEERs, but the definition of external balance based on *optimal* policy	None	As BEERs	As with FEERs, but with the assumption of portfolio balance (so domestic real interest rate is equal to the world rate)	Real exchange rate affected by supply and demand (but not nominal) shocks in the long term	Models designed to explore movements in real and/or nominal exchange rates in response to shocks
Short term (also forecast)	Medium term	Medium term	Medium/ long term	Medium term	Long term	Short (and long) term	Short and long term
Non-stationary	Non-stationary	Non-stationary	Non-stationary (extract permanent component)	Non-stationary (extract permanent component)	Non-stationary	As with theoretical	As with theoretical
Real	Real effective	Real effective	Real	Real	Real	Change in the real	Change relative to long term steady state
Direct	Underlying balance	Underlying balance	Direct	Direct	Direct	Direct	Simulation

jump to adjust for changes in expected real interest rate differentials, risk premia and the expected future level of the real exchange rate. In the longer term therefore the *level* of the real exchange rate must be determined by other factors. At first glance, this finding would appear to be at odds with the widely believed view that nominal exchange rates are primarily determined in the world's foreign exchange markets, where massive speculative capital flows swamp the flows associated with trade transactions. In fact, none of the above explanation is inconsistent with that view, indeed speculative transactions on the foreign exchange markets may well have an important role in the short term. However, we must look elsewhere for an explanation of the equilibrium real exchange rate itself.[27]

One of the problems with validating the existence of UIP itself is that in general expectations about the future value of exchange rates are unavailable and certainly are not measured with sufficient accuracy to be matched to real time interest rate differentials. In addition risk premia are unobservable. Most tests of UIP have concentrated on trying to establish whether *ex post* changes in exchange rates can be explained by interest rate differentials. In general the results from this type of exercise have had very limited success, as the interest rate differential is often found to be incorrectly signed; see, for example, the survey in Lewis (1995).[28] One final thing worth noting that in empirical terms UIP by itself has not been very successful at predicting exchange rate movements. One reason for this empirical failing might, of course, be shifts in the expected long-term equilibrium, or exchange rate which are not usually taken account of in UIP estimates. McCallum (1994) suggests one reason for the apparent failure of UIP may be policy behaviour, if policy makers attempt both to smooth interest rate changes and to resist big changes in the exchange rate. Christensen (2000) finds that this explanation no longer appears to hold empirically when the policy reaction function is estimated directly.

4.1.2 Why should the equilibrium exchange rate vary? – The role of PPP

The previous section discusses how one possible explanation for the failure to observe UIP might be shifts in the equilibrium exchange rate. However, another well known arbitrage condition, that of purchasing power parity (PPP) would suggest that in fact equilibrium exchange rates should be constant.[29]

PPP is a natural starting point to begin any consideration of equilibrium real exchange rates, not least because of its enduring popularity. In its strictest form, PPP predicts that price levels in different countries will always be equalised when they are measured in a common currency. In other words that the real exchange rate is constant and equal to unity.[30] The theoretical rationale behind PPP is often given as arbitrage in markets for individual goods. For example, if similar goods are priced differently in different countries, then demand will switch to the cheaper good. If sufficient arbitrage exists, then the forces of supply and demand will equalise prices, so that the Law Of One Price (LOOP) holds. At an economy wide level, deviations of the real exchange rate from PPP will lead to changes in supply and demand which will move the real exchange rate back to PPP. More generally, however, PPP may also hold as a result of the impact of changes in the competitiveness on the location of production. For example in the longer-term differential labour costs will have an impact on the desirability of different locations. There will tend to be a movement in production from the overvalued to the undervalued economy not as a result of consumer arbitrage, but because of arbitrage in capital.[31]

In this section the theoretical explanations for why PPP might not hold in practice are discussed.[32] The explanations fall into two parts. The first represents reasons why PPP may not hold, even if LOOP is observed. The second is based on reasons why LOOP itself may not hold. Finally it goes on to discuss the empirical evidence for PPP.

Although PPP is a distinct concept, it can be seen from above that it is closely linked to LOOP, whereby a process of international arbitrage causes the price of each and every good and service sold on international markets to be equalised. Of course if LOOP always holds, then PPP will also hold by definition provided (a) all goods and services are tradable, (b) the composition of goods bought by consumers in each country is identical, or in other words that consumer preferences are identical across countries, and (c) that countries produce the same goods. The trouble is that if any of these conditions are violated then even if LOOP holds, PPP may not, or at least not for all definitions of the real exchange rate.

(a) To start with consider a situation where *consumers' preferences in different countries differ.* This will influence the composition of their consumption basket and hence their consumer price index.[33] As inflation rates for different goods may differ, this implies that there may be trends in the real exchange rate.[34]

(b) Suppose instead consumer preferences are identical, but they also *include goods which are not traded internationally.* (The reasons why goods may be nontraded are discussed below.) LOOP only applies to traded goods and services. In principle, the existence of nontradables allows the exchange rate adjusted prices of goods sold in different countries to drift apart without any necessary tendency for the divergence to be corrected. Even so, under quite general assumptions, the existence of nontradables will not be sufficient to cause persistent real exchange rate divergences unless the relative price inflation of tradable to nontradable goods differs between countries. One way this can happen is via productivity differences between countries. The most widely cited example of this type of effect is the so called Balassa–Samuelson effect whereby countries with faster growing productivity in the tradable sector will have an appreciating real exchange rate (see section 4.1.3).

(c) Finally, *if countries specialise in producing different goods* that can potentially cause the breakdown of PPP even when LOOP holds, depending on the definition of the real exchange rate under consideration. In exactly the same way that relative prices of goods within a single economy can vary according to demand and supply conditions, so the relative price of different goods made in different countries can change. The real exchange rate will not be constant therefore if it is measured either using producer prices, or using the terms of trade (defined as the ratio of export prices to import prices).[35] In general therefore, where countries produce differentiated products, PPP can only hold for all possible definitions of the real exchange rate if trade elasticities are infinite.

WHY LOOP ITSELF MAY NOT HOLD

Of course there are also reasons why LOOP itself may not hold and this in turn could also be linked to the failure of PPP. The first of these reasons is the existence of trade barriers and transport costs. Of course, a nontradable good is simply an extreme example of this type of friction where the transportation cost is either infinitely high (e.g. the Eiffel Tower) or else it constitutes a disproportionately high fraction of the cost of the good or service (it is after all *possible* to travel from London to Paris to have a haircut).[36] So long as any of these frictions exist, it will be possible for prices to differ between countries in these markets by any amount up to the size of the transactions costs. More generally, there may be adjustment costs which imply that it takes time for consumers and/or producers to respond to a price differential between markets (see, for example, the discussion in Obstfeld and Rogoff (2000)).

Another reason why LOOP may fail is provided by the nature of the competitive structure of the markets for different goods. In general, most trade among OECD countries tends to be in differentiated manufactured goods.[37] If in addition firms have a degree of market power, this potentially gives them the possibility of pricing-to-market, see, for example, Krugman (1987). When pricing-to-market occurs any mark-ups become destination specific, so the full impact of any change in the exchange rate may not be fully passed-through and LOOP will not hold. The above are all reasons why PPP and LOOP may not hold in theory.[38] The next subsection considers whether PPP holds in practice.

EMPIRICAL SUPPORT FOR PPP

As was discussed above, one of the defining features of how to approach estimating equilibrium exchange rates is whether or not real exchange rates are stationary, or in other words whether they revert to a constant mean over some time frame. As this is what PPP implies, in statistical terms a test for PPP would be that real exchange rate series are stationary. Until the emergence of non-stationary panel techniques econometric studies on the real exchange rate typically confirmed the visual impression from the data that real exchange rate series are not stationary; see MacDonald (1995) and Breuer (1994), for surveys. In particular the results tend to depend on the length of the sample period, the degree of price variation observed and the choice of countries and in particular the choice of numeraire currency. Evidence in favour of PPP is more likely to be found if the tests include periods of substantial price variation (such as periods of hyperinflation); if they are based on long samples (of around

100 years) of annual data; and if the US dollar is not used as a numeraire. The first case may reflect statistical problems in identifying stationarity, but even if PPP does hold during periods of hyperinflation, it is difficult to argue that this represents a useful equilibrium. The distortions in the economy associated with hyperinflation mean that it is unlikely that the economy will be operating at its true potential. The second set of evidence provides support for long-term, as opposed to medium-term, PPP. The final factor undermines the case for PPP as a meaningful concept of equilibrium. If an equilibrium concept is to be useful then it must apply to the whole economy. If PPP holds for some currencies but not for others then it will not hold for effective exchange rates and it is the effective rate which is relevant for the whole economy.[39]

Given the enduring theoretical popularity of PPP, however, a variety of techniques have been used in an attempt to overturn these largely negative findings. One early trend was to use cointegration techniques to establish whether nominal exchange rates may be cointegrated with domestic and overseas price indices, leaving a stationary residual.[40] The estimated coefficients on prices in these cointegrating vectors, though, are often not unity. One interpretation of these results is that published price series are poor measures of 'true' prices, and so allowing non-unity coefficients allows the regressions to reveal true PPP. However, as Breuer (1994) points out, it is difficult to interpret these results as supporting PPP, particularly if the coefficients on the price series in the cointegrating vector are noticeably different from unity. They imply, of course, an absence of *measured* long-term neutrality.

More recently a spate of papers using more powerful non-stationary panel techniques have tended to overturn the single equation results, with the majority of such studies finding evidence in favour of PPP. Such studies include: Frankel and Rose (1996), MacDonald (1996), Oh (1996), O'Connell (1998), Papell (1997) and Coakley and Fuertes (1997). With the exception of O'Connell (1998) these papers have all tended to find in favour of the mean reversion of the real exchange rate, or the existence of PPP. Papell (1997) does find that the results tend to depend on the size of the panel, although even with panels as small as five countries the probability of rejecting a unit root increases significantly compared to the single equation results. The negative results from O'Connell (1998) stem from accounting for cross-sectional dependence. Chortareas and Driver (2001) find that the results of the panel unit root tests may well be test specific, which would suggest that the findings in favour of PPP should still be treated with a degree of scepticism.

The discussion above suggests that there are problems with the PPP approach.[41] Finally, even proponents of PPP accept that the rate of mean reversion is very slow (see MacDonald 2000). All this suggests that alternative approaches to equilibrium are needed.

4.1.3 Balassa–Samuelson

One of the explanations for why PPP may not hold revolves around the distinction between tradable and nontradable goods. If the forces underlying PPP relate to arbitrage in the goods markets then there would be no reason for PPP to hold for definitions of the real exchange rate which included goods and services which were not traded.

It is this insight which is behind the Balassa–Samuelson effect.[42] The Balassa–Samuelson model uses the decomposition of the price level into traded and nontraded prices, where α is the proportion of nontraded goods within the economy. Applying this to the real exchange rate and taking logs it can be shown that the real exchange rate can be written as:

$$e_t = (s_t + p_t^T - p_t^{T*}) - \alpha(p_t^T - p_t^{NT}) + \alpha^*(p_t^{T*} - p_t^{NT*}) \tag{9}$$

where a star indicates a foreign variable, the superscript T refers to traded goods and NT to nontraded goods. The real exchange rate therefore is a combination of the real exchange rate for traded goods and the ratio of the relative prices of traded to nontraded goods in the two economies. If productivity growth in the tradables sector is higher in one country, then relative nontradables-to-tradables prices will grow more quickly.[43] So its CPI-based real exchange rate will appreciate relative to other countries.[44] As with PPP, however, these effects are more likely to explain medium- and long-term movements in the real exchange rate, as they are not designed to capture cyclical differences.

Econometrically, the Balassa–Samuelson hypothesis has a simple interpretation. If PPP holds for tradables and Balassa–Samuelson effects are present, then the tradables real exchange rate should be stationary but the relative movements in the nontradables-tradables price ratio should cointegrate with the CPI-based real exchange rate. Of course if Balassa–Samuelson effects are absent then the observed non-stationarity in the CPI-based real exchange rate can be (at least partly) explained by the real exchange rate defined in terms of tradables.

Typically, empirical studies have tended to find that these types of effects do have some influence on real exchange rate movements but that these are not sufficiently large to explain the large movements in real exchange rates (see Engel (1993) and Rogers and Jenkins (1995)). In particular, there is little evidence that the real exchange rate for tradables is stationary. In addition, the volatility of the real exchange rate for tradables explains a far higher proportion of the volatility of the real exchange rate defined using CPIs than is explained by the volatility of the relative price of tradables to nontradables. However, there is evidence to support the hypothesis that movements in relative productivity can explain changes in the relative price of tradables to nontradables in the very long term (see, for example, Kohler (2000), Canzoneri *et al.* (1999) and Chinn (1997)).

4.2 Attempts to understand short-term exchange rate movements

In theoretical terms, the set of measures that aim to capture short run equilibrium exchange rate movements are often the hardest to pin down. This is particularly true because at very short frequencies the volatility of the exchange rate is much greater than the volatility of fundamentals.[45] Models of short run equilibrium exchange rate movements are therefore often based around the model's ability to forecast exchange rate movements, rather than an overriding theoretical framework. This emphasis on forecast performance came out of the Meese and Rogoff (1983) findings that the first category of short run models considered here, namely monetary models, were unable to beat a forecast of no change for the exchange rate.[46] The remaining three models considered within this section are loosely based around UIP, with the biggest differences linked to the treatment of the risk premia and long run movements in exchange rates.

4.2.1 Monetary models

Monetary models of the exchange rate can be traced to a desire to improve on the ability of PPP to explain the behaviour of nominal exchange rates and an acknowledgement that exchange rates will be influenced by asset markets as well as goods markets. The emphasis is therefore on how to explain short term movements in nominal exchange rates rather than the desirable properties for a medium-term equilibrium real exchange rate. Although Frenkel and Goldstein (1986) list the monetary/portfolio balance approach as a single methodology, in fact the concept covers a variety of differing approaches. This chapter will not attempt to provide a comprehensive summary of these (see Frankel (1993), MacDonald and Taylor (1992) and Taylor (1995) for more extensive surveys, as well as Groen (2000) and Rapach and Wohar (2002)). Basically, however, the models can be distinguished by the degree of capital substitutability and whether or not prices are sticky (see in particular Frankel (1993) on these distinctions).

The starting point of this literature can be traced to a notion of perfect capital mobility and the idea that if the foreign exchange market is working efficiently then covered interest parity (or that the interest differential will be equal to the forward discount) will hold. The monetary approach to the balance of payments takes as its basis perfect capital substitutability and the idea that uncovered interest parity will hold. However, the exact model that emerges depends on the assumptions made about price adjustment. The monetarist model assumes flexible prices and that PPP holds continuously, see, for example, Frenkel (1976). The alternative assumption of sticky prices with PPP holding only in the long term generates the overshooting model, see, for example, Dornbusch (1976).[47] The portfolio balance approaches are based on the assumption that there is imperfect substitutability of capital, so that the UIP condition only holds with the addition of a risk premium. Within the portfolio balance framework, models can be categorised depending on whether they employ a small country model, a preferred local habitat model, or a uniform preference model.

The monetary approach uses the fact that the nominal exchange rate can be seen as the relative price of two monies. Within the simplest version of this approach, the monetarist model, the money supply and demand conditions can be substituted into a PPP equation, so that nominal exchange rates, s_t, are solved by:

$$s_t = (m^{s*} - m^s)_t + \phi y_t - \phi^* y_t^* - \lambda r_t + \lambda^* r_t^* \tag{10}$$

where m^s is the money supply, y is real income, r is the nominal interest rate, * denotes a foreign variable and all variables except interest rates are in natural logarithms. Within this framework an increase in domestic interest rates will generate a depreciation in the exchange rate, even though domestic assets will be more attractive. This is because an increase in interest rates reduces the demand for domestic money creating an excess supply of money. To restore money market equilibrium prices must rise, and hence for PPP to hold a depreciation is needed. By assumption the model displays neutrality to the determination of nominal magnitudes. However, the assumption that PPP holds continuously implies that this model of exchange rates cannot explain or generate changes in real exchange rates, such as might be needed if there were a sustained relative productivity shock. This is also true of the long-term behaviour of the overshooting model, which also collapses to PPP. This 'long term' is likely to be equivalent to the medium-term time horizon appropriate for the FEER. This is because the monetary models do not consider the dynamics of asset accumulation.

Portfolio balance models also have the exchange rate determined by the demand and supply of financial assets. However, the models incorporate the fact that exchange rates determine the current account, which in turn affects net holdings of foreign assets and therefore wealth, which will influence the demand for assets and therefore the exchange rate. The models distinguish between short-term equilibrium exchange rates where demand and supply are equated by the asset market, and a long-term equilibrium which is a complete stock equilibrium where wealth is stable. This model resembles the FEER approach in many ways, and indeed the resulting long-term equilibrium exchange rate could be thought of as the long-term FEER. However, in terms of a method of calculation the approach is quite different, as the calculated equilibrium exchange rate is obtained from a relationship between the components of wealth rather than from equilibrium output and sustainable capital flows. As Taylor (1995) notes, this can cause practical difficulties for estimating portfolio balance models because of data issues. The approach is also cast in nominal terms, as prices and real wealth are assumed to be homogeneous.

4.2.2 Capital enhanced equilibrium exchange rates

An alternative approach to explaining the persistence of real exchange rates is to combine PPP theories with that of the UIP condition discussed earlier. MacDonald (2000) has dubbed such estimates as capital-enhanced equilibrium exchange rates (CHEERs). The idea underlying this approach is that while PPP may explain long-term movements in real exchange rates, the real exchange rate may be away from equilibrium as a result of nonzero interest rate differentials (and that these may be necessary to finance the capital account). The approach therefore supplements the nominal UIP condition, given in equation (6) but excluding any risk premia, with the assumption that the expected value of the nominal exchange rate can be predicted using relative prices if PPP holds. A cointegrating relationship is then estimated between relative prices, nominal interest rate differentials and the nominal exchange rate.[48]

In general, the CHEER approach has tended to suggest higher estimated speeds of convergence than is found for simple PPP estimates, see, for example, Johansen and Juselius (1992), MacDonald and Marsh (1997) and Juselius and MacDonald (2000). Partly for this reason the approach has been successful in forecasting movements in bilateral exchange rates, and has proved able to significantly out forecast a random walk even at horizons as short as two months (see MacDonald and Marsh (1997)). The approach is most closely linked to the first of the two concepts of short-term equilibrium given by equation (2) in section 2, as the emphasis is on forecasting and the speed of convergence so that dynamics are important. The implicit assumption behind the approach, however, is that in the very long term when interest rate differentials are zero, the real exchange rate will be constant, or in other words that PPP will hold.

4.2.3 Intermediate-term model-based equilibrium exchange rates

Another concept of equilibrium which emphasises forecasting has been suggested by Wadhwani (1999) who has proposed an intermediate-term model-based equilibrium exchange rate (ITMEER). The starting point is again nominal UIP, this time including a risk premium. This risk premium is made up of two components.[49] The first component is made up of returns on other assets (stocks and bonds) to help explain exchange rate movements. The idea is that all assets must be priced off the same set of underlying risks and should therefore help predict excess currency returns. The second component is motivated by the assumption that risk will also in part be a function of the deviation in the real exchange rate from its equilibrium level. This equilibrium is assumed to be a function of relative current accounts (as a percentage of GDP), relative unemployment,[50] relative net foreign assets to GDP ratios and the relative ratio of wholesale to consumer prices.[51] In each case the approach uses the actual levels of these variables, rather than either their levels relative to equilibrium or the equilibrium levels themselves. Unless the equilibrium associated with these variables is constant, their actual levels will be an imperfect proxy of disequilibrium. In addition, unlike most of the alternative approaches to directly estimating equilibrium exchange rates discussed here, the framework does not use cointegration analysis.

ITMEERs are essentially attempting to capture e^{ST} in equation (2) and so forecast the exchange rate. Indeed the emphasis is on forecasting nominal bilateral rather than real exchange rate movements and in that sense the approach appears relatively successful. Nonetheless this emphasis would make it difficult to back out any associated medium- or long-term equilibria.

4.2.4 Behavioural equilibrium exchange rates

Work on behavioural equilibrium exchange rates (BEERs) is associated with Clark and MacDonald (1997, 1999).[52] BEERs aim to use a modelling technique which captures movements in real exchange rates over time, not just movements in the medium- or long-term equilibrium level. Partly reflecting this, the emphasis in the BEER approach is largely empirical and captures what we have defined above as short-term equilibrium concepts.

The starting point for the BEER analysis is the real UIP condition.[53] This is adjusted for the existence of a time varying risk premium. In the empirical work this risk premium is proxied using the ratio of outstanding domestic government debt to foreign government debt, both as a percentage of GDP. However, even with the addition of a risk premium, the UIP relationship is difficult to implement as an empirical model because of the lack of observed expectations of future levels of the real exchange rate. Clark and MacDonald (1997 and 1999) therefore make the assumption that expected future exchange rates will be related to long-term fundamentals.[54] The variables that Clark and MacDonald (1997, 1999) use to represent long-term fundamentals are: the terms of trade (tot) or the ratio of the unit value of exports to the unit value of imports; the relative price of traded to nontraded goods (tnt), proxied by the ratio of CPI to PPI; and net foreign assets as a ratio of GNP. In each case these variables are measured as relative to their foreign counterparts.

The equation for the real exchange rate which underpins the BEER analysis is therefore a function of real interest differentials, tot, tnt, nfa and the ratio of government debt.[55] This collection of variables will also influence FEERs. However, both the reasons for their inclusion and the way in which they feature are slightly more *ad hoc* than would be true for most FEER calculations. For example the analysis does not impose any particular functional forms or links from economic theory. Instead the links are essentially data determined. The estimation technique employed by Clark and MacDonald (1997, 1999) is the cointegration analysis due to Johansen, which allows the variables to be modelled as a system and for the existence of more than one cointegrating vector. In their modelling of the US, Germany and Japan, Clark and MacDonald (1999) find two cointegrating vectors in each case, one reflecting real interest rate differentials and the other the remaining variables in the system.

4.3 Underlying balance models – thinking about the medium term

In the medium term it is assumed that countries should be in both internal and external balance, but that asset stocks may still be changing. These are the key features of the underlying balance approach. To illustrate the basis for the underlying balance models, consider a very simple model where all variables (except asset stocks) have settled down on their steady-state growth paths. Assuming that superneutrality holds it is possible to present the model in real terms. This obviously abstracts from pricing considerations, which will be important in the short term. However, under the assumption of superneutrality, abstracting from pricing considerations is justifiable in the medium and long term on the grounds that the real economy will be independent of monetary policy over these horizons. A real exchange rate is consistent with a whole range of nominal exchange rate and price combinations, and in this time frame monetary policy simply determines the price level.

In the long term it is conventional to assume that output supply (or potential output) is determined exogenously. The first equation therefore embodies output supply (y^S):

$$y_t^S = \overline{y}(A, K, \overline{L})_t \tag{11}$$

so that output depends on the level of technical progress (A), the capital stock (K) and labour supply ($\overline{L}$), where an overbar indicates the variables are at their equilibrium levels.[56]

For underlying balance to hold, output supplied will have to equal output demanded (since we are abstracting from capacity utilisation considerations), where the latter is given by:

$$y_t^D = DD_t + NT_t \tag{12}$$

where aggregate demand (y^D) is the sum of domestic demand (DD) and net trade (NT). Domestic demand will depend on income, wealth, the capital stock, the real interest rate and fiscal policy, while net trade will depend on income at home and abroad and the real exchange rate. In an open economy, UIP implies that the long-term real interest rate will be equal to the world real interest rate minus the risk premium and any additional effects from trends in the equilibrium real exchange rate. The real exchange rate must then move to reconcile aggregate demand and aggregate supply: the real exchange rate is playing the role of a relative price which, just like any other relative price, must move to equilibrate supply and demand given supply constraints and demand preferences.[57]

The final relationship which can be used to help pin down underlying balance and hence the equilibrium exchange rate is given by the current account (CA):

$$CA_t = NT_t + BIPD_t = \Delta NFA_t = S_t - I_t \qquad (13)$$

which is equal to net trade together with the balance of interest, profit and dividend flows plus net transfers $(BIPD)$. By definition the current account is also equal to the change in net foreign assets (NFA) as well as savings minus investment $(S - I)$ for the economy as a whole. The external balance component of the underlying balance model is usually given by the assumption that the savings and investment balance for each individual economy is in some sense sustainable. It does not, however, imply that there will be a full stock-flow equilibrium, as this could take decades to achieve. As such net foreign assets can still be changing over time.

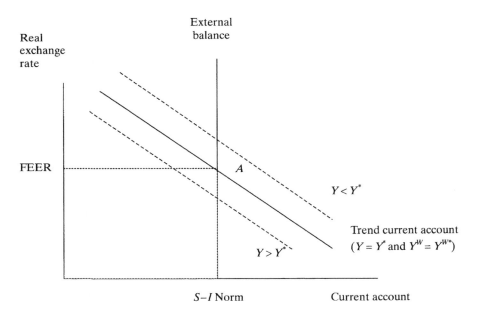

Figure 6.1 Stylised model of the underlying balance model.

Figure 6.1 represents a highly stylised view of the economy, but it is useful to illustrate the underlying balance approach. Consider the relationship between the current account and real exchange rates, where the real exchange rate is defined as units of foreign currency per unit of domestic, so that an increase represents an appreciation. For a given level of output, therefore, this relationship will be downward sloping so the current account improves (with imports falling and exports rising) as the real exchange rate depreciates. If domestic output increases this relationship will shift to the left as imports rise and therefore the current account deteriorates for any given real exchange rate. Similarly if foreign output were to increase then the relationship would shift to the right, with exports improving for a given real exchange rate.

The equilibrium exchange rate associated with the underlying balance models is the real exchange rate that reconciles the two conditions of external and internal balance, both of which are assumed to be invariant to the real exchange rate.[58] Internal balance occurs when output is at potential (or when $Y = Y^*$) and for this level of domestic output (as with any other) there is an upward sloping relationship between the current account and the real exchange rate. When output is equal to potential at home and abroad ($Y^W = Y^{W*}$) then this can be thought of as the trend current account. External balance is given by the level of savings minus investment (or current account) which is sustainable in the medium to long term. At point A, therefore, both internal and external balance will hold simultaneously, and the real exchange rate will represent underlying balance.

For the given combination of $S - I$ and Y^* and Y^{W*}, the equilibrium exchange rate implied by underlying balance will be constant. However, over time these factors will shift relative to each other and these shifts will be reflected in changes in the equilibrium. A simple example of such shifts would be if trend domestic growth were below world GDP growth, but that the world was otherwise symmetric. This would shift the trend current account to the right over time, so leading to an appreciation of the equilibrium exchange rate (for an unchanged $S - I$ norm).

What the underlying balance model gives is a path which pins down movements in the real exchange rate in the medium to long term. In other words the path for the exchange rate associated with underlying balance should act as an attractor for the real exchange rate, unless economies are permanently away from potential.[59] What the underlying balance model does not give is the path by which the economy returns to equilibrium. It is a model of the real exchange rate based on the assumption that all variables (except asset stocks) have settled down to their steady-state growth paths and abstracts from the pricing considerations which will be important in the short term.

The underlying balance approach involves the specification and estimation of equations in their structural form (i.e. in terms of trade equations, pricing relationships, expenditure functions, current account relationships, etc.), then inverting the model so that the real exchange rate is expressed in terms of fundamental variables. The equilibrium exchange rate will be determined as the (appropriate) long-term solution to the model.[60]

This type of approach can be implemented either using a fully specified macromodel, where all variables are endogenous, or a partial equilibrium model which looks at a subset of the equations of interest. If a large scale macroeconometric model is used, the real exchange rates which prevail at horizons once nominal inertia has washed out will be compatible with underlying balance, assuming that the model has a well defined long-term equilibrium. The advantage of pursuing this approach is that all the relationships within the model are endogenous. The disadvantages can sometimes be in terms of loss of transparency. In practice, using a full macromodel is rarely implemented because empirical macromodels are too large and it becomes hard to disentangle the different influences. Instead, the partial equilibrium approach is typically adopted. As this involves estimating on a country by country basis, the relationship for the external balance (either in terms of the current account or in terms of savings-investment balances) is usually estimated directly. Different choices regarding which structural trade equations should be modelled and how the external balance should be captured explains the differences between the empirical estimates that have been made. Since underlying approaches necessarily involves the use of trade-weighted effective exchange rate measures, equilibrium exchange rate estimates of this type will tend to be on an effective basis.[61]

Finally, one issue which is potentially important is the distinction between medium term and sustainability discussed in section 2 (above). One issue is the optimality and sustainability of fiscal policy, which is the key factor that distinguishes the FEER and DEER approaches (see below). An additional complication which occurs when agents' behaviour (for example consumption decisions) are influenced by persistent expectational errors that are not linked to cyclical factors. If, therefore, asset prices have risen based on an over optimistic assessment of future productivity growth, then this may boost consumption even though potential output itself has not changed. The associated outcome for medium-term consumption which is based on these expectational errors will therefore be reflected in the calculated medium-term exchange rate equilibrium. However, it will not represent the true, as in sustainable, medium-term equilibrium based on actual potential output. This distinction becomes important when macroeconometric model based approaches are used in estimation because these types of model, for example, often allow financial wealth to influence consumption. In contrast estimates based on a partial equilibrium approach will be largely immune from the problems associated with expectational errors assuming that there is no inconsistency between trend output and the calculated sustainable current account. Potentially both types of medium-term equilibrium are useful because while the calculated equilibrium linked to expectational errors may not be sustainable, it may well explain medium-term trends in exchange rates.

4.3.1 The fundamental equilibrium exchange rates approach

Possibly the most popular of the underlying balance models has been that of fundamental equilibrium exchange rates (FEERs). Wren-Lewis (1992) defines a FEER as 'a *method of calculation* of a real exchange rate which is consistent with *medium-term macroeconomic equilibrium*'. What is important in that statement is the notion of medium-term macroeconomic balance, as the FEERs approach does not actually impose a unified methodology on how these calculations are done. Indeed as noted above the calculations can either be made using a full scale macroeconometric model or using a partial equilibrium approach.[62] Under the partial equilibrium approach, which is most commonly used in the literature, the net trade and balance of interest, profit and dividend (ipd) relationships are specified and the trend current account is calculated under the assumption that real exchange rates are at their actual levels, but that output at home and abroad are at trend. The difference between the trend current account and the actual current account will therefore be the result of cyclical factors, together any errors in the specification of the trade and ipd equations. The FEER is then calculated as the real exchange rate that reconciles this trend current account with an assumption about the level of the savings and investment balance for each individual economy which will be in some sense sustainable.

Of the two components of macroeconomic balance, internal and external, it is external balance, or the sustainable level of savings and investment, which has attracted the most controversy. The earliest attempts to derive FEER estimates include Artis and Taylor (1995), Barrell and Wren-Lewis (1989), Currie and Wren-Lewis (1989a, 1989b), Williamson and Miller (1987), Williamson (1993, 1994), Frankel (1996) and Frenkel and Goldstein (1986). One distinguishing feature of these early FEER estimates was the relatively simple way that the equilibrium current account was modelled. This tended to be rationalised in terms of a measure of sustainable capital flows which were usually assumed to be a constant proportion of GDP and was often arrived at in a fairly *ad hoc* manner (see, for example, Williamson and Mahar (1998)).[63]

An alternative, less *ad hoc*, approach to deriving the equilibrium current account has more recently been developed by researchers at the IMF (see Faruqee and Debelle (1998) and Masson (1998)). Since net domestic savings and the current account of the balance of payments are by identity equal, they focus on the determinants of the difference between domestic savings and investment. Specifically, they explain medium-term net domestic savings in terms of demographic factors and the government deficit (adjusted for the cycle) (see also Bussiere *et al.* (2003), for a recent application of this approach).

One criticism of the FEER concept often made is that it does not constitute a true equilibrium since stock-flow equilibrium is not achieved. This criticism is misplaced, as it reflects a misunderstanding of the concept. However, one consequence of the fact that full stock-flow equilibrium has not been achieved is that FEERs will be subject to hysteresis effects since the medium-term current account will be affected by temporary shocks (see Artis and Taylor (1995) for an articulation of this criticism of FEERs). Shocks will cause wealth stocks to move away from equilibria and the time horizon over which these wealth-income ratios are restored to their target levels may be much longer than that required for internal and external balance to be achieved. In principle, of course, it would be possible to calculate the long-term equilibrium value of savings-investment balances and calculate the long-term equilibrium exchange rate accordingly. In practice, little interest has been shown in doing this mainly because such an equilibrium is probably only relevant to the very long term.

It is worth noting though that the process of deriving a FEER does not have to involve the estimation of a full dynamic model. Rather, FEER calculations are attempting to identify $\hat{e}$ in equation (3) above (where the relevant levels of the fundamentals are their medium-term equilibrium levels), not to model the process of how the economy might arrive at that exchange rate. This does not imply, however, that FEER calculations could not be used to calculate a version of exchange rate short-term equilibrium consistent with current values of economic fundamentals, but abstracting from transitory factors. This could be obtained using the values of actual output and the current account in place of potential output and sustainable capital flows. Such an exchange rate would not be a true equilibrium. For example there would be no guarantee that the actual value of the current account would be sustainable. However, it might help to distinguish the extent to which deviations from the FEER are the result of cyclical considerations.[64]

4.3.2 Desired equilibrium exchange rates

One additional potential shortcoming of the FEER concept can be the slightly arbitrary definition of 'medium-term' fundamentals. Depending on how the calculations are performed this potentially places a strong emphasis on an essentially normative issue, that of optimal policy, a link which is reinforced by Williamson's use in much of his work on FEERs of the phrase '*target* current account' to describe sustainable capital flows.[65] This link between the FEER and particularly fiscal policy has led many economists (including Williamson himself: Williamson 1994b: 181) to argue that the FEER is inherently normative, and tied to some kind of 'desired' policy trajectory.[66] In the light of this, some economists have preferred to use an alternative title to describe medium-term equilibrium known the desired equilibrium exchange rate (DEER) (see Bayoumi *et al.* (1994) and Artis and Taylor (1995)) where the real exchange rate is conditioned on some measure of optimal fiscal policy.

However, it is worth noting that just because a calculated medium-term equilibrium exchange rate is conditional on fiscal policy assumptions, does not imply that it has to be normative. A normative exercise would use the 'optimal' path. However, it would be just as easy to use the most likely path for fiscal policy, or structural fiscal policy, and where the two differed, so would the calculated FEER and DEER.

4.4 Measuring the long term

In this section a set of alternative ways of calculating long-term equilibrium exchange rates, which are distinct from PPP, are presented. In other words, these are measures that allow real exchange rate equilibrium to vary even in the long term. The measures are quite different in their approach, ranging from the purely statistical to a more model-based method of calculation. The statistical methods are categorised as long term because they aim to calculate permanent changes in the exchange rate. However, it is important to note that this definition of permanent is not based on any assumption about asset stocks being in equilibrium. As such it could be argued that they should be classified as medium term.

4.4.1 Statistical methods: APEERs

An alternative and rather different way to estimate equilibrium exchange rates is to use techniques which rely directly on the statistical properties of the real exchange rate. In particular, these methods aim to decompose the real exchange rate itself into its 'permanent' and 'transitory' components. For example, Huizinga (1987) and Cumby and Huizinga (1990) use Beveridge–Nelson decompositions to extract the permanent component of real exchange rate movements. This has been dubbed by MacDonald (2000) as the atheoretical permanent equilibrium exchange rate (APEER), because of the absence of any explicit theory about exchange rate behaviour.

4.4.2 Permanent equilibrium exchange rates

The emphasis in BEER approaches is on modelling the behaviour of exchange rates, and therefore BEER-type calculations do not require that fundamentals are at their equilibrium levels. As such, BEERs will only coincide with measures of medium-term equilibrium such as FEERs when the condition $Z_t - \hat{Z}_t = 0$ holds. Even at that point, however, exchange rates can still be misaligned, with the misalignment reflecting transitory factors and random errors.

Recognising this distinction Clark and MacDonald (2000) have more recently defined the permanent equilibrium exchange rate (PEER) which is derived directly from the BEER estimates but separates out the factors underlying the BEER into their permanent and transitory components.[67] This can be done using the statistical techniques due to Gonzalo and Granger (1995).[68] This technique makes no attempt to directly measure what the longer-term levels of the individual fundamentals are and as such is a statistical rather than an economic definition of equilibrium. An alternative would be to estimate the BEER in the normal way and then to replace the actual levels of fundamentals with estimates of their trend levels; see, for example, the discussion in Égert (2003) in the context of BEERs. However, despite the different estimation technique used in its derivation, the PEER concept is comparable with the FEER concept.

4.4.3   The natural real exchange rate approach

Another concept which is closely related to FEERs is that of the natural real exchange rate (NATREX). Work on the NATREX is mainly due to Jerome Stein (see Stein (1994), Stein and Allen (1995) and Stein and Paladino (1998)). Stein defines the NATREX as 'the rate that would prevail if speculative and cyclical factors could be removed while unemployment is at its natural rate' (1994: 135). In addition, the NATREX is the real exchange rate which equates the current account to *ex ante* saving and investment, where these are evaluated at the level implied by fundamentals, where fundamentals relate to productivity and thrift and are exogenous. On this basis, this definition is very similar to the medium-term equilibrium concept embodied in the FEER. However, in addition, the NATREX is also defined by its proponents as that real exchange rate which is consistent with portfolio balance, so that domestic real interest rates equal world real interest rates.[69] This implies that the NATREX should be interpreted as a long-term equilibrium concept. Indeed, in discussing the NATREX, Stein and Paladino (1998) distinguish between medium- and long-term considerations. For example, in the medium term an increase in social consumption (for example, because government consumption increases) implies that the associated real exchange rate must appreciate to reduce excess demand. This in turn implies that the current account will deteriorate. In the longer term the decline in the current account implies that there will be a related deterioration in net interest flows on foreign debt because of the impact on net foreign assets. This implies a further worsening of the current account. Therefore at the prevailing exchange rate there will now be a short fall in demand relative to the planned level of savings minus investment. In the longer term therefore the real exchange rate needs to depreciate until net foreign assets are stabilised. This process has to be associated with a change in the planned level of savings less investment (so that they become zero). Such arguments are similar to those associated with the long-term FEER. In discussing the long-term FEER, Wren-Lewis and Driver (1998) speculate that this could take decades to achieve as there may be good reasons even in the medium term for capital flows to take place.

In estimation the NATREX model considers a variety of fundamentals, which depend in part on whether the economy is considered small or large. In the analysis of the US given in Stein (1994) fundamentals are defined as productivity at home and abroad (given by real GDP growth) and the rate of time preference, given by the ratio of social consumption (or private and government consumption) to GNP in the US. In each case these fundamentals are measured using a 12-quarter moving average of the underlying series in order to eliminate cyclical elements. The change in fundamentals is measured using the real long interest differential. In the analysis of Australia presented in Lim and Stein (1995) the list of fundamentals is given by productivity, the terms of trade, the real foreign interest rate and social thrift (for Australia).

The definition of the real exchange rate used in empirical work on the NATREX also varies. For large countries the nominal exchange rate is deflated either using GDP deflators or CPI, while for small countries unit labour costs are used, see Stein and Paladino (1998). The reason for this distinction is the argument that for small open economies prices are determined on world markets. In fact if countries produce differentiated products under imperfect competition this does not necessarily have to be true.

Empirical work on the NATREX is also done over two time horizons, the medium and the long term. In the medium term, the real exchange rate responds to real interest rate differentials, as well as being dependent on exogenously determined fundamentals. Stein (1994) models this relationship for the US by estimating an equation which relates the real exchange rate to real US GNP growth, real foreign GNP growth, the current account to GNP ratio for the US and the real long-term interest rate differential. The growth rates are proxies for the growth of the capital stock at home and abroad, while the current account is a proxy for the rate of change of foreign debt. The growth rates and current account are set to their 12 quarter moving average, while the real interest rate differential is lagged one period.

In the long term the capital stock and foreign debt are also endogenous and will be related, together with the real exchange rate, to long-term fundamentals, or productivity at home and abroad and the rate of time preference at home and abroad. However, it is not always possible to obtain measures of the appropriate variables. Therefore the modelling strategy for the long term of the US, Stein (1994) relates the real exchange rate and foreign debt to productivity at home and abroad and the rate of time preference at home. Foreign debt is again proxied using the ratio of the US current account to GNP. Productivity at home and abroad are proxied by the 12-quarter moving average of the GNP growth rate to abstract from cyclical elements. In the case of the rate of time preference in the US, this is given by social consumption (i.e. private and public consumption) as a proportion of GNP. As this is a ratio, cyclical factors should cancel. In addition, Stein (1994) finds that the 12-quarter moving average of this variable is not useful in the regressions. The focus of the empirical analysis is on the trajectories, not the steady states, which might take decades to achieve.

Although the variables considered are similar, it is clear that the estimation strategy employed for the NATREX differs from methods of calculating medium-term equilibrium exchange rates. Indeed it belongs more naturally in our discussion on direct methods which relate actual real exchange rates to the actual level of the appropriate variables.[70] Such estimation can either be in the form of single equations, or could encompass more complex models. The hope, however, is that it will produce an unbiased and efficient estimate of the parameters which make up the β vector associated with the fundamentals, Z, in equation (1). The equilibrium exchange rate is obtained by inserting the equilibrium levels of the relevant fundamentals, $\hat{Z}$ or $\overline{Z}$ (see equations (3) and (4)). An alternative that is used in the NATREX analysis is to attempt to estimate β using $\hat{Z}$ or $\overline{Z}$ directly, so that the calculated equilibrium is obtained directly by setting the regression residuals to zero. Given the problems associated with adequately measuring $\hat{Z}$ and $\overline{Z}$, this may have implications for the efficiency of estimates of β.

4.5 *Understanding the role of shocks*

An important empirical and theoretical question is what impact will shocks (for example, to supply) have on real exchange rates. In this section two general methods (one empirical and one theoretical) are highlighted which aim to answer this type of question. These are not methods which can be used to calculate a level of the real exchange rate. Nonetheless they are important tools for allowing us to understand why exchange rates move in the way that they do.

4.5.1 *Structural vector autoregressions (SVARs)*

In considering how the real exchange is determined, it is useful to adopt as general a framework as possible. Of course, because the real exchange rate is endogenous to the whole macroeconomic system, we should expect it to be affected by all the shocks which impinge on the economy. A variety of techniques exist which allow us to obtain a reduced-form expression that captures all or some of these effects. For example, by estimating a structural vector autoregression (SVAR), we can make assumptions about how different shocks will affect the exchange rate and hence decompose the value of the real exchange rate into its different components (see, for example, Clarida and Gali (1995) and Astley and Garratt (1998)). Such techniques therefore require the researcher to have theoretical prior views on how particular shocks affect the exchange rate. So it is inevitably necessary to consider a structural model of the economy.

For example, Clarida and Gali (1994) use SVAR techniques to decompose the *change* in real exchange rate movements into the effects of supply, demand and nominal shocks.[71] Typically this type of approach finds that real demand shocks or nominal shocks can explain a far higher proportion of exchange rate movements than supply shocks. However, these findings will be sensitive to decomposition used, see Labhard and Westaway (2002).

MacDonald and Swagel (2000) suggest that the permanent component of movements in the real exchange rate will be that given by the contribution of the supply shocks, thus stripping out the influence of the demand and nominal shocks (see also Detken *et al.* (2002)). In some senses these estimates are related to medium-term FEER-type measures. The correspondence is not exact however: first, because theory would suggest that equilibrium exchange rates may also be influenced by permanent demand shocks; second, because even if the effects of demand shocks were to be included, these SVAR-based methods will tend to incorporate the short-term dynamic effects of the demand and supply shocks which would be stripped out from conventional measures of the medium-term equilibrium; and finally, because the SVAR methodology is related to the change in the exchange rate rather than its level it is difficult to translate the methodology into levels space as it will depend on an arbitrary start point, which may or may not represent equilibrium.

4.5.2 Dynamic stochastic general equilibrium approaches to the exchange rate

Dynamic stochastic general equilibrium (DSGE) models have proved to be extremely popular within the so-called New Open Economy literature, see Lane (2001) for a survey. For all its popularity, this class of model cannot provide information about the level of the real exchange rate, because results from DSGE models are typically presented as deviations from steady state. However, they are ideally suited to thinking about what impact shocks will have on exchange rates and relative prices. As such they can provide valuable insights into the likely source of shocks hitting the economy, based on the observed correlations between variables and how these match up to the predictions from the models. In addition, because they include explicit expressions for consumers' utility they can also be used for welfare analysis.

Probably the best known model within this class is the so-called Obstfeld–Rogoff *Redux* model, see Obstfeld and Rogoff (1995, 1996). This uses a very simple two country model, where firms' prices are sticky for one period in the producers' currency and where the law of one price holds for individual goods, so that PPP holds continuously and the real exchange rate defined in consumer prices is constant. Consumer preferences are the same in both countries, but because countries produce different goods both nominal exchange rates and the terms of trade will shift following shocks to the money supply, productivity and government spending. Clearly the assumption that PPP holds even in the short term is very strong (see the evidence in section 4.1.2). Benigno and Thoenissen (2002) suggests various ways to break this link, at least in the short term, including the existence of nontraded goods, home bias in consumption and pricing-to-market.

While one of the attractions of DSGE models is that they have a strong theoretical basis, changes to the theoretical priors can often yield very different results.[72] Ultimately which version of the transmission mechanism makes most sense is an empirical question, so that the results from DSGE models are often compared to those from SVARs in order to determine whether the impact of shocks is the one expected. One of the most controversial aspects of the transmission mechanism within this class of model is the choice between producer currency versus local currency pricing. See section 3.2.1 above for a discussion of the implications of these two approaches to trade pricing. See also Bergin (2003) for an attempt to test the importance of this assumption empirically in the context of a DSGE model.

5   Conclusions

This chapter has examined the concept of equilibrium real exchange rates. In theoretical terms, it has explained why the assumption of purchasing power parity, frequently adopted in simple theoretical models, may be inadequate when various real world complications are introduced. Importantly these richer models imply that the real exchange rate is ultimately determined as an endogenous variable in the macroeconomy. And while acknowledging that speculative factors may have an important role to play in determining short-term exchange rate movements, the chapter has argued that the exchange rate will ultimately be determined by 'fundamental' factors relating to the real economy.

The chapter has emphasised the distinction between short-, medium- and long-term exchange rate equilibria. It has argued that 'misalignment' with respect to these different equilibrium concepts may have quite different policy implications. A measure of the real exchange rate may be away from its medium-term equilibrium because the fundamental factors on which it depends are themselves away from equilibrium: for example monetary policy maybe temporarily tight in response to a demand shock causing the exchange rate to appreciate above its medium-term equilibrium. On the other hand, the exchange rate may diverge from its equilibrium despite the fact that the fundamentals are in equilibrium themselves. In these circumstances, the policy implications will depend on what the source and nature of the shock to the exchange rate is perceived to be. Deliberately, this chapter does not set out to explore these important policy-related issues in depth. Rather it is designed to convey the message that exchange rate misalignments can be defined in a variety of ways and for any given definition the link between the misalignment and the policy response is not mechanical.

In the final section, the chapter has examined the different approaches that have been taken to deriving empirical estimate of these equilibrium concepts. Previously, there have been few attempts to explain how these different empirical estimates and their associated acronyms can be related to each other. For the first time, a taxonomy of the different approaches is provided explaining what horizon each equilibrium concept refers to, what theoretical assumptions are adopted in its construction and how the measure has been estimated. This description is not intended to provide a recommendation of which approach is best. Rather it is to emphasise that different measures of *the* equilibrium real exchange rate may be conceptually distinct.

This chapter covers a lot of ground both in terms of describing the underlying theoretical basis for equilibrium exchange rate concepts and for the associated empirical estimates. As such this chapter is designed to provide a conceptual framework for ongoing work related to both the theoretical and empirical aspects of equilibrium exchange rates.

Notes

1 See the summary of this debate in Milgate (1998).
2 This can be linked to the work of Marshall (1890), who distinguished between three periods: 'market', 'short' and 'long'; see the discussion in Milgate (1998).
3 An alternative measure of short-term equilibrium would simply take account of current levels of fundamentals and would abstract from transitory factors.
4 Arguably, this characterisation of external balance may be slightly confusing since the only true position of balance is that associated with the full stock-flow equilibrium.
5 Real rigidities are not, of course, the only reason why asset stocks take time to adjust to long-term equilibrium. Alternative explanations for protracted asset stock adjustment include the Blanchard–Yaari style consumption model with overlapping generations.
6 This would not be true if hysteresis effects are important. In addition, although the economy may naturally return to equilibrium, the period over which it does so may not be short enough from a welfare point of view, and so an activist policy may assist in restoring balance.
7 Unless there is complete certainty that the method of obtaining estimates of ϵ completely captures the impact of the relevant fundamentals and the transition

path generated by past shocks, this can only be an indication. In addition it assumes that any risk premium (see below) is defined as being dependent on fundamentals, rather than simply the unexplained part of any empirical estimate.

8 The question of whether any misalignment of the exchange rate is appropriate or not therefore needs to be considered in the more general context of whether the monetary policy response itself is appropriate or optimal.

9 The same is true for the difference between medium- and long-term values of fundamentals.

10 In practice, in the short term at least, real and nominal exchange rates tend to move very close together.

11 This point is often confused in discussion of the equilibrium value of particular exchange rates. For example, in choosing a particular bilateral exchange rate which sterling might lock into vis-à-vis the euro upon entering EMU, it is too simplistic to argue, as is often done, that a particular nominal exchange rate is economically unsustainable. In principle, any initial value of the nominal exchange rate is sustainable so long as relative inflation rates can adjust so as to bring about a movement in the real exchange rate to its warranted equilibrium. Of course, that is not to deny that if the initially chosen rate is misaligned in real terms, this transition may be potentially costly in terms of lost output.

12 In general effective exchange rate indices are calculated as a geometric rather than an arithmetic mean. This has the useful property that any calculation of percentage change will be independent of the base year chosen.

13 The sum of ϖ_{ij} will be unity by construction. If the real exchange rate of interest is a bilateral exchange rate there will only be one j.

14 See Pagan (2003) for an excellent discussion of the strengths and weaknesses of different approaches along this spectrum in the context of forecasting inflation.

15 One caveat is that it is assumed that macroeconomic fundamentals are the key driving variables underlying movements in the exchange rate. In practice, particularly in the short term, this may not be true. Andersen *et al.* (2003) and Faust *et al.* (2003) both find that the news component of macroeconomic announcements has an impact on the exchange rate in the immediate aftermath (measured in minutes) of the announcement. However, these movements only represent a small fraction of daily exchange rate volatility, making the impact of the announcements harder to detect at longer frequencies.

16 In general there has been less theoretical work on equilibrium exchange rates, in part because of the attractions, not least in terms of analytical tractability, of assuming PPP (see below). A notable exception to this is Benigno and Thoenissen (2002).

17 This implies that firms have a degree of market power and therefore earn monopoly rents.

18 Of course the finding that the real exchange rate is stationary may occur because the fundamentals it depends on are themselves stationary. However, as PPP is not a theory of exchange rate determination (it contains no information on how exchange rates and prices adjust) this is perfectly compatible with PPP.

19 The tests in Murray and Papell (2002) are conducted using both wholesale and consumer prices to measure the real exchange rate.

20 In cases where more structural models have been used, one test of their validity is whether the resulting estimates cointegrate with the real exchange rate; see section 3.3.

21 Taylor and Allen (1992) and Cheung *et al.* (2000) present evidence for the prevalence of different types of trading strategies employed in the FOREX market. While fundamentals are seen as important by some, they are by no means the dominant consideration.

22 As the underlying balance models make clear, it is generally thought that flow equilibrium will be reached before stock equilibrium because of the slow speed of adjustment for capital.

23 In addition we make no attempt to compare the estimates of equilibrium that are given by the different methodologies; see Koen *et al.* (2001) for a comparison of estimates for the euro. Detken *et al.* (2002) compare estimates from four different approaches to calculating equilibrium.

24 Real interest rates are typically defined using consumer prices, suggesting CPI should be used, see Chortareas and Driver (2001).

25 This UIP decomposition is explained in greater detail in the context of the nominal exchange rate in Brigden *et al.* (1997).

26 Although UIP appears to embody quite a specific assumption about how exchange rates evolve, it is actually consistent with a wide range of models if we are prepared to interpret the expectations formation mechanism in a number of ways and if we interpret the risk-premium sufficiently flexibly. For example, the UIP condition can be interpreted as a limiting case of a portfolio balance model.

27 It is also important not to confuse UIP considerations with capital flows which are ultimately determined by the net balance of saving and investment flows within a country; see Niehans (1994) on this point. The choice of portfolio composition will be influenced by many things, including, for example, tax considerations.

28 Naturally there are exceptions. Flood and Rose (2001), for example, find that the interest rate differential is correctly signed over the 1990s, although the coefficients are often small and occasionally insignificant.

29 Given its basis is generally given by goods market arbitrage, assuming that countries produce a roughly similar range of goods, the most natural definition of the real exchange rate in the PPP context uses tradable or output prices. However, consumer prices are also often used, but for this to be valid relies on the assumption that all goods are traded.

30 In practice most measures of the real exchange rate use price indices, rather than price levels, and therefore PPP will simply imply that the real exchange rate will be constant. In addition, most empirical tests of PPP only assume that the real exchange rate will be constant in the long term.

31 This mechanism is likely to be long term rather than medium term in duration.

32 See MacDonald (1995), Breuer (1994) and Froot and Rogoff (1995) for surveys on PPP.

33 Differences in the construction of price indices across countries cause additional complications which may also mean that PPP will be violated in practice. These include differences in indirect taxation and the treatment of housing costs.

34 Obstfeld and Rogoff (2000) show how transport costs may provide an explanation for home country bias in the goods countries consume.

35 In the case where consumer preferences are identical and there are no non-traded goods then PPP will hold when the real exchange rate is defined using consumer prices, providing LOOP holds.

36 Bergin and Glick (2003) explore the implications of the fact that at the margin the decision to trade or not to trade a good is endogenous.

37 This happens because countries specialise according to the Ricardian principle of comparative advantage (see, for example, Obstfeld and Rogoff (1996: Chapter 4)). Note the presence of transactions costs will imply that some goods are produced by more than one country.

38 In fact, even if none of these factors are present Noussair *et al.* (1997) show within an experimental environment that both LOOP and PPP may not hold

due to a combination of perceived exchange rate risk and differing speeds of convergence towards equilibrium. For LOOP and PPP to hold, markets must be in equilibrium simultaneously.

39 In general the results for PPP are less favourable when the US is used as a numeraire currency. This may reflect the fact that the US is relatively closed and therefore that the forces of arbitrage are not as strong.

40 Michael *et al.* (1997) argue that cointegration tests may be biased against finding evidence of long-term PPP because they ignore the non linearities implied by the presence of transaction costs (see also Dumas (1992), on this point).

41 The empirical evidence has concentrated on PPP, rather than LOOP because it is the former which is actually related to exchange rate equilibrium. However, the evidence in favour of LOOP is if anything even weaker (see, for example, Frankel and Rose (1995) and Haskel and Wolfe (2001)). Evidence also suggests that there is more to the problem than simply transport costs (see, for example, Engel and Rogers (1996)).

42 The basic Balassa–Samuelson model assumes that there are constant returns to scale in production, that labour is mobile between the traded and nontraded sectors, but is fixed internationally, while capital is internationally mobile. Balassa–Samuelson effects are also based on the assumption that PPP holds within the tradables sector.

43 This is because the rising wages in the tradables sector associated with increased productivity will spillover into the nontradables sector, causing prices to rise.

44 Devereux (1998) shows that these effects may go in the opposite direction if strong productivity growth in the tradables sector feeds through into the distribution sector.

45 De Grauwe and Grimaldi (2002) present a model which suggests that one explanation of this may be the existence of traders in the market who use chartist methods rather than fundamentals to forecast exchange rates (see also Jeanne and Rose (2002)).

46 Cheung *et al.* (2002), suggest that newer models such as behavioural equilibrium models may not, in fact, do any better in this respect than their traditional alternatives. It is worth noting however that Cheung *et al.* (2002) separate out the dynamics when they conduct these tests and these dynamics are often thought of as an integral part of behavioural equilibrium exchange rates, or BEERs.

47 See Rogoff (2002) on the Dornbusch overshooting model.

48 This type of approach usually models bilateral exchange rates and hence will not represent whole economy equilibrium.

49 The variables used to represent these components varies across currencies and in that sense are relatively *ad hoc*.

50 A rise in relative unemployment in country A is expected to cause its exchange rate to depreciate. Although this is motivated using the FEERs literature, the effect of this type of impact within that framework would have the opposite sign.

51 This last term aims to capture productivity differentials between the traded and nontraded sectors and is based on the assumption that Balassa–Samuelson effects will explain internal inflation differentials, see Kohler (2000).

52 Other examples of BEER estimates include Alberola *et al.* (1999), Clostermann and Schnatz (2000), Maeso-Fernandez *et al.* (2001), Osbat *et al.* (2003) and Schnatz *et al.* (2003).

53 Clark and MacDonald (1997, 1999) look at real effective exchange rates. Other researchers have used very similar approaches to model bilateral exchange rates, see, for example, Clostermann and Schnatz (2000).

54 Conceptually, Clark and MacDonald (1999) in fact subdivide the Z_t in equation (1) into medium- and long-term fundamentals. However, in estimation this sub-

tlety is ignored. In practice it is sometimes difficult to determine which variables will influence expected future exchange rates and which will determine the risk premia. Researchers have therefore placed differing emphasis on these two factors, although similar variables are used within estimation.

55 Clark and MacDonald (2000), suggest that in some cases it may be important to concentrate simply on the role of fundamentals, in order to understand the impact of the real interest rate differential. See also the arguments in MacDonald (1999).

56 The supply equation will often be written in terms of a simple price adjustment mechanism such as a Phillips curve whereby inflation changes according to the gap between demand and supply but the long-term solution of that relationship collapses to equation (11).

57 In terms of the solution for the real exchange rate, demand conditions become particularly important once a model incorporates factors such as differences in consumer preferences and (depending on the real exchange rate under consideration) differentiated goods.

58 Barrell and Wren-Lewis (1989) and Driver and Wren-Lewis (1999) investigate the results of relaxing the assumption that potential output is invariant to the level of the real exchange rate. In general the impact on the FEER calculations of relaxing this assumption is found to be very small.

59 Work by Barisone *et al.* (2003) suggests that FEERs (the most popular of the underlying balance approaches) do have this attractor property.

60 Given the important role of trade relationships in underlying balance model, the measure of the real exchange rate used in calculations typically links world trade prices to the price of domestic tradables. However, in principle any definition of the real exchange rate that links domestic and foreign prices could be used.

61 If equilibrium exchange rates have been calculated on a consistent basis for more than one country, then estimates of the associated bilateral exchange rates can be derived using trade weights, see Alberola *et al.* (1999). Alternatively if the model includes more than one country then bilaterals can also be estimated directly, see, for example, Wren-Lewis (2003).

62 Such partial equilibrium calculations are typically only performed for a single point in time and this leads to the accusation that there was no way of determining how much relevance FEERs have in explaining movements in real exchange rates over time. Barisone *et al.* (2003) investigate this issue and find that FEERs have more success than PPP in explaining movements in real exchange rates over time. This is demonstrated by the fact that while real exchange rates themselves are found to be nonstationary, the difference between FEERs and real exchange rates are stationary.

63 Driver and Wren-Lewis (1999) examine the sensitivity of the resulting FEER estimates to these assumptions about sustainable capital flows (see also Dvornak *et al.* (2003) and Brook and Hargreaves (2000)).

64 One problem is that in the short term it is not possible to invoke neutrality, implying that dynamics will matter. Depending on the model used to calculate the FEER, such dynamics may, or may not, be available.

65 In this sense the term sustainable is possibly also misleading. Within this context it refers to medium-term (average) capital flows rather than an upper limit for the absolute size of the current account.

66 In the case of Williamson, there is an additional reason why the FEER is seen as an essentially normative concept, which is because:

> FEERs are intended to be used as intermediate targets in securing the international coordination of economic policy.
>
> (Williamson, 1994b: 185)

67 Other examples of PEER estimates include Alberola *et al.* (1999), Hansen and Roeger (2000) and Maeso-Fernandez *et al.* (2001).
68 Hansen and Roeger (2000) warn that in some cases the estimated equilibrium will be sensitive to the decomposition method and that the Gonzalo and Granger (1995) may exaggerate the 'goodness of fit'.
69 If real UIP is assumed (equation (7)) then this last condition implies that changes in the real exchange rate will only occur if there is a risk premium.
70 Not all NATREX calculations take this approach. Detken *et al.* (2002) estimate a NATREX model using structural rather than reduced form methods.
71 In the case of Clarida and Gali (1994) the SVAR also contains the change in relative foreign output and relative inflation. The identification scheme used is one whereby output is only affected by supply shocks in the long term, while real exchange rates can be influenced by both demand and supply shocks. It is the fact that these models are specified in terms of the change in the real exchange rate, allowing researchers to use normal SVAR or VAR analysis, rather than forcing them to estimate a cointegrating (VECM) relationship which distinguishes them from the BEER and PEER methodology discussed earlier.
72 This is one reason why Krugman (2000) argues strongly in favour of using relatively *ad hoc* models for empirical investigations because of their proven ability to fit key stylised facts.

References

Alberola, E.S., Cervero, S., Lopez, H. and Ubide, A. (1999), 'Global equilibrium exchange rates: euro, dollar, "ins", "outs" and other major currencies in a panel cointegration framework', IMF Working Paper no. 99/175.

Andersen, T.G., Bollerslev, T., Diebold F.X. and Vega, C. (2003), 'Micro effects of macro announcements: real-time price discovery in foreign exchange', *American Economic Review*, 93: 38–62.

Artis, M. and Taylor, M. (1995), 'The effect of misalignment on desired equilibrium exchange rates: some analytical results', in Bordes, C., Girardin, E. and Mélitz, J. (eds), *European Currency Crises and After*, Manchester University Press.

Astley, M. and Garratt, A. (1998), 'Exchange rates and prices: sources of sterling real exchange rate fluctuations 1973–94', Bank of England Working Paper no. 85.

Barisone, G., Driver, R. and Wren-Lewis, S. (2003), 'Are our FEERs justified?', *Journal of International Money and Finance*, forthcoming.

Barrell, R. and Wren-Lewis, S. (1989), 'Fundamental equilibrium exchange rates for the G7', CEPR Discussion Paper no. 323.

Bayoumi, T., Clark, P., Symansky, S. and Taylor, M. (1994), 'The robustness of equilibrium exchange rate calculations to alternative assumptions and methodologies', in Williamson, J. (ed.), *Estimating Equilibrium Exchange Rates,* Washington, DC: Institute of International Economics.

Benigno, G. and Thoenissen, C. (2002), 'Equilibrium exchange rates and supply-side performance', Bank of England Working Paper no. 156.

Bergin, P.R. (2003), 'Putting the "new open economy macroeconomics" to a test', *Journal of International Economics*, 60: 3–34.

Bergin, P.R. and Glick, R. (2003), 'Endogenous nontradability and macroeconomic implications', NBER Working Paper no. 9739.

Bernanke, B.S. and Gertler, M. (1999), 'Monetary policy and asset price volatility', *Federal Reserve Bank of Kansas City Economic Review*, Fourth Quarter: 17–51.

Breuer, J.B. (1994), 'An assessment of the evidence on purchasing power parity', in Williamson, J. (ed.), *Estimating Equilibrium Exchange Rates*, Washington, DC: Institute of International Economics.

Brigden, A., Martin, B. and Salmon, C. (1997), 'Decomposing exchange rate movements according to the uncovered interest parity condition', *Quarterly Bulletin*, 37: 377–388.

Brook, A.-M. and Hargreaves, D. (2000), 'A macroeconomic balance measure of New Zealand's equilibrium exchange rate', Reserve Bank of New Zealand Discussion Paper no. 2000/09.

Bussiere, M., Chortareas, G. and Driver, R.L. (2003), 'Current accounts, net foreign assets and the implications of cyclical factors', *Eastern Economic Journal*, 29: 269–286.

Canzoneri, M.B., Cumby, R.E. and Diba, B. (1999), 'Relative labour productivity and the real exchange rate in the long run: evidence for a panel of OECD countries', *Journal of International Economics*, 47: 245–266.

Cecchetti, S.G., Genberg, H., Lipski, J. and Wadhwani, S. (2000), 'Asset prices and central bank policy', Geneva Report on the World Economy no. 2.

Cheung, Y.-W. and Chinn, M.D. (1998), 'Integration, cointegration and the forecast consistency of structural exchange rate models', *Journal of International Money and Finance*, 17: 813–830.

Cheung, Y.-W., Chinn, M.D. and Marsh, I.W. (2000), 'How do UK based foreign exchange dealers think their market operates?', NBER Working Paper no. 7524.

Cheung, Y.-W., Chinn, M.D. and Pascual, A.G. (2002), 'Empirical exchange rate models of the nineties: are any fit to survive?', *Journal of International Money and Finance*, forthcoming.

Chinn, M.D. (2002), 'The measurement of real effective exchange rates: a survey and applications to East Asia', in DeBrouwer, G. and Kawai, M. (eds), *Exchange Rate Regimes in East Asia*, Routledge, forthcoming.

Chinn, M.D. (1997), 'Sectoral productivity, government spending and real exchange rates: empirical evidence for OECD countries', NBER Working Paper no. 6017.

Chortareas, G.E. and Driver, R.L. (2001), 'PPP and the real exchange rate-real interest rate differential puzzle revisited: evidence from nonstationary panel data', Bank of England Discussion Paper no. 138.

Christensen, M. (2000), 'Uncovered interest parity and policy behaviour: new evidence', *Economics Letters*, 69: 81–87.

Clarida, R.H. and Gali, J. (1994), 'Sources of real exchange rate fluctuations: how important are nominal shocks?', *Carnegie Rochester Series of Public Policy*, 41: 1–56.

Clark, P.B. and MacDonald, R. (2000), 'Filtering the BEER: a permanent and transitory decomposition', IMF Working Paper no. WP/00/144.

Clark, P.B. and MacDonald, R. (1999), 'Exchange rates and economic fundamentals: a methodological comparison of BEERs and FEERs', in MacDonald, R. and Stein, J. (eds), *Equilibrium Exchange Rates*, Boston: Kluwer Academic Publishers.

Clark, P.B. and MacDonald, R. (1997), 'Exchange rates and economic fundamentals: a methodological comparison of BEERs and FEERs', Paper presented at Conference on Exchange Rates, Strathclyde University.

Clostermann, J. and Schnatz, B. (2000), 'The determinants of the euro–dollar exchange rate: synthetic fundamentals and a nonexisting currency', Deutsche Bundesbank Discussion Paper no. 2/00.

Coakley, J. and Fuertes, A.M. (1997), 'New panel unit root tests of PPP', *Economics Letters*, 57: 17–22.

Cumby, P. and Huizinga, J. (1990), 'The predictability of real exchange rate changes in the short run and the long run', NBER Working Paper no. 3468.

Currie, D. and Wren-Lewis, S. (1989a), 'An appraisal of alternative blueprints for international policy coordination', *European Economic Review*, 33: 1769–1785.

Currie, D. and Wren-Lewis, S. (1989b), 'Evaluating blueprints for the conduct of international macro policy', *American Economic Review*, 79(2): 264–269.

De Grauwe, P. and Grimaldi, M. (2002), 'The exchange rate and its fundamentals in a complex world', Paper presented at CCBS Workshop on Capital Flows, June 2002.

Detken, C., Dieppe, A., Henry, J., Marin, C. and Smets, F. (2002), 'Model uncertainties and the equilibrium value of the real effective euro exchange rate', European Central Bank Working Paper no. 160.

Devereux, M.B. (1998), 'Real exchange rate trends and growth: a model of East Asia', *Review of International Economics*, 7: 509–521.

Devereux, M.B. and Engel, C. (2002), 'Exchange rate pass-through, exchange rate volatility, and exchange rate disconnect', *Journal of Monetary Economics*, 49: 913–940.

Dornbusch, R. (1976), 'Expectations and exchange rate dynamics', *Journal of Political Economy*, 84: 1161–1176.

Driver, R.L. and Wren-Lewis, S. (1999), 'FEERs: a sensitivity analysis', in MacDonald, R. and Stein, J. (eds), *Equilibrium Exchange Rates*, Boston: Kluwer Academic Publishers.

Dumas, B. (1992), 'Dynamic equilibrium and the real exchange rate in a spatially separated world', *Review of Financial Studies*, 5(2): 153–180.

Dvornak, N., Kohler, M. and Menzies, G. (2003), 'Australia's medium-run exchange rate: a macroeconomic balance approach', Reserve Bank of Australia Research Discussion Paper no. 2003-03.

Égert, B. (2003), 'Assessing equilibrium exchange rates in CEE acceding countries: can we have DEER with BEER without FEER? A critical survey of the literature', Oesterreichische Nationalbank, *Focus on Transition*, 2/2003: 38–106.

Engel, C. (1993), 'Real exchange rates and relative prices: an empirical investigation', *Journal of Monetary Economics*, 32: 35–50.

Engel, C. and Rogers, J. (1996), 'How wide is the border?', *American Economic Review*, 86: 1112–1125.

Faruqee, H. and Debelle, G. (1998), 'Saving-investment balances in industrialised countries: an empirical investigation', in Isard, P. and Faruqee, H. (eds), *Exchange Rate Assessment: Extensions to the Macroeconomic Balance Approach*, IMF Occasional Paper no. 167.

Faust, J., Rogers, J.H., Wang, S.-Y.B. and Wright, J.H. (2003), 'The high-frequency response of exchange rates and interest rates to macroeconomic announcements', Federal Reserve Board, International Finance Discussion Paper no. 784.

Finn, M.G. (1999), 'An equilibrium theory of nominal and real exchange rate comovement', *Journal of Monetary Economics*, 44: 453–475.

Flood, R.P. and Rose, A.K. (2001), 'Uncovered interest parity in crisis: the interest rate defense in the 1990s', IMF Working Paper no. WP/01/207.

Frankel, J.A. (1996), 'Recent exchange-rate experience and proposals for reform', *American Economic Review*, 86(2): 153–158.

Frankel, J.A. (1993), *On Exchange Rates*, Cambridge, MA: MIT Press.

Frankel, J.A. and Rose, A.K. (1996), 'A panel project on purchasing power parity: mean reversion within and between countries', *Journal of International Economics*, 40: 209–224.

Frankel, J.A. and Rose, A.K. (1995), 'Empirical research on nominal exchange rates', in Grossman, G.M. and Rogoff, K. (eds), *The Handbook of International Economics, Volume 3*, Amsterdam: Elsevier Science Publishers B.V.

Frenkel, J. (1976), 'A monetary approach to the exchange rate: doctrinal aspects and empirical evidence', *Scandinavian Journal of Economics*, 78: 200–224.

Frenkel, J.A. and Goldstein, M. (1986), 'A guide to target zones', *IMF Staff Papers*, 33: 633–673.

Froot, K.A. and Rogoff, K. (1995), 'Perspectives on PPP and long-run real exchange rates', in Grossman, G.M. and Rogoff, K. (eds), *The Handbook of International Economics, Volume 3*, North-Holland: Elsevier Science Publishers B.V.

Gonzalo, J. and Granger, C. (1995), 'Estimation of common long-memory components in cointegrated systems', *Journal of Business and Economic Statistics*, 13: 27–35.

Groen, J.J.J. (2000), 'The monetary exchange rate model as a long-run phenomenon', *Journal of International Economics*, 52: 299–319.

Hansen, J. and Roeger, W. (2000), 'Estimation of real equilibrium exchange rates', European Commission, Economic Papers no. 144.

Haskel, J. and Wolfe, H. (2001), 'The law of one price: a case study', *Scandinavian Journal of Economics*, 103: 545–558.

Huizinga, J. (1987), 'An empirical investigation of the long run behaviour of real exchange rates', *Carnegie Rochester Conference Series on Public Policy*, 27: 149–214.

Jeanne, O. and Rose, A.K. (2002), 'Noise trading and exchange rate regimes', *Quarterly Journal of Economics*, 117: 537–569.

Johansen, S. and Juselius, K. (1992), 'Testing structural hypotheses in a multivariate cointegration analysis of the PPP and the UIP for the UK', *Journal of Econometrics*, 53: 211–244.

Juselius, K. and MacDonald, R. (2000), 'International parity relationships between Germany and the United States: a joint modelling approach', Institute of Economics, University of Copenhagen, mimeo.

Kilian, L. and Taylor, M.P. (2003), 'Why is it so difficult to beat the random walk forecast of exchange rates?', *Journal of International Economics*, 60: 85–107.

Kim, S. (2001), 'International transmission of US monetary policy shocks: evidence from VARs', *Journal of Monetary Economics*, 48: 339–372.

Koen, V., Boone, L., de Serres, A. and Fuchs, N. (2001), 'Tracking the euro', OECD Economics Department Working Paper no. 298.

Kohler, M. (2000), 'The Balassa–Samuelson effect and monetary targets', in Mahadeva, L. and Sterne, G. (eds), *Monetary Policy Frameworks in a Global Context*, London: Routledge.

Krugman, P.R. (2000), 'How complicated does the model have to be?', *Oxford Review of Economic Policy*, 16(4): 33–42.

Krugman, P.R. (1987), 'Pricing-to-markets when the exchange rate changes', in Arndt, S.W. and Richardson, J.D. (eds), *Real Financial Linkages among Open Economies*, Cambridge MA: MIT Press.

Labhard, V. and Westaway, P. (2002), 'What is shocking exchange rates', Paper presented at the European Economic Association Conference, Venice.

Lane, P.R. (2001), 'The new open economy macroeconomics: a survey', *Journal of International Economics*, 54: 235–266.

Lewis, K.K. (1995), 'Puzzles in international financial markets', in Grossman, G.M. and Rogoff, K. (eds), *The Handbook of International Economics, Volume 3*, North-Holland: Elsevier Science Publishers B.V.

Lim, G.C. and Stein, J.L. (1995), 'The dynamics of the real exchange rate and current account in a small open economy: Australia', in Stein, J.L. and Allen, P.R (eds), *Fundamental Determinants of Exchange Rates*, Oxford: Clarendon Press.

MacDonald, R. (2000), 'Concepts to calculate equilibrium exchange rates: an overview', Economic Research Group of the Deutsche Bundesbank Discussion Paper no. 3/00.

MacDonald, R. (1999), 'What determines real exchange rates? The long and the short of it', in MacDonald, R. and Stein, J. (eds), *Equilibrium Exchange Rates*, Boston: Kluwer Academic Publishers.

MacDonald, R. (1996), 'Panel unit root tests and real exchange rates', *Economic Letters*, 50: 7–11.

MacDonald, R. (1995), 'Long-run exchange rate modelling: a survey of the recent evidence', *IMF Staff Papers*, 42(3): 437–489.

MacDonald, R. and Marsh, I.W. (1997), 'On casselian PPP, cointegration and exchange rate forecasting', *Review of Economics and Statistics*, 79: 655–664.

MacDonald, R. and Swagel, P. (2000), 'Real exchange rates and the business cycle', IMF Working Paper, forthcoming.

MacDonald, R. and Taylor, M.P. (1992), 'Exchange rate economics: a survey', *IMF Staff Papers*, 39: 1–57.

Maeso-Fernandez, F., Osbat, C. and Schnatz, B. (2001), 'Determinants of the euro real effective exchange rate: a BEER/PEER approach', European Central Bank Working Paper no. 85.

Mark, N. (1995), 'Exchange rates and fundamentals: evidence on long horizon predictability', *American Economic Review*, 85: 201–218.

Marsh, I.W. and Tokarick, S.P. (1994), 'Competitiveness indicators: a theoretical and empirical assessment', IMF Working Paper no. WP/94/29.

Marshall, A. (1890), *Principles of Economics*, London: Macmillan.

Masson, P. (1998), 'A globally consistent conceptual framework', in Isard, P. and Faruqee, H. (eds), *Exchange Rate Assessment: Extensions to the Macroeconomic Balance Approach*, IMF Occasional Paper no. 167.

McCallum, B.T. (1994), 'A reconsideration of the uncovered interest parity relationship', *Journal of Monetary Economics*, 33: 105–132.

Meese, R. and Rogoff, K. (1983), 'Empirical exchange rate models of the seventies: do they fit out of sample?', *Journal of International Economics*, 14: 3–24.

Michael, P., Nobay, A.R. and Peel, D.A. (1997), 'Transactions costs and nonlinear adjustment in real exchange rates: an empirical investigation', *Journal of Political Economy*, 105(4): 862–879.

Milgate, M. (1998), 'Equilibrium: development of the concept', in Eatwell, J.,

Milgate, M. and Newman, P. (eds), *The New Palgrave: A Dictionary of Economics*, Basingstoke, UK: Macmillan Press.

Murray, C.J. and Papell, D.H. (2002), 'The purchasing power parity persistence paradigm', *Journal of International Economics*, 56: 1–19.

Niehans, J. (1994), 'Elusive capital flows: recent literature in perspective', *Journal of International and Comparative Economics*, 3: 21–43.

Noussair, C.N., Plott, C.R. and Riezman, R.G. (1997), 'The principles of exchange rate determination in an international finance experiment', *Journal of Political Economy*, 105(4): 822–861.

Obstfeld, M. (2002), 'Exchange rates and adjustment: perspectives from the new open economy macroeconomics', University of California, Berkeley, mimeo.

Obstfeld, M. and Rogoff, K. (2000), 'The six major puzzles in international macroeconomics: is there a common cause?', NBER Working Paper no. 7777.

Obstfeld, M. and Rogoff, K. (1996), *Foundations of International Macroeconomics*, Cambridge, MA: MIT Press.

Obstfeld, M. and Rogoff, K. (1995), 'Exchange rate dynamics redux', *Journal of Political Economy*, 103: 624–660.

O'Connell, P.G.J. (1998), 'The overvaluation of purchasing power parity', *Journal of International Economics*, 44: 1–19.

Oh, K.-Y. (1996), 'Purchasing power parity and unit root tests using panel data', *Journal of International Money and Finance*, 15: 405–418.

Osbat, C., Rüffer, R. and Schnatz, B. (2003), 'The rise of the yen vis-à-vis the ("synthetic") euro: is it supported by economic fundamentals?', European Central Bank Working Paper no. 224.

Pagan, A. (2003), 'Report on modelling and forecasting at the Bank of England', *Bank of England Quarterly Bulletin*, 43(1): 60–88.

Papell, D.H. (1997), 'Searching for stationarity: purchasing power parity under the current float', *Journal of International Economics*, 43: 313–332.

Rapach, D.E. and Wohar, M.E. (2002), 'Testing the monetary model of exchange rate determination: new evidence from a century of data', *Journal of International Economics*, 58: 359–385.

Rogers, J.H. and Jenkins, M. (1995), 'Haircuts or hysteresis? Sources of movements in real exchange rates', *Journal of International Economics*, 38: 339–360.

Rogoff, K. (2002), 'Dornbusch's overshooting model after twenty-five years', IMF Working Paper no. WP/02/39.

Rogoff, K. (2001), 'The failure of empirical exchange rate models: no longer new, but still true', *Economic Policy* Web Essay.

Rogoff, K. (1996), 'The purchasing power parity puzzle', *Journal of Economic Literature*, 34: 647–668.

Schmitt-Grohe, S. and Uribe, M. (2003), 'Closing small open economy models', *Journal of International Economics*, 61: 163–185.

Schnatz, B., Vijselaar, F. and Osbat, C. (2003), 'Productivity and the ("synthetic") euro–dollar exchange rate', European Central Bank Working Paper no. 225.

Stein, J.L. (1994), 'The natural real exchange rate of the US dollar and determinants of capital flows', in Williamson, J. (ed.), *Estimating Equilibrium Exchange Rates*, Washington, DC: Institute of International Economics.

Stein, J.L. and Allen, P.R. (1995), 'Fundamental determinants of exchange rates', Oxford: Clarendon Press.

Stein, J.L. and Paladino, G. (1998), 'Recent developments in international finance: a guide to research', *Journal of Banking and Finance*, 21: 1685–1720.

Taylor, M.P. (1995), 'Exchange-rate behaviour under alternative exchange rate arrangements', in Kenen, P.B. (ed.), *Understanding Interdependence: the Macroeconomics of the Open Economy*, Princeton: Princeton University Press.

Taylor, M.P. and Allen, H. (1992), 'The use of technical analysis in the foreign exchange market', *Journal of International Money and Finance*, 11: 304–314.

Taylor, M.P., Peel, D.A. and Sarno, L. (2001), 'Nonlinear mean-reversion in real exchange rates: towards a solution to the purchasing power parity puzzles', *International Economic Review*, 42: 1015–1042.

Von Neumann, J. and Morgenstern, O. (1944), *Theory of Games and Economic Behavior*, Princeton: Princeton University Press.

Wadhwani, S.B. (1999), 'Currency puzzles', Speech delivered at the LSE, 16 September.

Williamson, J. (1994), 'Estimates of FEERs', in Williamson, J. (ed.), *Estimating Equilibrium Exchange Rates*, Washington, DC: Institute for International Economics.

Williamson, J. (1993), 'Exchange rate management', *Economic Journal*, 103: 188–197.

Williamson, J. (1983, *revised* 1985), 'The exchange rate system', Institute of International Economics, Washington, DC: Policy Analyses in International Economics no. 5.

Williamson, J. and Mahar, M. (1998), 'Current account targets', in Wren-Lewis, S. and Driver, R.L. (eds), 'Real exchange rates for the year 2000', Institute for International Economics, Washington, DC: Policy Analyses in International Economics no. 54.

Williamson, J. and Miller, M. (1987), 'Targets and indicators: a blueprint for the international coordination of economic policy', Institute for International Economics, Washington, DC: Policy Analyses in International Economics no. 22.

Wren-Lewis, S. (2003), 'Estimates of equilibrium exchange rates for sterling against the euro', *H.M. Treasury, EMU Study*, London: HM Treasury.

Wren-Lewis, S. (1992), 'On the analytical foundations of the fundamental equilibrium exchange rate', in Hargreaves C.P. (ed.), *Macroeconomic Modelling of the Long Run*, Aldershot, Hants: Edward Elgar.

Wren-Lewis, S. and Driver, R.L. (1998), 'Real exchange rates for the year 2000', Institute for International Economics, Washington, DC: Policy Analyses in International Economics no. 54.

Wren-Lewis, S., Westaway, P., Soteri, S. and Barrell, R. (1991), 'Evaluating the UK's choice of entry rate into the ERM', *Manchester School*, 59 (Supplement): 1–22.

7 Fundamental equilibrium exchange rates and currency boards

Evidence from Argentina and Estonia in the 1990s

*Kalin Hristov**

1 Introduction

Over the last decade of the twentieth century currency boards regained popularity. Initially seen as a colonial monetary regime applicable only to very small, open and well integrated countries, currency boards made a come back, becoming popular in both small- and medium-size economies. There are two different explanations of the revival of currency boards in the 1990s.

First, proponents of currency boards say that the revival of this monetary regime is part of a global tendency of hollowing out of the middle part of the distribution of exchange rate regimes. As intermediate regimes become unsustainable, countries move towards either flexible exchange rates or hard exchange rate commitments (Hanke and Schuler 1999).[1] These authors regard currency boards as a permanent means of achieving a stable monetary standard. According to this view currency boards ensure monetary discipline and instil confidence in the domestic currency and indeed provide important anti-inflationary benefits. In addition currency boards are successful in maintaining high growth and low inflation. This explanation of the revival of currency boards regards them as a permanent monetary regime.

The second, explains revival of currency boards with their ability to stabilise economies, which have a long history of monetary instability or lack the institutions and expertise to conduct independent monetary policy. Indeed the adoption of a currency board is a solution for countries in transition from a centrally planned to a market economy (Estonia and Lithuania); which desperately need to import monetary stability due to the history of hyperinflation or absence of stable institutions (Argentina and Bulgaria); or who are in the process of post-war reconstruction (Bosnia and Herzegovina). This explanation views currency boards as a transitory monetary regime. Once the economy is stabilised and credibility in the national currency and monetary authority is rebuilt, the country needs to find an exit strategy from the existing currency board arrangement. The reason for this is that currency board arrangements are very rigid. Since the nominal exchange rate is irrevocably fixed, changes in the real exchange rate can only take place through differential price movements. Such adjustment is likely to be slow and partial (if prices and wages are sticky), which could lead to continuous overvaluation of the real exchange rate. This exchange rate misalignment implies a loss of competitiveness, a worsening current account balance and eventually speculative attacks and a collapse of the fixed exchange rate. Countries should therefore follow different exit strategies in order to avoid the collapse of the fixed exchange rate. Exit can be to a simple peg to the same or to a different currency, and at the same or different parity; to a floating rate; or to a different monetary standard including joining monetary union or adopting foreign currency as legal tender. For the Central and Eastern European countries which have currency boards the path of exchange rate regime transition looks predetermined. Baltic countries (Estonia and Lithuania) joined the EU in the beginning of 2004 and Bulgaria is in a process of negotiations and expects to become a member of the EU in 2007. Since new member countries can not use an opt-out clause, eventually they have to join EMU.

On joining EMU, currency board countries will need to decide at what parities to enter the monetary union (Gulde *et al.* 2000). One option is to stick to the current parity and to join monetary union at the existing rate. This means that they will need to quantify their equilibrium exchange rate and the deviation from this rate to assess whether the current parity would be sustainable. If it is overvalued, then for some years inflation will be lower than in other member states, and output growth will be sluggish. If the current parity is undervalued then for some years inflation in the economy will be higher than in the other members of the monetary union and output growth will be buoyant, and there may be some permanent gain in market share. In evaluating risk these countries need to know the sustainable rate between the euro and the dollar, and that this is independent from their policies.

Another option is to change the current parity in the order to narrow the gap between the equilibrium real exchange rate and the current level of the real exchange rate. This change could be done when they enter ERM II. Since ERM II is a multilateral commitment to fix the exchange rate within a 15 per cent band, the change in the parity might not lead to loss of credibility and currency crisis.

There was intense discussion about whether Central and Eastern European countries should adopt the euro as legal tender before joining EU (euroisation). Since euroisation is practically irreversible these countries would have to choose very carefully the level of the exchange rate at which they adopt the euro as legal tender.

The collapse of Argentina's currency board at the end of 2001 intensified the discussion on sustainability of currency board arrangements and possible exit strategies from this monetary regime. Many things contributed to the collapse of Argentine currency board, but overall there are two main explanations. First, the chronic inability of the Argentine authorities to run a responsible fiscal policy was the fundamental cause of economic disaster (Mussa 2002). The ratio of total public debt to GDP in Argentina rose from 29.2 per cent to 41.4 per cent between 1993 and 1998 and to 53.7 per cent at the end of 2001. "During 1993–98, when the Argentine economy was generally performing very well and the government was receiving substantial non-recurring revenues from privatisation and enjoyed other temporary fiscal benefits, the public sector debt to GDP ratio nevertheless rose by 12.2 percentage points."[2] Between 1999 and 2001 when economy went into recession the debt to GDP ratio rose by an additional 12.3 percentage points. These facts were a signal of unsustainable fiscal policy. Much of Argentina's fiscal problems arose from inadequate fiscal discipline in the provinces for which the central government ultimately had to take responsibility. Indeed, the Argentine system – enshrined in the Constitution and in decades of practice – was fundamentally where the provinces retained much of the initiative and incentive for public spending, but the responsibility for raising of revenue and payment of debt was passed off largely to the central government.

Second, a more conventional explanation stresses the rigidity of the currency board system and accumulated overvaluation of the peso due to higher inflation in Argentina than in the USA. The overvaluation of the peso, the strong dollar and continuous devaluation of Argentina's main trade partners undermined the competitiveness of its exports and exerted a negative effect on growth.

In this chapter we estimate equilibrium exchange rates for Argentina and Estonia and calculate misalignments of the exchange rates in order to address the issue of sustainability of these currency boards, possible path of transition for the exchange rate regimes and to answer whether misalignment of the peso was the main cause of the collapse of the Argentine currency board.

The plan of the chapter is as follows. Section 2 provides a short discussion of the appropriate methodology for estimating equilibrium exchange rates and the definition of the real exchange rate. Section 3 provides an explanation of the assumptions underlying the calculation of fundamental equilibrium exchange rate. The results are presented in section 4. Section 5 offers some brief conclusions.

2 Which measure of equilibrium?

In this chapter we try to address two related questions. First, does the adoption of a currency board arrangement lead to a prolonged appreciation of the real exchange rate and big misalignments, which affect the country's export competitiveness and growth performance? Second, we try to calculate quantitative measures of the deviation of real exchange rates from equilibrium, which will give us valuable information about possible channels of correction of cumulated misalignments.

To find answers to these questions we need a concept of equilibrium real exchange rates against which to measure actual exchange rate changes. Traditionally the purchasing power parity (PPP) doctrine is viewed as a model of the long-term real exchange rate. Under PPP the equilibrium real exchange rate is a constant. Recent studies, which emphasise purchasing power parity as a long-term concept, allow short-term deviation from the equilibrium rate. In this case the real exchange rate need only be stationary rather than a constant. Stationarity implies that the real exchange rate returns to its mean in the long term. The mean is considered to be the long-term equilibrium real exchange rate, which is fixed. Thus the model of long-term PPP admits changes in the real exchange rate, but not in its mean.

The chapter by Driver and Westaway in this volume present the theoretical explanations for why PPP might not hold in practice providing reasons why the equilibrium exchange rate might not be constant. Factors described by them all show the need for a richer model of equilibrium real exchange rate.

Given existing shortcomings of the PPP in this chapter we utilise an alternative concept of the equilibrium real exchange rate. The underlying balance methodology addresses the issue of the relationship between equilibrium real exchange rates and macroeconomic fundamentals. This approach expresses the equilibrium exchange rate in terms of fundamental variables.[3] The most popular and widely applied in empirical work on the underlying balance model is the fundamental equilibrium exchange rate (FEER) approach. The concept of FEERs was introduced by Williamson (1983). It is the real exchange rate, which is consistent with internal and external equilibrium of the economy. Within this framework internal equilibrium is a situation where demand for domestic output is equal to its supply. This implies that there will be no output gap either in the domestic economy or abroad. External balance is defined as a position where saving minus investment in the economy is at a sustainable level. The definition of external balance does not imply that the economy has to achieve full stock-flow equilibrium, where net foreign assets are constant and sustainable current account is equal to zero. The FEER is therefore a medium-term rather than long-term concept of equilibrium exchange rates. The medium-term nature of the FEER is consistent with a neutrality assumption that implies that the real economy will be independent of nominal variables. Therefore the FEER is a real exchange rate, which is consistent with a range of combinations of nominal exchange rates and prices.

Before moving to the next section, which explains in detail the methodology applied to estimate equilibrium exchange rates, we need to clarify which measure of real exchange rate will be used as a basis for the FEER calculations. The measure needs to be a multilateral real exchange rate construction, as the FEER represents equilibrium in the whole economy. This choice implies that we will estimate multilateral equilibrium exchange rates and cannot derive bilateral equilibrium exchange rates directly. It is possible to back out the associated bilateral equilibrium exchange rates if estimates of equilibrium exchange rates are also available for the country's main trade partners.[4] Since we estimate FEERs only for two countries (Argentina and Estonia) this does not allow us to back out estimates of bilateral exchange rates. In terms of the price indices used for the construction of the real exchange rate we used indices which focus on traded good prices.

The definition of real exchange rate used in this chapter is given by:

$$R = \frac{WPXG^*r}{PD}$$

Where r is the nominal exchange rate (local currency per US dollar), $WPXG$ is world export price in US dollars and PD is domestic price expressed in domestic currency, given by producer price. An increase in R represents depreciation. This is the definition of the real exchange rate used in most of the existing work on fundamental equilibrium exchange rates.[5]

Using this definition of the real exchange rate allows us to abstract from the Balassa–Samuelson effect, which accounts for productivity differentials between traded and nontraded sectors of the economy. Since there is substantial empirical support for the Balassa–Samuelson effect, especially in comparisons between developed and developing countries, the choice of real exchange rate definition that excludes nontraded goods will significantly affect our estimation of FEERs for currency board countries.[6] Figures 7.9 and 7.10 in Appendix C show the real effective exchange rates and R for Argentina and Estonia.

3 Calculating FEERs

There are two main approaches to estimating FEERs. The first uses a complete macroeconomic model and generates the FEER as a solution to that model. This can be done with a single country model, under given assumption about the rest of the world or a multicountry model.[7] The main advantage of this approach is that it derives estimates of the equilibrium exchange rate, which are consistent with all macroeconomic variables. However it can sometimes lack transparency. The second and most widely used method to calculate FEERs takes a partial equilibrium approach. The approach estimates trend output and sustainable current accounts separately and solves for the real exchange rate which is consistent with these estimates. The main advantage of this approach is its simplicity and clarity. It allows one to identify the factors that particularly affect the FEER estimation and permits different sensitivity tests.[8] The disadvantage of the partial equilibrium approach is that there is no model that ensures consistency between estimates of trend output and the sustainable current account. In addition this approach does not allow for any feedback from the FEER to the inputs for trend output and saving minus investment relationships. This implies that trend output and saving minus investment influence FEER, but there is no feedback from the equilibrium exchange rate to the rest of the model.[9]

Since we do not have complete macroeconomic models for the countries of interest we are going to use the "partial-equilibrium" model following the Barrell and Wren-Lewis (1989) and Wren-Lewis and Driver (1998) methodologies to estimate FEERs.

The methodology applied in this chapter for the calculation of FEERs can be broken down in three stages. Each of these stages illustrates the importance of the assumptions made about external and internal equilibrium of the economy. The first stage is to calculate the trend current account, which differs from actual current account. The difference between the actual and trend current account depends on the accuracy of the model of trade equations and IPD flows and estimation of the output gap. The difference between actual and predicted trade flows can be described as an outcome of shocks, which are viewed as temporary shocks and can be stripped out in calculations of the trend current account. Then we use the estimated trade equations to calculate what exports and imports would have been if output were equal to potential output (zero output gap). This allows us to derive a trend current account that is consistent with existence of internal balance within economy.[10] The first stage shows what the medium current account would be if the real exchange rate remained unchanged. However the real exchange rate must move to clear the balance of payments, so the trend current account matches the medium-term sustainable current account. A critical element in estimating FEER is the assumption of the medium-term sustainable current account (also called structural capital flows if we look from the capital account point of view).[11] The second stage involves calculation of a sustainable level of current account that corresponds to the external equilibrium of the economy. The final stage involves calculation of the real exchange rate that produces medium-term current account, which is equal to sustainable current account (structural capital flows) (see Appendix A for a full equation listing for the model of the current account).

3.1 Modelling aggregate trade

Trade is disaggregated into eight components: prices and quantities of imports and exports of goods and services. Trade volumes are modelled in traditional "demand curve" approach. This approach has a long tradition in empirical macroeconomics and remains the standard way of modelling trade flows.[12] There are three arguments in trade volume equation: a measure of the total demand, a measure of competitiveness, and an exogenous time trend. The functional form is the traditional log-linear specification. We use domestic income as the variable which captures the impact of activity for both goods and services imports. For goods exports we use world trade, while for services exports we use world income approximated by OECD real GDP. Export competitiveness is measured by the ratio of world trade prices converted in domestic currency and domestic export prices. Import competitiveness is measured by real exchange rate defined as a ratio of world trade prices expressed in domestic currency and domestic producer prices. Export and import competitiveness for services is captured by the real exchange rate for services defined as a ratio of world consumer prices (approximated by OECD consumer prices) and domestic consumer prices multiplied by nominal effective exchange rate.

The estimation technique, which we apply, is a simple error correction mechanism (ECM). As we are not interested in short-term dynamics (FEERs are a medium-term concept) it would be preferable to use cointegration techniques. Since our sample is quite short (1993:Q1–2001:Q4) we do not test for cointegration for trade volumes. A crucial ingredient in the estimation of an ECM is the assumption that the term capturing the disequilibrium effect is correctly specified. If estimation of the ECM does not produce residuals that are stationary it might be because the levels of variables are not cointegrated, and this in turn may be because a variable had been inadvertently omitted. To control this we perform a variety of diagnostic tests to check for misspecification in the equations. These tests are for serial correlation, functional form, normality and heteroskedasticity.[13] Results from this estimation are reported in Appendix B.

Price elasticities have a big impact on the FEER calculations because their size determines how much the real exchange rate has to change in order to bring economy into internal and external balance. Higher price elasticities mean that smaller changes in real exchange rate are needed in order to correct disequilibrium. In the extreme case, where price elasticities are infinite, the equilibrium real exchange rate is a constant and PPP holds.

Theoretically the Marshall–Lerner condition is regarded as the dividing line for the size of price elasticities. It requires the sum of the price elasticities for imports and exports volumes (in absolute terms) to be greater than unity. Under this condition the nominal trade balance (in domestic currency) will improve following a depreciation of the real exchange rate.[14] For both countries the results for goods exports and imports show that the Marshall–Lerner condition is satisfied (see Table 7.1). For Argentina we found higher elasticities for goods imports and exports prices than for Estonia. These relatively high price elasticities imply that for a given change in saving-investment norm relatively small changes in the FEER will be needed to reach a new equilibrium.

In both cases the prices elasticities with respect of services exports and

Table 7.1 Normalised elasticity estimates for goods exports and imports

	Argentina	Estonia
Export		
Price elasticity	−1.4	0.85
Income elasticity	3.4	3.8
Import		
Price elasticity	−3.9	−1.2
Income elasticity	2.2	3.5

imports are relatively low. Exception is the price elasticity of Argentina's services export (see Table 7.2).

Activity elasticities give the amount by which trade volumes respond to a change in output. If they are greater than one then this implies that trade volumes will be rising as a proportion of associated activity variable. Activity elasticities play an important role in the determination of the FEER because they transmit changes in the potential output into changes of the equilibrium exchange rate. A change in potential output at home will trigger changes in the FEER (for an unchanged level of sustainable current account) and the size of these changes will be determined by the size of the activity elasticities of trade volume. The higher the activity elasticities are then the bigger the resulting change in the trend current account for a given change in potential output. In other words the size of the change in the FEER associated with a change in trend output is increasing function of the size of the activity elasticities.

The activity variable associated with goods import volumes is given by domestic output. No restrictions are imposed on this elasticity. Export goods volumes are modelled as a function of world trade. Any prior belief in unit elasticity is not supported by the data. In both countries (Argentina and Estonia) the estimated activity elasticities are much bigger than unity. This makes FEER very sensitive to changes in trend output at home and abroad and to world trade. For Estonia the estimated activity elasticities are higher than for Argentina, which reflects the fact that Estonia is smaller and a more open economy.

Table 7.2 Normalised elasticity estimates for services exports and imports

	Argentina	Estonia
Export		
Price elasticity	−1.6	0.4
Income elasticity	4.9	3.8
Import		
Price elasticity	−0.1	−0.4
Income elasticity	2.5	3.0

In the case of services exports and imports the activity variables are given by domestic output and world output respectively. No restrictions are imposed on the associated activity elasticities.

Trade prices are modelled separately for goods and services. Goods prices are divided into two groups: commodity prices and manufacturing prices.

Commodity prices are broken down into four categories: oil prices, food prices, world agricultural non-food prices and world metals and mineral prices. Commodity prices for imports and exports are defined as a weighted function of these four commodity prices groups, where country specific weights are based on the relevant shares of commodity exports and imports in total trade. Coefficients A_1 and B_1 give the share of all commodities within total goods exports and imports, respectively. Data are derived from the UNCTAD Handbook of International Trade and Development Statistics and for each country the totals are for 1995 (see Table 7.3).

Manufacturing export and import prices are modelled as a weighted average of world export prices and domestic producer prices. The elasticities for import and export prices to world trade prices are obtained using an error-correction mechanism model. In each case, the models are estimated using quarterly data from 1993:Q1 to 2001:Q4. Results of estimated and chosen price elasticities to world trade prices are presented in Table 7.4. In the case of Argentina we found an estimate for the elasticity of

Table 7.3 Coefficients on commodity prices

	Argentina	Estonia
Exports: B_1	0.66	0.32
Oil: b_1	0.16	0.18
Food: b_2	0.75	0.48
Non-food: b_3	0.07	0.26
Metals: b_4	0.02	0.08
Imports: A_1	0.14	0.29
Oil: a_1	0.29	0.33
Food: a_2	0.40	0.54
Non-food: a_3	0.14	0.09
Metals: a_4	0.17	0.04

Table 7.4 The impact of world prices within trade price equations

	Import prices		Export prices	
	Estimated A_2	Chosen A_2	Estimated B_2	Chosen B_2
Argentina	1.09	1.0	0.44	0.44
Estonia	0.55	0.55	0.15	1.0

import prices to world trade prices, which is slightly higher than 1. In this case we impose coefficient of 1. The estimate for the elasticity of Estonian export prices to world trade prices is very low. This result implies that Estonia's exports are composed of goods whose prices are independent of world export prices. The evidence of the structure of Estonian exports does not seem to support the view of that the country exports goods whose prices are independent of world trade prices. Taking into account the fact that Estonia is very small and open economy, we impose export price elasticity to world trade prices of 1.

For trade in services, export prices are assumed to be identical to domestic consumer prices and import prices to OECD consumer prices.

In addition to the trade price equations, we also assume simple relations between domestic GDP deflators and domestic producer prices; domestic consumer prices and domestic producer prices; world consumer prices and world trade prices (specifications of these relationships are given in Appendix A3).

Since the current account is not only made up of net trade flows we need to model interest, profit and dividend flows and net transfers.

In this chapter we take IPD flows as exogenous because over the historical period, actual foreign assets and liabilities will determine IPD flows. If we assume that foreign assets are denominated in foreign currency then IPD credits will be in foreign currency (this is a plausible assumption for both Argentina and Estonia). On the other side, if foreign liabilities are denominated in domestic currency, then IPD debits will be in domestic currency. Here we assume that foreign liabilities are also denominated in foreign currency.[15] When these flows are denominated in foreign currency we need to allow for exchange rate revaluation effects since changes in real exchange rate will affect IPD flows. We also smooth the series for IPD flows using a four-quarter moving average. An equation describing the balance of IPD flows as a proportion of GDP is presented in Appendix A6.

Net transfers are modelled simply as an exogenous variable with trend, and are expressed as a proportion of GDP (in Appendix A5 we present equation for net transfers).

3.2 *Estimating the trend output*

An important element of estimation of FEERs is the calculation of trend output. Since the FEER is a concept, which is compatible with exogenously determined values for internal balance, we need to model potential output in order to set output gaps (at home and abroad) to zero. In the literature three different methodologies are widely used for estimation of potential output and output gap.[16] The first two approaches are based on mechanical times series smoothing of GDP series. These are the time trend method and the Hodrick–Prescott filter. Estimates of potential output and output gaps derived by these two techniques use no information about the structure of the economy or economic inter-relationships. The third approach is based on a Cobb–Douglas production function constructed by using a measure of equilibrium unemployment and the whole economy capital stock. This structural framework is less mechanical and reflects structural factors, which affect potential output. The disadvantage is that the production function estimation of potential output demand data for capital stock within the whole economy and the measure of potential employment, which in most cases are unavailable for developing countries.

In this chapter we use time series approach for estimation of the trend output and output gap. Trend output is modelled as exogenous with a time trend, and is given by:

$$Y = \lambda_0 e^{\lambda_1 T}$$

Where λ_0 is a measure of trend GDP for a given period (in the case of this chapter, 1995) and is equal to actual GDP plus output gap; λ_1 is a measure of potential output growth and T is time trend (1995:Q1 = 0).

As an alternative to the time trend method we use the HP filter to calculate trend output and the output gap. In general, the results produced by the HP filter method for trend output and the output gap are very similar to that produced by the time trend method. The difference is that at the end of the sample the HP filter method generates a level of trend output, which is slightly higher than that produced by time trend method. In the calculation of the trend current account we prefer to use trend output estimations generated by time trend method as the HP filter suffers from a well-known end point problem. We apply this method to calculate domestic trend output, world trend output and trend world trade. In Appendix C we present estimated output gaps for Argentina and Estonia using time trend method (see Figures 7.7 and 7.8).

Once we have estimates of trend output and trend world trade we use the estimated trade equations to calculate the levels of exports and imports when there is no output gap at home and abroad. The trend current account obtained is consistent with internal balance within economy.

3.3 Estimating sustainable current account

In order to estimate FEERs, we need a measure of the sustainable level of the current account, or in other words the level of the current account that corresponds to external balance. Since the notion of sustainability in the FEERs calculation is associated with the medium term, assets stocks may still be adjusting over time towards a long-term steady state. This implies that our estimation of sustainable current account need not be zero (net foreign assets are not constant).

There are two different approaches applied in the empirical work to estimate sustainable current accounts. The first approach derives measures of sustainable (structural) capital flows, which finance current account imbalances (Williamson and Mahar 1998). These structural capital inflows are not speculative flows, which move from country to country in search of high short-term rates of return, but inflows or outflows that are likely to persist for a considerable period of time. This measure of sustainable capital flows is usually assumed to be a constant proportion of GDP. The sustainable level of current account derived at this fairly *ad hoc* manner is highly criticised.

The second approach to estimating sustainable currents account is developed by Masson (1998) and implemented by Faruqee and Debelle (1998).[17] Since saving minus investment in the economy and current account are by identity equal, this approach focuses on the determinants of net domestic savings. Savings minus investment norms provide an assessment of what might be the sustainable level of the current account in the medium term if the economy were in internal balance. This methodology does not aim to account for short-term cyclical movements in the current account. The estimates for long-term saving minus investment are calculated by setting the output gap equal to zero.

In this chapter we estimate sustainable current accounts based on savings minus investment norms. Within the savings minus investment framework the determinants of current account are given by:

- The fiscal position. An improving fiscal position (rising surplus or falling deficit) reduces investment and increases saving, which leads to an improvement in the current account. As we are interested in current accounts in the medium term, we have to use a structural, cyclically adjusted measure of fiscal balance. In order to obtain such a measure we regress the actual fiscal position on the output gap and then subtract the estimated impact of the output gap. There is also work, which suggests that it is not only the size of fiscal surplus that matters but also its composition. To control for this effect we follow Bussiere *et al.* (2003) and include taxation as a proportion of GDP as an explanatory variable. This will also capture any effects due to the overall size of the government within the economy.
- The demographic structure, which affects savings behaviour for life cycle reasons. Countries where young and retired people dominate the population will have a low level of savings. Countries with a big share of the population of working age will have higher levels of saving. The demographic profile of countries is proxied by dependency ratio, defined as population younger than 14 and older than 65 as a proportion of the population aged between 14 and 65 years.
- The stage of development, proxied by GDP per head. This has implications for the amount of capital which countries need to import.

Poor countries (low levels of GDP per head) have a low capital–labour ratio and high marginal return on capital. Countries with access to international capital markets borrow from abroad and over time the country builds up its capital stock and international debt. The higher level of capital increases output, part of which is diverted into servicing foreign debt. As countries became more developed they started to export capital and to run current account surpluses. Income per capita is in US dollars converted using PPP exchange rates.

- The world real interest rate, which will equilibrate saving and investments for the world. As an approximation of world real interest rates we are using a US real interest rate.[18]

We derive a sustainable current account level for Argentina and Estonia within a panel framework. In the case of Estonia the panel consists of eleven Central and Eastern European transition countries for the period 1993–2001.[19] The time span is chosen taking into account data availability for the countries within the panel. For most of them we have data since 1993.[20] Since all variables are calculated relative to their sample, average estimation can be conducted only on a balanced panel. All the countries except Croatia are in the process of accession to the European Union, which means that these countries form a homogenous group. We do not include former Soviet Union countries in the panel (except Baltic countries), taking into account the fact that these countries lag behind Central and Eastern European countries in the process of economic transformation from centrally planned to market economies and are very different from accession countries in terms of development of macroeconomic variables. In the case of Argentina we again use a regional panel, which consists of twelve Central and Latin American countries for the period 1985–2001.[21] The selection of the countries included in the panel and time span were based on data availability.

All explanatory variables are measured relative to their sample averages, which give us two advantages. First, any shock which is common for all countries in the panel and hits them simultaneously will not affect the current account. Second, measuring explanatory variables relative to their sample averages would allow the world real interest rate to be substituted out from the equation specification (see Masson 1998). Dropping out the world real interest rate is based on the assumption that position of transition countries, which are in the sample, relative to the rest of the world does not change over time. At the same time one can think of the inclusion of the aggregate variables as capturing the equilibrium effects of changes in the world real interest rate on saving and investment (Obstfeld and Rogoff 1996: 76–78). Based on this argument we include world real interest rate in the estimation of the equation of sustainable current accounts for countries of interest.

The use of fixed effects, does, however, imply that the current account position of each panel with respect to the rest of the world does not have to be zero. The disadvantage of applied panel data framework for estimation of sustainable current account is that this approach assumes homogeneous coefficients across countries. The preferred equation for sustainable current accounts for Argentina and Estonia are presented in Table 7.5.

Here, CA_i is the current account as a proportion of GDP and is the dependent variable, RDR is a dependency ratio relative to sample average; RYPC is GDP per capita relative to sample average; RSFB is the structural fiscal surplus relative to sample average; and RTY is taxation as a percentage of GDP relative to sample average. c_i is a constant which captures country specific effects (fixed effects).

In the transition countries panel, demographic factors are omitted because the dependency ratio proves insignificant. World real interest rate approximated by US real interest rate also proves to be insignificant. As we mentioned above, panel data methodology which we apply allows us to drop out real interest rate from the model of savings minus investment norms. All explanatory variables are significant and the signs of the coefficients are consistent with those expected from the theory. The results show that stage of development variable proxied by GDP per head relative to sample average plays the most important role in determining savings minus investment norms in transition countries. This result is expected, since all of these countries need to import capital in order to finance the restructuring of their economies and to converge to developed countries. Fiscal policy development has a marginal effect, but its compositional effect is highly significant, with increases in the fiscal surplus from rising taxation having less of a contractionary effect than falls in government spending.[22]

In the Latin American panel the results suggest that the relative dependency ratio and relative GDP per capita give the best model. Vari-

Table 7.5 Panel estimates of current account equation

	Argentina	Estonia
c_i	0.02	0.37
RDR	0.17 (1.78)	–
RYPC	−0.12 (−2.99)	−0.24 (−2.89)
RSFB	–	0.01 (−1.75)
RTY	–	−0.23 (−3.7)
Adj. R^2	0.22	0.24
DW	1.85	1.89
S.E.E.	0.040	0.039

Note
T-statistics are given in parentheses.

ables are significant and the signs of the coefficients are consistent with those predicted from the theory. Structural fiscal balance and taxation as a percentage of GDP proved to be insignificant and were not included in the model. As with the transition country panel the world real interest rate is also insignificant in the Latin American panel. This allows us to exclude the real interest rate from the estimation of sustainable current accounts.

In the next section we present charts with actual, trend and estimated sustainable current accounts for Argentina and Estonia; see Figures 7.1 and 7.3 respectively.

Since we have estimates for trend current accounts, which are compatible with internal balance of the economy and for sustainable current account we can now solve the model in order to get the level of real exchange rate that match these two estimates. The next section provides overview of the results of the historic FEERs for Argentina and Estonia, as well as some discussion of policy implications.

4 Results and discussion

This section presents results of our estimates of FEERs for Argentina and Estonia. We have estimated only historic FEERs covering the sample of 1993:Q1–2001:Q4;[23] see Figures 7.2 and 7.4 respectively.

Essentially actual and trend current accounts may differ for several reasons: domestic and world (OECD) outputs differ from trend output; world trade differs from the trend; commodity prices differ from trend prices; and existence of unexplained deviations (residuals) from the model's relationship for trade.

In the case of Argentina the difference between trend current account and actual current account represents mainly the effects of deviation of output from its trend (output gaps). Between 1993:Q3 and 1994:Q3 output growth was above trend and output gap reached a positive 5 per cent. This pushed the actual current account below the trend current account. At that time the trend current account was below the sustainable current account and therefore the real effective rate needed to appreciate in order to reach the FEER (the real exchange rate was undervalued).

From the last quarter of 1994 until the last quarter of 1995 contagion effects from the Mexican crisis caused Argentina to have negative growth and a negative output gap. The result was a sharp reduction of imports and a massive improvement of actual current account during 1995. The trend current account was therefore below actual current account. However it was still higher than the sustainable current account so that real exchange rate needed to appreciate to get to the FEER.

Since the beginning of 1996 the Argentinean economy started to recover from the crisis and to grow faster. This higher growth combined with relatively high magnitudes of the activity coefficients in the trade volume caused a deterioration of the actual and trend current accounts.

At the same time the current account deficit implied by savings minus investments norms started to narrow. This led to a depreciation in the FEER and until the end of 1998 an overvalued exchange rate. In the first quarter of 1998 Argentine output growth started to decline reflecting the effect of the Asian crisis. Negative output growth caused by the negative effect of the big devaluation of Argentina's main trade partner (in the beginning of 1999 Brazil devalued by 50 per cent) persisted between 1999 and 2001. Despite the negative impact on the competitiveness of Brazil's devaluation during this period the Argentine export of goods and services continued to grow. Negative growth of domestic economy decreased the import of goods and services, which combined with continuous growth of export, led to improvement of the actual current account. The gap between FEER and actual real exchange rate increased between 1999 and 2000 due to a faster increase of sustainable current account compared to trend current account. From 1998 to 1999 the budget deficit doubled reaching 3 per cent of GDP and remained at that level until the end of the period of interest. This policy caused the permanent shift of the sustainable current account. At the end of the period the gap between the trend and sustainable current account closed and actual real exchange rate converged to FEER.

The model for Estonia produces results which are more volatile. This is due to the fact that Estonian economy was changing very fast during the period following the path of transition from a planned to a market economy. This was a period of price and trade liberalisation, which

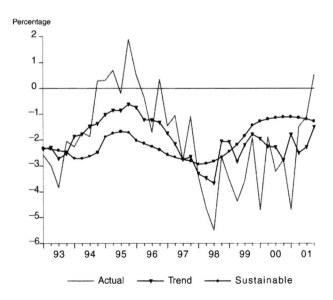

Figure 7.1 Argentina actual, trend and sustainable current accounts.

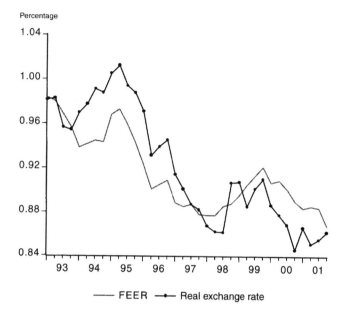

Figure 7.2 Argentina real exchange rate and FEER.

affected the development of trade flows. The structural changes in economic environment were also relevant and caused permanent shifts in the real exchange rate level.

During the period of 1994 to 1996 Estonian output growth was below trend output growth and so the trend current account was below actual current account. However the estimated sustainable current account was much higher, with the gap between the two reflecting a large overvaluation of the real exchange rate. The slight increase in the sustainable current account over this period was reflected in the sharp appreciation in the FEER.

Since the beginning of 1997 and during 1998 the Estonian economy had higher than trend output growth which caused the actual current account on average to be lower than the trend current account. The effect of Russian crisis reversed this trend pushing the actual current account back above the trend current account. At the beginning of 1997, the sustainable current account started to fall, due to high budget surplus run by the government (2.5 per cent of GDP).

Since the first quarter of 1998 sustainable current account started to increase steadily as the government fiscal position was reversed to a permanent deficit. After the Russian crisis and the decline in GDP growth trend current account was improving faster than sustainable current account increased, which closed the gap between FEER and actual real

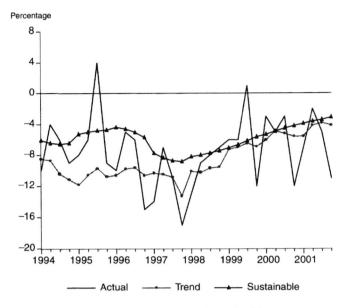

Figure 7.3 Estonian actual, trend and sustainable current accounts.

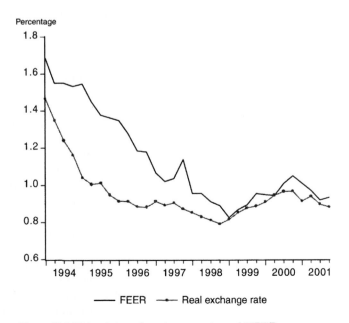

Figure 7.4 Estonian real exchange rate and FEER.

exchange rate. An analysis of the equilibrium real exchange rates has implications for the sustainability of the currency boards. Conventional criticism of the currency boards states that this monetary regime is associated with big misalignments, which eventually led to the collapse of the fixed exchange rate (Roubini 1998). Comparison of the FEER dynamics relative to the actual real exchange rate can give us an idea as to what extent conventional criticism is supported by the empirical evidence.

In the case of Argentina development of the ratio of actual real exchange rate relative to the FEER can be broken down into three main periods: 1993:Q3–1997:Q4 (undervaluation); 1998:Q1–2000:Q4 (overvaluation) and 2001:Q1–2001:Q4 (returning to equilibrium) (see Figure 7.5).[24]

Overall the dynamics of the Argentine real exchange rate and FEER during the period of the existence of the currency board arrangement does not show the persistent overvaluation critics of fixed exchange rates predict. Indeed the overall size of any misalignment is remarkably small, significantly less than the 10 per cent band Williamson (1983) felt was warranted by the uncertainty of FEER calculations. Even in 1999 when Argentine economic performance started to deteriorate the real exchange rate was roughly at equilibrium. This is the period when severe economic problems in Argentina started and eventually led to the collapse of the currency board arrangement. At that time there were proposals for the adoption of the US dollar as legal tender at the existing parity (Calvo 2000; Hanke and Schuler 1999). The main argument against official dollarisation was that Argentine real exchange rate was massively overvalued and adoption of the US dollar would not solve the problems of uncompetitiveness of Argentinean export (Sachs and Larrain 1999). Even worse

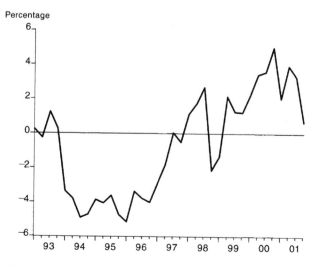

Figure 7.5 Argentina actual real exchange rate relative to the FEER.

dollarisation would aggravate the problems as it is an irreversible process, which would lock the country to the wrong exchange rate parity and would have a permanent negative effect on the Argentine economy. Our results show that the Argentine real exchange rate was not severely misaligned. At the end of 1999 real exchange rate was close to equilibrium exchange rate (FEER) with misalignment of the magnitude of about 1 per cent. Official dollarisation at the beginning of 2000 might have helped to prevent the deeper crisis faced by Argentina at the end of 2001. Dollarisation brings two big advantages.[25]

First, the formation of a monetary union (symmetric or asymmetric) stimulates trade among member countries, which makes goods produced in different countries closer substitutes for one another (Rose and Van Wincoop 2001; Rose 2001).[26] This should have the effect of raising the relative price elasticities in mutual trade relationships. The greater these elasticities are the less the adjustment of the real exchange rate is required in response to any shock of given size. A second and more important benefit for Argentina might be the reduction of interest rates since the devaluation premium will disappear with adoption of the US dollar.

In the case of Estonia development of the ratio of actual real exchange rate relative to the FEER can be broken down into three main periods: 1994:Q1–1994:Q4 (increasing overvaluation); 1995:Q1–1998:Q4 (decreasing overvaluation) and 1999:Q1–2001:Q4 (overvaluation fluctuating in a range of 10 per cent) (see Figure 7.6).

In general the size of the misalignments has been much larger than in the case of Argentina. Of course the uncertainties surrounding the calculation of equilibrium exchange rates for Estonia will also be higher. Estonia

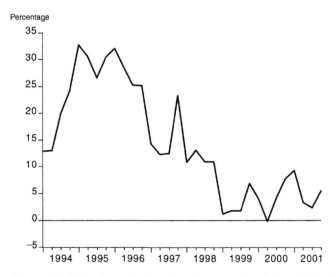

Figure 7.6 Estonian actual real exchange rate relative to the FEER.

launched the currency board at the beginning of 1992 with an exchange rate that deliberately undervalued the kroon.[27] As a result they had higher inflation in 1992. The results of this analysis suggest that, at the beginning, the kroon was already overvalued versus FEER, so the gain from deliberate undervaluation did not last long. This result might suggest how quickly the advantage from deliberate undervaluation disappears.

During the early period the trend current account is far below sustainable levels, which produces a big overvaluation. Over time the gap between the trend current account and sustainable current account was closing bringing the real exchange rate close to equilibrium (FEER).

Since the beginning of 1998 the continuous improvement of the trend current account reduced overvaluation of the real exchange rate to about 10 per cent. The real exchange rate needed to appreciate in order to reach FEER.

Between 1999 and 2001 overvaluation of the real exchange rate fluctuated within a range of 10 per cent.

Real exchange rate misalignments can be one important determinant and an indicator of a currency crisis. Our estimates of misalignments of the Estonian real exchange rate of magnitude of about 10 per cent are far less than critics of fixed exchange rates and currency boards would expect.

In contrast to Argentina, for Estonia the end point of the exchange rate regime path is clear – the adoption of the euro. The main issue here is whether a currency board can serve Estonia well through the process leading up to adoption of the euro. New entrants are envisaged to undergo three stages: EU accession, participation in ERM II and joining the euro zone. For countries with currency board the main question is whether this regime is compatible with participation in ERM II.[28] During this phase it is important that exchange rate regime fulfils several objectives: facilitating nominal convergence; allowing a market test for exchange rate stability; ensuring that countries enter the euro zone at an appropriate exchange rate and preparing central banks for operating within the euro zone (European Commission). Perhaps the most important of these is to ensure that countries enter the euro zone at an appropriate exchange rate.

Estonia, which joined the EU and ERM II in 2004, chose to preserve the existing regime of currency board. The Estonian authorities state that a currency board is compatible with ERM II and they want to maintain it until full participation in EMU. This implies that Estonia will enter the monetary union at the existing parity. Since entry into monetary union is practically irreversible, entry at the wrong level of the nominal exchange rate could have a permanent negative effect on the country's economic performance (Barrell and In't Velt 1991).[29] Entry at an overvalued exchange rate will result in losses of both export markets and foreign direct investment. Such losses may not be reversible and the country may be permanently affected if it chose the wrong entry level of exchange rate.

Our results show that the Estonian real exchange rate is not severely overvalued relative to equilibrium level. Indeed at the end of the sample period it is overvalued by 10 per cent. Based on these results we might expect that Estonia could sustain the existing nominal parity and preserve its currency board during the second stage of the accession process. Of course taking into account the relatively short sample of our work and the fact that any decision about Estonian entry rate into EMU will be taken around 2007 we can not answer the question of whether the current parity is appropriate for entry into EMU with any certainty.

5 Conclusions

Hard pegs and especially currency boards have been criticised as a policy tool for fighting inflation, as over the medium to long term period they are thought to lead to an overvalued exchange rate and to a significant worsening of the current account. Locking a country's exchange rate for too long a period to a misaligned nominal parity is bound to lead to a speculative attack and the collapse of the currency board (currency boards carry seeds of their own destruction).

In order to verify this criticism we calculate historic FEERs for two countries which have introduced currency boards in the beginning of 1990s namely Argentina and Estonia. FEERs are measures of medium-term equilibrium real exchange rates and they are not intended to explain short-term movement in exchange rates. Rather we use the calculated FEERs to assess medium- and long-term movements in real exchange rates and to assess sustainability of currency board arrangements.

Our analysis suggests that there were no severe misalignments of real exchange rate in currency board countries at least in the recent past. Overall since the introduction of the currency board the Argentine real exchange rate has had periods of relatively small undervaluation and overvaluation. These misalignments are in the magnitude of 6 per cent, which is far from the severe misalignments that might have been expected. At the end of sample period (2001) Argentine real exchange rate was virtually equal to equilibrium rate (FEER). The analysis suggests that it is not the currency board arrangement and the overvaluation of real exchange rate that is at the root of the economic disaster in Argentina. Based on this result we could expect that official dollarisation at the beginning of 2000 might have helped to prevent the economic collapse faced by Argentina at the end of 2001.

In Estonia the size of the misalignments has been much larger than in the case of Argentina. Of course the uncertainties surrounding the calculation of equilibrium exchange rate for Estonia will also be higher. The results of this analysis suggest that, despite the fact that the parity at which Estonia entered the currency board was deliberately undervalued by the beginning of 1994, the kroon was already overvalued versus FEER.

However, the process of transformation has allowed Estonia to improve its competitiveness. At the end of the sample period (2001) the Estonian real exchange rate was overvalued by around 5 per cent. Based on these results we might expect that Estonia could sustain the existing nominal parity and preserve its currency board during the second stage of the accession process. Of course taking into account the relatively short sample of our work and the fact that any decision about Estonian entry rate into EMU will be taken around 2007 we cannot answer the question of whether the current parity is appropriate for entry into EMU with any certainty.

Appendices

Appendix A: the model

This appendix presents the structure of the model used to estimate FEER for Argentina and Estonia. It is based on Barrell and Wren-Lewis (1989) and Wren-Lewis and Driver (1998).

A1 Trade volumes

Exports

$$Goods: XGI = \gamma_0 RX^{-\gamma_1} S^{\gamma_2} e^{\gamma_3 T}$$
$$Services: XS = \theta_0 RS^{-\theta_1} YW^{\theta_2} e^{\theta_3 T}$$

Imports

$$Goods: MGI = \delta_0 R^{\delta_1} Y^{\delta_2} e^{\delta_3 T}$$
$$Services: MS = \psi_0 RS^{\psi_1} Y^{\psi_2} e^{\psi_3 T}$$

Where:

RX is export competitiveness given by: $RX = \dfrac{WPXG*r}{PXG}$

r is nominal exchange rate (local currency per US dollar)
$WPXG$ is world export prices expressed in US dollars

RS is real exchange rate for services given by: $RS = \dfrac{PCW}{PC*NEER}$

PCW is world consumer prices, approximated by OECD consumer prices
PC is domestic consumer prices expressed in domestic currency

NEER is nominal effective exchange rate
S is world trade volume
YW is world real GDP, approximated by OECD real GDP

R is real exchange rate given by: $R = \dfrac{WPXG*r}{PD}$

PD is domestic prices, approximated by producer prices expressed in domestic currency
Y is domestic real GDP
T is time trend (1995: Q1 = 0).

A2 Trade prices

Exports

> All goods: $PXGA = (PCOMX*r)^{B_1}PXG^{1-B_1}$
> Manufacturing: $PXG = (WPXG*r)^{B_2}PD^{1-B_2}$
> Commodities: $PCOMX = WPO^{b_1}WPFD^{b_2}WPANF^{b_3}WPMM^{b_4}$
> Services: $PXS = PC$

Imports

> All goods: $PMGA = (PCOMM*r)^{A_1}PMG^{1-A_1}$
> Manufacturing: $PMG = (WPXG*r)^{A_2}PD^{1-A_2}$
> Commodities: $PCOMM = WPO^{a_1}WPFD^{a_2}WPANF^{a_3}WPMM^{a_4}$
> Services: $PMS = PCW*r$

Where:
PCOMX is country's commodity export prices
PXG is country's manufacturing export prices
WPO is oil prices, in US dollars
WPFD is world food prices, in US dollars
WPANF is world agricultural non-food prices, in US dollars
WPMM is world metals and minerals prices, in US dollars.

A3 Price equations

> Domestic GDP deflator: $PY = \omega_0 PDe^{\omega_1 T}$
> Domestic consumer prices: $PC = \omega_2 PDe^{\omega_3 T}$
> Foreign consumer prices: $PCW = \omega_4 WPXGe^{\omega_5 T}$

Where:
PY is domestic GDP deflator and all other variables are previously defined.

A4 Trade balance

The equations above can be combined to give a single expression for the trade balance as a proportion of nominal output:

$$bgs = \frac{BGS}{PY^*Y} = \frac{\gamma_0 RX^{-\gamma_1}S^{\gamma_2}e^{\gamma_3 T}(PCOMX^*r)^{B_1}PXG^{(1-B_1)}}{PY^*Y}$$

$$+ \frac{\theta_0 RS^{-\theta_1}YW^{\theta_2}e^{\theta_3 T}PC}{PY^*Y}$$

$$- \frac{\delta_0 R^{\delta_1}Y^{\delta_2}e^{\delta_3 T}(PCOMM^*r)^{A_1}PMG^{(1-A_1)}}{PY^*Y}$$

$$- \frac{\psi_0 RS^{\psi_1}Y^{\psi_2}e^{\psi_3 T}(PCW^*r)}{PY^*Y}$$

The number of relative price measures in this expression can be reduced to three: our measure of real exchange rate and two terms in real commodity prices using information of trend in relative pricing behaviour between different sectors. These pricing trends are given by equations in section A3. The balance of goods and services as a proportion of nominal GDP can therefore be simplified to:

$$bgs = c_0 RCOMX^{c_1}R^{c_2}S^{c_3}Y^{-1}e^{c_4 T} + c_5 R^{c_6}YW^{c_7}Y^{-1}e^{c_8 T} \\ - c_9 RCOMM^{c_{10}}R^{c_{11}}Y^{c_{12}}e^{c_{13}T} - c_{14}R^{c_{15}}Y^{c_{16}}e^{c_{17}T}$$

Where:

$$RCOMX = \frac{RCOMX}{WPXG}$$

$$RCOMM = \frac{RCOMM}{WPXG}$$

A5 Net transfers

$$NTRAN = \eta_0 e^{\eta_1 T}$$

A6 IPD flows

The balance of IPD flows as a proportion of GDP for the historic period can therefore be given as:

$$bipd = \left[1 + \rho^*\left(\frac{FEER - R}{R}\right)\right]^*(ipdc - ipdd)$$

Where:
   ipdc is IPD credits as a percentage of GDP
   ipdd is IPD debits as a percentage of GDP
   ρ is the proportion of the revaluation effect (1 for both Argentina and Estonia)
   FEER is fundamental equilibrium exchange rate
   R is actual real exchange rate.

A7   *The current account*

The full model of the current account in domestic currency, and as a proportion of nominal GDP, can therefore be given by:

$$cbs = \frac{CA}{PY*Y} = bgs + bipd + ntran$$

Where:
   cbs is current account balance (proportion of GDP)

   $ntran = \dfrac{NTRAN}{Y}$ is balance of net transfers (proportion of GDP).

Appendix B: estimation results

B1   *Trade volumes*

This appendix presents results of the error correction estimations (ECM) of the elasticities for the trade volume equations discussed in section 3. The definition of the variables is given in Appendix A. L indicates the variable is in natural logarithms and D indicates the first difference. See Appendix D for the data sources.

Table 7.6 Error correction estimation of goods export volume elasticities (dependent variable DLXGI)

	Argentina	Estonia
DLRX	−0.55 (−0.90)	0.24 (0.38)
DLS	2.53 (1.73)	2.95 (1.77)
Constant	−11.8 (−1.86)	−17.9 (−1.99)
$LXGI_{-1}$	−0.26 (−1.99)	−0.39 (−2.39)
LRX_{-1}	−0.37 (−1.87)	0.33 (1.75)
LS_{-1}	0.89 (1.83)	1.47 (2.05)
SQ1	0.37 (1.81)	−0.10 (−0.47)
SQ2	0.72 (9.57)	−0.01 (−0.09)
SQ3	0.23 (1.58)	0.01 (0.03)
Adj. R^2	0.92	0.68
Serial correlation	1.28	0.80
Functional form	0.86	0.79
Normality	0.15	0.20
Heteroskedasticity	1.02	0.89

Note
T-statistics are given in parentheses.

Table 7.7 Error correction estimation of services export volume elasticities (dependent variable DLXS)

	Argentina	Estonia
DLRS	−0.42 (−0.67)	1.11 (2.65)
DLYW	0.96 (0.28)	−7.98 (−1.12)
Constant	−23.9 (−1.86)	−20.0 (−1.18)
LXS_{-1}	−0.30 (−1.75)	−0.33 (−2.18)
LRS_{-1}	−0.48 (−1.86)	0.13 (1.46)
LYW_{-1}	1.46 (1.95)	1.26 (1.26)
SQ1	0.14 (5.29)	−0.09 (−2.17)
SQ2	−0.24 (−5.25)	0.24 (3.91)
SQ3	0.03 (0.93)	0.13 (3.20)
Adj. R^2	0.97	0.88
Serial correlation	0.99	0.97
Functional form	2.67	0.37
Normality	1.55	3.9
Heteroskedasticity	0.69	1.19

Note
T-statistics are given in parentheses.

Table 7.8 Error correction estimation of goods import volume elasticities (dependent variable DLMGI)

	Argentina	Estonia
DLR	−2.75 (−2.36)	−0.54 (−0.73)
DLY	2.72 (2.68)	3.37 (4.14)
Constant	8.64 (0.66)	−12.9 (−2.86)
$LMGI_{-1}$	−0.32 (−3.46)	−0.51 (−2.75)
LR_{-1}	−1.26 (−2.28)	−0.63 (−1.55)
LY_{-1}	0.69 (2.63)	1.81 (2.80)
SQ1	−0.02 (−0.32)	−0.01 (−0.01)
SQ2	−0.14 (−1.51)	−0.10 (−1.95)
SQ3	0.14 (2.42)	−0.01 (−0.02)
Adj. R^2	0.70	0.80
Serial correlation	1.42	2.50
Functional form	1.23	3.47
Normality	0.31	0.49
Heteroskedasticity	1.20	0.54

Note
T-statistics are given in parentheses.

Table 7.9 Error correction estimation of services import volume elasticities (dependent variable DLMS)

	Argentina	Estonia
DLRS	1.02 (1.58)	0.62 (1.15)
DLY	1.11 (2.38)	0.66 (0.77)
Constant	−3.84 (−1.12)	−6.61 (−1.48)
LMS_{-1}	−0.39 (−2.03)	−0.29 (−2.08)
LRS_{-1}	−0.05 (−1.27)	−0.11 (1.74)
LY_{-1}	0.98 (1.76)	0.88 (2.04)
SQ1	0.33 (8.84)	−0.16 (−1.12)
SQ2	−0.32 (−3.90)	0.02 (0.41)
SQ3	0.04 (1.18)	−0.01 (−0.03)
Adj. R^2	0.96	0.63
Serial correlation	2.40	0.52
Functional form	1.20	0.86
Normality	0.93	0.74
Heteroskedasticity	3.72	3.97

Note
T-statistics are given in parentheses.

Appendix C: charts

Percentage

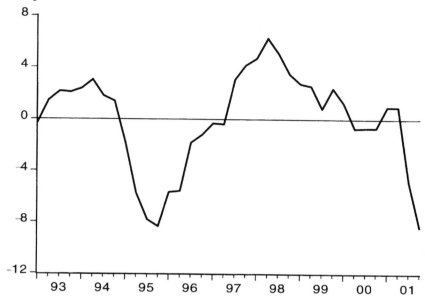

Figure 7.7 Argentina's output gap.

Percentage

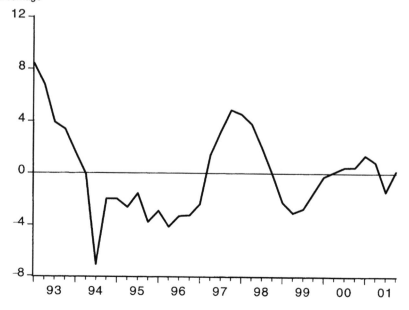

Figure 7.8 Estonia's output gap.

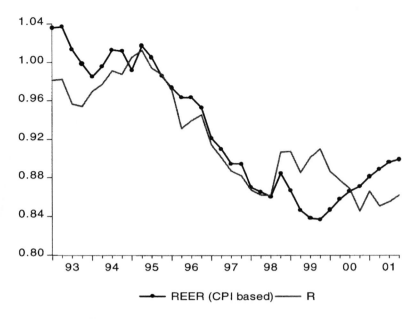

Figure 7.9 Argentina's real effective exchange rate and R.

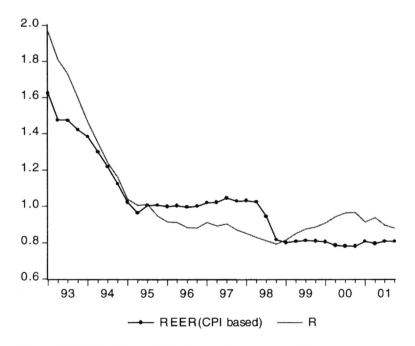

Figure 7.10 Estonia's real effective exchange rate and R.

Appendix D: data and data sources.

Most of the data are taken from International Financial Statistics (IFS) published by IMF, World Development Indicators 2002 published by World Bank, and the Quarterly National Accounts (QNA) and Monthly Economic Indicators (MEI) published by OECD. Additional sources of information for Argentina is the Ministry of the Economy, Secretariat of Economic Policy (http://www.mecon.gov.ar/prgmacri.htm) and Secretariat of Finance (http://www.mecon.gov.ar/finance/). For Estonia additional data sources are the Bank of Estonia web site (http://www.ee/epbe/) and the Statistical Office of Estonia web site (www.stat.ee). The base period for the constant price series is 1995 and all indices are for 1995 = 100.

XGI: Domestic goods export volume
IFS line 72, volume of exports for Argentina. For Estonia data are taken from the Statistical Office of Estonia. Turned from an index into constant price series using 1990 average for merchandise exports in US dollars (IFS line 78aa) converted into domestic currency using 1990 average for *r*. Sample period is 1993:Q1 to 2001:Q4 both for Argentina and Estonia.

WPXG: World export prices in US dollars
IFS line 74, unit value of world exports in US dollars (1993:Q1 to 2001:Q4).

r: Nominal dollar exchange rate (local currency/US dollars)
IFS line rf, average exchange rate, national currency units per US dollar. For both countries the sample period is 1993:Q1 to 2001:Q4.

S: World trade volume
IFS line 70, total world exports, US dollars current prices (1993:Q1 to 2001:Q4). Deflated using *WPXG*.

XS: Domestic export services volume
IFS line 78ad, services credits in US dollars. Converted into domestic currency using *r* and into a volume series by deflating by *PC*. For both countries the sample period is 1993:Q1 to 2001:Q4.

PCW: World consumer prices
MEI, OECD consumer price index (1993:Q1 to 2001:Q4).

PC: Domestic consumer prices, domestic currency
IFS line 64, consumer price index. For both countries the sample period is 1993:Q1 to 2001:Q4.

NEER: Nominal effective exchange rate
Nominal effective exchange rate index. For Argentina data are taken from the Ministry of the Economy, Secretariat of Economic Policy. For Estonia data are from Bank of Estonia. For both countries the sample period is 1993:Q1 to 2001:Q4.

YW: World (OECD) real GDP
QNA, total OECD GDP at constant market prices in US dollars (adjusted from annual to quarterly rate) (1993:Q1 to 2001:Q4).

MGI: Domestic import goods volume
IFS line 73, volume of imports, FOB (for Argentina). For Estonia data are taken from the Statistical Office of Estonia. Turned from an index into constant price series using 1990 average for merchandise imports in US dollars (IFS line 78ab) converted into domestic currency using 1990 average for *r*. For both countries the sample period is 1993:Q1 to 2001:Q4.

PD: Domestic prices, domestic currency
IFS line 63, producer prices. For both countries the sample period is 1993:Q1 to 2001:Q4.

Y: Domestic real GDP
IFS line 69b. For Estonia GDP at 1995 prices in national currency. For Argentina GDP at 1993 prices in national currency. Adjusted from base year 1993 to 1995. For both countries the sample period is 1993:Q1 to 2001:Q4.

MS: Import services volume
IFS line 78ae, services debits in US dollars. Converted into domestic currency using *r* and into a volume series by deflating by *PCW* converted into domestic currency terms using NEER. For both countries the sample period is 1993:Q1 to 2001:Q4.

WPO: Oil prices, dollars
IFS, index constructed from Saudi Arabian light oil spot price (US dollars/barrel), end period (1993:Q1 to 2001:Q4).

WPFD: World food prices, dollars
IFS, food commodity price index, market prices, US dollars (1993:Q1 to 2001:Q4).

WPANF: World agricultural non-food prices, dollars
IFS, agricultural raw materials commodity price index, market prices, US dollars (1993:Q1 to 2001:Q4).

WPMM: World metals and minerals prices, dollars
IFS, base metals commodity price index, market prices, US dollars (1993:Q1 to 2001:Q4).

PY: Domestic GDP deflator
For Argentina the source is the Ministry of the Economy, Secretariat of Economic Policy. Implicit price index calculated as a relation between GDP at current prices and at 1995 prices. For Estonia implicit price index calculated from Y and GDP at current market prices. For both countries the sample period is 1993:Q1 to 2001:Q4.

NTRAN: Net transfers, domestic currency
IFS, lines 78aj and 78ak, current transfers credits and current transfers debits, both in US dollars, converted into domestic currency using r and into real terms using PY. For both countries the sample period is 1993:Q1 to 2001:Q4.

CA: Current account, domestic currency
IFS line 78al, current account, current prices in US dollars. Converted into domestic currency using r. For both countries the sample period is 1993:Q1 to 2001:Q4.

IPDC: Interest, profits and dividends credits
IFS line 78ag, income credit in US dollars. Converted into domestic currency using r, and into real terms using PY. For both countries the sample period is 1993:Q1 to 2001:Q4.

IPDD: Interest, profits and dividends debits
IFS line 78ah, income debit in US dollars. Converted into domestic currency using r, and into real terms using PY. For both countries the sample period is 1993:Q1 to 2001:Q4.

PXG: Domestic export prices
IFS line 74, unit value of all exports (for Argentina). For Estonia data are taken from Statistical Office of Estonia. For both countries the sample period is 1993:Q1 to 2001:Q4.

PMG: Domestic import prices
IFS line 75, unit value of all imports (for Argentina). For Estonia data are taken from Statistical Office of Estonia. For both countries the sample period is 1993:Q1 to 2001:Q4.

REER: Real effective exchange rate
Real effective exchange rate index. For Argentina data are taken from the Ministry of the Economy, Secretariat of Economic Policy. For Estonia

data are from Bank of Estonia. For both countries the sample period is 1993:Q1 to 2001:Q4.

DR: Dependency ratio
Dependency ratio defined as population younger than 14 and older than 65 as a proportion of the population aged between 14 and 65 years. Data are taken from World Bank World Development Indicators 2002.

YPC: GDP per head
GDP per head, PPP current international US dollars. Data are taken from World Bank World Development Indicators 2002.

FB: Fiscal balance
Fiscal position as a proportion of GDP. Data are taken from World Bank World Development Indicators 2002.

TY: Taxation
Taxation as a proportion of GDP. Data are taken from World Bank World Development Indicators 2002.

WR: US real interest rate
US real interest rate defined as Treasury bill rate minus consumer price inflation. Data for US Treasury bill rate and consumer price inflation are taken from IFS. IFS line 60c Treasury bill rate, and IFS line 64 consumer price inflation.

Notes

* This chapter was written while at the Centre for Central Banking Studies, Bank of England. The author would like to thank Peter Sinclair, Rebecca Driver, Paul Robinson, Gill Hammond, Ray Barrell, Larry Schembri, Kurt Schuler, Steve Hanke, Martin Zaimov, Nikolay Gueorguiev, Boris Petrov, Rasmus Pikkani and Raoul Lattemae and one anonymous referee for their helpful comments and support. They are however not responsible for any errors. The views in this chapter are those of the author and not necessarily those of the Bulgarian National Bank or the Bank of England.
1 Fischer (2001) states that empirical evidence shows that in the last decade there has been a tendency of hollowing out the middle of the distribution of exchange rate regimes and moving towards either flexible exchange rates or hard exchange rate commitments ("two poles"). There is an opposite view that "intermediate solutions are more likely to be appropriate for many countries rather than corner solutions" (Frankel 1999). Masson (2001) rejects the hypothesis that there are only transitions towards the two poles (floating or firm fixed) using a wide set of countries. According to Masson (2001) the evidence of exchange rate regimes transitions suggest that intermediate regimes will continue to constitute an important fraction of actual exchange rate regimes.
2 Mussa 2002: 15.
3 For a review of a wide variety of concepts and empirical approaches to estimat-

ing equilibrium exchange rates see Driver and Westaway in Chapter 6 of this book.

4 See Alberola *et al.* 1999; Faruqee 1998.

5 See, for example, Barrell and Wren-Lewis 1989; Wren-Lewis and Driver 1998.

6 A definition of the real exchange rate that uses relative output or trade prices rather than consumer prices is also more appropriate when countries produce different goods. Obstfeld and Rogoff (1995) show that PPP holds for relative consumer prices, but not for relative producer prices. This occurs even though all consumers are identical across countries, there is no home bias in consumption, no pricing to market and the law of one price holds for each individual good.

7 Wren-Lewis *et al.* (1991) estimate FFER for UK economy using complete macroeconomic model. Bayoumi *et al.* (1994) calculate equilibrium real exchange rates for major industrial countries using IMF's multicountry macro-model MULTIMOD.

8 For discussion of how sensitive FEER estimation is to exogenous assumptions and weaknesses in the underlying structure see Driver and Wren-Lewis (1999).

9 Barrell and Wren-Lewis (1989) and Driver and Wren-Lewis (1999) investigate the impact of relaxing this assumption in the case of trend output. They allow trend GDP to vary with the real exchange rate. The results show that allowing for output endogeneity does not make a large difference.

10 For simplicity we use actual IPD flows, smoothed using a four-quarter moving average.

11 Driver and Wren-Lewis (1999) show that FEER estimates are much more sensitive to sustainable current account norms and trade parameters than to estimates of trend output.

12 For a survey see Goldstein and Kahn (1985). The demand curve specification has serious empirical and theoretical inadequacies. First, this approach does not account for nonprice competitiveness factors so the demand curve approach does not account for variety and quality of goods produced in the economy. Second, modelling trade volumes with demand curve equation neglects supply side factors, in particular, decisions over the location of production.

13 The test for serial correlation is the Lagrange multiplier test; for functional form Ramsey's RESET test; for normality Jarque-Bera test, and for heteroskedasticity, White's heteroskedasticity test. The tests are all distributed as χ^2 and null is accepted when the test statistics is less than critical value.

14 This condition assumes that trade balance is initially zero. If the trade balance is in deficit, then for the nominal balance (expressed in domestic currency) to improve, the amount by which the sum of the trade price elasticities must exceed unity increases. The size of this increase will be determined by the relative size of the export and import price elasticities (see, for example, Goldstein and Kahn 1985; Hooper and Marquez 1995).

15 For example, in the case of Argentina federal government debt is denominated 96 per cent in foreign currency (70 per cent in US dollars, 20 per cent in euros and 5 per cent in Japanese yen) and only 4 per cent in domestic currency – pesos (information from Argentinean Ministry of Economy, Undersecretariat of Financing).

16 For a short review and comparison of the estimation properties of these methodologies see Giorno *et al.* (1995).

17 For recent application of the IMF methodology see Chinn and Prasad (2003).

18 US real interest rate is defined as Treasury bill rate minus consumer price inflation.

19 Bulgaria, Croatia, Czech Republic, Estonia, Hungary, Latvia, Lithuania, Poland, Romania, Slovak Republic and Slovenia.
20 Croatia and Slovenia gained independence from Yugoslavia in June 1991. Lithuania became independent of the Soviet Union in March 1990, Estonia in August 1991 and Latvia in September 1991. In January 1993 the former Czechoslovakia has split into Czech and Slovak republics (EBRD 2000).
21 Argentina, Brazil, Chile, Colombia, Costa Rica, Ecuador, Mexico, Panama, Paraguay, Peru, Uruguay and Venezuela.
22 In the long term one would expect supply effects which differed substantially from short-term demand effects of a Keynesian nature.
23 The choice of the sample was based solely on data availability.
24 Measures the difference between actual real exchange rate and FEER as a percentage of the FEER $(FEER - R)FEER$. A negative number indicates an under-valuation, so that the real exchange rate needs to appreciate to reach the FEER.
25 For a discussion of the pros and cons of dollarisation see, for example, Bogetic (2000).
26 Rose and Van Wincoop (2001) and Rose (2001) estimate that having a common currency can boost trade among countries participating in monetary union by a factor of three.
27 Thanks to Kurt Schuler for this useful information.
28 When a country with a currency board pegged to the euro wishes to join ERM II, the decision on the compatibility of a particular currency board arrangement with ERM II could only be taken on the basis of a profound assessment of the appropriateness and sustainability of the said currency board. This conclusion logically follows from the procedure foreseen in the ERM II resolution concerning the adoption of the central rates. Although the currency board arrangements can not be regarded as an acceptable substitute for participation in ERM II, they may in particular circumstances constitute an appropriate unilateral commitment within ERM II. Such unilateral commitment would not impose any additional obligations on the ECB beyond those deriving from the ERM II resolution and the Central Bank Agreement.
29 This decision has also implications for the sustainability of the monetary union. The monetary union will be easier to hold together the less the relative price adjustments that take place among countries (Barrell and In't Velt 1991; Barrell and Pain 1998).

References

Alberola, E.S., Cervero, S., Lopez, H. and Ubide, A. (1999), 'Global equilibrium exchange rates: euro, dollar, "ins", "outs" and other major currencies in a panel cointegration framework', IMF Working Paper no. WP/99/175.

Barrell, R. and Wren-Lewis, S. (1989), 'Fundamental equilibrium exchange rates for the G7', CEPR Discussion Paper no. 323.

Barrell, R. and In't Veld, J.W. (1991), 'FEERs and the path to EMU', *National Institute Economic Review*, N137: 51–58.

Barrell, R. and Pain, N. (1998), 'Choosing the rate again: If we join EMU what would be the right entry rate?', *New Economy*, 5(2): 109–113.

Bayoumi, T., Clark, P., Symansky, S. and Taylor, M. (1994), 'The robustness of equilibrium rate calculations to alternative assumptions and methodologies', in Williamson, J. (ed.) *Estimating Equilibrium Exchange Rates*, Washington DC: Institute of International Economics.

Bogetic, Z. (2000), 'Official dollarization: current experiences and issues', *CATO Journal*, 20(2): 179–213.

Bussiere, M., Chortareas, G. and Driver, R. (2003), 'Current accounts, net foreign assets and the implications of cyclical factors', Bank of England Working Paper no. 173.

Calvo, G. (2000), 'Testimony on dollarization', Presented before the Subcommittee on Domestic and Monetary Policy, Committee on Banking and Financial Services, Washington DC, 22 June.

Chinn, M. and Prasad E. (2003), 'Medium-term determinants of current accounts in industrial and developing countries: an empirical exploration', *Journal of International Economics*, 59: 47–76.

Driver, R.L. and Wren-Lewis, S. (1999), 'FEER's: a sensitivity analysis', in MacDonald, R. and Stein, J. (eds), *Equilibrium Exchange Rates*, Boston: Kluwer Academic Publishers.

EBRD Transition Report 2000, London.

European Commission (2001), 'Exchange rate aspects of enlargement, European economy', 1 (February) (Supplement C): 1–3.

Faruqee, H. (1998), 'Methodology for calculating equilibrium exchange rates and questions of global consistency., in Isard, P. and Faruqee, H. (eds), 'Exchange rate assessment: extensions to the macroeconomic balance approach', IMF Occasional Paper no. 167.

Faruqee, H. and Debelle, G. (1998), 'Saving-investment balances in industrialised countries: an empirical investigation', in Isard, P. and Faruqee, H. (eds), 'Exchange rate assessment: extensions to the macroeconomic balance approach', IMF Occasional Paper no. 167.

Fischer, S. (2001), 'Exchange rate regimes: Is the bipolar view correct?', *Journal of Economic Perspectives*, 15(2) (Spring): 3–24.

Frankel, J.A. (1999), 'No single currency regime is right for all countries or at all times', NBER Working Paper no. W7338.

Giorno, C., Richardson, P., Roseveare, D. and Van den Noord, P. (1995), 'Potential output, output gaps and structural budget balances', *OECD Economic Studies*, 24: 167–209.

Goldstein, M. and Kahn, M. (1985), 'Income and price effects in foreign trade', in Jones, R.W. and Kenen, P.B. (eds), *Handbook of International Economics, Volume 2*, Amsterdam: Elsevier Science Publishers B.V.

Gulde, A.M., Kahkonen, J. and Keller, P. (2000), 'Pros and cons of currency board arrangements in the lead-up to EU accession and participation in the euro zone', IMF PDP/00/01.

Hanke, S. and Schuler, K. (1999), 'Monetary constitution for Argentina: rules for dollarization', *CATO Journal*, 18(3): 405–419.

Hanke, S. and Schuler, K. (2002), 'How to dollarize in Argentina now?', www.cato.org.

Hooper, P. and Marquez, J. (1995), 'Exchange rates, prices, and external adjustment in the United States and Japan', in Kenen, P. (ed.), *Understanding Interdependence: The Macroeconomics of the Open Economy*, Princeton: Princeton University Press.

Masson, P. (2001), 'Exchange rate regime transitions', *Journal of Development Economics*, 64: 571–586.

Masson, P. (1998), 'A globally consistent conceptual framework', in Isard, P. and

Faruqee, H. (eds), 'Exchange rate assessment: extensions to the macroeconomic balance approach', IMF Occasional Paper no. 167.

Mussa, M. (2002), 'Argentina and the fund: from triumph to tragedy', *Institute for International Economics Policy Analyses in International Economics*, 67 (May).

Obstfeld, M. and Rogoff, K. (1995), 'Exchange rate dynamics redux', *Journal of Political Economy*, 103(3): 624–660.

Obstfeld, M. and Rogoff, K. (1996), *Foundation of International macroeconomics*, Cambridge, MA: The MIT Press

Rose, A. and Van Wincoop, E. (2001), 'National money as a barrier to trade: the real case for currency union', *American Economic Review, Papers and Proceedings*, 91(2): 386–390.

Rose, A. (2001), 'Currency unions and trade: the effect is large', *Economic Policy*, 33: 449–461.

Roubini, N. (1998), 'The case against currency boards: debunking 10 myths about benefits of currency boards', www.stern.nyu.edu/~nroubini.

Sachs, J. and Larrain, F. (1999), 'Why dollarization is more straitjacket than salvation', *Foreign Policy*, 99(116) (Fall): 80–93.

Williamson, J. (1983), *The Exchange Rate System*, Washington, DC: Institute for International Economics.

Williamson, J. and Mahar, M. (1998), 'Current account targets', in Wren-Lewis, S. and Driver, R.L. (eds) *Real Exchange Rates for the Year 2000*, Washington DC: Institute for International Economics, Policy Analyses in International Economics, no. 54.

Wren-Lewis, S., Westaway, P., Soteri, S. and Barrell, R. (1991), 'Evaluating the UK's choice of entry rate into the ERM', *The Manchester School*, 59 (Supplement): 1–22.

Wren-Lewis, S. and Driver, R.L. (1998), *Real Exchange Rates for the Year 2000*, Washington, DC: Institute for International Economics.

8 Revisiting the border

An assessment of the law of one price using very disaggregated consumer price data

*Charles Engel, John H. Rogers and
Shing-Yi Wang*

1 Introduction

Prices that households pay for consumer goods should not be very different across a pair of markets if those markets are well integrated. "Integration" means that barriers to commerce of all sorts – formal trade barriers, transportation costs, exclusivity of distribution networks, etc. – are low. Engel and Rogers (1996) (hereinafter referred to as ER) examined prices across a number of North American cities in an attempt to assess the integration of Canadian and American markets for goods. Their finding was that the markets were not as well integrated as one might have expected. Cities within each country showed much greater harmony in prices even if they were very distant markets compared to pairs of cities that lie across the U.S.–Canada border, even if the cities were nearby geographically. There was, in the words of that study, a large "border" effect.

The literature suggests two ways in which this imperfect synchronization of prices might influence exchange rate and monetary policy. On the one hand, following Mundell (1961), two countries that are highly integrated commercially are apt to be strong candidates for a common currency. One of the most powerful gains from a common currency is from lowering transactions costs for cross-border trade. Money eases trade, so a common money would ease trade across borders.[1] The more transactions that occur between economies, the more integrated the goods markets, and the greater the gains from a common currency.

On the other hand, short-term deviations from the law of one price across national borders might reflect nominal exchange rate misalignment. That is, in each country nominal goods prices might be set in the local currency. Nominal exchange rates reflect not only current market conditions but also expectations of the future. As the nominal exchange rate fluctuates but goods prices adjust only slowly, there arise deviations of prices (expressed in a common currency) across borders. That is, let $P_i^{US\$}$ be the U.S. dollar price of good i sold in the U.S., and $P_i^{CA\$}$ the Canadian dollar price of the same good sold in Canada. Both of these prices might adjust sluggishly to changes in demand or supply. As $S_{US\$/CA\$}$ the U.S. dollar per

Canadian dollar exchange rate, fluctuates as the market learns news of future economic conditions, there will be deviations from the law of one price condition, $P_i^{US\$} = S_{US\$/CA\$}P_i^{CA\$}$. Devereux and Engel (2003) have argued that under these circumstances, there are gains to stabilizing nominal exchange rates. When there is local-currency pricing, changes in the nominal exchange rate do not change relative prices faced by consumers. Prices of foreign-produced and domestically-produced goods are both sticky in the local currency. There is no "expenditure switching" effect of exchange rate changes, so a flexible exchange rate does not help facilitate goods market adjustment. On the contrary, because short-term fluctuations in the nominal exchange rate induce price wedges between countries, they lead to inefficient allocation of resources. Exchange-rate stability can minimize these distorting deviations from the law of one price.

Thus if deviations from the law of one price are short-term, there may be a case for fixing nominal exchange rates, perhaps in the ultimate form of a common currency. On the other hand, if the deviations from the law of one price are large in the long term, then the markets are not well integrated, and they are poor candidates for a common currency in Mundell's framework.

The tests of ER do not permit the evaluation of long-term deviations from the law of one price. They use price index data. This means that ER cannot compare price levels in U.S. cities to price levels in Canadian cities. They are only able to compare rates of inflation. ER can only measure the extent of short-term deviations from the law of one price. That is, they can compare $\pi_{i,j}^{US\$}$ – the inflation rate of good i, in U.S. dollars, in U.S. city j – to $\delta_{US\$/CA\$} + \pi_{i,k}^{CA\$}$, where $\delta_{US\$/CA\$}$ is the rate of depreciation of the U.S. dollar relative to the Canadian dollar, and $\pi_{i,k}^{CA\$}$ is the Canadian dollar inflation rate of good i in some Canadian city. ER use official consumer price data from Statistics Canada and the U.S. Bureau of Labor Statistics, which publish price data only in index form. Moreover, their data is disaggregated by categories of consumer goods, but not highly disaggregated. Their prices are subindexes of fairly broad categories of goods such as food at home, women's and girls' clothing, footwear, transportation, etc.

Here, we make use of data from the Economist Intelligence Unit (EIU) that includes actual prices of 100 consumer goods in 13 U.S. cities and four Canadian cities. The cities are listed in Table 8.1. The data is annual (recorded in December) from 1990 to 2002. The data is collected by EIU as a way to compare costs of living for cities throughout the world. The data is for a wide variety of products. There is heavy concentration on food items – 42 of the 100 goods are food or drink, such as tomatoes, ground beef, or six-year aged Scotch whiskey. There are nine clothing items, such as women's cardigan sweaters. A half-dozen of the items are consumer durables, including a 2-slice electric toaster and a low priced car (900–1299cc). Nontradable services such as men's haircut (including tip) or one hour's babysitting constitute 21 of the items. The remaining 22 prices are for miscellaneous (tradable) products such as insect-killer spray (330 g) and aspirin (100 tablets). So the items are narrowly defined, and the EIU attempts to price comparable products across cities. They report prices according to type of outlet (supermarket, mid-priced store, etc.) Table 8.1 lists the products and outlets that we use in this study.[2]

Because we can compare actual price levels, we can investigate long-term differences in price levels among North American cities, as well as the behavior of short-term price changes. Our empirical work, therefore, estimates a simple model to explain price level differences between cities: the absolute value of the difference in the price between two cities is modeled as a function of the log of distance between the cities, the absolute value of the population difference (since larger cities tend to have higher prices), a measure of the absolute value of the difference in sales taxes between cities, and a dummy variable that indicates whether or not the two cities are in different countries.[3] We use the same set of explanatory variables in a separate set of regressions in which the dependent variable captures the short-term movements in prices, and is thus similar to that used by ER: A typical observation might be $|\pi_{i,j}^{US\$} - (\delta_{US\$/CA\$} + \pi_{i,k}^{CA\$})|$ if cities j and k are in different countries (where $|x|$ refers to the absolute value of x), or, for example, $|\pi_{i,j}^{US\$} - \pi_{i,k}^{US\$}|$ if cities j and k are both located in the U.S.

There are drawbacks both to our measurement of long-term price differences and short-term differences. Our data span only 13 years. If transitory price differences disappear slowly, then our 13-year sample might not be long enough to eliminate the effects of transitory deviations from the law of one price. Specifically, it may be the case that the U.S. dollar was "overvalued" compared to the Canadian dollar during a sizable fraction of our 13-year span, which would induce higher average prices in the U.S. that do not reflect permanent barriers to integration. However, one might suspect that there must be some significant commercial barriers if transitory price differences can persist for years. On the other side of the coin, one-year changes might be too low frequency to capture the most significant transitory fluctuations in relative prices that emerge from volatile nominal exchange rates. But since the data is only annual, we cannot measure price changes at any higher frequency.

There may be a large degree of measurement error in these prices. The EIU does not publish full details of its methodology, and one suspects that the prices are not as comparable as prices collected by the official agencies. However, the price data is used as the dependent variable in our regression, so any measurement error should not affect the consistency of our parameter estimates. There may be a lot of "noise" in the inter-city price comparisons for a particular item, which might make it difficult to assess the role of the border for comparisons of prices for a single good. But, we gain power by using panel estimation, assessing the role of the border for the entire collection of 100 goods. In addition, we estimate

Table 8.1 List of cities, goods and type of retail outlet

U.S. cities Atlanta, Boston, Chicago, Cleveland, Detroit, Houston, Los Angeles, Miami, New York, Pittsburgh, San Francisco, Seattle, Washington, DC
Canadian cities Calgary, Montreal, Toronto, Vancouver
Goods (type of retail outlet) ("average" refers to the average of mid-priced and discount outlets, as reported by EIU)

White bread (1 kg) (supermarket)	Drinking chocolate (500 g) (supermarket)	Women's dress, ready to wear, daytime (chain store)
Butter (500 g) (supermarket)	Coca-Cola (1 l) (supermarket)	Women's shoes, town (chain store)
Margarine (500 g) (supermarket)	Tonic water (200 ml) (supermarket)	Women's cardigan sweater (chain store)
White rice (1 kg) (supermarket)	Mineral water (1 l) (supermarket)	Women's tights, panty hose (chain store)
Spaghetti (1 kg) (supermarket)	Wine, common table (750 ml) (supermarket)	Child's shoes, sportswear (chain store)
Flour, white (1 kg) (supermarket)	Beer, local brand (1 l) (supermarket)	Girl's dress (chain store)
Sugar, white (1 kg) (supermarket)	Beer, top quality (330 ml) (supermarket)	Hourly rate for domestic cleaning help (average)
		Babysitter's rate per hour (average)
Cheese, imported (500 g) (supermarket)	Scotch whisky, six years old (700 ml) (supermarket)	
Cornflakes (375 g) (supermarket)	Soap (100 g) (supermarket)	Compact disc album (average)
Milk, pasteurized (1 l) (supermarket)	Laundry detergent (3 l) (supermarket)	Television, colour (66 cm) (average)
Olive oil (1 l) (supermarket)	Toilet tissue (two rolls) (supermarket)	Kodak colour film (36 exposures) (average)
Peanut or corn oil (1 l) (supermarket)	Dishwashing liquid (750 ml) (supermarket)	Cost of developing 36 colour pictures (average)
Potatoes (2 kg) (supermarket)	Insect-killer spray (330 g) (supermarket)	Daily local newspaper (average)
Tomatoes (1 kg) (supermarket)	Batteries (two, size D/LR20) (supermarket)	Paperback novel (at bookstore) (average)
Oranges (1 kg) (supermarket)	Frying pan (Teflon or good equivalent) (supermarket)	Three-course dinner at top restaurant for four people (average)
Apples (1 kg) (supermarket)	Electric toaster (for two slices) (supermarket)	Four best seats at cinema (average)
Lemons (1 kg) (supermarket)	Laundry (one shirt) (mid-priced outlet)	Low priced car (900–1299cc) (low)
Bananas (1 kg) (supermarket)	Dry cleaning, man's suit (mid-priced outlet)	Family car (1800–2499cc) (low)

Lettuce (one) (supermarket)	Dry cleaning, woman's dress (mid-priced outlet)	Deluxe car (2500cc upwards) (low)
Peas, canned (250 g) (supermarket)	Dry cleaning, trousers (mid-priced outlet)	Cost of a tune up (but no major repairs) (low)
Peaches, canned (500 g) (supermarket)	Aspirins (100 tablets) (supermarket)	Hilton-type hotel, single room, one night including breakfast (average)
Sliced pineapples, canned (500 g) (supermarket)	Razor blades (five pieces) (supermarket)	Moderate hotel, single room, one night including breakfast (average)
Beef: steak, entrecote (1 kg) (supermarket)	Toothpaste with fluoride (120 g) (supermarket)	One drink at bar of first class hotel (average)
Beef: stewing, shoulder (1 kg) (supermarket)	Facial tissues (box of 100) (supermarket)	Two-course meal for two people (average)
Beef: roast (1 kg) (supermarket)	Hand lotion (125 ml) (supermarket)	Simple meal for one person (average)
Beef: ground or minced (1 kg) (supermarket)	Lipstick (deluxe type) (chain store)	Regular unleaded petrol (11) (average)
Pork: chops (1 kg) (supermarket)	Man's haircut (tips included) (average)	Taxi: initial meter charge (average)
Pork: loin (1 kg) (supermarket)	Woman's cut and blow dry (tips included) (average)	Taxi rate per additional kilometre (average)
Ham: whole (1 kg) (supermarket)	Cigarettes, Marlboro (pack of 20) (supermarket)	Taxi: airport to city centre (average)
Chicken: fresh (1 kg) (supermarket)	Cigarettes, local brand (pack of 20) (supermarket)	International foreign daily newspaper (average)
Fresh fish (1 kg) (supermarket)	Electricity, monthly bill for family of four (average)	International weekly news magazine (Time) (average)
Instant coffee (125 g) (supermarket)	Men's business suit, two piece, medium weight (chain store)	One good seat at cinema (average)
Ground coffee (500 g) (supermarket)	Men's business shirt, white (chain store)	
Tea bags (25 bags) (supermarket)	Socks, wool mixture (chain store)	

smaller panels for the different categories of goods described above: food, clothing, miscellaneous products, durables, and services.

Estimation of panels allows us to compare price levels of individual goods across countries, and reduce the problems of low power introduced by measurement error. Official statistical agencies do not make price data on individual goods publicly available, in part because of their concerns about measurement error. Instead they only report indexes, because the variance of the measurement error is reduced when the prices are averaged into an index. But once the data is averaged, we can no longer compare price levels of individual goods across locations.

We find significant evidence of border effects both in the levels of (logs of) prices and the percentage change in prices. Even accounting for distance between cities and relative population sizes, we find that the absolute difference between prices in the U.S. and Canada in our data (annual from 1990 to 2002) is greater than 7 percent. This difference exists among tradables and nontradables, though for some categories of tradables (clothing and durables) the difference is smaller. The findings are similar for annual changes, though the magnitude is smaller – the border accounts for a difference in 1.5 percent in annual (log) price changes. Relative population sizes and distance are helpful in explaining price level differences (between Canadian and U.S. cities) for traded goods, but are less helpful in explaining price level differences for nontraded goods or in accounting for differences (between U.S. and Canadian cities) in price changes for either traded or nontraded goods.

What does all of this mean for the desirability of a common currency or fixed exchange rates for Canada and the U.S.? Probably nothing. In the first place, the adoption of a common currency is almost certainly a non-starter politically. Second, we have no standard by which to assess the magnitude of this border effect. Is a seven percent average difference in prices small or large? This study is not intended to yield a definitive conclusion, but instead is meant to encourage further study and to provide the starting point for a methodology that can assess the integration of markets. It is our hope that government and central bank researchers will work in cooperation with official statistical agencies to analyze very disaggregated price level data so that we can get a broader picture of the "border" effect among a collection of countries.

2   Estimation strategy

Our measure of integration of two locations – the dependent variable in our regressions – is the absolute value of the log price difference of good i between locations j and k: $|p_{i,j,t} - p_{i,k,t}|$, where $p_{i,j,t}$ refers to the log of the price expressed in U.S. dollars of good i, in city j, at time t. Note that we express all prices in U.S. dollars so that we can compare prices across all cities.[4] The price data is annual, measured in December, for 1990–2002.

The dimensions of our panel then are: 100 goods; 17 cities, which means 136 city pairs; and 13 time periods. The panel consists of 176,800 observations. Prices are inclusive of tax.

When we consider changes in prices, the dependent variable is $|\pi_{i,j,t} - \pi_{i,k,t}|$, where $\pi_{i,j,t} \equiv p_{i,j,t} - p_{i,j,t-1}$. This data then runs from 1991–2002, for a time dimension of 12 periods. This panel has 163,200 observations.

The first explanatory variable in the regression is the log of the distance between locations j and k, $dist_{jk}$. Distance has proven to be a very useful explanatory variable for the volume of trade between two locations, as in the "gravity model" of trade. ER explain how it might also help explain deviations from the law of one price. The gravity model suggests that since transportation costs increase with distance, trade volumes will be greatest among nearby locations. When we consider the consumer prices of goods in two locations, it is very unlikely that either city is the exporter of the good. For example, we compare the price of olive oil between Washington, DC and Toronto, but neither city is known for its extensive groves of olive trees. Nonetheless, transportation costs might play a role in making prices more similar between nearby cities. The transport costs of olive oil from Greece to two close cities is probably very similar, while it may be very different for two distant cities.

Distribution costs are a large component of the final consumer price. Distribution costs are more likely to be similar for neighboring locations. Distribution of some goods is very labor intensive, and labor markets may be more tightly integrated if they are nearer geographically.

Also, ER point out that the mark-up on certain products might be more alike for nearby communities, perhaps because of regional determinants of demand.

The second explanatory variable is the absolute value difference in the log of the population between cities j and k, $pop_{jk,t}$. This variable is included because larger cities tend to have higher prices. For the U.S. the data refer to Metropolitan (MSA) Population Data. For Canada, the data are described as "Total Population, Census Div/Metro Areas." The population variable is time varying in the panel regressions, with data in each year from 1990–2002.[5]

We also introduce a measure of the difference in sales taxes between two locations as a possible explanatory variable for price differences. It is conceivable that markets are integrated to the extent that pre-tax prices are nearly equal but that differences in local sales taxes drives a wedge between prices in different locations. The tax rates used in the regressions are retail sales tax rates. For Canada, there are both national and provincial components to the rate. For the U.S., there is of course no national sales tax, so we simply use the state sales tax rates.[6] The absolute value of the tax rate difference between cities j and k is labeled tax_{jk} This variable is not time varying because we use a single tax rate for each city for the entire period. We were not able to construct a full panel of tax rates, and so averaged the data we were able to compile for each city. There appears to be very little time variation in sales tax rates.

The variable that is meant to capture the degree of integration between U.S. and Canadian markets is $bord_{jk}$ This is a dummy variable that takes on the value of 1 if cities j and k lie on opposite sides of the national border between the U.S. and Canada. The coefficient on the border dummy captures the absolute average log price difference between U.S. and Canadian cities that is not explained by distance or city size (or one of the dummy variables described below.)

As in ER, we include dummy variables for each city, $citdum_j$ This variable takes on the value of 1 if one of the cities in the city pair is city j. It is intended to capture any idiosyncratic aspects of the price of a given city that tends to make it different. We also performed regressions using time dummies, but the introduction of time dummies had little influence on our other parameter estimates. We also felt that there might be problems of interpretation when time dummies are included, so we report only results from regressions with no time dummies.

Thus, when we estimate equations for differences in price levels, our regression takes the form:

$$|p_{i,j,t} - p_{i,k,t}| = \beta_1 dist_{jk} + \beta_2 pop_{jk,t} + \beta_3 tax_{jk} + \beta_4 bord_{jk} + \sum_{h=1}^{N} \alpha_h citdum_h + u_{i,jk,t} \tag{1}$$

For changes in prices, the equation is similar:

$$|\pi_{i,j,t} - \pi_{i,k,t}| = \eta_1 dist_{jk} + \eta_2 pop_{jk,t} + \eta_3 tax_{jk} + \eta_4 bord_{jk} + \sum_{h=1}^{N} \lambda_h citdum_h + u_{i,jk,t} \tag{2}$$

As has been noted, we estimate these equations as a panel using all 100 goods. We also estimate using panels that have prices from each of 5 categories of goods: food, clothing, durables, miscellaneous products, and services.

3 Empirical results

Table 8.2 reports regression results for equation (1) when the full sample of 100 items is used in the panel. The sales tax variable proved not to be statistically significant in our regressions, so we report results only for those specifications that drop that variable. The three remaining variables – $dist_{jk}$, $pop_{jk,t}$, and $bord_{jk}$ – are highly significant, and the coefficients all have the expected sign. The coefficients on $dist_{jk}$ and $pop_{jk,t}$ have interpretations as elasticities. A 10 percent increase in the distance between two cities *ceteris paribus* increases the absolute price difference between the cities by 3.2 one-hundredths of 1 percent. Similarly, the effect of a 10 percent increase in relative population between two cities is to increase

Table 8.2(a) Panel regression, levels, all items

Dependent variable	Coefficient	Std. err.	t-stat
$dist_{jk}$	0.003208	0.000941	3.41
$bord_{jk}$	0.073104	0.001736	42.12
$pop_{jk,t}$	0.009451	0.001597	5.92

Notes
The equation was estimated using the full panel of 100 items, for 136 city-pairs, with annual data for 1990–2002. The dependent variable is $|p_{i,j,t} - p_{i,k,t}|$, the absolute value of the difference in the log of the price (expressed in U.S. dollars) of good i, between cities j and k, at time t. $dist_{jk}$ is the log of the distance (measured in miles as the great circle distance) between cities j and k. $bord_{jk}$ is a dummy variable that takes on the value of one if the two cities j and k are in different countries. $pop_{jk,t}$ is the absolute value of the difference in the logs of the populations of cities j and k in the year 2000. Also included in the regression, but not reported, are dummy variables for each city.
Std. err. denotes Huber–White robust standard errors.
Number of observations equals 176,800.

Table 8.2(b) Panel regression, first differences, all items

Dependent variable	Coefficient	Std. err.	t-stat
$dist_{jk}$	0.000857	0.000579	1.48
$bord_{jk}$	0.014425	0.001026	14.07
$pop_{jk,t}$	0.002255	0.000938	2.40

Notes
The equation was estimated using the full panel of 100 items, for 136 city-pairs, with annual data for 1990–2002. The dependent variable is $|\pi_{i,j,t} - \pi_{i,k,t}|$, the absolute value of the difference in the log of the inflation (expressed in U.S. dollars) of good i, between cities j and k, at time t. The regression uses the same independent variables as the regression reported in Table 8.2(a).
See Table 8.2(a) for definitions.
Sample size equals 163,200.

the absolute value of the price differential by 9.5 one-hundredths of 1 percent.

The coefficient on the border gives us the absolute average difference in prices in the U.S. versus Canada, holding other explanatory effects constant. We see from Table 8.2(a) that the difference is 7.3 percent. Note also that the border effect is very precisely estimated, with a *t*-statistic over 40. While this magnitude of price difference appears to be large in economic terms, it is difficult to interpret it as a measure of economic integration without having similar statistics for other country pairs for comparison.

To get a sense of the usefulness of panel estimation, we can compare the findings from the panel with our findings when we estimate equation (1) for each item individually. We find that out of 100 individual regressions, the coefficient on distance was significant at the 5 percent level and correctly signed for only 23 items; on relative population for 27 items; and, on the border dummy for 70 goods. (There were eight items for which the distance variable was significant but incorrectly signed, five in which population was significant but with the wrong sign, and zero such cases for border.) At the 10 percent significance level, the number of significant and correctly signed coefficients were: 27 for distance, 30 for population and 72 for the border (with 10 incorrectly signed significant coefficients on distance, 11 on population, but none on border).

The estimated coefficients for equation (2) when all items are included in the panel are reported in Table 8.2(b). As one should expect, all of the coefficients are smaller in magnitude when these short-term changes are examined. While the border dummy and relative population are still statistically significant, distance no longer is. That is, changes in the absolute price differences are not significantly linked to distance, which contrasts with the finding of ER.

The coefficient on the border dummy tells us that, *ceteris paribus*, the influence of the border effect is to increase the absolute value of the difference in price changes in U.S. cities relative to Canadian cities by 1.4 percentage points. Again, more data from other countries are needed before we can assess the economic significance of this finding.

We also estimated regression (equation (2)) individually for each of the 100 items, with this outcome: The coefficient on distance was significant at the 5 percent level and of the correct sign for 1 item (5 at the 10 percent level); relative population for 5 (6) items; border for 50 (56) items. For no items was a variable significant but of the incorrect sign.

The panel estimation is restrictive in that it imposes the same coefficients in regressions (1) and (2) for all items. Tables 8.3–8.8 report results for regressions estimated on smaller panels.

Tables 8.3(a), 8.4(a), 8.5(a), and 8.6(a) report results of estimation of equation (1) on price level differences for four mutually exclusive groupings of items: food, miscellaneous products, clothing, and durables, respectively. The border dummy is the only variable that was significant and of

Table 8.3(a) Panel regression, levels, food items only

Dependent variable	Coefficient	Std. err.	t-stat
$dist_{jk}$	0.005839	0.001477	3.95
$bord_{jk}$	0.079617	0.002508	31.74
$pop_{jk,t}$	0.018186	0.002493	7.29

Notes
The equation was estimated using the 42 items that are food items, for 136 city-pairs, with annual data for 1990–2002. The dependent variable is $|p_{i,j,t} - p_{i,k,t}|$, the absolute value of the difference in the log of the price (expressed in U.S. dollars) of good i, between cities j and k, at time t. The regression uses the same independent variables as the regression reported in Table 8.2(a).
See Table 8.2(a) for definitions.
Sample size equals 74,256.

Table 8.3(b) Panel regression, first differences, food items only

Dependent variable	Coefficient	Std. err.	t-stat
$dist_{jk}$	0.001037	0.001028	1.01
$bord_{jk}$	0.014520	0.00181	8.02
$pop_{jk,t}$	0.003325	0.001697	1.96

Notes
The equation was estimated using the 42 items that are food items, for 136 city-pairs, with annual data for 1990–2002. The dependent variable is $|\pi_{i,j,t} - \pi_{i,k,t}|$, the absolute value of the difference in the log of the inflation (expressed in U.S. dollars) of good i, between cities j and k, at time t. The regression uses the same independent variables as the regression reported in Table 8.2(a).
See Table 8.2(a) for definitions.
Sample size equals 68,544.

Table 8.4(a) Panel regression, levels, miscellaneous products only

Dependent variable	Coefficient	Std. err.	t-stat
$dist_{jk}$	−0.000040	0.002026	−0.02
$bord_{jk}$	0.089489	0.004126	21.69
$pop_{jk,t}$	0.006415	0.003344	1.92

Notes
The equation was estimated using the 22 items that are miscellaneous products, for 136 city-pairs, with annual data for 1990–2002. The dependent variable is $|p_{i,j,t} - p_{i,k,t}|$, the absolute value of the difference in the log of the price (expressed in U.S. dollars) of good i, between cities j and k, at time t. The regression uses the same independent variables as the regression reported in Table 8.2(a).
See Table 8.2(a) for definitions.
Sample size equals 38,896.

Table 8.4(b) Panel regression, first differences, miscellaneous products only

Dependent variable	Coefficient	Std. err.	t-stat
$dist_{jk}$	0.000973	0.001072	0.91
$bord_{jk}$	0.017147	0.001984	8.64
$pop_{jk,t}$	0.002032	0.001727	1.18

Notes
The equation was estimated using the 22 items that are miscellaneous products, for 136 city-pairs, with annual data for 1990–2002. The dependent variable is $|\pi_{i,j,t} - \pi_{i,k,t}|$, the absolute value of the difference in the log of the inflation (expressed in U.S. dollars) of good i, between cities j and k, at time t. The regression uses the same independent variables as the regression reported in Table 8.2(a).
See Table 8.2(a) for definitions.
Sample size equals 35,904.

Table 8.5(a) Panel regression, levels, clothing items only

Dependent variable	Coefficient	Std. err.	t-stat
$dist_{jk}$	0.004589	0.002740	1.67
$bord_{jk}$	0.019125	0.006292	3.04
$pop_{jk,t}$	−0.010780	0.004587	−2.35

Notes
The equation was estimated using the 9 items that are clothing items, for 136 city-pairs, with annual data for 1990–2002. The dependent variable is $|p_{i,j,t} - p_{i,k,t}|$, the absolute value of the difference in the log of the price (expressed in U.S. dollars) of good i, between cities j and k, at time t. The regression uses the same independent variables as the regression reported in Table 8.2(a).
See Table 8.2(a) for definitions.
Sample size equals 15,912.

Table 8.5(b) Panel regression, first differences, clothing items only

Dependent variable	Coefficient	Std. err.	t-stat
$dist_{jk}$	0.000838	0.001607	0.52
$bord_{jk}$	0.004700	0.003315	1.42
$pop_{jk,t}$	0.002460	0.002656	0.93

Notes
The equation was estimated using the 9 items that are clothing items, for 136 city-pairs, with annual data for 1990–2002. The dependent variable is $|\pi_{i,j,t} - \pi_{i,k,t}|$, the absolute value of the difference in the log of the inflation (expressed in U.S. dollars) of good i, between cities j and k, at time t. The regression uses the same independent variables as the regression reported in Table 8.2(a).
See Table 8.2(a) for definitions.
Sample size equals 14,688.

Table 8.6(a) Panel regression, levels, durables only

Dependent variable	Coefficient	Std. err.	t-stat
$dist_{jk}$	0.000036	0.002962	0.01
$bord_{jk}$	0.029864	0.005344	5.59
$pop_{jk,t}$	−0.009670	0.005046	−1.92

Notes
The equation was estimated using the 6 items that are durables, for 136 city-pairs, with annual data for 1990–2002. The dependent variable is $|p_{i,j,t} - p_{i,k,t}|$, the absolute value of the difference in the log of the price (expressed in U.S. dollars) of good i, between cities j and k, at time t. The regression uses the same independent variables as the regression reported in Table 8.2(a).
See Table 8.2(a) for definitions.
Sample size equals 10,608.

Table 8.6(b) Panel regression, first differences, durables only

Dependent variable	Coefficient	Std. err.	t-stat
$dist_{jk}$	−0.000380	0.001685	−0.22
$bord_{jk}$	0.008923	0.003289	2.71
$pop_{jk,t}$	−0.00014	0.002671	−0.05

Notes

The equation was estimated using the 6 items that are durables, for 136 city-pairs, with annual data for 1990–2002. The dependent variable is $|\pi_{i,j,t} - \pi_{i,k,t}|$, the absolute value of the difference in the log of the inflation (expressed in U.S. dollars) of good i, between cities j and k, at time t. The regression uses the same independent variables as the regression reported in Table 8.2(a).
See Table 8.2(a) for definitions.
Sample size equals 9,792.

Table 8.7(a) Panel regression, levels, services only

Dependent variable	Coefficient	Std. err.	t-stat
$dist_{jk}$	0.001664	0.002078	0.80
$bord_{jk}$	0.078399	0.003627	21.61
$pop_{jk,t}$	0.009293	0.003696	2.51

Notes

The equation was estimated using the 21 items that are services, for 136 city-pairs, with annual data for 1990–2002. The dependent variable is $|p_{i,j,t} - p_{i,k,t}|$, the absolute value of the difference in the log of the price (expressed in U.S. dollars) of good i, between cities j and k, at time t. The regression uses the same independent variables as the regression reported in Table 8.2(a).
See Table 8.2(a) for definitions.
Sample size equals 37,128.

Table 8.7(b) Panel regression, first differences, services only

Dependent variable	Coefficient	Std. err.	t-stat
$dist_{jk}$	0.000734	0.001008	0.73
$bord_{jk}$	0.017125	0.001468	11.67
$pop_{jk,t}$	0.000943	0.001499	0.63

Notes

The equation was estimated using the 21 items that are services, for 136 city-pairs, with annual data for 1990–2002. The dependent variable is $|\pi_{i,j,t} - \pi_{i,k,t}|$, the absolute value of the difference in the log of the inflation (expressed in U.S. dollars) of good i, between cities j and k, at time t. The regression uses the same independent variables as the regression reported in Table 8.2(a).
See Table 8.2(a) for definitions.
Sample size equals 34,272.

Table 8.8(a) Panel regression, levels, goods only

Dependent variable	Coefficient	Std. err.	t-stat
$dist_{jk}$	0.003619	0.001050	3.45
$bord_{jk}$	0.071696	0.001968	36.44
$pop_{jk,t}$	0.009493	0.001762	5.39

Notes
The equation was estimated using the 79 items that are goods, for 136 city-pairs, with annual data for 1990–2002. The dependent variable is $|p_{i,j,t} - p_{i,k,t}|$, the absolute value of the difference in the log of the price (expressed in U.S. dollars) of good i, between cities j and k, at time t. The regression uses the same independent variables as the regression reported in Table 8.2(a).
See Table 8.2(a) for definitions.
Sample size equals 139,672.

Table 8.8(b) Panel regression, first differences, goods only

Dependent variable	Coefficient	Std. err.	t-stat
$dist_{jk}$	0.000889	0.000673	1.32
$bord_{jk}$	0.013707	0.001215	11.28
$pop_{jk,t}$	0.002603	0.001105	2.36

Notes
The equation was estimated using the 79 items that are goods, for 136 city-pairs, with annual data for 1990–2002. The dependent variable is $|\pi_{i,j,t} - \pi_{i,k,t}|$, the absolute value of the difference in the log of the inflation (expressed in U.S. dollars) of good i, between cities j and k, at time t. The regression uses the same independent variables as the regression reported in Table 8.2(a).
See Table 8.2(a) for definitions.
Sample size equals 128,928.

the correct sign in all four regressions. Its magnitude varies across categories. The border effect implies approximately an 8 percent difference in prices of food items, and a 9 percent difference in prices of miscellaneous products; but only a 2 percent difference in the price of clothing and a 3 percent difference in the price of durable items. Population is only significant and of the correct sign for food items. Apparently prices are higher in larger cities only for food. Similarly, distance is only significant and of the correct sign for food items. This suggests that perhaps shipping costs are important in determining price differences, since these costs are apt to be a relatively high fraction of total value for food.

Table 8.7(a) reports the results of regression (equation (1)) for a panel that only includes prices of services. The border coefficient and relative population are significant and of the correct sign. The border accounts for an 8 percent difference in prices across the U.S./Canadian border, *ceteris paribus*. The fact that both the border coefficient and relative population are significant explainers of price differences for services most likely accounted for by the differences in labor markets across locations. One can surmise that wages are relatively high in large cities, and in the U.S. compared to Canada, thus making services prices higher.

It is interesting to compare the findings in Table 8.7(a) to those in Table 8.8(a). The latter table reports the results of a panel regression in which only goods – food, miscellaneous products, clothing, and durables – are included. First, note that distance is significant in explaining price differences for goods but not services. This seems to indicate that shipping costs are an important reason why distance matters for prices, since the effect is restricted to goods that are traded. (And, recall that this effect mostly arises from food items.)

Second, the border effect is quite similar in magnitude for both services and goods. Perhaps this represents the influence of higher wages in the U.S. compared to Canada. This might push up the cost of all products, including goods (because of the labor input into distribution) in the U.S. Alternatively, it may be that the mark-up is higher in the U.S. as a consequence of price discrimination by sellers. But another possibility that we cannot rule out is that this difference represents a persistent overvaluation of the U.S. dollar relative to the Canadian dollar in the 1990s. That is, perhaps the price wedge is not the result of equilibrium factors, but instead arises because of a very long-lived, but transitory disequilibrium.

We also note that the magnitude of the relative population variable is almost identical for goods and for services, which may lend support for the notion that the local wage is a large determinant of retail prices even for goods.

Tables 8.3(b), 8.4(b), 8.5(b), and 8.6(b) report the results of estimation of equation (2) for price changes for food, miscellaneous products, clothing, and durables, respectively. The border dummy is significant and of the correct sign for all of these categories except clothing. As we found with price levels, the border effect on price changes is largest for food items and miscellaneous products, and is especially small for clothing. Distance is never a significant explanatory variable in these regressions, and population is significant only for food items.

Comparing the effects of distance, relative population, and the border on relative price changes between cities for services and goods (from Tables 8.7(b) and 8.8(b)), we again find little difference. The magnitude of the border coefficient is very similar – it accounts for a 1.7 percentage points difference in price changes for services, and 1.4 percentage points difference for goods. The coefficients on distance are small and insignificant in both panels. One slight distinction is that the coefficient on relative population is slightly larger and significant in the goods panel.

4 Caveats and conclusions

We have found that distance and relative population play a significant role in explaining price level differences between the U.S. and Canada, but only a minor and usually insignificant role in the regressions explaining differences in price changes. The major exception to this is that distance does not play an important part in explaining price level differences for service items. But the border dummy is almost universally significant, both statistically and apparently in economic magnitude. The price differences across borders exist among tradables (i.e., goods) and nontradables (services), though for some categories of tradables (clothing and durables) the difference is smaller. Roughly, the magnitude of the border effect is a 7 percent difference in the absolute prices between Canada and the U.S., and a 1.5 percent difference in price changes.

We do not view the findings of this study as conclusive. The precision of our estimates is limited by the precision of the measurement of prices; the lack of availability of prices for more than four cities in Canada; the number of goods for which we have a full time series from 1990–2002 of prices (only 100 goods); the frequency of observation of prices (annual); and, the time span of the data (only the most recent 13 years). It would also be helpful to be able to use data on other explanatory variables for price differences, such as wages in the service sector by city. And, as we have noted, this study only examines price differences for one pair of countries. There is no set of results for other countries to use as a gauge for comparisons. Most of the data for more refined study probably lies in the files of national statistical agencies. There are significant potential benefits to analyzing that data as a way of measuring the economic integration of economies and the significance of short-term fluctuations in exchange rates.

Acknowledgement

The views expressed in this chapter are those of the authors and do not necessarily represent the views of the Board of Governors of the Federal Reserve or the Federal Reserve System. Engel acknowledges research support from a grant from the National Science Foundation to the University of Wisconsin.

Notes

1 This simple idea finds empirical backing in the work of Rose (2000), who finds that adoption of a common currency greatly expands the volume of trade between nations.
2 In a typical year, the EIU reports prices on many more products. We chose to work with these 100 items because there is price data for all of them for each city for every year, thus allowing us to use balanced panels.
3 There are also city dummies, and in some regressions, time dummies, as we explain in section 1.
4 This means that the Canadian dollar price of goods sold in Canadian cities is converted into U.S. dollar values by multiplying by the U.S. dollar per Canadian dollar exchange rate. The EIU survey reports prices in U.S. dollar terms, converted using "the market exchange rate on the date of the survey."

5 The U.S. data is from the Census Bureau, and the Canada data from Statistics Canada. The U.S. data was downloaded from the site: http://recenter.tamu.edu/ Data/popm, and the Canadian data from Haver in the Cansimr database (Regional Canadian Economic Indicators).

6 We do not include any measure of city-specific sales taxes for any U.S. cities. The data on sales taxes are compiled from a variety of sources: U.S. data (on-line): Center on Budget and Policy Priorities; Urban Institute State database. Canadian data: Canadian Tax Foundation's Finances of the Nation; Price Waterhouse; http://www.ca.taxnews.com/tnnpublic.nsf/notespages/4652A712797CB4AC85256 959006AB77E/$file/FactsFigures2002.pdf, http://www.bus.ualberta.ca/CIBS-WCER/ WCER/pdf/43.pdf, and http://freespace.virgin.net/john.cletheroe/usa_can/taxes/.

References

Devereux, Michael B. and Engel, Charles (2003), "Monetary policy in the open economy revisited: exchange rate flexibility and price-setting behavior," *Review of Economic Studies*, 70: 765–783.

Engel, Charles and Rogers, John H. (1996), "How wide is the border?," *American Economic Review*, 86: 1112–1125.

Mundell, Robert (1961), "A theory of optimum currency areas," *American Economic Review*, 51: 657–665.

Rose, Andrew (2000), "One money, one market: estimating the effect of common currencies on trade," *Economic Policy*, 30: 7–45.

9 An asset market integration test based on observable macroeconomic stochastic discount factors

P.N. Smith, S. Sorensen and M.R. Wickens[1]

1 Introduction

There are a number of tests and measures of the degree of financial market integration in the literature. An example is the idea that integrated markets should provide rates of return that are highly correlated with one another and that a measure of correlation provides an appropriate test. This particular idea is clearly false; for substantial periods of time we do not even see stocks that are traded on the same market moving together. Specific models of what prices risk in individual markets could provide the basis of a test of integration. However, as has been widely shown, any differences between these pricing models will be subject to arbitrage by informed traders and so cannot form the basis for a test. Adam *et al.* (2002) provide a recent survey of tests of integration between various stock markets.

In this chapter we exploit the absence of arbitrage possibilities and the operation of the 'Law of One Price' in stochastic discount factor (SDF) theory to construct a test of integration based on a common approach to pricing assets in all markets, not only for stocks. The SDF approach that we adopt says that one SDF should price all assets – the model is not market or asset-specific. Unlike much of the literature, we adopt a direct parametric approach which takes estimates of an identical SDF from two asset markets and asks whether the price of risk associated with this SDF is the same for the two assets as SDF theory says it should. Another distinctive feature of our approach is that we employ observable macroeconomic factors. This allows us to estimate and compare the estimated risk premia in the markets concerned, with and without the integration restriction being applied.[2]

The chapter uses this methodology to test market integration between the UK equity and FOREX markets. This approach tests a joint hypothesis of the integration of the two markets and the specification of the SDF. Hence, to mitigate the potential corruption of the test of integration by misspecification of the SDF, we exploit the extensive analysis in two previous papers on the two individual markets of the specification of the SDF (see Wickens and Smith (2001) and Smith *et al.* (2003)). Potentially, there are a large number of consumption-based models, as well as broader SDF models, that could be analysed in the environment that is proposed in this chapter. The results from previous work suggest, however, that this number can be reduced substantially. In a study of the US and UK equity risk premia, Smith *et al.* (2003) find that the simple positive relationship between the level of the excess return and the variance implied by the static model capital asset pricing model (CAPM) is not supported by the evidence. Nor is there much evidence in favour of the consumption-based CAPM model with power utility, or of generalisations to allow for time-non-separable preferences. Instead, two-variable SDF models that include a role for inflation in addition to consumption growth perform much better in terms of providing significantly priced sources of risk. There is, in addition, some evidence of alternative multiple-factor SDF models also providing priced factors. Similar results for the FOREX risk premium are found by Wickens and Smith (2001). Even allowing for different versions of the model that allow for complete and incomplete markets and take the perspectives of domestic US or UK investors, the evidence suggests that the CCAPM with power utility does not provide a good model of the FOREX risk premium. There is, however, some evidence in favour of two-factor SDF models of a similar type to those employed to model equity returns. In particular, evidence is found in favour of a two-factor model with money and output growth as factors.

In this chapter we confine ourselves to analysing the two-factor SDF models for UK investors but we include the CCAPM for comparability. Given their importance in our previous work, we consider nominal sources of risk. It should be emphasised that all of the models we examine impose the absence of arbitrage possibilities.

Our approach can be contrasted with that of Chen and Knez (1995). Following the work of Hansen and Jagannathan (1991), Chen and Knez reverse-engineer the set of possible SDFs that could generate observed asset returns and then compare these SDFs across assets. The extent to which they are different provides a test of market integration. While this type of analysis can provide some tests of integration, it cannot provide a measure of the importance of different sources of risk in the markets concerned. By estimating the risk premia directly, our approach does provide such measures.

In the next section we set out the SDF approach and the set of asset pricing equations that result. Subsequent development of the CCAPM and other SDF models produces the individual and joint models for asset returns that we estimate. These form the basis of the test for integration. Following description of the data, section 3 presents the estimation and testing results and measures of the risk premia. Our conclusions are presented in the final section.

2 Theoretical models of the risk premium

2.1 The SDF model of asset pricing for asset returns

The SDF model is based on the simple idea that P_t, the price of a one-period asset at the beginning of period t, is determined by the expected discounted value of its payoff at the start of period $t+1$, namely, X_{t+1}:

$$P_t = E_t(M_{t+1}X_{t+1}) \tag{1}$$

where M_{t+1} is the stochastic discount factor, or pricing kernel (see Cochrane (2001) for a survey of SDF theory). For equity, the payoff is $X_{t+1} = P_{t+1} + D_{t+1}$, where D_{t+1} are dividend payments assumed to be made at the start of period $t+1$. The pricing equation can also be written

$$1 = E_t\left[M_{t+1}\frac{X_{t+1}}{P_t}\right] = E_t[M_{t+1}R_{t+1}], \tag{2}$$

where $R_{t+1} = 1 + r_{t+1} = X_{t+1}/P_t = (P_{t+1} + D_{t+1})/P_t$ is the gross return and r_{t+1} is the return. For FOREX the domestic investor can receive the risky return $R_{t+1} = S_{t+1}(1 + i^*_{t+1})/S_t$ from investing in one unit of the overseas asset. This has the risk-free component i^*_{t+1} denominated in foreign currency and the risky component resulting from the change in the exchange rate S_{t+1}/S_t. i^*_{t+1} is the nominal interest rate and the exchange rate S_t is defined as the price of foreign currency. The pricing equation ((1) or (2)) has an identical form for all assets.

For any return R_{t+1} taking logarithms and assuming log-normality – and noting that if $\ln x$ is $N(\mu, \sigma^2)$ then $\ln E(x) = \mu + \sigma^2/2$ – we obtain

$$\begin{aligned}
0 &= \ln E_t(M_{t+1}R_{t+1}) \\
&= E_t(\ln(M_{t+1}R_{t+1})) + V_t(\ln(M_{t+1}R_{t+1}))/2 \\
&= E_t(m_{t+1}) + E_t(r_{t+1}) + V_t(m_{t+1})/2 + V_t(r_{t+1})/2 + cov_t(m_{t+1},r_{t+1})
\end{aligned}$$

where $m_{t+1} = \ln M_{t+1}$. Hence the pricing equation can be written

$$E_t(r_{t+1}) + E_t(m_{t+1}) + V_t(m_{t+1})/2 + V_t(r_{t+1})/2 = -cov_t(m_{t+1},r_{t+1})$$

If the asset is risk-free then its return is known at the start of period t implying $r_{t+1} \equiv r^f_t$, $E_t(r_{t+1}) = r^f_t$ and $V_t(r_{t+1}) = 0$. The pricing equation for the risk-free asset can therefore be written

$$E_t(m_{t+1}) + r^f_t + \frac{1}{2}V_t(m_{t+1}) = 0.$$

Subtracting the two pricing equations gives the expected excess return on the risky asset

$$E_t(r_{t+1} - r_t^f) + \frac{1}{2}V_t(r_{t+1}) = -cov_t(m_{t+1}, r_{t+1}). \tag{3}$$

This is the key no-arbitrage condition that all correctly priced assets must satisfy *when their returns are log-normally distributed*. The right-hand side is the risk premium and $1/2V_t(r_{t+1})$ is the Jensen effect. We note that $V_t(r_{t+1}) = V_t(r_{t+1} - r_t^f)$ and $cov_t(m_{t+1}, r_{t+1}) = cov_t(m_{t+1}, r_{t+1} - r_t^f)$ as r_t^f is known at time t.

2.1.1 Real versus nominal returns

The pricing equation (1) and the no-arbitrage condition (3) hold whether the variables, including the discount factor, are expressed in nominal or real terms. Although it is common to specify the discount factor in real terms, as a real risk-free rate does not exist in practice, we shall specify returns in nominal terms. Assuming no default risk, the nominal risk-free rate is a Treasury bill rate. We therefore need to re-express the no-arbitrage condition accordingly.

We assume that equations (1) and (3) are expressed in real terms with M_{t+1} as the real *ex post* discount factor and r_{t+1} and r_t^f as real *ex post* rates of return. We now let i_{t+1} and i_t^f be the respective nominal rates of return and we let P_t^c be the consumer price index at the start of period t. Equation (2) can therefore be written

$$1 = E_t(M_{t+1}.(1 + r_{t+1}))$$

$$= E_t\left(M_{t+1}.\frac{1 + i_{t+1}}{1 + \pi_{t+1}}\right)$$

$$= E_t\left(\frac{M_{t+1}}{1 + \pi_{t+1}}.(1 + i_{t+1})\right)$$

where $1 + r_{t+1} = 1 + i_{t+1}/1 + \pi_{t+1}$ and $1 + \pi_{t+1} = P_{t+1}^c/P_t^c$. It can be shown that the no-arbitrage condition for nominal returns and a real discount factor is

$$E_t(i_{t+1} - i_t^f) + \frac{1}{2}V_t(i_{t+1}) = -cov_t(m_{t+1}, i_{t+1}) + cov_t(\pi_{t+1}, i_{t+1}). \tag{4}$$

Thus there is an extra term in the conditional covariance of inflation with the nominal (excess) return.

2.2 Asset market integration

The key feature of the SDF approach is that if markets are integrated, equation (4) applies to all assets – i.e. if the Law of One Price prevails and arbitrage drives risk-adjusted returns together. In the case of equity and FOREX their nominal returns should satisfy:

$$E_t(i^e_{t+1} - i^f_t) + \frac{1}{2}V_t(i_{t+1}) = -cov_t(m_{t+1}, i^e_{t+1}) + cov_t(\pi_{t+1}, i_{t+1}) \tag{5}$$

$$E_t(i^{fx}_{t+1} - i^f_t) + \frac{1}{2}V_t(i_{t+1}) = -cov_t(m_{t+1}, i^{fx}_{t+1}) + cov_t(\pi_{t+1}, i_{t+1})$$

where the nominal return on equity is i^e_{t+1} and the nominal return on FOREX is i^{fx}_{t+1}. In order to create a test of integration we need to specify m_{t+1}. We consider two models of the real discount factor.

2.3 Consumption-based models: CCAPM with power utility

The canonical model of the discount factor is the CCAPM. We consider this for nominal asset returns. Asset prices derive their value from the expected consumption streams of investors who choose to

$$\max_{C_t} \mathcal{U}_t = U(C_t) + \beta E_t(\mathcal{U}_{t+1})$$

subject to the nominal budget constraint

$$P^c_t C_t + W_{t+1} = P^c_t Y_t + W_t(1 + i_t)$$

where C_t is real consumption, Y_t is real non-asset income and W_t is nominal financial wealth at the start of period t. The solution is the Euler equation

$$E_t\left(\frac{\beta U'(C_{t+1})}{U'(C_t)} \frac{P^c_t}{P^c_{t+1}} (1 + i_{t+1}) \right) = 1.$$

which was first estimated by Hansen and Singleton (1983). This implies that the CCAPM has implicitly defined the real SDF as

$$M_{t+1} = \frac{\beta U'(C_{t+1})}{U'(C_t)}$$

For the power utility function $U = (C^{1-\sigma}_t - 1)/(1 - \sigma)$ with constant co-efficient of relative risk aversion σ, the real discount factor, or marginal rate of substitution between periods t and $t + 1$, is

$$M_{t+1} = \beta\left(\frac{C_{t+1}}{C_t} \right)^{-\sigma}$$

Since real consumption is usually defined in *ex post* terms, the discount factor will also be in real *ex post* terms. Taking logarithms, and ignoring all constants, we obtain

$$m_{t+1} = -\sigma \Delta c_{t+1}$$

where $c_t = \ln C_t$. The no-arbitrage condition in real terms becomes

$$E_t(r_{t+1} - r_t^f) + \frac{1}{2}V_t(r_{t+1}) = \sigma cov_t(\Delta c_{t+1}, r_{t+1})$$

The interpretation of the real equity risk premium is that investors lose utility today by not consuming. To compensate investors who defer the utility from an extra unit of consumption today they need additional marginal utility from future consumption. Because marginal utility declines as consumption increases, a higher level of consumption is needed in the future. The return on the investment must be large enough to generate the required consumption in the future. The greater the consumption needed, the larger the return must be, hence the risk premium is larger the greater the predicted covariance between consumption and returns.

In nominal terms the no-arbitrage condition can be written

$$E_t(i_{t+1} - i_t^f) + \frac{1}{2}V_t(i_{t+1}) = \sigma cov_t(\Delta c_{t+1}, i_{t+1}) + cov_t(\pi_{t+1}, i_{t+1}) \qquad (6)$$

Thus the nominal risk premium involves the nominal return and has a second covariance term associated with consumer price inflation. The greater the covariance between nominal returns and inflation, the larger the risk premium. We have argued that the larger the future consumption needed, the higher real returns must be. This is also true for nominal returns. The extra risk is that nominal returns will be larger solely due to inflation.

The power utility version of the CCAPM is a restricted version of more general representations of preferences. Campbell (2003), amongst others, argues for the time non-separable preferences originally proposed by Kreps and Porteus (1978) and implemented in CES form by Epstein and Zin (1989, 1990, 1991). The results in Smith *et al.* (2003) provide a direct test of this specification of preferences in the context of the method employed in this chapter. These results demonstrate that this generalisation adds little to the explanation of the behaviour of equity returns as the extra parameters are not statistically significant. Here, therefore, we provide estimates based only on the CCAPM with power utility.

2.4 CAPM and the monetary model

In Wickens and Smith (2001) the CCAPM for FOREX risk is found to be dominated by an implementation of the one-period CAPM. In this chapter we consider how well CAPM might do as a model of equity risk. The argument in Wickens and Smith is that in practice mean-variance analysis is often used to hedge FOREX risk. The key issue is then how to measure the uncertainty that arises from the future return to the portfolio. According to monetary models of the exchange rate, pure currency risk can be expected to be a function of domestic and foreign money supplies and output. Wickens and Smith find that for the UK domestic investor the behaviour of domestic money and output were the most important. Using the argument that the same SDF should be relevant for pricing all assets, we also consider the potential role for money and output to be the fundamental sources of risk for the equity market. An additional rationale for the choice of these two risk factors in the domestic equity market is the general equilibrium argument that money and output growth represent the fundamental sources of nominal and real activity.

One could view such models from a general SDF perspective. If $z_{it}(i = 1, \ldots, n)$ are n factors which are jointly log-normally distributed with equity returns then the discount factor can be written

$$m_{t+1} = -\sum_{i=1}^{n} \beta_i z_{i,t+1}$$

This implies the no-arbitrage condition

$$E_t(r_{t+1} - r_t^f) + \frac{1}{2} V_t(r_{t+1}) = \sum_i \beta_i cov_t(z_{i,t+1}, r_{t+1}) \tag{7}$$

$$= \sum_i \beta_i f_{it},$$

where the f_{it} are known as *common factors*.

In the absence of the sort of clear theoretical foundations provided by general equilibrium theories of asset pricing, the problem is to identify potential sources of risk to include in the SDF model. The latent factor literature simply assumes that unobserved processes can be specified for the factors. As noted above, general equilibrium models imply that investors are concerned with future consumption, and in particular, consumption next period. The main holders of equity are financial institutions, especially pension funds. They act on behalf of investors' consumption at a much more distant point in the future. In assessing risk, financial institutions focus largely on short-term performance, and on the value of the portfolio. This suggests that the market equity risk premium may be more influenced by short-term price risk than longer-term considerations of consumption. The sort of factors that are likely to affect the price of equity in the short term are associated with the business cycle and inflation. Output and money could be good measures of these sources of risk.

2.5 Alternative related approaches

While our analysis of a market integration is made from the perspective of alternative versions of the SDF model, others have chosen to rely on a single representation of the SDF model without providing evidence of its adequacy. Flood and Rose (2003) present a panel-data test of the integration of US equity markets using the level of the Fama–French return factors: market return, HML and SMB. They assume that the conditional covariance between the SDF and the risky return is a linear function of the factors. The theory provides no restrictions on the parameters on the factors in these linear pricing equations; the coefficients on the factors are allowed to vary between assets. The only parameter that Flood and Rose can identify across assets is that on the risk-free rate, and so this forms the basis of their test of integration. Despite their success in relating the Fama–French factors to returns, it would seem unlikely that such linear relations provide a proper basis for carrying out the test. According to SDF theory, risk premia are based on the conditional covariances between the underlying discount factor and the risky return, and not on the return itself. It is only in models such as the Vasicek latent affine factor model that the risk premium is a linear function of the return. Our approach, which is more general, by contrast works directly with such covariances (compare with equation (7)). Furthermore, given that the Fama–French factors are all portfolio returns themselves, and so may be asset-specific, tests based on these 'mimicking portfolios' are essentially tests based on relationships between relative rates of return rather than tests based on fundamental sources of risk. It would seem unlikely therefore that the factors chosen by Flood and Rose would be suitable for testing, for example, the integration of equity and FOREX markets.

3 The econometric framework

3.1 Multivariate conditional heteroskedasticity models

We need to model the distribution of the excess return on equity jointly with the macroeconomic factors in such a way that the mean of the conditional distribution of the excess return in period $t+1$, given information available at time t, satisfies the no-arbitrage condition. The conditional mean of the excess return involves selected time-varying second moments of the joint distribution. We therefore require a specification of the joint distribution that admits a time-varying variance–covariance matrix. A convenient choice is the multi-variate GARCH-in-mean (MGM) model.

Let $\mathbf{x}_{t+1} = (i^e_{t+1} - i^f_t, \; i^{fx}_{t+1} - i^f_t, \; z_{1,t+1}, \; z_{2,t+1}, \; \ldots)'$, where $z_{1,t+1}, \; z_{2,t+1}, \; \ldots$ include the macroeconomic variables that give rise to the factors in the SDF through their conditional covariances with the excess return. In principle, they may also include additional variables that are jointly distributed with these macroeconomic variables as this may improve the estimate of the joint distribution. The MGM model can then be written

$$\mathbf{x}_{t+1} = \alpha + \Gamma\mathbf{x}_t + \Theta\mathbf{g}_t + \epsilon_{t+1}$$

where

$$\epsilon_{t+1}|I_t \sim D[0, \mathbf{H}_{t+1}]$$

$$\mathbf{g}_t = vech\{\mathbf{H}_{t+1}\}$$

The *vech* operator converts the lower triangle of a symmetric matrix into a vector. The distribution is the multivariate t-distribution. The first equation of the model is restricted to satisfy the no-arbitrage condition. Thus, in general, the first two rows of Γ are zero and the first two rows of Θ are $(-\frac{1}{2}, 0, \; -\beta_{11}, \; -\beta_{12}, \; -\beta_{13}, \ldots)$ and $(0, \; -\frac{1}{2}, \; -\beta_{11}, \; -\beta_{12}, \; -\beta_{13}, \ldots)$.

It will be noted that the theory requires that the macroeconomic variables display conditional heteroskedasticity. This is not something traditionally assumed in macroeconometrics, but seems to be present in our data. Ideally, we would like to use high frequency data for asset returns, but very little macroeconomic data are published for frequencies higher than one month, and then only a few variables are available. Although more macroeconomic variables are published at lower frequencies, they tend not to display conditional heteroskedasticity.

While the MGM model is convenient, it is not ideal. First, it is heavily parameterised which can create problems for the numerical convergence of the maximum likelihood due to the surface being relatively flat, and hence uninformative. Second, asset returns tend to be excessively volatile. Assuming a non-normal distribution such as a t-distribution can sometimes help in this regard by dealing with thick tails. The main problem, however, is not thick tails, but a small number of extreme values. The coefficients of the variance process of the MGM model have a tendency to produce a near unstable variance process in their attempt to fit these extreme values. In principle, a stochastic volatility model, which includes an extra random term in the variance, could capture these extreme values. Unfortunately, as far as we are aware, no multivariate stochastic model with mean effects in the conditional covariances has been proposed in the literature.

In view of the need to restrict the number of coefficients to estimate, a commonly used specification of $\mathbf{H}_{t+1}$ is the constant conditional correlation (CCC) model discussed in Ding and Engle (2001) where the dynamics of the conditional covariances are driven by individual GARCH processes for the variances of each variable. Given that the SDF approach focusses on the importance of the contribution of covariances, restricting their dynamics in this way, and not allowing the correlations to be time-varying, seems too restrictive.[3]

As a result, we specify $\mathbf{H}_{t+1}$ using the BEKK model originally proposed by Engle and Kroner (1995). This takes the form:

$$vech(\mathbf{H}_{t+1}) = \Lambda + \sum_{i=0}^{p-1} \Phi_i vech(\mathbf{H}_{t+1}) + \sum_{j=0}^{q-1} \Theta_j vech(\epsilon_{t-j}\epsilon_{t-j}')$$

where Λ, Φ and Θ may be unrestricted. With $n - 1$ factors z_{it} then Φ and Θ are both square matrices of size $n(n + 1)/2$ and Λ is a size $n(n + 1)/2$ vector. A formulation of this model which can make implementation easier is the error-correction formulation or VECM BEKK:

$$\mathbf{H}_{t+1} = \mathbf{V}'\mathbf{V} + \mathbf{A}'(\mathbf{H}_t - \mathbf{V}'\mathbf{V})\mathbf{A} + \mathbf{B}'(\epsilon_t\epsilon_t' - \mathbf{V}'\mathbf{V})\mathbf{B}$$

where the first term on the RHS is the long-term or unconditional covariance matrix. This can be initialised with starting values from sample averages. The remaining terms capture short-term deviations from this long term. A restricted version of this formulation is to specify $\mathbf{V}$ to be lower triangular, the ARCH matrix $\mathbf{B}$ to be fully parameterised to allow for full generality in the transmission of shocks and the GARCH matrix $\mathbf{A}$ to be a symmetric matrix which reduces parameter numbers but allows for correlation over time in elements of the covariance system. A further restriction is that we require that the covariance function is stationary. This is satisfied if the absolute value of the eigenvalues of $(A \otimes A) + (B \otimes B)$ lie inside the unit circle where $\otimes$ is the Kronecker product.

We employ two alternative structures for the VECM BEKK model for the models that we estimate. In the first case we condition on consumption growth and inflation and in the second case on money and output growth. Thus the vector $\mathbf{x}_{t+1}$ for the first models of the nominal equity and FOREX returns are $\mathbf{x}_{t+1} = (i_{t+1}^e - i_t^f, i_{t+1}^{fx} - i_t^f, \pi_{t+1}, \Delta c_{t+1})'$ while that for the second model is $\mathbf{x}_{t+1} = (i_{t+1}^e - i_t^f, i_{t+1}^{fx} - i_t^f, \Delta m_{t+1}, \Delta y_{t+1})'$. A first order vector autoregression for the macroeconomic variables is found to be sufficient to capture the serial dependence in their means, a VECM BEKK(1,1) model is found to be adequate for the multivariate variance–covariance process.

For greater generality, instead of assuming that ϵ_t has a multivariate Normal distribution, we assume that it has a multivariate t-distribution. This introduces a technical problem: unlike the Normal distribution, the moment generating function of the t-distribution does not exist and hence, strictly, the logarithm of the Euler equation does not exist.

4 Results, tests and risk premia

4.1 The data

The data are monthly (1975.6–2002.6). The equity returns are constructed from the MSCI total equity return index, the FOREX returns are formed from the spot exchange rate of Sterling relative to the US dollar and one-month Treasury Bill interest rates for the two countries. The Retail Price Index (RPI) is used to construct price inflation. M0 is the narrow definition money supply and output is measured by the volume index of industrial production all from Datastream. Total real non-durable consumption growth is especially provided by the NIESR. All data are expressed in equivalent annual percentages.

4.2 Estimation results and integration tests

The estimation results for two versions of each of the three models outlined above are presented in Table 9.1. These are the CCAPM, the two factor SDF model with consumption growth and inflation as the two factors and a second two-factor SDF model with output growth and money growth as the two factors. In the first two models the restriction on the coefficient on the covariance of the risky return with inflation to -1 is applied. The estimate of the coefficient on the covariance with consumption growth is therefore an estimate of the coefficient of relative risk aversion. The coefficients are estimated with less precision than those presented in our earlier work reflecting the loss of degrees of freedom implied by a joint model of pricing equity and FOREX risk using the same sample size. Taking the first model where this estimate is allowed to differ between assets, we obtain estimates of the CRRA that are large and implausible from the perspective of the theory. The estimate for the equity market is somewhat larger than that for FOREX. The test of integration of the two markets for the CCAPM is a test, therefore, of whether these two coefficient estimates are the same. Estimates for the restricted model are presented as model 2. The value of the likelihood ratio test of integration is 15.78 which is significant at less than the 0.05 per cent level given that the test is distributed $\chi^2(1)$ in this case.

The CCAPM is dominated by the two factor SDF models presented as models 3–6. These are models where no restriction is applied on the coefficients on the two conditional covariances between the risky excess return and the macroeconomic factor. The likelihood ratio test for the CCAPM restriction between models 1 and 3 has a value of 16.04 which is also significant at less than the 0.05 per cent level given that the test is distributed $\chi^2(2)$ in this case. In the equation for equity returns the coefficients on consumption growth and inflation reflect the estimates presented in Smith *et al.* (2003) in that the coefficient on the inflation covariance far exceeds that implied by the power-utility CCAPM in real terms. Likewise the coefficient on the consumption covariance is again much larger than would be regarded as a plausible measure of the degree of relative risk aversion implied by the CCAPM in real terms. The coefficients in the FOREX return equation are also representative of our earlier work reported in Wickens and Smith (2001). For the UK investor the coefficient on the consumption covariance is very large and positive as is that on the inflation covariance. It should be noted that the major disagreement on coefficient sign between the two parts of the model is on the inflation covariance. This is the main source of the rejection of market integration implied by the test statistic comparing model 3 with model 4 that imposes identical prices of risk in both markets. The LR test of integration has a value of 7.3 which is significant at the 2.5 per cent level given that the statistic is distributed $\chi^2(2)$. This rejection is quite decisive given the relative imprecision of the coefficient estimates themselves.

The second set of estimates take output and money growth as the SDF. In model 5 the results for both excess returns in the model imply a positive relation with the covariance with money growth and a negative relation with the output growth. This model is found in Wickens and Smith (2001) to be the best description of the FOREX return – again in the current environment the coefficients are estimated with less precision. The integration test for this model has a value of 11.88 which is significant at the 0.25 per cent level again providing a clear rejection of integration.

The estimation results also provide some comparative information about the nature of the risk premium in the two markets. For models apart from the CCAPM, we see that the risk premium on the FOREX market is smaller on average than that for equity at 2 per cent or less rather than more than 8 per cent for equity. This is also reflected in lower excess returns for FOREX than equity. Unconditional analysis might suggest therefore that the FOREX risk premium is less economically important. However, the FOREX risk premium has a larger variance, in some cases much larger. As a result, the proportion of the variance of the observed excess return explained by variation in the FOREX risk premium is greater than 15 per cent compared with less than 10 per cent for the equity risk premium. This is given that the variability of the underlying returns series are similar in order of magnitude terms: the sample standard deviation of the FOREX return at 38.11 is, however, smaller than 54.01 of the equity return. These results are further illuminated by examination of Figures 9.1 to 9.6 which show the estimated risk premia and the conditional covariances that they are constructed from. Figure 9.1 shows the equity return and the estimated risk premium from model 3. The estimated risk premium is predominantly positive although there are short periods, mainly in the 1970s when the risk premium is negative. These episodes appear to be when there are negative shocks to the covariance between the excess return to equity and consumption growth (see Figure 9.3).

Table 9.1 Estimates of various no-arbitrage equations for equity and FOREX returns

Model	1		2	
dependent variable	i^e_{t+1}	i^{fx}_{t+1}	i^e_{t+1}	i^{fx}_{t+1}
$V_t(i^e_{t+1})$	−0.5		−0.5	
$V_t(i^{fx}_{t+1})$		−0.5		−0.5
$C_t(\Delta c_{t+1}, i^e_{t+1})$	153.45 (1.95)		39.46 (1.22)	
$C_t(\Delta c_{t+1}, i^{fx}_{t+1})$		69.93 (1.21)		39.46 (1.22)
$C_t(\pi_{t+1}, i^e_{t+1})$	−1		−1	
$C_t(\pi_{t+1}, i^{fx}_{t+1})$		−1		−1
$C_t(\Delta q_{t+1}, i^e_{t+1})$				
$C_t(\Delta q_{t+1}, i^{fx}_{t+1})$				
$C_t(\Delta m_{t+1}, i^e_{t+1})$				
$C_t(\Delta m_{t+1}, i^{fx}_{t+1})$				
Dummy, d_t	−0.308 (1.25)		−0.280 (2.52)	
Degrees of freedom	10.55 (3.68)	12.00 (3.35)	8.223 (4.48)	7.341 (5.26)
Log-likelihood	3658.53	3650.64	3666.55	3662.90
Mean risk premium	5.36%	−0.852%	1.56%	−0.850%
$\|\lambda_{max}\|$	0.988	0.984	0.980	0.979
$\bar{\epsilon}_{t+1}$	3.16	1.02	6.90	0.983
$V(\phi_{t+1})$	39.69	10.61	8.60	5.03
$\dfrac{V(\phi_{t+1})}{V(i^{j}_{t+1} + \frac{1}{2}V_t(i^j_{t+1}) - \hat{\alpha}D)}$	0.0137	0.00732	0.00295	0.00346

Note
Absolute t-statistics are in parentheses.

3		4		5		6	
i^e_{t+1}	i^{fx}_{t+1}	i^e_{t+1}	i^{fx}_{t+1}	i^e_{t+1}	i^{fx}_{t+1}	i^e_{t+1}	i^{fx}_{t+1}
−0.5		−0.5		−0.5		−0.5	
	−0.5		−0.5		−0.5		−0.5
244.18 (1.30)		74.80 (0.49)					
	151.55 (1.36)		74.80 (0.49)				
−1840.7 (1.89)		1824.60 (3.76)					
	1149.50 (2.95)		1824.60 (3.76)				
				−173.33 (1.65)		−97.04 (1.16)	
					−121.32 (1.07)		−97.04 (1.16)
				120.38 (0.53)		1003.50 (2.17)	
					1472.50 (2.44)		1003.50 (2.17)
−0.269 (6.71)		−0.312 (3.62)		−0.343 (5.89)		−0.338 (3.05)	
12.86 (3.67)	12.24 (3.66)						
3506.31	3500.37						
8.78%	2.96%	10.08%	1.97%	8.02%	−2.14%	10.56%	−0.404%
0.988	0.990						
−0.524	−2.89	−1.51−1.89	0.526	2.14	−2.02	0.455	
253.52	286.89	90.16	239.2	43.05	246.24	42.29	158.71
0.0869	0.1975	0.0311	0.1651	0.0148	0.1699	0.0146	0.1095

Figure 9.4 is the corresponding plot for inflation. The conditional covariance between excess equity returns and consumption are generally positive and that with inflation mainly negative. In order to produce a positive equity risk premium, the signs of the coefficients must reflect those of the conditional covariances. The covariances with the FOREX return are somewhat different to those for equity. While they are not expected to be

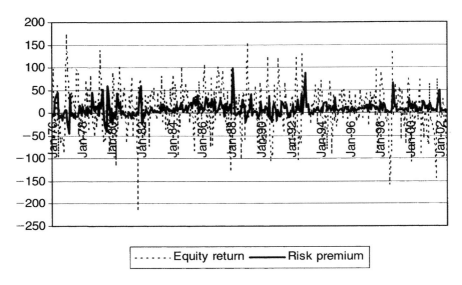

Figure 9.1 Equity return and risk premium for model 3.

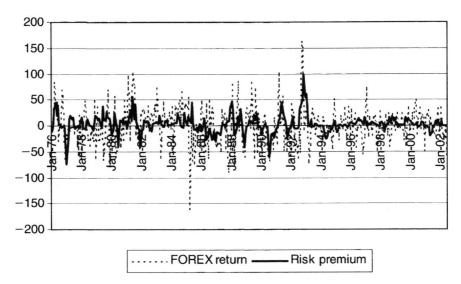

Figure 9.2 FOREX return and risk premium for model 3.

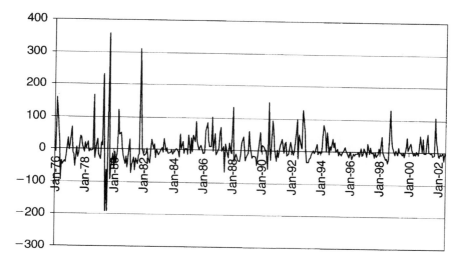

Figure 9.3 Conditional covariance between equity return and consumption growth.

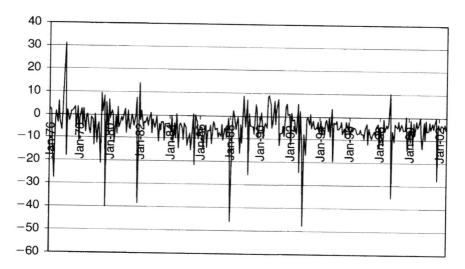

Figure 9.4 Conditional covariance between equity return and inflation.

the same, the fact that the covariance with inflation in Figure 9.6 is predominantly positive explains the difference in the estimated price of risk which generates the rejection of market integration.

In the case of model 5, the output and money growth model, the risk premia are shown in Figures 9.7 and 9.8. The variance of the equity risk premium in this model is much smaller than in model 3 reflecting lower

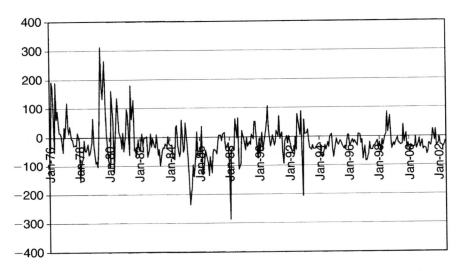

Figure 9.5 Conditional covariance of FOREX return and consumption growth.

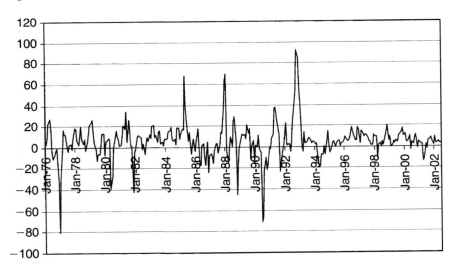

Figure 9.6 Conditional covariance between FOREX return and inflation.

prices of risk and lower variability in the conditional covariances. The risk premium in the FOREX market is, however, as variable as in the consumption growth and inflation model. This is due to the large positive price of risk associated with money growth. This feature which was also found to be of importance in the more general study of FOREX risk in Wickens and Smith (2001) contributes greatly to the rejection of market integration.

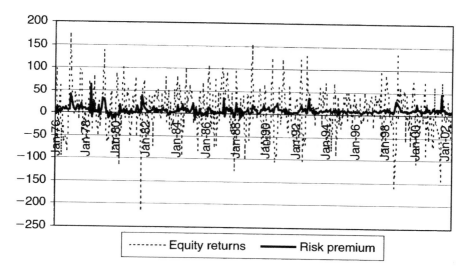

Figure 9.7 Equity return and risk premium for model 5.

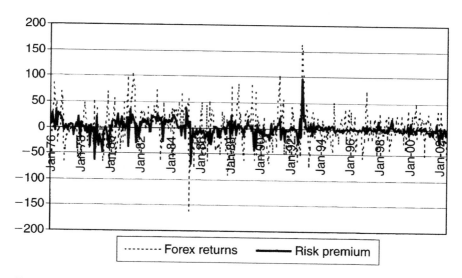

Figure 9.8 FOREX returns and risk premium for model 5.

5 Conclusions

In this chapter we present a test of asset market integration based upon a very general approach to asset pricing, the SDF approach. Our test is constructed from parametric estimation of three models of the SDF. We show that this approach allows us to examine the sources and prices of risk and therefore the likely sources of rejection of integration. This represents an improvement over existing, including recently proposed, tests. Most of these tests have been applied to various stock markets and some are not applicable to non-equity markets. The application of the test in this chapter is to the possible integration of the UK equity and FOREX markets. We find strong evidence against integration in the case of all three of the models we examined. While the testing of asset market integration cannot be model free, we show that our result is robust in the face of all three alternative models. Further work will examine whether this result can be extended across further markets and across additional countries.

Notes

1 We are grateful to the ESRC for providing financial support for this research in grant No. L13830100140. The first author is grateful for the hospitality of the Economics Program, RSSS, Australian National University over the period during which this chapter was written. JEL classification: G12, C32, C51, E44.
2 The widely used unobserved factor approach is discussed in detail in Smith and Wickens (2002).
3 The attraction of the reduction in parameterisation offered by the CCC model has led to an extension to the dynamics in the DCC proposed recently by Engle (2000).

References

Adam, K., Jappelli, T., Menichini, A., Padula, M. and Pagano, M. (2002), 'Analyse, compare and apply alternative indicators and monitoring methodologies to measure the evolution of capital market integration in the European Union', University of Salerno, mimeo.

Campbell, J.Y. (2003), 'Consumption-based asset pricing', in Constantinides, G., Harris, M. and Stulz, R. (eds) *Handbook of the Economics of Finance*, Amsterdam: Elsevier.

Chen, Z. and Knez, P.J. (1995), 'Measurement of market integration and arbitrage', *Review of Financial Studies*, 8(2): 287–325.

Cochrane, J. (2001), *Asset Pricing*, Princeton: Princeton University Press.

Ding, Z. and Engle, R.F. (2001), 'Large scale conditional covariance matrix modelling, estimation and testing', Academia Economic Papers, June, mimeo.

Engle, R.F. (2000), 'Dynamic conditional correlations – a simple class of multivariate GARCH model', University of California, San Diego, mimeo.

Engle, R.F. and Kroner, K.K. (1995), 'Multivariate simultaneous generalised GARCH' *Econometric Theory*, 11: 122–150.

Epstein, L.G. and Zin, S.E. (1989), 'Substitution, risk aversion and the temporal behaviour of consumption and asset returns: a theoretical framework', *Econometrica*, 57: 937–968.

Epstein, L.G. and Zin, S.E. (1990), 'First order risk aversion and the equity premium puzzle', *Journal of Monetary Economics*, 26: 387–407.

Epstein, L.G. and Zin, S.E. (1991), 'Substitution, risk aversion and the temporal behaviour of consumption and asset returns: an empirical investigation', *Journal of Political Economy*, 99: 263–286.

Flood, R.P. and Rose, A.K. (2003), 'Financial integration: a new methodology and an illustration', National Bureau of Economic Research Working Paper no. 9880.

Hansen, L.P. and Jagannathan, R. (1991), 'Implications of security market data for models of dynamic economies', *Journal of Political Economy*, 99(2): 225–262.

Hansen, L.P. and Singleton, K. (1983), 'Stochastic consumption, risk aversion and the temporal behaviour of asset returns', *Journal of Political Economy*, 91: 249–263.

Kreps, D. and Porteus, E. (1978), 'Temporal resolution of uncertainty and dynamic choice theory', *Econometrica*, 46: 185–200.

Smith, P.N., Sorensen, S. and Wickens, M.R. (2003), 'Macroeconomic sources of equity risk', University of York, mimeo.

Smith, P.N. and Wickens, M.R. (2002), 'Asset pricing with observable stochastic discount factors', *Journal of Economic Surveys*, 16(3): 397–446.

Wickens, M.R. and Smith, P.N. (2001), 'Macroeconomic sources of FOREX risk', University of York, mimeo; http://www-users.york.ac.uk/~pns2/forex.pdf.

10 Real exchange rates, current accounts and the net foreign asset position*

Christoph Thoenissen

1 Introduction

What is the relationship between a country's current account and its real exchange rate? Is an exchange rate appreciation positively correlated with a current account deficit? Much discussion of exchange rate movements in recent years, especially among policy makers and market commentators, has linked exchange rate appreciations with capital inflows or current account deficits.[1] The implication is that capital inflows used to finance a country's current account deficit raise the demand for assets denominated in that country's currency, causing the domestic currency to appreciate. An example of this kind of reasoning among policy makers is given by the following quote:

> The bilateral [exchange] rates that are frequently quoted in fact tell us very little about sterling: they are essentially a reflection of the persistent general strength of the dollar on the one hand and the persistent general weakness of the euro on the other, *resulting from* [emphasis added] sustained capital inflows to the United States in large part from the Eurozone.[2]

This chapter examines the theoretical link between the real exchange rate and the current account using a dynamic two-country stochastic New Open Economy Macroeconomics model. The two key variables of interest in this analysis, the real exchange rate and the current account, are modelled by assuming local currency pricing by firms and the absence of a complete set of state-contingent claims in financial markets, respectively. Modelling both the real exchange rate and the current account in this kind of framework is relatively new. A notable recent example is Bergin (2002), whose focus is however different from ours.

When firms are able to set prices in local currency, as opposed to their domestic currency, the law of one price need not hold at all times. This failure of the law of one price leads to deviations from purchasing power parity and drives the dynamics of the real exchange rate in our analysis.

Engel (1999) shows that for the United States real exchange rate, deviations from the law of one price of traded goods are the most important source of real exchange rate variability.

When financial markets are incomplete, in the absence of a complete set of state-contingent claims, the current account plays a major role in the transmission of shocks between countries. A shock that results in a current account surplus redistributes wealth from the country experiencing a current account deficit to the country experiencing a current account surplus. This redistribution of assets is called a wealth effect.

When using standard linear techniques to solve this kind of model, the presence of wealth effects proves to be problematic. Models such as ours are linearised around a well defined and stationary steady state, such that the second moments of the model are based on small deviations from this steady state. Because wealth effects redistribute assets they also affect the steady state of the model, causing it to change in response to temporary shocks. In other words, the steady state can become non-stationary. One simple way to overcome this non-stationarity problem has been put forward by P. Benigno (2001), who assumes that domestic holdings of foreign bonds are subject to transactions costs, which are increasing in the difference between a country's actual and steady-state net foreign asset positions. The further away a country is from its steady-state net foreign asset position, the more expensive it becomes to take positions in the foreign bond market, thus ensuring that in the long run the country returns to its initial net foreign asset position.

The attraction of this approach is that it does not require the steady-state net foreign asset position to be zero, which accords well with empirical evidence.[3] A steady-state net foreign asset position different from zero affects the dynamics of the current account in an important way. A change in the exchange rate will have a different effect on the current account if the country is a net creditor than if it is a net debtor. For example, if the country is a net creditor, a depreciation of the home currency will increase the value of its foreign-currency denominated assets, in terms of domestic currency. Other things remaining equal, this will improve the country's current balance. If on the other hand, the country is a net debtor, a depreciation will increase the value of its liabilities, worsening the current balance.

We show that in our model, the size as well as sign of the cross-correlation between the real exchange rate and the current account depends on (a) the net foreign asset position, (b) the type of shock and (c) a set of key parameters.

These results differ from those of the previous literature. Bailey *et al.* (2001) focus on the same set of variables, but do so using a deterministic, two-period, two-good endowment model as presented in Obstfeld and Rogoff (1996: Chapter 1). In their case, the real exchange rate deviates from purchasing power parity (PPP) because of changes in the relative price of nontraded goods. Given the structure of their model, they find that a real appreciation linked to a productivity improvement in the traded sector always implies a current account deficit, thus implying a positive cross-correlation.

The remainder of this chapter is structured as follows: section 2 outlines the structure of our model; section 3 derives the linearised current account equation; section 4 draws out the intuition for the relationship between the current account and the real exchange rate by making a set of simplifying parameter restrictions; sections 5 and 6 relax these restrictions and analyse the cross-correlation between the real exchange rate and the current account for a more general calibration; and section 7 highlights some of the caveats of our approach and concludes.

2 Structure of the model

This section reviews the main building blocks of the model. To capture the dynamics of the current account, we set up a stochastic new Keynesian two-country general equilibrium model with incomplete financial markets. In modelling our economy with incomplete financial markets, we follow P. Benigno (2001). Our main departure from P. Benigno (2001) is that we allow for deviations of the real exchange rate from PPP by assuming that firms display local-currency pricing behaviour.[4]

The key building blocks of our model are the following:

1   Households make optimal choices between consumption and leisure and receive utility from the holding of real money balances.
2   Each household is also a monopolistic producer who sets a profit maximising price. In their maximisation exercise, households face a budget constraint.
3   The structure of the asset market provides domestic agents with limited possibilities to pool consumption risk with foreign agents by holding domestic as well as foreign-currency denominated risk-free bonds.
4   The model is closed by modelling monetary policy through interest rate feedback rules.

The remainder of this section sets out these building blocks in some detail.

2.1 Household preferences

We consider a two-country economy where both 'home' and 'foreign' are explicitly modelled. The home economy produces a continuum of differentiated tradable goods indexed on the interval $(0, n)$, where n is the relative measure of country size. The foreign economy's goods are indexed on the interval $(n, 1)$. In each country, there is a continuum of economic agents, with population size normalised to the range of domestically produced goods.[5] Consumers are infinitely lived, and behave according to the permanent income hypothesis. Each consumer consumes two types of goods: a domestically-produced good and a foreign-produced good. All goods are tradable.

Each individual j maximises the following utility function which is separable in its three arguments: where $U(.)$ and $N(.)$ represent flows of utility from consumption and real money balances respectively and $V(.)$ flows of disutility from supplying labour,[6]

$$U_t^j = E_t \sum_{s=t}^{\infty} (\beta)^{s-t} \left[U(C_s^j, \xi_{C,s}) + N\left(\frac{M_s^j}{P_s}\right) - V(L_s^j) \right] \tag{1}$$

where ξ_C is a shock to preferences towards consumption, and C is a consumption index defined over home and foreign-produced goods:

$$C = \left(n^{1/\theta} C_H^{\frac{\theta-1}{\theta}} + (1-n)^{1/\theta} C_F^{\frac{\theta-1}{\theta}} \right)^{\frac{\theta}{\theta-1}} \tag{2}$$

where n represents the relative weight that a Home individual puts on domestically-produced goods, as well as the relative country size of the home economy. Money is deflated by a consumption-based price index that corresponds to the above specifications of preferences:

$$P = (nP_H^{1-\theta} + (1-n)P_F^{1-\theta})^{\frac{1}{1-\theta}} \tag{3}$$

where θ is the intratemporal elasticity of substitution between home and foreign-produced goods. Foreign individuals have analogous tastes towards domestic and imported goods.

Next, we define the following consumption sub-indices:

$$C^h = \left[\left(\frac{1}{n}\right)^{\frac{1}{\sigma}} \int_0^n c(z)^{\frac{\sigma-1}{\sigma}} dz \right]^{\frac{\sigma}{\sigma-1}}, \ C^f = \left[\left(\frac{1}{1-n}\right)^{\frac{1}{\sigma}} \int_n^1 c(z)^{\frac{\sigma-1}{\sigma}} dz \right]^{\frac{\sigma}{\sigma-1}} \tag{4}$$

where h and f denote the set of domestic and foreign production. Specifically Home produces a good, which we refer to as H, for the home market, and as H^* for the export market. Thus, $h = H, H^*$, analogously $f = F, F^*$ where $\sigma > 1$ is the elasticity of substitution for individual goods produced in the two countries. If we denote with $p(j)$ and $p^*(j^*)$ the individual price of the single differentiated good in domestic and foreign currency respectively, then it can be shown that domestic and foreign demand for the same good are given respectively by:

$$c_H(j) = \frac{1}{n} \left(\frac{p(j)}{P_H}\right)^{-\sigma} C_H, \ c_H^*(j) = \frac{1}{n} \left(\frac{p^*(j)}{P_H^*}\right)^{-\sigma} C_H^* \tag{5}$$

where P_H and P_H^* are the price indices corresponding to the consumption subindices (equation (4)) for $h = H, H^*$.

2.2 The asset market and budget constraint

The budget constraint and asset market structure follow directly from P. Benigno (2001), and needs only a limited exposition here. We assume that domestic agents can allocate their wealth between domestic money and home and foreign-currency denominated bonds. Both bonds are risk-free and mature after one period. Foreign agents allocate their wealth between foreign money and the foreign-currency denominated bond.

Formally the Home households' budget constraint is given by:

$$
P_t C_t^j + M_t^j - M_{t-1}^j + \frac{B_{H,t}^j}{(1 + i_t)} + \frac{S_t B_{F,t}^j}{(1 + i_t^*)\Theta\left(\frac{S_t B_{F,t}}{P_t}\right)} \leq B_{H,t-1}^j + S_t B_{F,t-1}^j
$$

$$
+ G_t^j + W_t^j L_t^j + \frac{1}{n}\int_0^n \pi_t^j dj \tag{6}
$$

The household j's risk-free one period bond denominated in units of domestic currency, $B_{H,t}^j$, yields a nominal rate of return of i_t. Home-currency denominated bonds are in zero net supply. The price of the foreign-currency denominated bond, $B_{F,t}^j$ held by household j is proportional to the gross nominal rate of return of the bond, $1 + i^*$. The factor of proportionality is the function $\Theta(.)$ which depends on the real holdings of foreign-currency denominated assets of the entire economy. Hence individual agents take the function $\Theta(.)$ as given when choosing their optimal level of foreign-currency denominated bond holdings. P. Benigno (2001) derives a set of restrictions on the function $\Theta(.)$ that ensure the stationarity of the steady state of the model which allows us to log-linearise the model around a well defined steady state. Specifically, the function $\Theta(.)$ captures a cost faced by domestic agents of taking a position in the foreign asset market. The cost is designed such that when the economy-wide real holdings of foreign-currency denominated bonds are above (below) the steady state level, $\bar{b}$, individual agents receive less (more) than the gross rate of return. The factor of proportionality is only equal to unity when economy-wide asset holdings are at their steady-state level. This setup ensures that in the steady state, when the gross rates of return on domestic and foreign bonds are equal, agents on aggregate hold only the exogenously determined steady-state level of foreign-currency denominated bonds.[7] M_t^j are the individual's holdings of money and $W_t^j L_t^j$ is the wage income received by individual j. The profits generated by domestic firms, $\int_0^n \Pi_t^j dj$, are distributed equally among home agents.

The fiscal authority in the home country rebates seigniorage revenues to households in the form of transfers, G_t^j.

$$\int_0^n [M_t^j - M_{t-1}^j] dj = \int_0^n G_t^j dj \tag{7}$$

To determine the resource constraint for the Home economy, we need to consolidate the public and private sectors. The public sector is described by the government budget constraint (equation (7)) and the behaviour of the private sector is described by aggregating the individual budget constraints (equation (6)) over all agents residing in the home economy. In our model the difference between total income and domestic consumption is defined as the current account:

$$\frac{S_t B_{F,t}}{P_t (1 + i_t^*) \Theta\left(\frac{S_t B_{F,t}}{P_t}\right)} = \frac{S_t B_{F,t-1}}{P_t} + \frac{P_t Y^d}{P_t} + \frac{S_t P_t^* Y_t^{d*}}{P_t} - C_t \tag{8}$$

which in our analysis is also the negative of the gross capital account.

By assuming that all households have the same initial level of assets and receive an equal share of the profits of all firms, we ensure that all households face the same budget constraint. Households choose their optimal path of consumption and bond holdings by maximising intertemporal utility, (equation (1)) with respect to the budget constraint (equation (6)). This yields two Euler equations for domestic agents: one describing the optimal holding of home bonds, the other the optimal holdings of foreign bonds. Agents in the foreign economy face a similar budget constraint which differs from that faced by home agents in two respects, first they hold only their own-currency denominated bonds and second, they receive the profits from the cost of intermediation that home agents face when taking positions in the foreign asset market.

2.3 The consumer's problem

Households' equilibrium conditions are described by the following equations:

$$U_C(C_t, \xi_{C,t}) = (1 + i_t)\beta E_t\left[U_C(C_{t+1}, \xi_{C,t+1})\frac{P_t}{P_{t+1}}\right] \tag{9}$$

$$U_C(C_t, \xi_{C,t}) = (1 + i_t^*)\Theta\left(\frac{S_t B_{F,t}}{P_t}\right)\beta E_t\left[U_C(C_{t+1}, \xi_{C,t+1})\frac{S_{t+1} P_t}{S_t P_{t+1}}\right] \tag{10}$$

Equations (9) and (10) represent the home consumer's optimal holdings of home and foreign-currency denominated bonds, respectively. Note that the rate of return on foreign-currency denominated bonds depends on the foreign gross rate of interest, $(1 + i_t^*)$ and on a factor of proportionality, $\Theta(S_t B_{F,t}/P_t)$, which is equal to unity only when the home country's holdings of net foreign assets are at their steady-state level.

The foreign consumer's optimal choice of bond holdings yields the following condition:

$$U_C(C_t^*, \xi_{C,t}^*) = (1 + i_t^*)\beta E_t\left[U_C(C_{t+1}^*, \xi_{C,t+1}^*) \frac{P_t^*}{P_{t+1}^*} \right] \tag{11}$$

2.4 Firms' price-setting behaviour

Each firm is a monopolistic producer of a single differentiated good. Firms use labour as their primary input. The production function is subject to shocks to the level of total-factor productivity (TFP), A. Under price flexibility a monopolistic producer sets prices as a mark-up over unit cost. An important dynamic element in our model consists of modelling the price-setting behaviour according to a partial adjustment rule *à la* Calvo (1983). At each point in time, each firm can change its price with probability $1 - \alpha$. This probability is independent of the time elapsed since the last price change, so the average time over which a price is fixed is given by $1/(1 - \alpha)$.

The firms in our model set price in the local currency of their market. This assumption requires a degree of market segmentation, which prevents goods market arbitrage from equalising the price of traded goods, when expressed in a common currency. This opens up an important channel of deviation of the real exchange rate from PPP.

If we denote by $p_t^H(j)$ the price chosen at time t and with $\tilde{y}_{t,t+k}^{Hd}(j)$ the demand for the individual good H at home, produced by producer j at time $t + k$, conditional on keeping the price fixed at the level chosen at time t, the first-order condition for the domestic goods producer is given by:

$$E_t\left\{ \sum_{k=0}^{\infty} (\alpha\beta)^k U_C(C_{t+k}) \frac{P_{Ht+k}}{P_{t+k}} \tilde{y}_{t,t+k}^{Hd}(j)\left[\frac{\tilde{p}_t^H(j)}{P_{H,t+k}} - \left(\frac{\sigma}{\sigma-1}\right)\frac{W_{t+k}^j}{P_{H,t+k}A_{H,t+k}} \right] \right\} = 0 \tag{12}$$

Domestic producers selling goods in the foreign market perform similar optimisations:

$$E_t\left\{ \sum_{k=0}^{\infty} (\alpha\beta)^k U_C(C_{t+k}) \frac{P_{Ht+k}}{P_{t+k}} \tilde{y}_{t,t+k}^{Hd*}(j)\left[\frac{\tilde{p}_t^{H*}(j)}{P_{H*,t+k}} \frac{P_{H*,t+k}S_{t+k}}{P_{H,t+k}} - \left(\frac{\sigma}{\sigma-1}\right) \right. \right.$$
$$\left. \left. \frac{W_{t+k}^j}{P_{H,t+k}A_{H,t+k}} \right] \right\} = 0 \tag{13}$$

where S_{t+k} is the nominal exchange rate defined as the domestic price of a unit of foreign currency at time $t + k$ and $\tilde{y}_{t,t+k}^{Hd*}(j)$ is the demand for the individual good H abroad, produced by producer j at time $t + k$.[8]

2.5 The real exchange rate

In this model, we allow for only one channel of deviation from PPP.[9] Due to local currency pricing, the real exchange rate in our model deviates from PPP via deviations from the law-of-one-price. We define the consumption-based real exchange rate as:

$$RS = \frac{SP^*}{P} \tag{14}$$

where P and P^* are the home and foreign price levels and S is the nominal exchange rate, defined as the home-currency price of a unit of foreign currency. Hence, an increase (decrease) in the real exchange rate represents a real depreciation (appreciation).

2.6 Monetary policy

In this model, as in many other recent contributions, we make the simplifying assumption that monetary policy is characterised in terms of an interest rate feedback rule. Each monetary authority sets the nominal interest rate according to current economic conditions. In particular, we assume that the monetary authorities in both countries follow a Taylor-type rule with interest rate smoothing. Under these rules, monetary policy reacts to current inflation and to the output gap. In log-linearised form, the monetary policy reaction functions can be expressed as follows:

$$i_t = \lambda_i i_{t-1} + (1 - \lambda_i)\lambda_\pi \pi_t + (1 - \lambda_i)\lambda_y (y_t - \bar{y}_t) + \epsilon_t^M$$

$$i_t^* = \lambda_i^* i_{t-1}^* + (1 - \lambda_i^*)\lambda_\pi^* \pi_t^* + (1 - \lambda_i^*)\lambda_y^* (y_t^* - \bar{y}_t^*) + \epsilon_t^{M*} \tag{15}$$

where CPI inflation, π and the deviation of sticky-price output form its flexible-price level, $(y - \bar{y})$ are the set of target variables for the home (foreign) country, given the information set at time t. ϵ_t^M and ϵ_t^{M*} are monetary policy shocks that in this setting represent deviation from the systematic component of the interest rate rule.

2.7 Log-linear equilibrium

We log-linearise the equations of the model around a well defined and stationary steady state. The linearised model is solved using a technique put forward by King and Watson (1998). The solved model is used to extract impulse response functions and for stochastic simulations subject to total factor productivity, monetary policy and preferences shocks.

3 The linearised current account

The structure of the asset market ensures that the steady state is well defined for our incomplete markets model. By introducing a cost of intermediation in the foreign bond market, we ensure that the level of foreign bond holdings relative to consumption is stationary. It is this feature which allows us to linearise around a well defined steady state.

The most important equation for our analysis is the log-linearised current account equation:

$$
\begin{aligned}
\beta(1 + \bar{a}\delta)\hat{b}_t = \ & \bar{a}(\beta i_t^* - \pi_t + \Delta s_t) + \hat{b}_{t-1} \\
& + (1-n)\widehat{RS}_t - (1-n)[\hat{C} - \hat{C}_t^*] \\
& + (1-n)(\theta-1)[n\hat{T}_t + (1-n)\hat{T}_t^*] \\
& + \bar{a}(\beta-1)[\hat{C}_t^* + \widehat{RS}_t + (1-n)(\theta-1)\hat{T}_t^*]
\end{aligned}
\tag{16}
$$

where $\hat{b} = (S_t B_{F,t}/P_t - \bar{b})\bar{c}$ is the deviation of real holdings of foreign-currency denominated bonds from their steady-state level, relative to the domestic steady-state level of consumption. $\delta \equiv -\Theta'(\bar{b})\bar{C}$ is the cost of intermediation in the foreign bond market and measures the spread of the domestic rate (in the foreign currency market) over the foreign rate. $\bar{a}$ is the steady state level of foreign bond holding divided by the steady-state level of consumption: $\frac{\bar{b}}{\bar{c}}$. Any variable $\hat{X}_t$ denotes the log deviation of X_t from its steady-state level.

In the general specification (equation (16)), the current account depends on the deviation of the return of the foreign asset, $(\beta i^* - \pi_t + \Delta s_t)$, on deviation in the terms of trade, $\hat{T}$ at home and abroad (where $T = \frac{P_f}{P_h}$ and $T^* = \frac{P_f^*}{P_h^*}$), on the deviation of consumption at home and abroad, $\hat{C}, \hat{C}^*$ and on the deviation of the real exchange rate, $\widehat{RS}$, all from their steady-state levels. Having set out the current account equation in its general form, we now consider a few simple special cases to facilitate our analysis.

4 Some special cases

Before we proceed to analyse the cross-correlation between the current account and the real exchange rate generated by our calibrated model economy, this section looks at some special cases, which highlight the role of some key parameters. Specifically, we examine the role of the *inter*temporal elasticity of substitution, and the *intra*temporal elasticity of substitution between imports and exports, and the net foreign asset position.

4.1 Baseline calibration

We start with a perfectly symmetric calibration, where preferences over goods (equation (2)), are Cobb–Douglas, i.e. $\theta = 1$ and the steady-state asset position, $\bar{a}$, is zero. Applying these parameter restrictions to (equation (16)) yields the following simplified expression for the current account:

$$\beta\hat{b}_t = \hat{b}_{t-1} + (1-n)\widehat{RS}_t - (1-n)[\hat{C}_t - \hat{C}_t^*] \tag{17}$$

In this simple case, the dynamics of the current account depend on those of the real exchange rate and on those of relative consumption in the two economies. *Ceteris paribus* a depreciation of the real exchange rate (a positive $\widehat{RS}$) results in a positive current account balance ($\hat{b}$ is positive). A rise in relative consumption, on the other hand, worsens the current account balance.

The cross-correlation between the current account and the real exchange rate thus depends on the relationship between the real exchange rate and the relative consumption. The theoretical determinants of this cross-correlation are analysed in Benigno and Thoenissen (2003b). They find that the data show no consistent pattern for this cross-correlation, which, depending on the sample of countries chosen, can be either positive or negative, with a mean close to zero. A key theoretical determinant of the relationship between the real exchange rate and the current account in our model is the intertemporal elasticity of substitution. Throughout this chapter, we assume that preferences, U, are of the constant relative risk aversion (CRRA) type, such that $-U_{cc}(C)\bar{C}/U_c(C)$ is equal to ρ, the inverse of the intertemporal elasticity of substitution. Figure 10.1 shows the impulse responses of the real exchange rate and the current account following a one-off one standard deviation increase in domestic total-factor productivity. Throughout, the real exchange rate is shown to depreciate following an increase in domestic total-factor productivity. As the supply of home-produced goods increases, their relative price must fall to clear the market. Because of local-currency pricing behaviour of firms, changes in the nominal exchange rate are not fully passed through into prices, causing the real exchange rate to depreciate.[10] The first column replicates this simulation for the symmetric baseline calibration for various values of ρ. When the intertemporal elasticity of substitution is equal to unity, the current account remains unchanged following a supply side shock. This is because under supply side shocks, relative consumption and the real exchange rate are perfectly correlated for this set of parameters.[11] As ρ increases and the intertemporal elasticity of substitution declines, agents are less willing to substitute consumption across states of nature and time. As a result, relative consumption moves by less than the consumption-based real exchange rate, so that the current account improves following an increase in TFP. The cross-correlation between the current account and the real exchange rate is thus positive. For values of ρ below unity, when the intertemporal elasticity of substitution is greater than one, relative consumption is more volatile than the real exchange rate, such

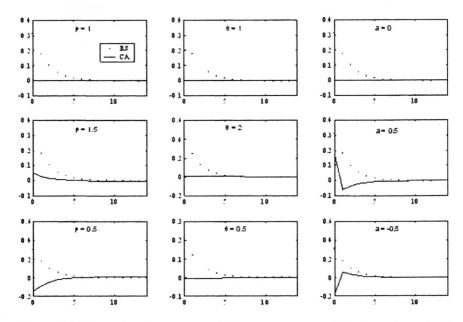

Figure 10.1 The real exchange rate and the current account following a 1 standard
deviation shock to domestic total factor productivity for various parameters combinations.

that a TFP improvement results in a current account deficit and thus a
negative cross-correlation between the real exchange rate and the current
account. In this case, the current account becomes counter-cyclical.

The empirical evidence on the size of the ρ is inconclusive. Fernandez-
Corugedo and Cromb (2002) suggest values for $(1/\rho)$ of between zero and
2, encompassing both positive as well as negative correlations between the
current account and the real exchange rate.

4.2 The elasticity of substitution between home- and foreign-produced traded goods

Starting from our baseline calibration, this section relaxes the assumption
that the elasticity of substitution between imports and exports, θ, is
unitary. This adds a further term to our current account equation, namely
the terms of trade, $\hat{T}$.

$$\beta b_t = b_{t-1} + (1-n)(\theta-1)(n\hat{T}_t + (1-n)\hat{T}_t^*) - (1-n)(\hat{C}_t - \hat{C}_t^* - \widehat{RS}) \quad (18)$$

Ceteris paribus, when the elasticity of substitution is greater than unity,
$\theta > 1$, such that domestic- and foreign-produced goods are substitutes in

consumption, there is a positive correlation between the terms of trade, defined as $\frac{P_t}{P_{tt}}$ and $\frac{P_t^*}{P_{tt}^*}$ and the current account. When the relative price of imported goods increases, consumers substitute away from imported-towards home-produced goods which, other things remaining constant, improves the current account. When $\theta < 1$, such that domestic- and foreign-produced goods are complements in consumption, a depreciation of the terms of trade (a rise in T), all things remaining equal, leads to a worsening of the current account.

The second column of Figure 10.1 shows the response of the current account and the real exchange rate to a 1 standard-deviation shock to home TFP for various values of θ. If $\theta > 1$ the cross-correlation is positive, whereas if $\theta < 1$ the model generates a negative cross-correlation.

Empirical evidence suggests values of θ of around and above unity. For instance, Backus *et al.* (1995) choose a value of 1.5, whereas Heathcote and Perri (2002) choose a value of 0.9.

4.3 Steady-state net foreign assets

So far we have focused our analysis on cases where the steady-state level of net foreign assets is zero. In this section, we assume our baseline calibration, but let $\bar{a}$, the steady-state level of foreign-currency denominated bonds relative to steady-state consumption be different from zero.

$$\beta(1 + \bar{a}\delta)b_t = \bar{a}(\beta i_t^* - \pi_t + \Delta s_t) + b_{t-1} - (1 - n)[\hat{C}_t - \hat{C}_t^* - \widehat{RS}_t]$$
$$+ \bar{a}(\beta - 1)[\hat{C}_t^* + \widehat{RS}_t] \tag{19}$$

Letting steady-state net foreign assets differ from zero introduces additional terms to our current account equation. The first of these terms captures the effects of changes in the real rate of return on foreign-currency denominated bonds. The real return on foreign-currency denominated bonds is positively affected by the foreign policy rate, i_t^*, and the rate of depreciation of the nominal exchange rate, Δs_t. An increase in domestic inflation, on the other hand, reduces the real return from holding foreign-currency denominated assets. If the domestic economy is a net creditor in the steady state, such that $\bar{a} > 0$, an increase in the return on bonds improves the current account. If the domestic economy is a net debtor in the steady state, such that $\bar{a} < 0$, an increase in the return payable on foreign bonds will worsen the current account.

The third column of Figure 10.1 shows that the inclusion of a non-zero steady-state asset position does not qualitatively alter the dynamics of the real exchange rate, but it does change the dynamics of the current account. If the economy is net creditor, the real exchange rate and the current account initially move in the same direction. In the period following the shock, the current account moves into deficit, from which it gradually returns to equilibrium along the adjustment path. When the net foreign asset position is negative, the dynamics of the current account are reversed, while those of the real exchange rate remain largely unchanged.

For our symmetric baseline calibration, a positive (negative) $\bar{a}$ results in a positive (negative) cross-correlation between the current account and the real exchange rate.

Lane and Milesi-Ferretti (2001) provides estimates of net foreign asset positions relative to GDP for a variety of economies. Values of $\bar{a}$ (the steady-state net foreign asset position relative to home consumption) between -0.5 and 0.5 appear reasonable for OECD countries.

Having analysed the correlations between the real exchange rate and the current account under some special cases, the next section offers a more general calibration, which allows us to derive the cross-correlation between the current account and the real exchange rate generated by our model.

5 Calibration

Our calibration serves only as an illustration of the properties of the model and is not intended to match any particular pair of economies. We assume that the Home and Foreign economies are equal in size, so $n = 0.5$. For simplicity, we also assume that both economies are symmetric. We set $\beta = 0.99$ which implies a steady-state real interest rate of about 4 per cent in a quarterly model. We follow Rotemberg and Woodford (1997) in setting the inverse of the elasticity of labour supply, $\eta = 0.47$. We choose 1.5 for the inverse of the intertemporal elasticity of substitution ρ which lies within the range suggested by the literature. The degree of monopolistic competition is also taken from Rotemberg and Woodford (1997), who set $\sigma = 7.88$ which implies an average mark-up of some 15 per cent. We assume an elasticity of substitution between home- and foreign-produced traded goods, θ of 1.5. The average duration of price contracts in both countries is assumed to be 4 quarters, implying $\alpha = 0.75$. For our monetary policy rule, we choose a standard Taylor rule with lagged inflation with the following weights: 1.5, 0.5 and 0.75 for the response to inflation, λ_π, the output gap, λ_y and lagged inflation, λ_i, respectively. Finally, in setting the cost of intermediation in the foreign bond market, we choose $\delta = 0.001$ which implies a 10 basis point spread of the domestic rate (in the foreign bond market) over the foreign rate.

We calibrate three types of shocks: shocks to total factor productivity, shocks to the preference for consumption, and interest rate shocks. The associated shock processes take on the following form:

$$A_t = \omega_1 A_{t-1} + u_{1,t}$$
$$\xi_{C,t} = \omega_2 \xi_{C,t-1} + u_{2,t}$$
$$\epsilon^M = u_{3,t}$$

where u_1, u_2 and u_3 are white noise processes and ω_1 and ω_2 measure the persistence of shocks. In calibrating productivity shocks, we follow Chari *et al.* (2002) such that $\omega_1 = \omega_1^* = 0.95$, $var(u_1) = var(u_1^*) = (0.007)^2$ and $corr(u_1, u_1^*) = 0.25$. For the remaining two shocks we assume that these are un-correlated across countries, have unit variance and that $\omega_2 = 0$.

6 Cross-correlation between the current account and the real exchange rate

In this section we consider the cross-correlations between the real exchange rate and the current account that are generated by the calibrated model defined as:

$$Corr(RS,CA) = \frac{Cov(RS,CA)}{\sqrt{Var(RS) \times Var(CA)}}$$

We analyse this cross-correlation for two types of shocks, asymmetric or country specific shocks as well as symmetric or global shocks.

6.1 Asymmetric shocks

We start our analysis with asymmetric or relative shocks originating in the home economy. Table 10.1 looks at TFP, interest rate as well as preference shocks for three levels of steady-state foreign-currency denominated bonds relative to steady-state consumption. A value of $\bar{a} = \pm 0.5$ corresponds to assets/debts of 50 per cent of consumption.

Under TFP or interest rate shocks, the real exchange rate is positively correlated with the current account in the zero net foreign asset case, as well as in the case when $\bar{a}$ is equal to 0.5. This corresponds to the common prior that real exchange rate appreciations are positively correlated with current account deficits or gross capital account surpluses. However, when we assume that the home economy is a net debtor in the steady state, assuming that $\bar{a} = -0.5$ the correlation becomes negative. In this case, the direct effect on the current account coming from the return on foreign-currency denominated debt, outlined above, dominates. Under preference shocks, the correlation is negative for all analysed levels of $\bar{a}$. A positive

Table 10.1 Asymmetric shocks

	TFP shocks Corr(RS,CA)	Interest rate shocks Corr(RS,CA)	Preference shock Corr(RS,CA)
$\bar{a} = 0$	0.855	0.981	−0.601
$\bar{a} = 0.5$	0.756	0.698	−0.605
$\bar{a} = -0.5$	−0.008	−0.217	−0.596

shock to home preferences over consumption raises home consumption relative to foreign consumption and results in a current account deficit. The real exchange rate, on the other hand, depreciates. A preference shock in the home country raises relative consumption and thus relative inflation. If home inflation rises above foreign inflation, the nominal exchange rate will tend to depreciate to bring relative prices back into line. Under full pass-through, the nominal exchange rate exactly offsets the inflation differential, thus leaving the real exchange rate unchanged. In this model we find that the lower the degree of pass-through, the more the nominal exchange rate will react to inflation differentials, over-depreciating in response to a positive inflation differential; as a result the real exchange rate depreciates.

For all these shocks, the qualitative relationship between the real exchange rate and the shock does not change, it is the link between the shock and the current account that depends on the net foreign asset position.

6.2 Symmetric shocks

In this section, we analyse the cross-correlation between the real exchange rate and the current account under 'global' or symmetric shocks. Since we have chosen a symmetric calibration, where both countries are essentially identical, a global shock in a setting where the net foreign asset position, $\bar{a}$, is zero would leave both the current account balance and the real exchange rate unchanged. In order for either the current account or the real exchange rate to respond to a symmetric shock, we require some form of asymmetry in the model. As a result we limit our analysis to non-zero values of $\bar{a}$. Furthermore, we focus only on TFP and interest rate shocks, which are easier to interpret as global shocks.[12]

Our analysis of symmetric shocks focuses on two findings: For our model and calibration, we find, in Table 10.2, that under symmetric shocks the sign of the cross-correlation between the real exchange rate and the current account depends on the type of shock and not on the net foreign asset position, as we saw in the previous example. TFP shocks are associated with negative cross-correlations, whereas global interest rate shocks are associated with positive cross-correlations between the real exchange rate and the current account.

Table 10.2 Symmetric shocks

	TFP shocks *Corr(RS,CA)*	*Interest rate shocks* *Corr(RS,CA)*
$\bar{a} = 0.5$	−0.015	0.548
$\bar{a} = -0.5$	−0.448	0.538

Unlike under asymmetric or country specific shocks, Figure 10.2 illustrates that the initial response of the real exchange rate following a symmetric shock depends on the steady-state net foreign asset position. Figure 10.2 shows that for positive (negative) net foreign asset positions, the real exchange rate depreciates (appreciates) following an increase in either global TFP or interest rates.

Following a symmetric or global shock to TFP, we find that home consumption increases by more than foreign consumption if home is a net creditor in the steady state, i.e. $\bar{a}>0$. If home is a net debtor in the steady state, i.e. $\bar{a}<0$, home consumption rises by less than foreign consumption. The increase in relative consumption in the net creditor country has two effects. First, the current account will show a negative balance throughout the transition path. Second, relative inflation will be higher. The nominal exchange rate in our model moves in such a way as to bring relative prices at home and abroad back towards equilibrium. Thus, if home inflation exceeds foreign inflation the nominal exchange rate tends to depreciate. In the presence of local-currency pricing, the nominal exchange rate will depreciate by more than the amount required to bring the real exchange rate back to equi-

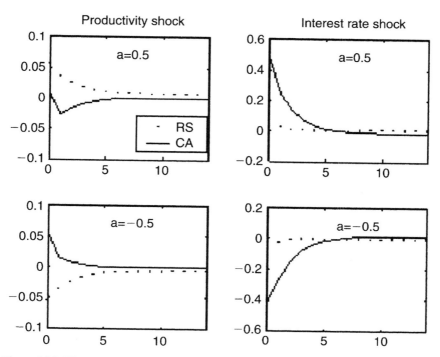

Figure 10.2 The real exchange rate and the current account following a symmetric 1 standard deviation shock to total factor productivity and interest rates for positive and negative net foreign assets.

librium, thus leading to a depreciation of the real exchange rate. This explains both the negative cross-correlation between the real exchange rate (rises) and the current account (falls) and why the response of the real exchange rate depends on the net foreign asset position.

The behaviour of the real exchange rate following a global interest rate rise can be explained in the same way as the response to a global TFP shock. The current account dynamics, on the other hand, and thus the cross-correlation between the real exchange rate and the current account, are different. A rise in home and foreign interest rates directly increases the rate of return from holding assets in the steady state. This effect dominated the factors that move the current account in the case of an increase in TFP. If the economy is a net creditor, so $\bar{a} > 0$, the current account moves into surplus following a shock, gradually returning to balance in the transition. If the economy is a net debtor, the increase in the return payable on foreign-currency denominated debt worsens the current account. For these reasons, the real exchange rate and the current account are positively cross-correlated under symmetric interest rate shocks.

7 Caveats and conclusions

Summarising our results, we find that in our simple two-country dynamic stochastic new open economy macroeconomics model the real exchange rate and the current account are not linked in a structural way. We analyse productivity, interest rate as well as preference shocks and show that the correlation between the real exchange rate and the current account depends on the types of shocks hitting the economy, as well as a set of key structural parameters. In particular, we highlight the role of the steady-state net foreign asset position. In our model, shocks to the interest income from holding foreign assets have significant effects on the dynamics of the current account. In our simple model there is no *a priori* reason to assume that real exchange rate appreciations are caused, or indeed correlated with current account deficits or capital inflows. Future work could fruitfully test to what extent this result reflects the simplifications made here.

Indeed, the model presented here is highly stylised; as a result some of our simplifications could affect our results. Perhaps the most obvious feature missing from our model is investment dynamics. Woodford (2003) shows how to correctly incorporate capital accumulation in a model with Calvo pricing. Whereas including capital accumulation is unlikely to significantly affect the dynamics of the real exchange rate, it most likely will have an effect on the dynamics of the current account, making the current account more countercyclical, as Backus *et al.* (1994) point out.

Another caveat concerns how we model deviations from PPP. In order to keep the model tractable, we have focused only on local-currency pricing as a source of real exchange rate deviations. This feature of our model causes the law of one price to fail. Engel (1999) shows that fluctuations in the law of one price account for most of the variability of the US real exchange rate. Modelling real exchange rate dynamics through changes in the relative price of nontraded goods, may result in different responses of the real exchange rate to productivity shocks. Specifically, if the intratemporal elasticity of substitution between home- and foreign-produced traded goods is high, then a productivity shock to the traded goods sector can result in a real appreciation of the real exchange rate – via the Balassa–Samuelson effect whereas such a shock results in a real depreciation in our model. How the Balassa–Samuelson effect would affect the current account is, however, not immediately obvious.

Another possible caveat concerns the way we model monetary policy. Sensitivity analysis, not reported here, has however found that changing the weights on inflation and the output gap as well as the degree of interest rate smoothing in either or both of the countries does not change the qualitative results of this chapter.

Notes

* I thank Rebecca Driver, Peter Sinclair and participants at a CCBS workshop on international capital movements for insightful comments. The usual disclaimer applies.
1 See Bailey *et al.* (2001) for a policy oriented perspective on this issue.
2 Speech by Sir Edward George, Governor of the Bank of England, delivered at the Lord Mayor's Dinner for Bankers and Merchants of the City of London, 20 June 2001.
3 See Lane and Milesi-Ferretti (2001) for evidence on net foreign asset positions across countries.
4 Purchasing power parity holds in Benigno (2001) due to the assumptions that (a) all goods are traded, (b) preferences for home and foreign-produced traded goods are the same in both economies and (c) exports set prices in their producer currency, implying full pass-through from exchange rate changes to consumer prices.
5 Home agents lie on the interval $(0, n)$, while foreign agents lie on $(n, 1)$.
6 We assume that U is increasing and concave in C_t, N is increasing and concave in $\frac{M}{P}$, and V is increasing and convex in L. E_t denotes the expectation conditional on information at time t, while β is the intertemporal discount factor $0 < \beta < 1$).
7 In this model, we simply postulate a given level of net foreign assets relative to consumption. In an overlapping generations model, the equilibrium net foreign asset position is determined by the lifecycle characteristics of agents.
8 See G. Benigno (2001) for a derivation and discussion of local-currency-pricing Phillips curves.
9 See Benigno and Thoenissen (2003a) for a similar model which analyses three separate channels of deviation from PPP.
10 See Benigno and Thoenissen (2003a) for an analysis of the real exchange rate response to supply-side improvements in a model with local-currency pricing, consumption home bias and nontraded goods.
11 See P. Benigno (2001) and Benigno and Thoenissen (2003b).
12 Specifically, we analyse cases where home and foreign shocks are perfectly correlated, such that $corr(u_1, u_1^*) = corr(u_3, u_3^*) = 1$.

References

Backus, D.K., Kehoe, P.J. and Kydland, F.E. (1994), 'Dynamics of the trade balance and the terms of trade: the J-curve?', *American Economic Review*, 84(1) (March): 84–103.

Backus, D.K., Kehoe, P.J. and Kydland, F.E. (1995), 'International business cycles: theory and evidence', in Cooley, Thomas F. (ed.) *Frontiers of Business Cycle Research*, Princeton: Princeton University Press, pp. 331–356.

Bailey, A., Millard, S. and Wells, S. (2001), 'Capital flows and exchange rates', *Bank of England Quarterly Bulletin*, Autumn, pp. 310–318.

Benigno, G. (2001), 'Real exchange rate persistence and monetary policy rules', London School of Economics, *Journal of Monetary Economics*, forthcoming.

Benigno, G. and Thoenissen, C. (2003a), 'Equilibrium exchange rates and supply-side performance', *Economic Journal*, 113(486): 103–124.

Benigno, G. and Thoenissen, C. (2003b), 'On the consumption-real exchange rate anomaly', unpublished manuscript, LSE and University of St Andrews.

Benigno, P. (2001). 'Price stability with imperfect financial integration', CEPR Working Paper no. 2854.

Bergin, P. (2002). 'How well can the new open economy macroeconomics explain the exchange rate and current account?', UC Davis, mimeo.

Calvo, G.A. (1983), 'Staggered prices in a utility-maximising framework', *Journal of Monetary Economics*, 12: 383–398

Chari, V.V., Kehoe, P.J. and McGrattan, E.R. (2002), 'Can sticky price models generate volatile and persistent real exchange rates?', *Review of Economic Studies*, 69(5): 533–563.

Engel, C. (1999), 'Accounting for US real exchange rate changes', *Journal of Political Economy*, 107(3): 507–538.

Fernandez-Corugedo, E.W. and Cromb, R. (2002), 'Interest rates and consumption when there is no uncertainty', unpublished manuscript, Bank of England.

Heathcote, J. and Perri, F. (2002), 'Financial autarky and international business cycles', *Journal of Monetary Economics*, 49: 601–627.

King, R. and Watson, M. (1998), 'The solution of singular linear difference systems under rational expectations', *International Economic Review*, 39(4): 1015–1026.

Lane, P.R. and Milesi-Ferretti, G.M. (2001), 'The external wealth of nations: measures of foreign assets and liabilities for industrial and developing countries', *Journal of International Economics*, 55: 263–294.

Obstfeld, M. and Rogoff, K. (1996), *Foundations of International Macroeconomics*, Cambridge, MA: MIT Press.

Rotemberg, J.J. and Woodford, M. (1997), 'An optimization-based econometric framework for the evaluation of monetary policy', in Bernanke, B.S. and Rotemberg, J.J. (eds) *NBER Macroeconomic Annual*, Cambridge, MA: MIT Press.

Woodford, M. (2003), *Interest and Prices: Foundations of a Theory of Monetary Policy*, Princeton: Princeton University Press, Chapter 5.

11 The macroeconomics of international financial trade

*Philip R. Lane**

1 Introduction

In this chapter, I provide a selective overview of recent research on the spectacular growth in international financial trade and its implications for the macroeconomic behaviour of open economies. The motivation for this research topic is quite basic, in that a driving factor in any open-economy macroeconomics model is the degree of international financial integration. This suggests that understanding the sources of the recent explosive growth in cross-border asset trade and the impact of the upscaling in gross and net international investment positions on key open-economy macro-economic variables such as the trade balance and the real exchange rate is critically important for policy analysis. Accordingly, the goal of this chapter is to introduce the reader to some of the main results emerging from this fast-expanding research field. However, it is beyond the scope of this chapter to provide a comprehensive survey of the literature: the following material is intentionally selective and indeed heavily draws on my ongoing collaboration with Gian Maria Milesi-Ferretti of the International Monetary Fund.

The rest of the chapter is organized as follows. Section 2 surveys the determinants of the growth in international financial trade: both the scale of gross investment positions and the emergence of large net foreign asset imbalances. The macroeconomic implications are explored in section 3, in terms of the impact of net imbalances on the trade balance, the real exchange rate and real interest rate differentials. In addition, the potential impact of large cross-holdings for risk-sharing, growth and business cycles is also reviewed. Section 4 offers some concluding remarks.

2 The rise in international financial trade

In this section, we first briefly discuss data issues before turning to the empirical analysis of gross and net foreign asset positions.

2.1 Data sources

Data limitations provide one reason why quantitative analysis of international financial trade has been relatively limited. This is especially the case, if one wishes to focus on accumulated stock holdings, rather than just examining international financial flows. Some countries (e.g. the United States, the United Kingdom and Canada) have long provided high-quality national data on foreign assets and liabilities. However, the International Monetary Fund only began reporting the details of international investment positions for a small number of countries in 1997. Its coverage has broadened since then but, especially for developing countries, its data do not go far back in time.

To redress this gap, Lane and Milesi-Ferretti (2001a) set out to construct estimates of gross foreign assets and foreign liabilities for a large number of industrial and developing countries over 1970–1998. In addition to the broad aggregates, the composition of the international balance sheet (debt, portfolio equity, FDI) was also addressed. The stock estimates were derived by cumulating gross financial flows but corrected for the valuation changes that result from movements in financial markets, currencies and price levels. Moreover, it is also important to allow for one-off capital transfers and the impact of debt reduction and debt cancellation programmes for some countries.

The importance of valuation changes in driving the evolution of net foreign asset positions is well illustrated by Table 11.1 (adapted from Lane and Milesi-Ferretti 2001a), which shows that the correlation between the current account and the change in the net foreign asset position is typically far from unity. As such, the simplistic method of capturing net foreign asset positions by simply cumulating current account imbalances can prove highly misleading.

2.2 Determinants of gross international investment positions

As is emphasized by Lane (2000), Lane and Milesi-Ferretti (2001a, 2001b, 2003a) and Obstfeld and Taylor (2004), the size of international balance sheets have grown very rapidly in recent decades. Although many countries display net foreign asset positions that are close to zero, this is consistent with having a large gross foreign asset position that is counterbalanced by offsetting gross foreign liabilities.

Even if net positions are small, large gross positions have important macroeconomic implications. First, the potential for international risk-sharing is largely a function of the scale of international balance sheets. For instance, domestic risks can be partly laid off by issuing state-contingent foreign liabilities – accomplished, for example, by the sale of domestic equities to external investors. In the other direction, holding foreign assets provides diversification, since the returns on these foreign

Table 11.1 Correlation between current account and change in net foreign asset position

	$\rho(CA, \Delta NFA)$
The USA	0.53
The UK	0.53
Austria	0.87
Denmark	0.29
France	0.44
Germany	0.89
Italy	0.95
The Netherlands	−0.14
Norway	0.93
Sweden	0.66
Switzerland	−0.63
Canada	0.6
Japan	0.82
Finland	0.17
Greece	0.89
Iceland	0.98
Ireland	0.99
Portugal	0.98
Spain	0.51
Australia	0.34
New Zealand	0.22

Source: Lane and Milesi-Ferretti (2001a).

Notes
CA is current account to GDP ratio; ΔNFA is first difference of the ratio of net foreign assets to GDP.

assets will be determined by external events. Of course, the precise mechanics of risk sharing will depend on the composition of the international balance sheet as between debt and equity-type investments and also on the mix between assets and liabilities that are denominated in domestic currency versus foreign currencies.

Second, gross positions also affect the relation between asset price fluctuations (including currency fluctuations) and macroeconomic variables. The larger the scale of the international balance sheet, the more important are re-valuation effects. To give a simple example, if a country holds $1 billion in dollar-denominated assets, it is much more exposed to shifts in the value of the dollar and in US financial markets than if its position is only $100 million. In this way, the growth in international financial positions strengthens international linkages across economies through this revaluation mechanism.

Third, international asset cross-holdings may also influence the determination of asset prices. To the extent that wealth effects are important for asset pricing, the closer correlation in wealth dynamics across investors of different nationalities that is induced by greater international diversification may also generate higher international comovement in asset prices.

Fourth, the internationalization of capital ownership may also have political economy implications in that it may be increasingly difficult to distinguish between domestic and foreign owners of capital. In turn, this feeds into debates about optimal and feasible tax structures and international regulation of corporations and financial markets.

Finally, a high level of international financial integration may also alter long-term growth potential. This may be the case for a number of reasons. First, international risk-sharing permits domestic investors to take on riskier projects that may promise higher returns. Second, the internationalization of the capital stock may weaken incentives to over-tax or over-regulate investment. Third, the discipline effect of open capital markets may also improve monitoring and increase the efficiency of capital allocation. On the other side, however, a poor regulatory structure and/or an exposed external capital structure may adversely affect economic performance by permitting overborrowing and increasing vulnerability to output-destroying financial crises.

For these reasons, it is important to understand the determinants of the scale and composition of international balance sheets. Lane and Milesi-Ferretti (2003a) studied the dynamics of the level of international financial integration for a sample of industrial countries over 1983–2001. The volume-based measure considered is

$$IFIGDP_{it} = \frac{(FA_{it} + FL_{it})}{GDP_{it}} \tag{1}$$

where FA_{it}, FL_{it} denote the levels of gross foreign assets and gross foreign liabilities respectively. The growth in this ratio is modelled as

$$\Delta IFIGDP_{it} = \alpha_i + \gamma * X_{it} + \beta * \Delta Z_{it} + \epsilon_{it} \tag{2}$$

where X_{it}, Z_{it} are a set of country- and time-varying determinants. Table 11.2 shows the results for a panel of industrial countries over 1983–2001. At a broad level, the most important covariates of the growth in international financial integration are: (a) the growth in international trade in goods and services; (b) rising output per capita; and (c) domestic financial and stockmarket development. While the importance of each of these variables is intuitively appealing, an important direction for future research is to sort out the lines of causality in the dynamic relation between these factors and the growth in international financial integration.

Drawing on Lane and Milesi-Ferretti (2003a), Table 11.2 also shows that the external liberalization index loses its explanatory power once other determinants are included in the specification: this is attributable to the fact that the process of opening capital accounts in the industrial

Table 11.2 Determinants of international financial integration, 1982–2001

	(1)	(2)	(3)	(4)	(5)	(6)	(7)
External liberalization	0.29	0.06	0.04	−0.05	−0.06	0.08	0.05
	(5.3)***	(0.69)	(0.5)	(0.5)	(0.6)	(0.8)	(0.5)
Trade openness		4.18	4.95	3.08	3.89	3.29	2.72
		(3.2)***	(3.7)***	(3.71)***	(4.5)***	(3.63)***	(3.01)***
Log GDP per capita			2.65	1.56	2.76	2.82	2.71
			(2.5)**	(1.97)*	(3.51)***	(4.31)***	(4.06)***
Financial depth				0.24	0.56	0.62	0.75
				(1.58)	(1.68)	(1.88)*	(2.37)**
Stock market capitalization				1.27	1.3	1.32	1.35
				(5.86)***	(6.18)***	(6.35)***	(6.95)***
Cumulative privatization					−1.65	−9.67	−9.92
					(0.66)	(2.66)**	(2.87)***
Corporate tax rate						−1.47	−1.27
						(1.65)	(1.4)
Investor protection							0.19
							(1.4)
Adjusted R^2	0.17	0.35	0.39	0.69	0.72	0.7	0.7
Observations.	78	78	78	72	64	49	49

Source: Lane and Milesi-Ferretti (2003a).

Notes
External liberalization is an index of capital account openness. Trade openness is a ratio of exports plus imports to GDP. Financial depth is a ratio of liquid liabilities to GDP. Stock market capitalization is measured as a ratio to GDP. Cumulative privatization is a ratio of cumulative privatization revenues to GDP. Corporate tax rate is average tax rate on corporate profits. Investor protection is a dummy taking value 1 if a country has introduced a law prohibiting insider trading and zero otherwise. Fixed-effects panel estimation using averaged data for 1982–1985, 1986–1989, 1990–1993, 1994–1997, 1998–2001. White-corrected t-statistics in parentheses.

countries was largely completed by the end of the 1980s, whereas the most rapid growth in international financial cross-trade took place in the late 1990s. The result that privatization, all else being equal, is associated with a lower value of international financial integration is somewhat surprising: one candidate explanation is that the terms of privatization programmes favour domestic investors and induce a greater home bias in investment patterns. In terms of composition, Lane and Milesi-Ferretti (2003a) find that the growth of the domestic stockmarket is the single most important factor associated with an increase in the ratio of equity to debt positions in the aggregate international balance sheet.

Employing the dataset developed by Lane and Milesi-Ferretti (2001a), Lane and Milesi-Ferretti (2001b) find that trade openness is highly important in explaining the level of aggregate external liabilities for developing countries and also raises the ratio of equity to debt liabilities. Another significant finding from that study is that ratio of FDI to total private liabilities negatively covaries with country size: smaller countries disproportionately rely on FDI as source of external investment.

Clearly, much remains to be done to gain a comprehensive understanding of the growth in international cross-border financial holdings and the determination of the relative contributions of debt and equity (both portfolio and FDI) in the overall external capital structure. As time elapses and data collection efforts intensify, more can be done to test various hypotheses about this phenomenon. In one direction, Lane and Milesi-Ferretti (2003b) explore the geographical composition of international investment positions, drawing on the recently-released Comprehensive Portfolio Investment Survey that is coordinated by the International Monetary Fund.

2.3 Determinants of net foreign asset positions

Although much has been written about the cyclical behaviour of the current account, relatively less is known about the long-term behaviour of net foreign asset positions. This is unsatisfactory, since recent decades have seen the emergence of persistent net foreign asset imbalances that represent significant asymmetries in the world economy. As will be explored later in this chapter, non-zero long-term net foreign asset positions have implications for the behaviour of trade balances, real exchange rates and real interest rates. In addition, these asymmetries influence the transmission of monetary and fiscal policies and the calculus involved in proposals to improve international policy coordination.

To gain some insight into the empirical determination of long-term net foreign asset positions, Lane and Milesi-Ferretti (2002a) estimate a parsimonious fixed-effects panel model for samples of industrial and developing countries. Three factors are considered: relative output per capita; the level of public debt; and demographic structure. In general, we may expect a long-term increase in output per capita to be associated with an improve-ment in the net foreign asset position – savings may increase, while the decline in the domestic marginal product of capital may induce a switch towards overseas investment. However, at least for developing countries, an increase in output per capita may relax binding credit constraints, such that it permits an increase in external borrowing – for these countries, the net correlation may actually be negative.

Public debt is included, since a failure of Ricardian Equivalence implies a 'twin debts' outcome – the higher is public debt, the larger also is net external debt. Finally, demography may influence the net foreign asset positions, both via its impact on the rate of asset accumulation and also on the rate of domestic capital formation. For instance, a country with a large cohort in the 40–65 age bracket may accumulate net foreign assets, as the savings rate increases in anticipation of retirement and the investment rate falls on account of the relative scarcity of young workers.

Based on Lane and Milesi-Ferretti (2002a), Tables 11.3 and 11.4 report the results of the panel estimation of the determinants of net foreign asset positions for industrial and developing country samples respectively. For the industrial country sample, Table 11.3 shows that richer industrial coun-tries indeed have more positive net foreign asset positions, with the age profile of the population also exerting an influence and that higher public debt is associated with some deterioration in the external account.

For the developing country sample, Table 11.4 shows that the relation between output per capita and the net foreign asset position is in fact negative: higher output is associated with an increase in net external liabil-ities. In addition, there is a high 'pass-through' from net government liabil-ities to net external liabilities. Both of these results are consistent with the presence of external and internal credit constraints in developing

Table 11.3 Determinants of net foreign asset positions, industrial countries

	(1)	*(2)*
	1970–1998	*Balanced*
Log GDP per capita	0.91	0.94
	(12.63)**	(11.66)**
Public debt	−0.125	−0.18
	(3.1)**	(4.54)**
Demography	30.1	43.6
	(0.00)**	(0.00)**
Adjusted R^2	0.89	0.9
Observations	516	390
Countries	22	15

Source: Lane and Milesi-Ferretti (2002a).

Notes
Panel DOLS fixed-effects estimation. White-corrected *t*-statistics in parentheses.

Table 11.4 Determinants of net foreign asset positions, developing countries

	(1)	(2)
	1970–1998	*Balanced*
Log GDP per capita	−0.21	−0.26
	(4.59)**	(3.55)**
Public debt	−0.67	−0.5
	(14.03)**	(8.87)**
Demography	28.7	38.7
	(0.00)**	(0.00)**
Adjusted R^2	0.83	0.89
Observations	779	416
Countries	39	16

Source: Lane and Milesi-Ferretti (2002a).

Notes
Panel DOLS fixed-effects estimation. White-corrected t-statistics in parentheses.

countries. The demographic structure of developing countries again turns out to influence the net foreign asset position.

Importantly, these long-term factors are important for the overall dynamics of the net foreign asset position. Again based on Lane and Milesi-Ferretti (2002a), Table 11.5 reports the adjustment coefficient from an 'error correction mechanism' (ECM) representation

$$\Delta NFA_{it} = -\delta(NFA_{it-1} - NFA^*_{it-1}) + \beta * Z_{it} + \epsilon_{it} \tag{3}$$

where NFA^*_{it} is the desired long-term net foreign asset position and the control factors Z_{it} (not reported) include innovations to the factors driving NFA^*_{it} and a lag of the dependent variable. This simple ECM equation has good explanatory power: Lane and Milesi-Ferretti (2002a) show its capability to track actual net foreign asset positions for a wide range of industrial countries.

Table 11.5 Dynamics of net foreign asset position

	(1)	(2)
ECM	−0.11	−0.06
	(4.1)***	(2.36)**
Adjusted R^2	0.28	0.44
Observations	539	849
Countries	22	39

Source: Lane and Milesi-Ferretti (2002a).

Notes
OLS estimation. t-statistics in parentheses.

In summary, this section has addressed the factors underlying the growth in the scale of international investment cross-holdings and the determinants of net foreign asset positions. In the next section, we ask whether the increase in gross and net international financial trade has implications for the macroeconomic behaviour of open economies.

3 Macroeconomic implications of international financial trade

In this section, we turn to drawing out the macroeconomic implications of the rise in international financial trade and the emergence of large divergences in net foreign asset positions between creditor and debtor countries. We first consider trade balances before turning to real exchange rates and real interest rate differentials. We then briefly consider the relations between financial globalization and international risk sharing, long-term growth performance and business cycle analysis.

3.1 Trade balance adjustment

For sustainability, the trade balance must adjust to reflect the value of the net foreign asset position. Following Lane and Milesi-Ferretti (2002a, 2002b), we can write the ratio of the trade balance to GDP as

$$tb_t = -\left[\frac{r_t - g_t}{1 + g_t}\right]f_{t-1} + \epsilon_t \equiv \Psi_\tau + \epsilon_t \qquad (4)$$

where f_t is the net foreign asset position, r_t is the (common) rate of return on foreign assets and liabilities and g_t is the GDP growth rate. The disturbance term captures temporary deviations from this long-term value, reflecting cyclical disturbances and shifts in the desired net foreign asset position. If the rate of return exceeds the output growth rate $(r_t > g_t)$, then a long-term creditor country can run persistent trade deficits, while a debtor country must run trade surpluses.

The trade balance adjustment that is required depends on the rate of return, which in turn should reflect the composition of the international balance sheet. To develop this point, let us now relax the assumption that foreign assets and liabilities earn a common rate of return. We can rewrite equation (4) as

$$tb_t = -\left\{\left[\frac{r_t^A - g_t}{1 + g_t}\right]f_{t-1} + \left[\frac{r_t^L - r_t^A}{1 + g_t}\right]fl_{t-1}\right\} + \epsilon_t \qquad (5)$$

where r_t^A, r_t^L denote the rates of return on gross assets and gross liabilities (fl_t) respectively. For a debtor nation, a larger trade surplus must be maintained, the greater is the positive differential $(r_t^L > r_t^A)$. Conversely, a debtor country need not run a trade surplus at all if it earns sufficiently more on its foreign assets than it pays out on its foreign liabilities $(r_t^L \ll r_t^A)$. For instance, a country that primarily issues foreign liabilities in the form of short-term liquid debt securities but invests overseas in higher-risk higher-return foreign equity assets may find itself in this fortunate position.[1]

Lane and Milesi-Ferretti (2002b) confirm that equation (5) has empirical relevance: they find that (tb_t, Ψ_t) are cointegrated for a sample of industrial countries, with a growth in long-term investment income or capital gains associated with a long-term decline in the trade balance. In this regard, it is important to underline the importance of rates of return and growth rates in intermediating the relation between net foreign assets and the trade balance: the cross-country correlation between the 'raw' net foreign asset position and the trade balance is relatively weak, in view of the substantial variation in rates of return and output growth rates. For instance, drawing on Lane and Milesi-Ferretti (2002b), Table 11.6 shows the variation in rates of return on foreign assets and foreign liabilities for a selection of industrial countries over 1993–1998.

3.2 Real exchange rates

A classical principle in international economics is the 'transfer problem': a country that must engineer a net resource outflow (e.g. war reparations or investment income payments to foreign investors) may need an equilibrium

Table 11.6 Rates of return on foreign assets and foreign liabilities, 1983–1998

	Real rate of return	
	Foreign assets	Foreign liabilities
The US	11.3	8.1
The UK	6.6	7.1
Austria	6.5	8.3
France	8.5	8.9
Germany	2.9	4.3
Italy	8.3	9.6
The Netherlands	5.9	7.3
Sweden	11.7	11
Switzerland	6.9	8.7
Canada	3.6	4.2
Japan	7	9.6
Finland	0.4	7.2
Iceland	6	3.3
Spain	6.1	6.9
Australia	6.1	3.5

Source: Adapted from Lane and Milesi-Ferretti (2002b).

Note
Dollar-based real rates of return.

real exchange rate depreciation in order to achieve the required restructuring of the domestic economy. Lane and Milesi-Ferretti (2001b, 2001c, 2002b) provide a range of estimates for the size of the 'transfer problem' effect and show that the magnitudes are typically quite substantial, especially for the larger economies (the United States, Japan, Euroland).

Table 11.7 shows the baseline results from Lane and Milesi-Ferretti (2001b) which models the long-term CPI-based real exchange rate as depending on the net foreign asset position, relative output per capita and the terms of trade. In column (1), all countries are pooled together, whereas columns (2) and (3) report results for the separate industrial and developing country subsamples. Across the specifications, a significant association between net foreign assets and real exchange rates is evident: more indebted countries have more depreciated real exchange rates. Importantly, the evidence in Lane and Milesi-Ferretti (2001c, 2002b) is that the net foreign asset position influences the real exchange rate via the relative price of nontradables: it cannot be attributed to endogenous movements in the terms of trade. Further analysis in those papers shows that the magnitude of the transfer problem intuitively covaries with country size: the real exchange rate adjustment required for a large, closed economy is much bigger than for a smaller externally-orientated economy (see Figure 11.1, derived from Lane and Milesi-Ferretti 2002b). For a sample of industrial countries, Lane and Milesi-Ferretti (2002b) also take into account that rates of return and output growth rates influence the required trade balance adjustment for a given long-term net foreign asset position and show that this correction strengthens the estimated relation between the trade balance and the real exchange rate.

Table 11.7 Net foreign assets and real exchange rates

	(1)	*(2)*	*(3)*
	All	*Industrial*	*Developing*
NFA	0.28	0.19	0.29
	(7.98)***	(3.97)***	(6.56)***
YD	0.14	0.22	0.14
	(3.15)***	(3.13)***	(2.57)***
TT	0.04	0.17	0.02
	(1.21)	(4.12)***	(0.51)
Adjusted R^2	0.52	0.44	0.42
Observations	1558	548	1010

Source: Lane and Milesi-Ferretti (2001b).

Notes
Dependent variable is CPI-based multilateral real exchange rate. NFA is ratio of net foreign assets to GDP; YD is domestic GDP relative to basket of trading partners; TT is terms of trade. Panel fixed-effects DOLS estimation. White-corrected *t*-statistics in parentheses.

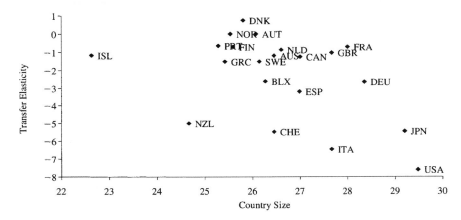

Figure 11.1 Scatter plot of estimated 'transfer elasticity' against country size (source: Lane and Milesi-Ferretti (2002b)).

3.3 *Real interest rate differentials*

Lane and Milesi-Ferretti (2002a) also study the comovement of real interest rate differentials and net foreign asset positions. In the portfolio-balance literature, it is hypothesized that a net debtor country must offer higher returns in order to induce global investors to hold its liabilities (see Frankel and Rose 1995 for a review). Table 11.8 reports the panel fixed-effects results: in panel A, all countries are included and the time dummies soak up the 'world real interest rate' that is common to all countries; in panel B, the dependent variable is the real interest rate differential vis-à-vis the US. In some of the specifications, we also control for the level of public debt and the rate of real exchange rate appreciation. The findings are quite suggestive: there is indeed some support for a portfolio-balance effect, with net creditor countries enjoying lower real interest rates than net debtors. The negative cross-sectional correlation is also evident in the scatter plot in Figure 11.2, also derived from Lane and Milesi-Ferretti (2002a).

In this subsection, we have focused on long-term relations in the data. Exchange rate adjustment to long-term equilibrium is unlikely to be perfectly smooth. Obstfeld and Rogoff (2001) analyse a number of scenarios for the dollar correction required in the event that global investors turn against funding the US external deficit. An important lesson from that research is that the existence of nominal rigidities sharply magnifies the required scale of short-term nominal depreciation in the event of a sharp reversal in capital flows.

Table 11.8 Determinants of real interest rate differentials

	(1)	(2)	(3)	(4)	(5)	(6)	(7)	(8)
A. Real interest rate								
NFA/exports	-1.06	-0.83	-1.36	-0.91	-1.5	-1.63	-2.87	-2.81
	(2.6)*	(2.0)*	(2.48)*	(1.66)	(2.45)*	(2.94)**	(4.48)**	(4.65)**
Public debt		3.82		7.1		2.98		3.56
		(2.1)*		(3.4)**		(2.03)*		(1.91)*
D(RER)		0.03		0.04		0.02		2.64
		(1.2)		(1.74)		(0.9)		(1.23)
Adjusted R^2	0.5	0.56	0.36	0.39	0.54	0.59	0.43	0.46
Countries	21	21	21	21	21	21	21	21
Observations	462	410	362	336	442	410	358	336
B. Real interest rate differential								
NFA/exports	-2.54	-2.44	-2.73	-2.22	-2.57	-2.77	-3.19	-3.24
	(5.41)**	(5.5)**	(4.3)**	(4.58)**	(4.03)**	(4.27)**	(4.83)**	(5.52)**
Public debt		3.18		7.79		2.23		3.18
		(1.76)		(4.82)**		(1.51)		(1.67)
D(RER)		-0.04		-0.014		0.012		0.015
		(2.15)*		(0.78)		(0.54)		(0.66)
Adjusted R^2	0.58	0.59	0.6	0.64	0.6	0.59	0.63	0.67
Countries	21	21	21	21	21	21	21	21
Observations	423	403	344	338	416	386	340	319

Source: Lane and Milesi-Ferretti (2002a).

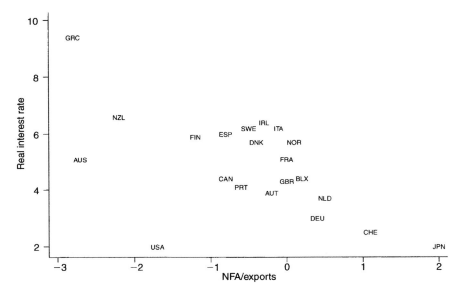

Figure 11.2 Scatter of real interest rate against ratio of net foreign assets to exports, average data over 1990–1998 (source: Lane and Milesi-Ferretti (2002a)).

3.4 International risk sharing

As was highlighted in section 2, an increase in the scale of international asset cross-holdings might be expected to lead to more international risk-sharing via a greater level of wealth diversification. Some studies have looked at this question in a partial and indirect manner by asking whether national incomes (GNP levels) are insulated from domestic output (GDP) shocks. For instance, in a study of the Irish economy, Lane (1998) finds that indeed the net factor income outflows are procyclical: GNP is less affected by cyclical fluctuations than GDP. However, for a broader sample of OECD countries, Sorensen and Yosha (1998) and Lane (2001) find little evidence of a smoothing role for international investment income flows.

A limitation of that approach is that risk-sharing may take place through the movements of capital gains rather than via investment income. Lane and Milesi-Ferretti (2003a) show that holding overseas assets indeed diversifies against domestic financial risks: although the correlations are typically positive, the degree of return comovement is far from perfectly correlated. In general, the capital gains component is far more volatile than the investment income component in overall financial returns, so that it is not too surprising that this factor is central in assessing the degree of diversification that is afforded by international financial integration. However, Sorensen *et al.* (2002) find that the investment income channel also becomes stronger, the greater is the degree of financial integration: the capacity of investment income flows to smooth GDP shocks is increasing in the level of foreign asset holdings.

Of course, the flip-side of acquiring insulation from domestic disturbances is greater exposure to externally-generated shocks. As is highlighted by Begg *et al.* (2002), the sharp reversals in US equity markets and in corporate profitability in 2000–2001 were quickly transmitted to Europe, in part due to the rapid acquisition of US assets by European investors during the late 1990s. It is also the case that financial integration alters the allocative impact of financial bubbles – Ventura (2002) explores the interrelation between bubbles and international capital flows.

3.5 Economic growth

During the 1990s, there was an extensive literature that attempted to identify the impact of capital account liberalization for economic growth, typically finding only weak effects (see Eichengreen 2002 for a review). In general, this is not too surprising since any positive effect may be overshadowed in the data by the impact of growth-impairing financial crises.

More recently, a number of studies have rather explored the relation between volume-based measures of financial integration and economic growth (Prasad *et al.* 2003; Durham 2003; O'Donnell 2003). These studies use variables similar to the *IFIGDP* measure defined in equation (1) above. Consistent with the earlier literature, the IMF study carried out by Prasad *et al.* (2003) also finds it difficult to detect a strong and robust causal relationship between financial integration and economic growth. However, there is some support for nonlinearity in the relationship: above a certain threshold level of domestic absorptive capacity, greater financial integration does indeed deliver high growth and lower volatility if an appropriate policy framework is in place.

Overall, it is perhaps too early to reach firm conclusions about the growth impact of greater financial integration. As the robustness of domestic financial sectors and regulatory institutions improve and adapt to a globalized financial system, the inherent capacity of financial integration to improve international resource allocation may come to the fore and deliver faster growth to capital-importing countries. Moreover, as is highlighted by Gourinchas and Jeanne (2003), the most significant gains from financial integration may accrue through indirect channels: for instance, by shifting the domestic political equilibrium in the direction of a more investment-friendly policy regime.

3.6 Business cycle analysis

Significant non-zero net foreign asset positions also have implications for business cycles and the analysis of macroeconomic stabilization policies.[2] Accumulated imbalances – regardless of their origin – may be important, since exchange rate and asset price fluctuations then also operate via a revaluation channel on the value of foreign assets and liabilities. For instance, Benigno (2001) shows that the business cycle response to shocks is quantitatively quite different if the initial net foreign asset position is say 30–50 per cent of GDP rather than zero as is assumed in most of the literature.

Moreover, the asymmetry created by non-zero net foreign asset positions also implies potentially large gains to international policy coordination. In Benigno's model, for zero initial net foreign asset positions, the first best can be well approximated a policy of targeting domestic producer price inflation.[3] However, such a policy induces excessive volatility in interest rates and hence inefficient cross-country wealth redistributions if initial net foreign asset positions are non-zero and policy coordination in this case can substantially improve welfare.

Tille (2003) provides a simple example about the impact of increasing financial integration on the transmission of exchange rate movements. Consider two cases with the same negative net foreign asset position of minus 100 billion. In case A, foreign assets and liabilities are 100 billion and 200 billion respectively; in case B, these stand at 1,000 billion and 1,100 billion. Let all foreign assets and liabilities be denominated in the domestic currency. A 10 per cent appreciation reduces the value of foreign assets by the same proportion in both cases. However, in case A, this translates into a wealth loss of 10 billion, whereas it represents a wealth decline of 100 billion in case B: a very significant difference, with corresponding implications for consumption and investment behaviour.

It should be recognized that a significant net external liability position also leaves a country vulnerable to a financing crisis, which can in itself be a source of business cycle volatility. In turn, a sharp turnaround in the trade balance may require a large real depreciation, especially in the presence of nominal rigidities. Such sudden stops in capital inflows have been a recurrent problem for emerging market economies in recent years. There is by now a large literature on the macroeconomics of 'liability dollarization' in developing countries (see, among others, Devereux and Lane 2003; Lane 2003). However, as indicated in the previous subsection, a financing crisis scenario is also potentially relevant for major industrial nations such as the United States, even if the currency composition profile of foreign liabilities is less risky for these countries.

In summary, to fully incorporate the implications of growing international balance sheets into the 'new open economy macroeconomics' modelling framework, more attention needs to be paid to the theoretical treatment of asset accumulation. It would be desirable to also allow for international trade in equities in addition to trade in bonds, without going all the way to a complete asset markets structure.[4] In related fashion, it may also be useful to re-incorporate portfolio-balance considerations into the baseline open-economy macroeconomic model.

4 Conclusions

This chapter has provided a tour d'horizon of some of the main research strands that have been pursued in analysing the macroeconomics of the recent rapid growth in international financial trade. As has been evident throughout the discussion, this research programme is quite immature. In part, this is due to the fact that the process of financial globalization is still in its early stages. As more data accumulate, more insights can be gained as to how macroeconomic relations are affected by international financial integration and how adjustment to larger net foreign asset positions imbalances will play out. For these reasons, this is likely to be an extremely active research field in the coming years and one that also has high relevance for policymakers.

Notes

* This chapter draws heavily on my joint work with Gian Maria Milesi-Ferretti. Useful comments were also received at CCBS workshops. I am grateful for the support provided by the IIIS. This chapter is also part of a research network on 'The analysis of international capital markets: understanding Europe's role in the global economy', funded by the European Commission under the Research Training Network Programme (Contract No. HPRN-CT-1999-00067).
1 However, such a country may leave itself exposed to a 'run' problem if creditors refuse to roll-over the short-term liquid liabilities.
2 Lane and Ganelli (2003) provide a more extensive discussion of this issue.
3 This is the optimal policy under complete financial integration. If initial net foreign asset positions are zero, it is also not far from the optimum with bond-only international asset trade.
4 See also Heathcote and Perri (2002) who focus more on the implications of financial globalization for models in the international real business cycle tradition.

References

Begg, David, Canova, Fabio, Fatas, Antonio, de Grauwe, Paul and Lane, Philip R. (2002), 'Surviving the slowdown: monitoring the European Central Bank 4', *Centre for Economic Policy Research*.

Benigno, P. (2001), 'Price stability with international financial integration', New York University, mimeo.

Devereux, Michael B. and Lane, Philip R. (2003), 'Exchange rates and monetary policy for emerging market economies', University of British Columbia and Trinity College Dublin, mimeo.

Durham, J. Benson (2003), 'Foreign portfolio investment, foreign bank lending, and economic growth', International Finance Discussion Paper no. 2003–757, Board of Governors of the Federal Reserve System.

Eichengreen, Barry (2002), 'Capital account liberalization: What do cross-country studies tell us?', *World Bank Economic Review*, 15(3): 341–365.

Frankel, Jeffrey and Rose, Andrew K. (1995), 'Empirical research on nominal exchange rates', in Grossman, G. and Rogoff, K. (eds), *Handbook of International Economics, Vol. 3.* Amsterdam: North-Holland.

Gourinchas, Pierre-Olivier and Jeanne, Olivier (2003), 'The elusive gains from international financial integration', CEPR Discussion Paper no. 3902.

Heathcote, Jonathan and Perri, Fabrizio (2002), 'Financial globalization and real regionalization', New York University, mimeo.

Lane, Philip R. (1998), 'International diversification and the Irish economy', *Economic and Social Review*, 31: 37–54.

Lane, Philip R. (2000), 'International investment positions: a cross-sectional analysis', *Journal of International Money and Finance*, 19(4): 513–534.

Lane, Philip R. (2001), 'Do international investment income flows smooth income?', *Weltwirtschaftliches Archiv*, 137(4): 714–736.

Lane, Philip R. (2003), 'Business cycles and macroeconomic policy in emerging market economies', *International Finance*, 6(1): 89–108.

Lane, Philip R. and Ganelli, Giovanni (2003), 'Dynamic general equilibrium analysis: the open economy dimension', in Altug, S., Chaddha, J. and Nolan, C. (eds), *Elements in Dynamic Macroeconomic Analysis*, Cambridge University Press, forthcoming.

Lane, Philip R. and Milesi-Ferretti, Gian Maria (2001a), 'The external wealth of nations: measures of foreign assets and liabilities for industrial and developing countries', *Journal of International Economics*, 55: 263–294.

Lane, Philip R. and Milesi-Ferretti, Gian Maria (2001b), 'External capital structure: theory and evidence', in Siebert, H. (ed.), *The World's New Financial Landscape: Challenges for Economic Policy*, Berlin: Springer-Verlag.

Lane, Philip R. and Milesi-Ferretti, Gian Maria (2001c), 'The transfer problem revisited: net foreign assets and long-run real exchange rates', CEPR Discussion Paper no. 2511.

Lane, Philip R. and Milesi-Ferretti, Gian Maria (2002a), 'Long-term capital movements', *NBER Macroeconomics Annual*, 16: 73–116.

Lane, Philip R. and Milesi-Ferretti, Gian Maria (2002b), 'External wealth, the trade balance and the real exchange rate', *European Economic Review*, 46: 1049–1071.

Lane, Philip R. and Milesi-Ferretti, Gian Maria (2003a), 'International financial integration', *International Monetary Fund Staff Papers*, forthcoming.

Lane, Philip R. and Milesi-Ferretti, Gian Maria (2003b), 'International investment patterns', Trinity College Dublin and International Monetary Fund, Mimeo.

O'Donnell, Barry (2003), 'International financial integration and economic performance', PhD Dissertation, Trinity College Dublin.

Obstfeld, M. and Taylor, A.M. (2004), *Global Capital Markets: Integration, Crisis, and Growth*, Cambridge: Cambridge University Press.

Obstfeld, Maurice and Rogoff, Kenneth (2001), 'Perspectives on OECD capital market integration: implications for U.S. current account adjustment', *Global Economic Integration: Opportunities and Challenges*, Federal Reserve Bank of Kansas City, pages 169–208.

Prasad, Eswar, Rogoff, Kenneth, Wei, Shang-Jin and Kose, M. Ayhan (2003), 'The effects of financial globalization on developing countries: some empirical evidence', IMF Occasional Paper no. 220, forthcoming.

Sorensen, Bent E. and Yosha, Oved (1998), 'International risk sharing and european monetary unification', *Journal of International Economics*, 45: 211–238.

Sorensen, Bent E., Wu, Yi-Tsung and Yosha, Oved (2002), 'Home bias and international risk sharing: twins separated at birth', University of Houston, mimeo,

Tille, Cedric (2003), 'The impact of exchange rate movements on U.S. foreign debt', *Current Issues in Economics and Finance*, 9(1): Federal Reserve Bank of New York.

Ventura, Jaume (2002), 'Bubbles and capital flows', CREI, mimeo.

12 External adjustment and debt sustainability

Douglas Hostland and Lawrence Schembri*

1 Introduction

Recent experiences in Argentina and Brazil have brought to the fore the question of the sustainability of external debt. The IMF defines a country's debt to be sustainable if the debt can be serviced without an unrealistically large future correction in the balance of income and expenditure.[1] Although this is a useful working definition, it does not address two key points. First, the question of sustainability only arises after economic conditions change unexpectedly for the worse. When the debt was incurred, both the lender and sovereign borrower must have shared the expectation that the debt would be sustained *sans* crisis; otherwise, the transaction would not have taken place. Consequently, the IMF should place more emphasis, instead, on assessing the *vulnerability* of a country's debt *before* an adverse shock strikes, rather than on the debt's sustainability after the shock's arrival. Second, the critical question to be asked in evaluating the vulnerability of a country's debt level to a potential negative shock is how is the necessary correction in the balance of income and expenditure (net exports) to be obtained to continue debt service? In practice, this correction can be achieved via two well-known channels: import compression or expenditure switching. Traditionally, the IMF focus has been on obtaining the necessary increase in trade balance via import compression, through a reduction in domestic aggregate demand. Economies, however, also endogenously adjust to adverse shocks through a real exchange rate depreciation that causes a shift in domestic and foreign expenditures towards domestically produced goods. Although this adjustment process via a real depreciation will almost always increase net exports, the outstanding question is whether this adjustment will be sufficiently vigorous to allow the country to meet its external debt service obligations and avoid a debt crisis.

The purpose of this chapter is to consider the vulnerability of a country's level of external debt to negative shocks by examining the country's ability to achieve the necessary adjustment in the real exchange rate and net exports.[2] If it is unlikely that an economy can achieve the required external adjustment in response to shocks of a realistic magnitude then the country's debt level is vulnerable and thus likely to be unsustainable. The analysis in the chapter focuses on an economy's ability to adjust to external shocks; in other words, how easily will an adverse shock, such as a sudden stop in capital inflows or a worsening in the terms of trade, translate into a real depreciation and an increase in the trade balance, in order to close the financing gap and to continue servicing its external debt. Although there are many factors that influence the economy's capacity to respond to a negative external shock, the analysis in the chapter concentrates on five:

1   The exchange rate regime: A flexible exchange rate regime will facilitate the adjustment of the real exchange rate to external shocks and avoid the currency crises and abrupt exchange rate movements that often occur under such circumstances with a fixed rate.
2   The currency denomination of external debt: Foreign-currency denominated debt leaves debtor countries more vulnerable to external shocks.
3   The magnitude of the import and export trade price elasticities: The Marshall–Lerner condition implies that larger price elasticities entail greater adjustment of trade volumes to real exchange rate movements.
4   The degree of pass-through of exchange rate movements into the domestic relative prices of traded goods (the lower the degree of pass-through, the greater the effect of a nominal exchange rate movement on the real exchange rate).
5   The size of the traded goods sector or the degree of openness to trade: The larger the traded goods sector, the greater would be the impact of a real exchange rate movement on net exports.

Emerging-market countries generally face two financing constraints, fiscal and external. The chapter considers only external debt because this constraint can be, in practice, more binding, especially since the bulk of external debt in emerging market countries is denominated in foreign currency. In addition, the fiscal constraint is often less constraining because countries have more scope to manage domestic currency indebtedness. First, the domestic authorities have more direct control over the fiscal balance than the trade balance. Second, since domestic entities tend to hold domestic debt while foreign entities hold foreign debt, moral suasion by the domestic authorities may be more effective in dealing with the fiscal financing constraint. Lastly, because the authorities can print domestic currency, they may be able to reduce the real burden of their domestic currency obligations through inflation. This option is not available with respect to external debt. As a final remark, the chapter's emphasis on external debt is consistent with a recent argument by Goldstein (2003: 9) who maintains that many of recent analyses of debt sustainability fail to incorporate fully the foreign exchange constraint.

Because the scope of the chapter is limited to the issues of adjustment and the vulnerability of external debt, it does not attempt to provide a complete analysis of the debt sustainability issue. In particular, like the IMF's recent work on sustainability, the chapter also avoids the distinction between solvency and liquidity because the distinction, is not meaningful in practice; a country's willingness to continue to service its debt often depends on political factors. Nonetheless, these political factors are often shaped by economic ones, such as the economy's capacity to absorb and adjust to adverse negative shocks. An economy lacking this flexibility will see interest groups pitted against one another in an effort to block needed economic adjustment and structural reform.

The next section of the chapter considers the current approach to debt sustainability assessment given the insights of the literature. Section 3 presents recent evidence on external debt levels and trade balance/current account adjustment for a set of important emerging market countries including Argentina, Brazil and Turkey. Section 4 provides a conceptual overview of the key factors that influence endogenous adjustment to adverse external shocks. Section 5 constructs and calibrates a dynamic partial equilibrium model of trade and current account adjustment and simulates the impact of an exchange rate devaluation under different parameterizations of the key factors. The final section of the chapter offers some concluding remarks.

2 Current approach reconsidered

The current approach to analyzing sustainability of external debt is based on the inter-temporal budget constraint (IBC).[3] The IBC relates interest rates, economic growth, the trade balance, and the debt/GDP level. In particular, the debt/GDP ratio will increase if:

$$(r - g)(D_t/Y_t) > (TB_t/Y_t) \tag{1}$$

where D_t is external debt, Y_t is output (real GDP), TB_t is the trade balance, r is the interest rate, and g is the growth rate of GDP.[4] Intuitively, this condition implies that if the interest rate on the debt exceeds the growth rate of output then the trade balance surplus must be sufficiently large to service the external debt; otherwise the debt/GDP will increase. This situation in which the interest rate exceeds the growth rate cannot persist indefinitely because interest payments will grow faster than the economy's capacity to generate net exports to pay them, and the debt level will become unsustainable. In contrast, if the economy is growing faster than the interest rate then the country can run a trade balance deficit and still maintain a constant debt/GDP ratio because the debt can be serviced from capital inflows. If the trade balance is zero, in a surplus or a small deficit position, then the debt/GDP ratio will decline.

The formal methodology recently proposed by the IMF (2002a, 2002b) to assess debt sustainability is based on the IBC. This approach incorporates the IMF's rule of thumb that the external debt level is considered to be sustainable if the debt/GDP ratio is declining. As a first step, the methodology entails generating a "baseline" economic projection conditional on policy settings that are designed to keep the debt/GDP ratio on a downward profile over a five-year planning horizon. Sensitivity analysis is then conducted using alternative projections for output growth, interest rates and exchange rates. This analysis illustrates the extent to which unfavorable economic developments (in the form of weaker economic growth for instance) could cause the debt/GDP ratio to deviate from the baseline projection and perhaps lead to a scenario in which the debt-to-GDP ratio is increasing and the debt unsustainable.

The Appendix to IMF (2002a) uses a sample of emerging market countries to estimate a rough approximation of the conditional probability distribution of a debt crisis for a given level of debt. The main findings are that debt crises typically occur at a debt/GDP ratio of 50–60 percent or more. For countries below the 40 percent level, the conditional probability of a debt crisis is only 2–5 percent. The conditional probability rises to 15–20 percent for countries above that threshold.

Although it is not surprising that this empirical evidence and similar evidence found by other researchers indicates the probability of default increases as the debt/GDP ratio rises, it casts doubt on the usefulness of assessing debt sustainability based on whether the debt to GDP ratio is declining. It is easily conceivable that while the debt/GDP ratio may be declining, it still may be "too high" to be sustainable because it is vulnerable to an adverse shock of a reasonable magnitude. For example, suppose the debt/GDP ratio was at a level that was perceived to be sustainable, e.g., 40 percent, and then rose significantly because of an unfavorable shock. Even if policy changes were implemented to put the debt/GDP ratio on a downward path it is not clear that the debt could continue to be serviced in the advent of another negative shock.

The IMF's approach to assessing debt sustainability based primarily on the path of the debt/GDP ratio does not place enough emphasis on the economy's capacity to adjust to these shocks in order to generate the level of net exports and the amount of foreign exchange necessary to continue to service the external debt. The stylistic model developed in this chapter will address both of these concerns.

3 Evidence on external debt and trade balance adjustment

3.1 External debt

The descriptive statistics reported in Table 12.1 provide a historical perspective on the variables in the intertemporal budget constraint (given by equation (1)) for 15 emerging market economies over the period 1970–2000.[5] Table 12.1 shows that there has been a wide variation in the external debt burden across the 15 countries.[6] The external debt/GDP ratio averaged 43 percent over the period 1970–2000, with a standard deviation of 22 percentage points and a range from 7 percent (Venezuela in

Table 12.1 Descriptive statistics for 15 emerging market economies

Interest rates, real GDP growth and inflation

	Sample: 1970–2000					2000	2001
	Average	Standard deviation	Minimum	Maximum	Median	Average	
Average interest rate	7.6	2.2	1.5	16.5	7.5	6.3	
Private sector	8.3	2.3	1.6	16.9	8.1	7.0	
Official sector	6.7	1.8	1.0	17.7	6.8	5.5	
Nominal GDP growth	9.5	16.0	−55.8	84.4	10.3	7.6	
Real GDP growth	4.5	4.7	−14.5	18.7	5.1	5.1	1.0
GDP deflator inflation	5.0	14.2	−44.4	86.8	5.0	2.4	

Percentage of GDP

	Sample: 1970–2000					2000	2001
	Average	Standard deviation	Minimum	Maximum	Median	Average	
External debt	43.4	22.3	6.8	167.9	40.9	52.7	52.0
Current account	−1.6	4.9	−14.5	19.2	−2.3	1.7	1.6
Trade balance	0.5	5.5	−11.3	25.1	−2.3	3.7	
Debt service	2.7	2.0	0.3	13.6	2.5	3.0	3.1

Percentage of exports

	Sample: 1970–2000					2000	2001
	Average	Standard deviation	Minimum	Maximum	Median	Average	
External debt	182.5	110.9	22.0	695.4	169.6	143.8	146.8

Source: World Bank, Global Development Finance database.

1975) to 167 percent (Indonesia in 1998). In 2001, the external debt/GDP ratio averaged 52 percent, with a range from 23 percent (for Mexico) to 90 percent (for Indonesia).

The implicit interest rate is measured using debt service payments as a percentage of external debt. This averaged 7.6 percent across all 15 countries over the period 1970 to 2000. This average combines average interest rates on private and official sector debt, which were 8.3 percent and 6.7 percent. These measures of implicit interest rates appear surprisingly low, particularly in light of the high interest rate spreads observed in recent years – the EMBI+ bond spread for these 15 countries averaged 7.1 percent from December 1997 to February 2003. The yields on one- and ten-year US Treasury bonds averaged about 4.3 percent and 5.3 percent, over the same period, implying an average yield on emerging market bonds in the range of 11.4 percent and 12.4 percent. The large difference between the implicit interest rate on external debt and emerging market bond yields reflect several factors, including the maturity structure of outstanding debt. Bond yields represent the immediate cost of debt refinancing. It may take several years for the implicit interest rate to adjust completely to a permanent increase in interest rates if the average duration of debt is long. Moreover, countries try to avoid issuing new debt when spreads widen by seeking alternative sources of financing (often from the official sector) and, in extreme cases by restructuring the terms of payment on outstanding debt.

Nominal GDP growth (g) averaged 9.5 percent over the period 1970 to 2000, with a standard deviation of 16 percentage points. This reflects an average rate of real GDP growth of 4.5 percent along with an average (GDP deflator) inflation rate of 5.0 percent.

The descriptive statistics reported in Table 12.1 provide a historical perspective on $(r - g)$, the interest rate–growth rate differential. These statistics indicate that the growth rate of nominal GDP growth (9.5 percent) exceeded the implicit interest rate (7.6 percent) by almost two percentage points on average over the period 1970 to 2000. This average differential across countries and over time implies favorable debt dynamics. In the simulation model developed in this chapter values of $(r - g)$ in the 0 percent to 8 percent range are considered for the purpose of analyzing the risk of an external debt crisis.

3.2 *Trade balance adjustment*

A number of empirical studies examine the question of whether large devaluations tend to be followed by an increase in the trade balance/current account. Cooper (1971) analyzed 24 major devaluations in the developing world over the period 1958 to 1969. He found that the current account balance increased in the year following large devaluations in 21 of the 24 episodes.

Krugman (1999), Calvo *et al.* (2003), Calvo and Reinhart (2002), and Ortiz (2002) document the sometimes sizable reversals in the current account observed during recent financial crises. Calvo *et al.* (2003) point out that the current account/GDP ratio in seven Latin American countries (Argentina, Brazil, Columbia, Mexico, Peru, and Venezuela) improved by almost five percentage points, on average, over a two-year period following the Russian crises in August 1998.[7] Statistics reported by Ortiz (2002) indicate that the current account/GDP ratio in five East Asian countries (Korea, Malaysia, Thailand, Indonesia, and the Philippines) increased by over 15 percentage points, on average, in the year (1998) following the Asian crises in 1997. Table 12.2 reports the change in the current account/GDP ratio following 11 recent financial crises.[8] The current account/GDP ratio increased by about 10 percentage points, on average, across the 11 episodes. What is worth noting, however, is the wide range of outcomes. The current account/GDP ratio rose by roughly two percentage points following the crises in Argentina (1995) and Brazil (1999), versus 20 percentage points in following the crisis in Thailand (1997). One of the objectives of this chapter is to shed some light on the reasons for these differences in external adjustment.

Recent developments in Argentina, Brazil, and Turkey display a similar pattern. Table 12.3 reports changes in the trade balance, current account and external debt, all expressed as percentages of GDP, in the same year as a large devaluation.[9] In the case of Turkey, the nominal effective exchange rate depreciated by 53 percent in 2001. External debt rose from

Table 12.2 Change in current account/GDP following financial crisis (percentage points)

Time Horizon	One year	Two years
Mexico (1995)	6.3	5.1
Argentina (1995)	1.9	0.2
Asian crisis		
The Philippines (1997)	15.3	17.7
Indonesia (1997)	7.4	7.3
Korea (1997)	17.1	10.4
Malaysia (1997)	17.5	20.3
Thailand (1997)	20.7	18.1
Russia (1998)	12.5	18.5
Brazil (1999)	2.2	2.7
Turkey (2001)	3.9	
Brazil (2001)	2.5	
Averages		
All 11 episodes	9.8	11.1
Asian crisis	15.6	14.8

Source: Calculation by authors

Table 12.3 Recent developments in Turkey, Brazil and Argentina

	Devaluation of effective exchange rate		Trade balance/ GDP	Current account/ GDP	External debt/GDP
	Nominal	*Real*	*Year-on-year change (in percentage points)*		
Turkey (2001)	53.1%	7.0%	10.7	7.3	17.2
Brazil (2002)	24.3%	15.6%	2.4	2.9	4.4
Argentina (2002)	69.0%	47.0%	4.6	10.6	80.8

Source: Calculation by authors.

60 percent of GDP in 2000 to 77 percent in 2001. The higher debt service costs in local currency terms were more than offset by the trade balance increase. The current account went from a deficit of 4.9 percent of GDP in 2000 to surplus of 2.4 percent in 2001. In Brazil, the nominal effective exchange rate depreciated by 24 percent in 2001. External debt rose from 41.7 percent of GDP in 2001 to 46.1 percent in 2002. The current account increased from a deficit of 4.6 percent of GDP in 2000 to a 1.7 percent deficit in 2001, an increase of 2.9 percentage points. In these two episodes, large devaluations have coincided with a rise in the current account. In the case of Argentina, the nominal effective exchange rate depreciated by 69 percent in 2002. External debt rose from 52 percent of GDP in 2001 to 133 percent in 2002. The current account increased from a deficit of 1.7 percent of GDP in 2001 to a surplus of 8.9 percent in 2002, a rise of 10.6 percentage points, due, in part, to the moratorium on debt service payments. The trade balance surplus went from 1.3 percent of GDP in 2001 to 5.9 percent in 2002, an increase of 4.6 percent percentage points. Once again, there was a wide variation in the adjustment of the trade balance in these three countries in response to the exchange rate movements. The possible reasons for these differences are explored in the next section.

4 Adjustment to external shocks

Market-based economies, even those in emerging-market countries, which are often fraught with government controls, have the capacity to adjust to negative external shocks, such as a worsening of the terms of trade or a sudden stop in capital inflows. Ultimately such shocks must translate into lower demand for domestic goods, services, labor, and capital and pressure will be put on domestic prices to adjust downwards. In so doing, domestic prices will become relatively lower than foreign prices (i.e., the real exchange rate would depreciate). Demand should shift toward domestic goods and services and net exports should rise to either offset the fall in domestic demand when the terms of trade decline or to fill the funding gap when capital flows are reduced.[10]

In general, there are myriad of factors that can influence the timing and magnitude of the external adjustment process. In this section, five key factors are considered that affect the transmission of the shock and the economy's response to it: the exchange rate regime, the currency denomination of external debt, the magnitude of the import and export trade price elasticities (as in the Marshall–Lerner condition (MLC)), the degree of pass-through of any exchange rate movements into the domestic relative prices of traded goods, and the relative size of the traded goods sector (openness to trade). Each of these factors is examined in more detail below.

4.1 Exchange rate regime

One of the classic arguments in favor of a flexible exchange rate regime put forward by Friedman (1953), among others, is the ability of the flexible exchange rate to translate external shocks into stabilizing real exchange rate movements, thus removing the burden of adjustment from domestic prices and wages, which are typically sticky downwards and thus slow and painful to adjust. By responding in this manner, the flexible rate accelerates adjustment and serves as a built-in shock absorber. Borda (2001) shows that flexible exchange rates do indeed play this role in less developed countries; he finds that countries with flexible rates have more stable output.

An important condition, however, for flexible exchange rates to work effectively in altering relative prices in response to external shocks is that monetary policy must attain a relatively low and stable inflation rate. In the absence of a well-anchored monetary policy, flexible exchange rate depreciations would be likely to translate into higher domestic inflation, leaving the real exchange rate unchanged. Indeed, in countries that have experienced high inflation rates, the indexation of domestic prices and wages is common and flexible exchange rates do not play a useful stabilizing role.

Goldstein (2003: 15) makes an interesting comparison between the pre-crisis Argentina and present-day Brazil in terms of the sustainability of their external debts. He argues that Brazil is more likely to avoid the debt service problems that Argentina encountered because, in part, Brazil has a floating exchange rate, which has encouraged domestic banks and firms to hedge their foreign exchange exposures to avoid currency mismatches, and will adjust to maintain the competitiveness of Brazilian exports. The flexible regime in Brazil contrasts starkly with that in pre-crisis Argentina. The Argentine currency board fixed the peso to the US dollar, and thus, precluded a timely real depreciation when the US dollar appreciated sharply relative to other major currencies and when the flow of capital into Argentina fell. The burden of adjustment to these shocks was placed on domestic wages and prices: as a result, unemployment increased dramatically and the economy collapsed. Furthermore, Goldstein remarks that Brazil's inflation targeting regime provides a good nominal anchor for monetary policy as well as allowing monetary policy the flexibility to respond to shocks.

4.2 Foreign currency denomination of external debt: the revaluation effect

The external debt of most emerging-market countries is denominated in foreign currency, primarily the US dollar.[11] By issuing debt in foreign currency, these countries gain access to foreign capital markets, but at the cost of bearing the risk associated with a possible exchange rate movement. In particular, an exchange rate depreciation/devaluation would raise the cost of servicing the debt in domestic currency. This risk is exacerbated under fixed exchange rate regime, because often the debt is incurred on the expectation that the exchange rate would remain fixed, or the expectation that if the exchange rate were to be devalued, government assistance would be forthcoming. As a result of this implicit guarantee, too much foreign currency borrowing may occur and much of it may be inadequately hedged, leading to situations of currency mismatches, in which liabilities are in foreign currency and assets are in local currency.

When the external debt is denominated in foreign currency, an exchange rate devaluation creates a revaluation effect as the debt/GDP ratio rises and the debt service costs in domestic currency increase. The size of this effect depends on the initial level of external debt and the implicit interest rate. Table 12.4 shows the implications of a 50 percent devaluation for debt service costs under four alternative scenarios. In scenario 1 the implicit interest rate (r) and nominal income growth rate (g) are equal to 6 percent, so that $(r-g)=0$ percent. The low value of the implicit interest rate (6 percent) corresponds to the average nominal interest rate in the United States over the past decade.[12] This serves as a benchmark for the case where default risk is minimal. Scenario 1 depicts a country with an average external debt burden (50 percent of GDP) and low implicit interest rate (6 percent). A 50 percent devaluation raises debt service costs from 3 percent of GDP to 4.5 percent, an increase of only 1.5 percentage points. Under scenario 2 the initial implicit interest rate is 14 percent, instead of 6 percent. In this case a 50 percent devaluation raises debt service costs from 7 percent of GDP to 10.5 percent, an increase of 3.5 percentage points. Scenario 3 illustrates the importance of openness to trade. The initial debt/export ratio is 100 percent in scenarios 1 and 2, which is about average for emerging market countries. In scenario 3 the initial debt/export ratio is 400 percent, which depicts the situation in Argentina in 2001. In this case, a 50 percent devaluation raises the debt service costs from 56 percent of exports to 84 percent. Scenario 4 illustrates the implications of a higher

Table 12.4 The revaluation effect under alternative scenarios

Percentage of GDP				
Scenario:	*1*	*2*	*3*	*4*
External debt	50	50	50	60
Trade balance	0	2	2	2
Debt service	3	7	7	8
Current account	−3	−5	−5	−6
Exports	45	45	13	22.5
Percentage of exports				
External debt	111	111	400	267
Debt service	7	16	56	37
Implications of a 50% exchange rate devaluation *Percentage of GDP*				
External debt	75	75	75	90
Trade balance	0	3	3	3.6
Debt service	4.5	10.5	10.5	12.6
Current account	45	45	12.5	12.5
Exports	100	100	100	100
Percentage of exports				
External debt	167	167	600	720
Debt service	10	23	84	10

Source: Calculation by authors.

initial debt burden – the initial debt level is 60 percent of GDP versus 50 percent in the previous three scenarios. In this case, a 50 percent devaluation raises debt service costs from 67 percent to 101 percent of exports. At this point the foreign currency constraint binds because all export earnings are required to service the external debt.

These simple calculations serve to illustrate the extent to which a country with a high external debt burden (denominated in foreign currency) and high interest rates may be vulnerable to a large devaluation. These calculations, however, overstate the impact of the revaluation effect because they implicitly assume that none of the foreign currency debt is hedged. In practice, exporters are hedged by the fact that their exports are sold in the world market, typically, in foreign currency. Thus, a devaluation may actually leave them better off to the extent that their costs are in local currency. For governments and other entities whose revenue is not in foreign currency or who are not otherwise hedged, the revaluation effect may pose serious problems. In particular, unhedged firms may see their capital eliminated and, thus, may be forced into bankruptcy. This, in turn, may have negative repercussions for the domestic banking sector, which may have extended these firms foreign currency loans. The prototypical examples of sharp exchange rate movements disrupting the corporate and financial sectors through these balance sheet effects were the East Asian financial crises in 1997–1998, chiefly Thailand and South Korea. The implosions of the corporate and banking sectors that these economies experienced greatly hindered the adjustment process as domestic firms could not easily increase their production of traded goods in response to the depreciation of the real exchange rate.

4.3 Trade elasticities – the modified Marshall–Lerner condition

As noted earlier, an adverse external shock will normally lead to a depreciation of the real exchange rate either due to a depreciation (devaluation) of the nominal exchange rate or as domestic prices fall. The next stage in an economy's adjustment to the shock is the response of trade volumes. The traditional method of characterizing this response is the MLC; it states that a real depreciation should cause an increase in the trade balance or net exports if the import and export demand elasticities are sufficiently large.

In this subsection, the classic version of the MLC is derived under the standard, albeit restrictive, assumptions on the model of an open economy and on behavior of international trade. Subsequently, some of these restrictions are relaxed and foreign-currency denominated external debt is introduced and a modified, more general version, of the MLC is derived.

The starting point for the derivation is equation (2); it defines the trade balance (or current account if the country has a zero net foreign asset position) measured in domestic currency terms.

$$TB = P_x X - EP_m M \tag{2}$$

Export and import values are given by the product of their prices (P_x and P_m) and volumes (X and M) where the prices are measured in domestic currency. The price of imports in domestic currency terms (P_m) is determined by the product of the nominal exchange rate expressed as the price of foreign exchange (E) and import prices measured in foreign currency P_{mf}.

Equation (3) states that export volumes are a positive function of foreign income (Y_f) and a negative function of the relative price of domestic exports in foreign currency to foreign exports (domestic imports).

$$X = f_x\{Y_f, (P_x/EP_{mf})\} \tag{3}$$

Similarly, equation (4) states that import volumes are a positive function of domestic demand (Y_d) and a negative function of the relative price of imports in domestic currency terms to exports (P_x).

$$M = f_m\{Y_d, (EP_{mf}/P_x)\} \tag{4}$$

The derivation of the classic version of MLC make the following assumptions:

- Export prices are constant in domestic currency terms. (For simplicity P_x set equal to 1.)
- Import prices are constant in foreign currency terms. (For simplicity P_{mf} is also set equal to 1.)
- There are only two goods: the domestic and foreign exports.
- Trade is initially balanced – $X = EM$.
- There is no debt.
- Domestic and foreign output/income are constant.[13]
- Import and export supply price elasticities are infinite.

Under these assumptions, equation (2) becomes:

$$TB = X - EM \tag{5}$$

Differentiating equation (5) with respect to the exchange rate and setting the change equal to zero obtains:

$$dTB/dE = dX/dE - M + EdM/dE = 0 \tag{6}$$

and multiplying through by (E/X) gives,

$$(E/X)[dX/dE - M + EdM/dE] = 0 \tag{7}$$

Making use of the definition of price elasticities for imports and exports (θ_m and θ_x) and that $M = X/E$ obtains the classic version of the MLC; that is, for the trade balance to improve as a result of an exchange rate depreciation/devaluation, the sum of the export and import elasticities has to be greater than 1.

$$\theta_m + \theta_x > 1 \tag{8}$$

When the assumption that trade is balanced is relaxed, the algebra is less elegant,

$$dTB/dE = \theta_x E^* X - (E_2 - E_1)M - E_2\theta_m E^* M, \tag{9}$$

where E^* is the percentage change in the exchange rate. Equation (9) says that in the case of a depreciation, the expansion of exports will be a function the price elasticity and the amount of the depreciation. The change in the value of imports is more complex. The term, $(E_2 - E_1)M$, denotes the increase in the cost of imports from the devaluation. The term, $E_2\theta_m E^* M$, represents the change in import volumes, the substitution effect. In this formulation, it can be seen that the current account will improve if expenditure switching, the substitution effects on export and import volumes, are more than enough to offset the cost effect. In general, price elasticities tend to be small in the short term so that there is a possibility that the trade balance could temporarily decline (the "J" curve effect). In the absence of additional capital inflows, there would be excess demand for foreign exchange and a further depreciation would likely result until the trade balance improved.

4.3 Adding external debt

If external debt denominated in foreign currency is added to the model and debt service in domestic currency terms is given by the product of the exchange rate, the interest rate (r) and the stock of debt (D). Equation (2) can be rewritten in terms of the current account:

$$CA = P_x X - EP_{mf} M - ErD \qquad (10)$$

Initially, assume once again that trade is balanced and that $P_x = P_{mf} = 1$. Differentiating equation (10) with respect to the exchange rate and setting it equal to zero gives,

$$dCA/dE = dX/dE - M + EdM/dE - rD \qquad (11)$$

Dividing through by (E/X) and rearranging gives a modified MLC,

$$\theta_m + \theta_x > 1 + ErD/X \qquad (12)$$

Equation (12) states that for the current account to improve following a devaluation, the sum of the price elasticities has to exceed 1 by an amount equal to the ratio of interest in local currency terms to exports.[14] Thus, for countries that are relatively closed (i.e. have low levels of imports), but that have contracted a relatively large amount of foreign currency debt, it becomes more difficult for a depreciation to lead to an improvement in the current account.

If trade is not balanced initially, equation (11) becomes,

$$dCA/dE = \theta_x E^* X - (E_2 - E_1)M - E_2 \theta_m E^* M - (E_2 - E_1)rD \qquad (13)$$

The simulation results displayed in Table 12.5 uses equation (13) to compare the sum of import and export price elasticities needed to improve the current account in the face of a devaluation for the classic MLC and for the MLC with debt, using data for Argentina in 2000 and assuming a 10 percent devaluation. If Argentina had no debt and a small trade balance surplus, then the sum of the export and import price elasticities would have to be greater than 0.994, or essentially what the classic MLC would predict (column 1) for the devaluation to increase the current account. Given that Argentina was US$146 billion in debt, which carried an average interest rate of 8 percent, the sum of the import and export elasticities would have to rise to 1.336 (column 2).[15]

4.4 Export pricing and exchange rate pass-through

The classic MLC assumes producer currency pricing which means that domestic (foreign) exporters set prices in domestic (foreign) currency and that this price would remain unchanged following a devaluation. Thus, for domestic exports, a devaluation would cause the price in foreign currency to decline and foreign demand for exports to increase.

For a small open economy, however, it is frequently assumed that it is a price taker for traded goods in world markets. Thus, export (and import) prices are set at the world level in foreign currency; for example, a country might sell oil at US$25 per barrel. Under this assumption, a devaluation would not influence the quantity of exports demanded abroad but would have a large impact on export values as the full effect of the devaluation is passed into domestic export prices.[16] Thus assuming,

$$P_x = EP_{xf} \text{ and } P_{xf} = 1 \text{ implies } P_x = E \tag{14}$$

where P_{xf} is the price of exports measured in foreign currency. Given that export prices increase by the same amount as the exchange rate, a much smaller import volume response is needed to bring the current account into balance. Column 3 of Table 12.5 shows that the required import price

Table 12.5 Modified Marshall–Learner conditions based on parameters for Argentina in 2000 and 10 percent devaluation

	1	*2*	*3*
	Classic MLC	*MLC with debt*	*MLC with debt and $P_x = E$*
M	30,968	30,968	30,968
X	33,929	33,929	33,929
E_1	1.00	1.00	1.00
E_2	1.10	1.10	1.10
$E*$	0.10	0.10	0.10
1	0	0	0
R		0.08	0.08
D		146,172	146,172
$E_1 rD/X$		0.38	0.38
$\theta_m + \theta_x$	**0.994**	**1.336**	
θ_m	**0.4970**	**0.668**	**0.393**

Notes
M, X, and D are measured in millions of pesos. $\theta_m + \theta_x$ are estimated jointly; θ_m in the last row is estimated as half of the total.

elasticity would fall to 0.393 from 0.668 under the alternative (small open economy) pricing assumption.[17]

Note that for emerging-market economies the setting of import prices is less controversial because it is generally true that these prices are set in foreign currency as the MLC assumes. What is more interesting, however, is the impact of an exchange rate devaluation/depreciation on consumer prices, in general. Although this issue is discussed in more detail later in the chapter, it is important to note that if monetary policy allows an exchange rate devaluation to increase wages and consumer prices across the board then the nominal exchange rate movement will have a smaller impact on the real exchange rate and thus will induce less external adjustment.

4.5 Openness to trade

The derivation of the classic MLC is based on a model with two traded goods, domestic exports and foreign exports (domestic imports), and the two countries in the model are completely specialized in the production of their own good. In reality, the bulk of domestic output is consumed at home, either as nontradable goods and services (i.e., goods and services that are prohibitively costly or impossible to trade) or as goods and services that are potentially tradable but because of relative prices (i.e., the real exchange rate and price distortions such as tariffs) are not. An economy's capacity to adjust to adverse external shock and increase net exports will critically depend on the amount of productive resources that can be re-allocated to the production of traded goods (i.e., exports and import-competing goods) in response to the resulting real depreciation. If many of these resources are tied up meeting domestic demand for non-tradable goods and services (and much of this demand may be driven by government purchases and therefore is price inelastic) then external adjustment in response to the adverse shock would be weaker than otherwise.

Equation (12) shows that for economies with foreign-currency external debt to service, the value of exports is crucial in determining the economy's ability to generate foreign exchange and meet the interest payments when a real depreciation in response to the shock occurs. Corsetti *et al.* (1998: 19) find in their recent study that "a large export sector (generating foreign currency receipts) strengthens the country's ability to service its debt obligation". Indeed, Argentina and Brazil provide a useful comparison; Argentina is a relatively closed economy and Brazil is more open. The responses of their trade balances to recent real depreciations are given in Table 12.3. The real depreciation experienced by Brazil was approximately one-third of that of Argentina, yet its trade balance improved by half as much. Although this is not an exact comparison because other factors are involved in determining the trade balance (chiefly, import compression), it is consistent with prevailing opinions on the extent of external adjustment in the two countries. Argentina's lack of openness has hindered the external adjustment process. This issue is explored further in the next section in which simulation experiments are used to compare the impact of openness on external adjustment.

5 Dynamic simulation: external adjustment

In this section, a dynamic partial equilibrium model is constructed to simulate the adjustment of the trade balance/current account following an adverse shock in the form of a sudden stop in capital flows that causes an exchange rate deprecation/devaluation. The model is designed to capture the dynamic response of imports and exports along with stock-flow identities that link the trade balance to debt service costs, the current account and external debt. The preference for a partial equilibrium framework reflects two main factors. First, the model's equations are specified to facilitate calibration. This enables the model to address the main issues with reference to the existing empirical evidence. Second, the analysis abstracts from intertemporal savings-investment decisions that also affects the trade balance. A sudden stop in capital flows acts as a credit constraint preventing borrowing from abroad and this essentially shuts off the intertemporal aspect of the current account.

5.1 Model specification

A number of simplifying assumptions are made to keep the model tractable and readily understandable. In particular, all external debt is assumed to be denominated in foreign-currency.[18] Moreover, there are no international reserves nor are there any other capital inflows such as portfolio or direct investment or lending from the official sector in the model. Thus, the simulation results can also be interpreted to indicate whether, and how much, alternative sources of financing would be required to replace a sharp decline in private capital flows.

Thus to focus the simulation analysis on the effect of an external shock on the foreign currency requirements necessary to maintain debt service, we redefine the expression for the current account given in (10) in terms of foreign currency:

$$CA/E = TB/E - rD = (P_x/E)X - P_{mf}M - rD \tag{15}$$

A devaluation affects the trade balance through three main channels in the model: trade volumes, traded goods, prices, and consumer prices.

5.1.1 Trade volumes

The dynamic adjustments of import and export volumes (m and x) are specified in logarithmic form using an error correction specification:[19]

$$\Delta m_t = \alpha_{11}\Delta y_{dt} + \alpha_{12}\Delta rpm_t - \lambda(m_{t-1} - \beta_m y_{t-1} - \eta_m rp_{mt-1}) \tag{16a}$$

$$\Delta x_t = \alpha_{21}\Delta y_{ft} + \alpha_{22}\Delta rpx_t - \lambda(x_{t-1} - \beta_x y_{ft-1} - \eta_x rp_{xt-1}) \tag{16b}$$

where y_d and y_f are domestic and foreign income. The variables rp_m and rp_x represent the relative price of imports and exports defined by:

$$rp_m = p_m - p_d \tag{17a}$$

$$rp_x = p_x - e - p_f \tag{17b}$$

where p_m is the price of imports, p_d is the price of the domestic consumption basket, p_x is the price of exports (in domestic currency), e is the nominal exchange rate and p_f is the price of the foreign consumption basket (in foreign currency).[20] The error correction dynamics underlying equations (17a) and (17b), which are calibrated to match the empirical evidence which indicates that trade volumes respond gradually to changes in relative prices (as per the MLC) and income.

5.1.2 Prices of imports and exports

Import and export prices are also modeled using an error correction specification to capture slow adjustment:

$$\Delta p_{mt} = \Delta p_{mt-1} - \rho(\Delta p_{mt-1} - \phi_m \Delta e_t - \Delta p_{dt}^*) \tag{18a}$$

$$\Delta p_{xt} = \Delta p_{xt-1} - \rho(\Delta p_{xt-1} - \phi_x \Delta e_t - \Delta p_{ft}^*) \tag{18b}$$

where Δp_d^* and Δp_f^* represent the domestic and foreign steady-state inflation rate, respectively, which are assumed to be exogenous, and ρ represents the dynamic error correction coefficient. The parameters ϕ_m and ϕ_x determine the long-term effect of exchange rate changes on import and export prices. Setting $\phi_m = \phi_x = 1$ implies that exports and imports are priced in foreign currency (the small open economy assumption). It implies that all exchange rate movements are ultimately passed-through into the domestic prices of traded goods, or in other words, exchange rate movements have no effect on the terms of trade. Setting $\phi_m = 1$ and $\phi_x = 0$ implies producer currency pricing (as under the derivation of the classic MLC). In this case, exchange rate changes affect import prices (there is full exchange rate pass-though), but not export prices (both measured in terms of the domestic currency). A devaluation, therefore, worsens the terms of trade.

The error correction dynamics underlying equations (18a) and (18b) are calibrated so that the prices of traded goods respond gradually to exchange rate changes. The adjustment can be thought of in terms of staggered contracts for imports and exports in which prices are fixed for the duration of each contract. Unanticipated changes in the exchange rate therefore have no effect on prices specified in outstanding contracts, but are fully incorporated into when subsequent contracts are negotiated. The staggered nature of the contracts implies that a proportion of contracts terminate in each period. For example, in the case of one-year contracts, 25 percent come due in each quarter. The dynamic adjustment of import and export prices is therefore determined by the average contract length. This pricing structure can be thought of as a generalization of sticky-price new open economy macroeconomic models where prices are reset each period. In our model, exchange rate changes affect import and export prices more gradually.

5.1.3 Consumer prices

The inflation rate based on domestic consumption basket p_{dt} is given by:

$$\Delta p_{dt} = (1 - \delta)\Delta p_{nt} + \delta\Delta p_{mt} \tag{19}$$

where δ and $1 - \delta$ represent the shares of imported goods and nontraded goods in the consumer price index. Thus, the direct effect of an exchange rate depreciation on the inflation rate depends on two factors: the impact on the price of imports (the degree of exchange rate pass-through) and the share of imported goods in the consumption basket.

The price dynamics for nontraded goods is determined by:

$$\Delta p_{nt} = \Delta p_{nt-1} - \omega_1(\Delta p_{nt-1} - \Delta p_d^*) + \omega_2(\Delta p_{mt} - \Delta p_d^*) \tag{20}$$

where Δp_d^* represents the domestic inflation target. In equation (20), an exchange rate movement affects nontraded goods prices to the extent that it causes the rate of increase of import prices to differ from the inflation target. Equations (19) and (20) represent a simple mechanism for modeling the inflation process as the interaction between expectations, intrinsic dynamics and monetary policy. The monetary authority implicitly sets monetary conditions such that consumer price inflation reverts to the target Δp_d^* over time. As a consequence, changes in import prices due to an exchange rate movement have only a transitory effect on nontraded goods prices and domestic inflation. The magnitude and duration of the transitory effect is jointly determined by the share of imported goods in the consumer price index (δ) and the error correction dynamics underlying equation (19).

5.2 Calibration

The parameters in the model are calibrated with reference to a wide variety of empirical work. The calibration approach avoids complications associated with estimating equations for emerging market economies where the quantity of data is often limited, and the quality of data is poor in many cases. The simulation experiments presented in the chapter are not intended to explain developments over history or to forecast future developments. The goal is to isolate a few key factors that determine the dynamic response of the current account to an adverse shock that causes an exchange rate depreciation.

5.2.1 Trade volume equations

For the trade volume equations (16a) and (16b), the calibration is based on recent econometric estimates in Hooper *et al.* (1998) and Marquez (2000), which provide extensive surveys of the existing empirical work on long-term trade elasticities in industrial countries. They report a wide range of estimates of long-term price elasticities, η_m and η_x. Hooper *et al.* report an average estimate of -0.66 for the G7 countries, with a range from -0.3 to -2.1 and a standard deviation of 0.5. Marquez reports estimates in the range of -0.3 to -4.8 for the US and -0.2 to -2.8 for Canada. Gylfason and Risager (1984) report estimates for 15 countries, with an average of -1.2, a standard deviation of 0.7 and a range from -0.4 to -2.5. In sum, the existing empirical evidence indicates that there is a high degree of uncertainty surrounding estimates of the long-term price elasticities. The model is calibrated using values of η_m and η_x set to 1.0 (in absolute value), which roughly corresponds to the center of the range of estimates.

A similar approach is taken to calibrate the long-term income elasticities, β_m and β_x. As before, the surveys by Hooper *et al.* (1998) and Marquez (2000) report a wide range of estimates. Marquez reports estimates in the range of 0.7 to 4.1 for the US, and 0.4 to 2.0 for Canada. His own estimates lie in the middle of this range: 1.5 for Canada and 1.3 for the US. Hooper *et al.* report an average estimate of 1.4 for the G7 countries, with range from 0.8 to 2.2 and a standard deviation of 0.4. The model is calibrated using values of β_m and β_x set to 1.4.

The other parameters $\{\alpha_{11}, \alpha_{12}, \alpha_{21}, \alpha_{22}, \lambda\}$ in the trade volume equations (16a) and (16b) are calibrated with reference to estimates of error correction models obtained by Hooper *et al.* for the G7 countries. Their estimates imply that about 50 percent of the adjustment in trade volumes is completed by the end of the first year, and about 70 percent by the end of the third year, following a change in relative prices. Trade volumes are found to respond much more rapidly to changes in income, with 96 percent of the adjustment completed in just one year. The model is calibrated to match these dynamic responses.

5.2.2 Import and export price equations

For the import and export price equations (18a) and (18b), the calibration is relatively straightforward. Imports are priced in foreign currency in all simulations; the domestic country is assumed to be a price taker in world markets for its imports. The parameter ϕ_m in equation (18a) is set to a value of 1, so that a 50 percent devaluation increases import prices by 50 percent in the long term. In the base case calibration of the model, exports are also priced in foreign currency, which implies setting the parameter ϕ_x in equation (18b) to a value of 1. In an alternative calibration of the model, only half of exported goods are priced in foreign currency; that is, ϕ_x is set to 0.5, so that a 50 percent devaluation increases export prices by only 25 percent in the long run.

Recent empirical studies by Goldberg and Knetter (1997), Campa and Goldberg (2002) and Burstein *et al.* (2002) generally find that the dynamic adjustment of trade prices to exchange rate changes is complete within a year or two. This empirical observation is incorporated into the analysis by calibrating the error-correction parameter ρ in equations (18a) and (18b) such that 95 percent of the adjustment is complete within a year. This implies that at each point in time 95 percent of contracts for imports and exports expire within a year. It is important to note that trade volumes adjust more gradually than trade prices – only 50 percent of the adjustment in trade volumes is completed within a year. This difference implies a "J-curve" dynamic response of the trade balance, which is consistent with the evidence in the aforementioned studies. An alternative specification is also tried in which the adjustment rates for trade volumes and prices are similar.

5.2.3 Consumer prices

Numerous empirical studies have examined the extent of pass-through of exchange rate devaluations/depreciations into the domestic consumer price level in emerging market economies and estimates are generally found to vary widely across countries and over time. For instance, Calvo and Reinhart (2000: Table 6) report estimates obtained from vector autoregressions (VARs) for 11 emerging market countries. They find an average estimate of 22.8 percent after two years, with a standard deviation of 27.6 percent. In an extensive panel study, Goldfajn and Werlang (2000) also report a wide range of estimates across regions, varying from 19 percent for Oceania countries to 124 percent for Latin American countries. Rabanal and Schwartz (2001) estimate a VAR using monthly data for Brazil over the period from January 1995 to September 2000 and report estimates in the range of 18 percent to 38 percent in the year following a depreciation, when 80 percent to 90 percent of the price adjustment is completed. Kfoury (2001) finds that estimates of rate of pass-through of exchange rate movements into domestic consumer prices in Brazil have decreased over time from 44 percent during 1980Q2–1994Q4 to 13 percent during 1995Q1–2001Q1. Burstein *et al.* (2002) examine the change in consumer price inflation following seven large exchange rate devaluations in emerging market countries. They obtain an average estimate of 30 percent in the first year (with a standard deviation of 11 percentage points) and 47 percent in the second year (with a standard deviation of 20 percentage points).

A few points are worth highlighting from the above discussion of estimates of exchange rate pass-through into domestic prices. First, the existing empirical studies imply a wide range of estimates. The estimates not only vary significantly across studies, but also across countries and over sample periods within studies. One explanation for this is that degree of pass-through is believed to depend on business cycle conditions. This point is of particular relevance for analysis here because large devaluations often coincide with financial crises and the resultant severe recessions, would imply a lower than average degree of pass-through. It is important to recognize, however, that this may largely be an issue about the timing of pass-through. Firms may initially attempt to preserve market share by foregoing price increases. One would not expect the implied reduction profit margins to be sustained permanently, however. In this case, weak business cycle conditions would act to delay the pass-through, but not reduce the long-term effects. Second, the point estimates reported in the various empirical studies are quite imprecise (in the sense that the standard errors are relatively large). The simulation experiments examine the implications of varying degrees of exchange rate pass-through. In the base case calibration, a 50 percent exchange rate devaluation increases consumer prices by 8 percent in the first year, implying 16 percent pass-through which is at the low range of the estimates outlined above. In an alternative calibration, a 50 percent devaluation increases consumer prices by 20 percent in the first year, implying 40 percent pass-through, which is at the high end of the range.

5.3 Dynamic simulation experiments

The simulation exercise examines the dynamic response of the current account to a 50 percent devaluation. The simulation results are illustrated with reference to "planned profiles" for the current account/GDP and external debt/GDP ratios shown in Figures 12.1 to 12.5. These profiles serve as a benchmark for gauging the size of the dynamic responses; they

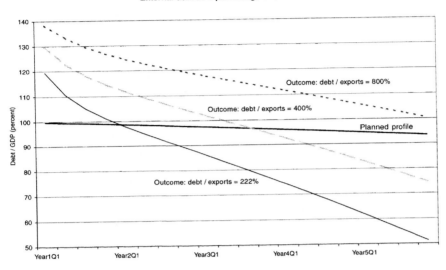

External debt as a percentage of GDP

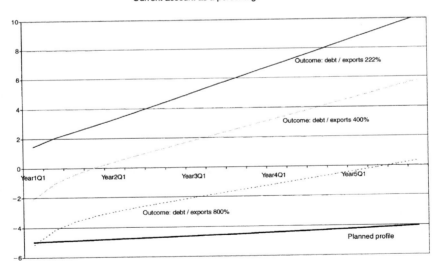

Current account as a percentage of GDP

Figure 12.1 Alternative debt/export ratios (dynamic responses to 50% exchange rate devaluation).

External debt as a percentage of GDP

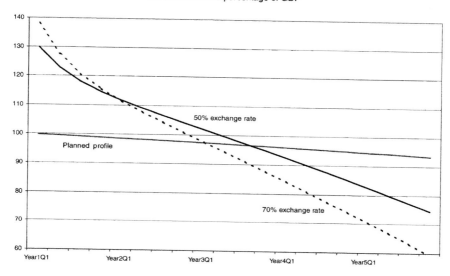

Current account as a percentage of GDP

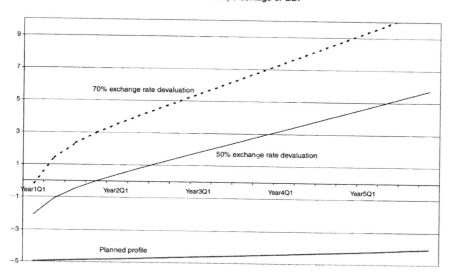

Figure 12.2 Exchange rate devaluation (dynamic responses to 50% versus 70%).

External debt as a percentage of GDP

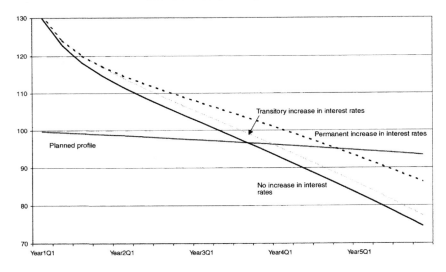

Current account as a percentage of GDP

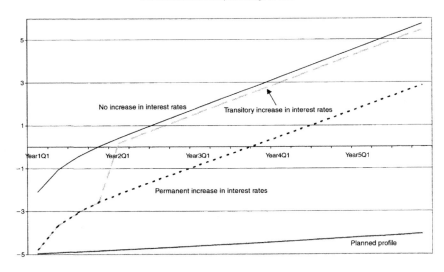

Figure 12.3 Implications of higher interest rates (dynamic responses to 50% exchange rate devaluation).

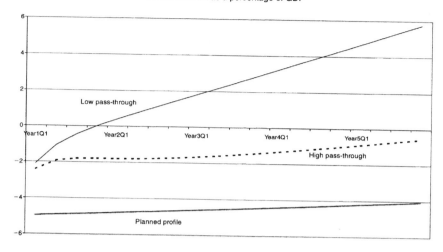

Response to 50% nominal devaluation
Current account as a percentage of GDP

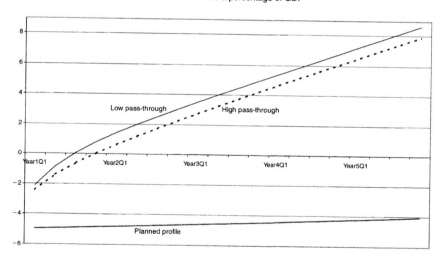

Response to 50% real devaluation
Current account as a percentage of GDP

Figure 12.4 Implications of pass-through from import prices to consumer prices.

External debt as a percentage of GDP

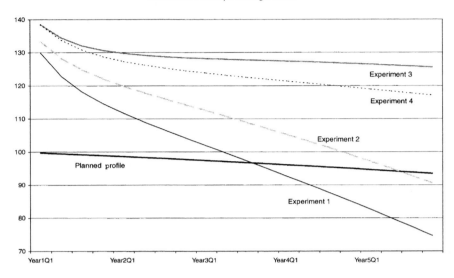

Current account as a percentage of GDP

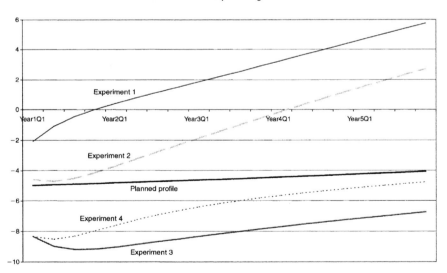

Figure 12.5 Implications of export pricing (dynamic responses to 50% exchange rate devaluation).

incorporate a real GDP growth rate of 3 percent, an inflation rate of 3 percent and a nominal interest rate of 10 percent. The nominal interest rate can be thought of as having three components: an expected inflation component of 3 percent, a real interest rate component of 3 percent, and a default risk premium of 4 percent. The real interest rate and real growth rate are assumed to be equal initially, and $(r-g)$ is determined by the default risk premium, which is set to 4 percent is the base case calibration. Prior to the devaluation, the external debt level is set equal to 100 percent of GDP and there is a current account deficit of 5 percent of GDP. The debt/GDP ratio declines by 6 percentage points over the five-year planning horizon, which is consistent with the general objective of keeping the external debt burden on a downward profile over time. The current account improves gradually over time with the decline in the debt service costs associated with the lower debt burden.

The analysis focuses on a few key structural factors that influence the dynamic response of the trade balance to a large devaluation. Monetary and fiscal policies do not play an explicit role in the analysis. The simulation experiments illustrate the response of the current account and the external debt burden in the absence of any policy changes. The simulations assume a fixed exchange rate regime in which the nominal exchange rate is devalued by 50 percent in response to a sudden stop in capital inflows. The devaluation persists over the entire five-year planning horizon. In one simulation, a flexible rate is assumed and the impact of a permanent depreciation in the equilibrium real exchange rate is examined to address the implications of exchange rate pass-through to consumer prices.

The simulation results of a 50 percent devaluation for the debt/GDP ratio and the current account with different debt/exports ratios are presented in Figure 12.1. The impact revaluation effects of the 50 percent devaluation are to raise the value of external debt from 100 percent to 150 percent of GDP and to increase the current account deficit (in absolute value) from 6 percent of GDP to 9 percent, as debt service costs increase. The model, however, predicts that a large devaluation would lead to a substantial increase in the trade balance, offsetting the revaluation effect on the external debt burden. The impact of these two counterbalancing effects is illustrated by comparing the solid lines corresponding to the planning profile and to the debt/exports ratio of 222 percent in Figure 12.1. The lower panel shows that the current account increases from a deficit of 4.9 percent of GDP in the benchmark planning profile case to a surplus of 2.2 percent in the first year, an increase of 7.1 percentage points. The upper panel shows that the debt/GDP ratio declines to the initial value of 100 percent level by the end of the first year.

5.3.1 Openness to trade

The importance of openness to trade to external adjustment can be easily seen in Figure 12.1 by comparing the simulation results across different debt-to-export ratios. These simulations are conducted using different values of exports as a percentage of GDP, while maintaining the initial debt/GDP ratio at 100 percent. As the share of exports increases the debt/exports ratio falls. The simulation results show that a higher share of exports or a lower debt/export ratio results in a larger improvement in the trade balance and current account, and hence, a more rapid decline in the debt/GDP ratio. For example, in the case of an initial debt/exports ratio of 222 percent, a 50 percent devaluation improves the current account/GDP ratio by 7.1 percentage points in the first year and the debt/GDP ratio reverts its initial 100 percent level by the end of the first year. With an initial debt/exports ratio of 400 percent, the current account/GDP ratio improves by 4.0 percentage points in the first year and the debt/GDP ratio reverts to the 100 percent level in 2.5 years. In the extreme case of an initial debt/exports ratio of 800 percent, the current account/GDP ratio improves by very little (less than one percentage point) in the first year and it takes over five years for the debt/GDP ratio to revert to the initial 100 percent level. The results of these simulations illustrate the fact that economies that are more open to trade have the capacity for more vigorous external adjustment.

It should be noted that the simulations conducted with initial debt/export ratios of 400 percent and 800 percent are extraordinary from a historical perspective. The debt/export ratio exceeded 400 percent in only two of the 15 emerging market economies (Argentina and Brazil) over the period 1970 to 2000. The highest value in the sample is 695 percent in Argentina in 1987. In 2001 only three countries had debt/export ratios over 200 percent: Argentina (383 percent), Brazil (296 percent) and Turkey (216 percent). Unless otherwise stated, the remainder of the simulations to be considered in the chapter are based on a debt/export ratio of 400 percent, which roughly corresponds to the ratio for Argentina in 2001.

5.3.2 Size of the devaluation

The next question to be investigated with the simulation model is suppose that capital inflows came to a complete stop so that no external financing were available, how large a devaluation would be necessary to cause the trade balance to adjust to fill the financing gap, continue debt service, and return the current account to zero balance? (Or in the event of a small financing gap, how many reserves or how much official lending would be needed to cover it?) In the case where the initial debt/export ratio is 222 percent, a 50 percent devaluation returns the current account to a surplus position within the first year. Hence, a 50 percent devaluation is more than what is needed. When the initial debt/export ratio is 400 percent, however, there would be a small financing gap of less than 1 percent of GDP cumulated over the first year. In the extreme case where the initial debt/export ratio is 800 percent, the financing gap would be substantial; over 9 percent of GDP cumulated over a four-year period. To illustrate the impact of a larger devaluation, Figure 12.2 compares the dynamic response of the current account and external debt to a 50 percent devaluation versus a 70 percent devaluation with a debt/exports ratio of 400 percent. The larger devaluation improves the current account by more, thus eliminating the financing gap. The model is linear in this dimension and hence, can be solved for the size of the devaluation required to make the adjustment of the current account consistent with the level of international reserves and (private and official sector) capital flows.

5.3.3 Aside: interest rate response

The simulation results discussed above assume that the exchange rate devaluation has no effect on interest rates. In practice, interest rates rise when an adverse shock such as a sudden stop of capital arises, most often during a financial crisis. Ideally, one would like to examine an endogenous interest rate response, reflecting several elements of the adjustment process including the possible inflationary consequences of the devaluation (the response of monetary policy) and the possible impact on the default risk premium. Modeling the endogenous response of interest rates to a large devaluation is a difficult task, however, and beyond the scope of the chapter. Instead, the implications of a large devaluation accompanied by a two percentage point increase in the implicit interest rate are examined. In one case, the interest rate increases for only one year; in the other case it persists for five years. Figure 12.3 shows the dynamic response of external debt and the current account in each case. The solid lines, labelled "no increase in interest rates", are generated using an initial debt/export ratio of 800 percent to serve as a benchmark. The upper panel shows that the *transitory* (one year) versus *permanent* (five year) distinction is quite important for debt dynamics over the five-year planning horizon. The *transitory* increase in interest rates raises the debt/GDP ratio by 2.7 percentage points after five years versus 10.8 percentage points for the *permanent* increase. The lower panel shows that a 2 percentage point increase in the implicit interest rate worsens the current account considerably. The current account deficit worsens from 0.9 percent to 3.5 percent of GDP in the first year. These simulations demonstrate that higher interest rates can curtail the adjustment of the current account, leaving countries vulnerable to a sudden stop in capital flows. In the case where the higher interest rates persist, the financing gap would amount to 5.5 percent of GDP over a three-year period.

5.4 Sensitivity analysis

The empirical evidence discussed earlier indicates that there is a high amount of uncertainty surrounding many of the parameters in the model. In this section, the sensitivity of the simulation results with respect to a few key parameters of interest is explored.

5.4.1 Pass-through from import prices to consumer prices

In the benchmark calibration of the model, a 50 percent devaluation increases consumer price inflation by 8 percentage points in the first year. This corresponds to the low end of the range of pass-through estimates discussed earlier. An alternative calibration is employed in which a 50 percent devaluation increases consumer price inflation by 20 percentage points in the first year. This corresponds to the high end of the range.

The upper panel in Figure 12.4 compares the dynamic response of the current account/GDP ratio to a 50 percent devaluation in the benchmark calibration ("low pass-through") and the alternative calibration ("high pass-through"). The simulations demonstrate that a higher degree of exchange rate pass-through into inflation decreases the current account. This is because higher pass-through leads to a smaller increase in the relative price of imports and hence, import volumes contract by less. Or to put it another way, a higher degree of pass-through widens the differential between the real and nominal exchange rate. The real exchange rate depreciates by 38 percent in the base case simulation, but only 8 percent in the alternative "high pass-through" simulation.

In these simulations, the devaluation takes place under a fixed exchange rate regime, which implies that because the nominal exchange rate is held fixed following the initial devaluation, subsequent changes in the real exchange rate arise solely from changes in consumer prices. Suppose instead that the depreciation of the real exchange rate occurs because of a nominal depreciation under a flexible exchange rate regime. Assume that the nominal exchange rate depreciates by 50 percent initially and then adjusts to changes in consumer prices in order to keep the real exchange rate constant at a 50 percent depreciation. This is an extreme assumption because it is unlikely that the nominal rate would always adjust to keep the real exchange rate constant, especially in the short term. Nonetheless, this scenario provides a useful benchmark. The lower panel in Figure 12.4 shows the response of the current account in this case and it indicates that the degree of pass-through has a relatively small effect on the adjustment of the current account. The rationale is that a higher degree of pass-through results in a smaller real exchange rate depreciation on impact, but no change thereafter because the nominal rate adjusts to offset the effect of pass-through on consumer prices. Ultimately, the behaviour of the real exchange rate is independent of the nominal exchange rate regime; therefore, these two sets of simulation exercises illustrate that the extent of exchange rate pass-through into inflation on the adjustment of the current account may depend on the exchange rate regime in the short term.

5.4.2 Pricing of exports

The benchmark calibration of the model assumes exports are priced in foreign currency. As a consequence, a devaluation raises the value of external debt and exports by the same proportion, having no effect on the debt/export ratio. Pricing exports in foreign currency provides a hedge against the revaluation of external debt resulting from a large devaluation because it implies that the nominal depreciation is completely passed through into the domestic currency price of exports. Thus, the value of exports in domestic currency increases one for one with the devaluation.

This assumption is relaxed by considering the case where only half of export goods are priced in foreign currency. This entails reducing the parameter ϕ_x in equation (18b) from a value of 1.0 to 0.5. For presentation purposes, the simulation conducted with exports priced in foreign currency ($\phi_x = 1$) is labeled Experiment 1. Experiment 2 refers to the simulation in which only half of exports are priced in foreign currency ($\phi_x = 0.5$). The lower panel in Figure 12.5 shows that pricing only half of exports in foreign currency substantially reduces the impact of the devaluation on the value of exports and the current account. The current account declines to 5.4 percent of GDP in the first year as opposed to 0.9 percent in the benchmark case Experiment 1.

5.4.3 Long-term trade price elasticities

Under the small economy assumption, domestic exports and imports are priced in foreign currency ($\phi_x = \phi_m = 1$). Therefore, a devaluation has no effect on the relative price of domestic exports and no impact on export demand, but it does raise export prices and export values one for one in domestic currency terms. For imports, however, a devaluation raises the relative price of imports, which leads to a decline in import volumes. As shown earlier in section 4, the net effect of the devaluation on the trade balance under the small open economy scenario is determined by the long-term import price elasticity η_M. In contrast, when some export goods are priced in domestic currency ($\phi_x < 1$), the relative price of exports declines, leading to higher export volumes. In this case, the net effect on the trade balance is jointly determined by the long-term elasticities trade price η_M and η_X in equations (16a) and (16b), as in the MLC. In the base case calibration (Experiment 1) η_M and η_X are set to a value of one and $\phi_m = \phi_x = 1$. Simulation Experiment 3 extends Experiment 2 (where $\phi_x = 0.5$) and examines the implications of reducing η_M and η_X to 0.5. The simulation results are illustrated in Figure 12.5. The lower panel shows that the trade balance and current account improves more gradually (compare Experiments 2 and 3). The current account GDP ratio decreases by 4.4 percentage points from 5.4 percent of GDP to 9.8 percent in the first year. This also has major implications for the external debt burden, shown in the upper panel of Figure 12.5. When η_M and η_X are set to a value of 1.0 (Experiment 2), the debt/GDP ratio reverts back to its initial level (100 percent) in the fifth year. When η_M and η_X are set to 0.5 (Experiment 3), the debt/GDP ratio declines very gradually, reaching only 126 percent in the fifth year. Thus, the magnitude of long-term trade elasticities have a large impact on trade balance and current account adjustment as would be expected from our earlier analysis of the modified MLC.

5.4.4 Trade dynamics

The dynamics of the trade equations represented by the error-correction coefficients, λ and ρ, also have an important influence on the response of the current account. Recall that in the benchmark calibration, the trade price equations (18a) and (18b) adjust more rapidly than the trade volume equations (16a) and (16b). In the year following a devaluation, 96 percent of the adjustment in trade prices is completed whereas only 50 percent of the adjustment in trade volumes is completed. This difference results in a "J-curve" dynamic adjustment pattern for the trade balance as seen in simulation Experiments 2 and 3. The significance of this specification is examined by considering an alternative calibration of the model where trade volumes adjust more rapidly to attenuate the "J-curve" response of the trade balance. In the alternative calibration, 70 percent (instead of 50 percent) of the adjustment in trade volumes is complete by the end of the first year. The simulation results are labeled Experiment 4, illustrated in Figure 12.5. (Note that the other settings for Experiment 4 are the same as for Experiment 3, i.e., $\eta_M = \eta_X = 0.5$ and $\phi_x = 0.5$.) The lower panel shows that diminishing the "J-curve" response of the trade balance improves the current account considerably, relative to that for Experiment 3. The debt burden also declines by more as shown in the upper panel.

5.5 Comparison with recent case studies

To assess the results of the simulation exercise further, it is useful to compare them to a recent set of case studies. Burstein *et al.* (2002) analyze seven episodes of large devaluations in emerging market countries.[20] The nominal effective exchange rate depreciated by 57 percent, on average. The descriptive statistics reported in the first line of Table 12.6 show the average response of trade values, volumes and prices in the first year following the devaluations. The value of exports increased by 67 percent, while the value of imports increased by only 33 percent, on average (in domestic currency terms). The large increase in export values largely

Table 12.6 Response of trade prices and volumes following large devaluations

	Devaluation (%)	Export growth (%)			Import growth (%)		
		Value	Volume	Price	Value	Volume	Price
Burstein et al. (2002)	57.0	66.6	10.1	54.8	32.3	−16.2	47.7
Turkey (2001)	114.6	113.0	6.4	106.6	52.2	−26.0	78.1
Brazil (2002)	24.3	27.5	7.4	20.1	8.1	−7.0	15.1
Argentina (2002)	69.0	62.6	−0.2	62.9	11.6	−53.5	65.2

Normalized to 50% devaluation	Devaluation (%)	Export growth (%)			Import growth (%)		
		Value	Volume	Price	Value	Volume	Price
Burstein et al. (2002)	50	58.4	10.3	48.1	28.3	−13.5	41.8
Turkey (2001)	50	49.3	2.8	46.5	22.8	−11.3	34.1
Brazil (2002)	50	56.6	15.2	41.4	16.7	−14.4	31.1
Argentina (2002)	50	45.4	−0.2	45.6	8.4	−38.8	47.2

	Real GDP growth (%)	
	Domestic	Foreign
Burstein et al. (2002)	−6.5	1.2
Turkey (2001)	−10.3	−0.2
Brazil (2002)	1.6	1.7
Argentina (2002)	−10.9	

reflects a 55 percent increase in export prices. The smaller increase in import values reflects a large decline in import volumes (16.9 percent on average).

It is important to note that these estimates are averages; there is considerable variation across the seven episodes. The estimates mentioned above have a standard deviation of about 25 percentage points across episodes. In the case of Korea for example, export prices increased by only 16.5 percent in 1998 following a 32.5 percent devaluation in 1997, implying that a 50 percent devaluation would only lead to a 25 percent increase in export prices within a year. In the case of Brazil, export prices increased by 39 percent in 2000 following a depreciation of 39 percent in 1999, implying a 50 percent devaluation would lead to a 50 percent increase in export prices within a year.[21]

Table 12.6 also reports changes in trade values, volumes, and prices that coincided with large devaluations in Turkey (2001), Brazil (2002), and Argentina (2002). The middle panel in Table 12.6 transforms the statistics to correspond to a 50 percent devaluation so that we can compare the responses of trade prices and volumes across episodes. The seven episodes examined by Burstein *et al.* imply that a 50 percent devaluation would lead to a 48 percent increase in export prices and 42 percent increase in import prices, on average. The response of export prices was quite similar in Argentina (46 percent) and Turkey (47 percent), though somewhat lower in Brazil (41 percent). The response of import prices was higher in Argentina (47 percent), but significantly lower in Brazil (31 percent) and Turkey (34 percent).

The calculations reported in Table 12.6 indicate that trade volumes tend to increase following large devaluations. The estimates reported by Burstein *et al.* (2002) imply a 10 percent increase in export on average, following devaluations that average 57 percent. Brazil (2002) provides a similar example. The nominal effective exchange rate depreciated by 24 percent in 2002 while export values increased by 27.5 percent. Moreover, the expansion in export volumes occurred at a time when foreign output declined by 0.2 percent.[22] The partial equilibrium model employed in this chapter cannot explain the expansion in export volumes that typically follow a large devaluation.[23]

One possible explanation for the strong expansion in export volumes is that income compression causes a major contraction in domestic consumption and as a consequence, domestic firms have a greater incentive to sell in foreign markets. Another possible explanation is that pricing exports in foreign currency leads to a substantial increase in profit margins when there is a large devaluation. The higher profit margins provide a strong incentive for firms to increase production and attract entry of more firms into the export sector. Our model does not take into account these supply side factors.

In the case of Argentina (2002), import volumes declined by 53.5

percent in 2002 even though there was little change in the relative price of imports. This was largely the result of income compression as real GDP declined by 10.9 percent. It is hard to reconcile the magnitude of this decline with empirical estimates of income effects on import volumes. This episode implies an income elasticity of about 5, which is well above most empirical estimates.[24] One possible explanation for this is that there was a foreign currency constraint in Argentina that prevented importers from purchasing goods priced in foreign currency.

6 Conclusion

To evaluate the sustainability of external debt it is critical to assess the vulnerability of the debt to adverse external shocks. The primary component of such an assessment must be the economy's ability to adjust to such shocks. This chapter has explored some of the key factors that determine an economy's capacity for external adjustment. The factors that are found to facilitate adjustment are: a flexible nominal exchange rate in conjunction with a monetary policy aimed at achieving stable, low inflation, openness to trade, large trade elasticities, and export pricing in foreign currency.

Clearly, there are other factors that also are important, which have been alluded to in this chapter, but not explored in detail. In particular, the degree of government involvement in the economy is critical because government policy can directly influence the capacity for external adjustment through several channels including the extent of government purchases, which affects the size of the traded goods sector, commercial policy, which affects trade openness, and the regulation of labor, goods, and other markets, which affects the performance of the price mechanism and the economy's ability to re-allocate productive resources. Another important factor is import compression that may result from immediate impact of the adverse shock on economic activity and may be aggravated by the possible contractionary response of government to the adverse shock in order to limit the shock's fiscal impact. Finally, adverse shocks also often create financial crises and a reduction in financial intermediation. These disruptions of financial sector also limit the economy's capacity to adjust. These issues are worthy of further study to provide a more complete assessment of an economy's capacity for external adjustment.

Notes

* The authors would like to thank Rebecca Driver, Mark Kruger, John Murray, and James Powell for their helpful comments. The views expressed in this chapter are those of the authors and not the Bank of Canada.
 1 IMF (2002a: 3).
 2 The focus of the chapter is on middle-income emerging market countries.
 3 For a useful derivation and analysis of the IBC, see Horne (1988).

4 Note that the interest rate and the growth rate of GDP can be expressed in real or nominal terms; the critical factor is the difference between them. Also, it may be more appropriate to assess the external debt-to-exports ratio than the external debt/GDP ratio. The latter ratio presumes that domestic output can be transformed at a fixed exchange rate into foreign currency to service the debt.

5 The 15 large emerging market economies include five from Latin America (Mexico, Brazil, Argentina, Venezuela, and Chile); five from East Asia (South Korea, Indonesia, Thailand, Malaysia, and the Philippines); and five from Eastern Europe/Asia (Russia, Poland, Turkey, Hungary, and the Czech Republic).

6 The data were obtained from the World Bank data base, documented in *Global Development Finance* 2002. The measures exclude situations where countries are in arrears (debt service payments are not being made). The external debt being measured is gross, not net, external debt.

7 See Figure 3 on p. 9 in Calvo *et al.* (2003).

8 Table 12.2 is adapted from the Appendix of Ortiz (2002). The numbers represent the change in the current account/GDP ratio from the year prior to the crisis to the first and second year following the crisis. Argentina (2001) is not included in Table 2 because the current account recorded in 2002 does not include debt service payments (following the moratorium announced in November 2001). Brazil (2001) is included instead.

9 The statistics reported in Table 12.3 correspond to changes in the trade balance, current account and external debt in the same year as a large devaluation; whereas those reported in Table 12.2 correspond to changes in the current account in the year following a large devaluation relative to the previous year.

10 Asset markets would also adjust to make investment in domestic assets more attractive.

11 The inability of most emerging-market countries to issue external debt in domestic countries has been interpreted as evidence of "original sin" – an irreversibly bad reputation for monetary instability (e.g., Eichengreen *et al.* (2002). Bordo *et al.* (2003) shows that many of the major western industrialized countries were not able to issue domestic currency external debt until well into the twenty-first century.

12 The yields on 3-month, 1-year, 5-year, 10-year, and 30-year US treasury bills/bonds averaged are 4.6 percent, 4.9 percent, 5.8 percent, 6.1 percent and 6.5 percent, respectively, over the period 1992–2001.

13 Under the small open economy assumption, an exchange rate depreciation and resulting adjustments in the domestic economy should have no impact on the foreign country. A depreciation, however, would, at less than full employment, cause domestic output and income to expand and increase imports.

14 For similar approaches to modifying the Marshall–Lerner Condition to incorporate external debt, see Nadkumar (1992) and Nguyen (1993).

15 In the simulation exercise, the import and export elasticities are assumed to be equal.

16 As profits in the export sector increase, resources will be drawn from elsewhere in the economy and export volumes could increase, if we assume that the country in question is too small to affect its terms of trade and that exporters' costs do not increase. Our analysis does not include this export supply effect and for this reason underestimates the response of the value of exports to a devaluation.

17 The degree to which a country prices its exports in domestic or foreign currency terms could be ascertained from the correlation of export prices with the

exchange rate. Pricing in domestic currency terms implies a correlation of 0, while pricing in foreign currency terms implies a correlation of 1.0.

18 The analysis could be generalized to include a portion of external debt denominated in domestic currency, which would be unaffected by exchange rate changes. This would not change the main results of the chapter.

19 All lowercase variables are measured in logs, with the exception of the interest rate (r) and the growth rate of nominal GDP (g).

20 The study by Burstein *et al.* (2002) actually examines episodes in nine countries. Episodes in Sweden and Finland are excluded from our calculations to focus on the emerging market countries.

21 Rabanal and Schwartz (2001) obtain a similar result for Brazil over an earlier period. They find that import prices moved virtually one-for-one with monthly changes in the exchange rate over the period from December 1998 to September 2000.

22 Foreign real GDP growth is measured using a trade-weighted average of real GDP growth for Brazil's major trading partners.

23 Complete pass-through from a devaluation to export prices implies no change in the relative price of exports. The estimates reported by Burstein *et al.* (2002) indicate that export prices increased by about 55 percent following large devaluations that averaged 57 percent. This implies 96 percent pass-through to export prices, on average, so that the relative price of exports declined by only 4 percent.

24 The long-term income elasticity of import volumes was set to 1.4 in the benchmark calibration.

References

Burstein, A., Eichenbaum, M. and Rebelo, S. (2002), "Why are rates of inflation so low after large devaluations?", NBER Working Paper no. 8748 (February).

Borda, C. (2001), "Coping with terms of trade shocks: pegs vs. floats", *American Economic Review Papers and Proceedings,* 91: 376–380.

Bordo, M., Meissner, C. and Redish, A. (2003), "How original sin was overcome: the evolution of external debt denominated in domestic currency and the United States and the British Dominions, 1900–2000", National Bureau of Economic Research Working Paper no. 9841, (July).

Calvo, G. and Reinhart, C. (2000), "Fixing for your life", NBER Working Paper no. 8006 (November).

Calvo, G., Izquierdo, A. and Talvi, E. (2003), "Sudden stops, the real exchange rate and fiscal sustainability: Argentina's lessons", National Bureau of Economic Research Working Paper no. W9828.

Campa, J. and Goldberg, L. (2002), "Exchange rate pass-through into import prices: A macro or micro phenomenon?", US Federal Reserve Bank of New York Staff Report no. 149 (May).

Cooper, R. (1971), "Currency devaluation in developing countries", *Princeton Essays in International Finance,* 86.

Corsetti, G., Pesenti, P. and Roubini, N. (1998), "What caused the Asian currency and financial crisis? Part I: A macroeconomic overview", NBER Working Paper no. 6833 (December).

Eichengreen, B., Hausmann, R. and Pinizza, U. (2002), "Original sin: the pain, the mystery and the road to redemption", Paper presented at IADB conference on "Currency and Maturity Matchmaking: Redeeming Debt from Original Sin" held in Washington, November 21–22.

Friedman, M. (1953), "The case for flexible exchange rates", *Essays in Positive Economics*, Chicago: Chicago University Press, pp. 175–203.

Goldberg, P. and Knetter, M. (1997), "Goods prices and exchange rates: What have we learned?", *Journal of Economic Literature*, 35 (September): 1243–1272.

Goldfajn, I. and Werlang, S. (2000), "The pass-through from depreciation to inflation: a panel study", Banco Central do Brasil Working Paper no. 5 (September).

Goldstein, M. (2003), "Debt sustainability, Brazil and the IMF", Institute for International Economics Working Paper no. WP 03-1 (February).

Gylfason, T. and Risager, O. (1984), "Does devaluation improve the current account?", *European Economic Review*, 25: 37–64.

Horne, Jocelyn (1988), "Criteria of external sustainability", IMF Working Paper no. WP/88/60.

Hooper, P., Johnson, K.H. and Marquez, J. (1998), "Trade elasticities for G-7 countries", Federal Reserve Board International Finance Discussion Paper no. 1998–609.

IMF (2002a), "Assessing sustainability", (May).

IMF (2002b), "Early warning system models: the next steps forward", *The Global Financial Stability Report* (March): Chapter IV.

Kfoury, M. (2001), "Inflation targeting in an open financially integrated emerging economy: the case of Brazil", Banco Central do Brasil Working Paper no. 26.

Krugman, P. (1999), "Balance sheets, the transfer problem, and financial crises," in Isard, P., Razin, A. and Rose, A. (eds), *International Finance and Financial Crises*, Boston: Kluwer Academic Publishers.

Marquez, J. (2002), *Estimating Trade Elasticities*, Boston: Kluwer Academic Publishers.

Nadkumar, Parameswar (1992), "Will devaluation reduce the debt-burden?" *Margin*. Oct.–Dec.

Nguyen, D.T. (1993), "The dynamic effect of devaluation on the balance of payments of a small debt-ridden open economy", *The Economic Record*, 69(206), Sept.

Ortiz, G. (2002), "Recent emerging market crises: What have we learned?", Per Jacobsson Lecture (July), Basel (Switzerland).

Rabanal, P. and Schwartz, G. (2001), "Exchange rate changes and consumer price inflation: 20 months after the floating of the real", in "Brazil: Selected Issues and Statistical Appendix", IMF Country Report no. 01/10.

13 What type of country restricts international capital movements?

Dan Huynh and Peter Sinclair

1 Introduction

This chapter explores the question of why some countries might wish to set up barriers to the international movement of capital. Much recent literature on international capital movements concentrates on three related issues – quantifying countries' net external asset positions,[1] why so little capital moves from rich to poor countries,[2] and whether capital mobility is beneficial or harmful in view of its various wider effects.[3] Exactly why some countries might not wish to participate in the globalization game has been less discussed. This is the main topic to be explored here. A theoretical preamble, in section 2, argues that countries in this position are likely to display one or more of the following characteristics: relatively high populations; *intermediate* levels of GDP per head, neither high nor low; and a strong penchant for protecting seignorage. These propositions are then tested against an index of restrictions on external transactions for a large number of countries, which is described in section 3. Empirical results are found to be consistent with the hypotheses.

2 Theoretical considerations

2.1 Do-it-yourself capital accumulation versus overseas borrowing

In a simple, one-good world of perfect foresight and competition, without technical progress or population growth, we should expect the stock of capital (k) and the level of output (y) to converge, eventually, on particular steady state values.[4] If everyone is alike in their preferences and technology, for example, and optimizes over an infinite horizon, the real rate of interest (before any tax), R, will equal the rate at which the utility from consumption is discounted (call this β).

In the absence of complicating factors such as tax and depreciation rates, the real rate of interest will equal the marginal product of capital (MPK). If capital depreciates at the rate δ, MPK should (eventually) equal

$\delta + R$. With a given production function linking output to capital, where the MPK is positive and declining, this condition will pinpoint a unique level of the capital stock. In the long run, consumption (c) should equal net product – that is output minus replacement investment (δk).

Population growth and (labour-augmenting) technical progress at given rates (n and x respectively, let us say) can easily be accommodated into this setting, with, in the latter case, an assumption that the instantaneous utility function for consumption displays a constant elasticity for the marginal utility of consumption (call this h). With no taxation, in the long run R (and MPK $- \delta$) will converge upon $\beta + n + hx$. This will identify unique ratios of capital to output and savings to income; aggregate real income, capital and consumption will all be growing at the rate of $n + x$.

There is a unique route to this steady state from any initial level of capital per head. If capital (per human efficiency unit) starts out low, both it, and consumption per human efficiency unit, will climb at decelerating rates until the steady state is reached. Capital is likely to grow a good deal more quickly than consumption. (This is certain if, as appears overwhelmingly probable, the parameter h exceeds the share of income accruing to capital under perfect competition).

Suppose all countries are alike in their values of h, β, n, x and δ, and let us continue to ignore complications such as taxation. Assume that each country accumulates capital independently, with no international borrowing or lending. Then the real rate of interest will eventually be the same everywhere. And so will levels of income and consumption per head, if levels of technology are common. There may, however, be very different starting points for capital at some initial date. A country that starts out with a very low level of capital per head will take much longer to converge. Suppose the rest of the world has already got (arbitrarily close) to the steady state well before our country – assume it is small – reaches this position.

The government of a country in that position will face a choice. It can stay accumulating capital gradually on its own. Call this the *closed* policy. Alternatively, it can opt to open up its capital market, allowing residents to borrow and lend at the now unique and steady state real interest rate ruling in the rest of the world. Call this the *open* policy. From what we have assumed, we can be sure that the real interest rate at home is *higher* than abroad, reflecting the fact that capital is scarcer there. How would adoption of the open policy affect the course of macroeconomic variables in the home economy? And which of these two policies is better, or liable to *appear* better, to countries with possibly different characteristics?

Adopting the open policy should lead to a jump in capital, and hence output, in response to capital imports. Consumption would also be expected to increase, too. Since absorbing and installing the extra capital would take some time, these changes would be phased. Subsequently, one would expect that output, consumption and capital would rise more slowly

– indeed close to, if not at their steady state trend rates of $n + x$. The country's domestic product would be higher than its national product, because capital imported from overseas would have to be serviced at the world interest rate, R.

The closed policy, by contrast, would see much slower convergence on the steady state, but, in the steady state, ultimately a higher level of consumption (because there would be no overseas borrowing costs). In the absence of distortions at least, the open policy is to be preferred to the closed one, on the grounds that agents opted deliberately for overseas borrowing: they did not have to incur it, and chose to because it offered a more attractive utility-from-consumption integral. So the gain in consumption early on is viewed by domestic residents as well worth the subsequent reduction, in terms of its impact on the stream of discounted utility.

The poorest countries should, on this logic, be further from their steady state if they have relied solely on domestic accumulation. So those countries should display the greatest scarcity of capital. This suggests that countries in this position will be rather keen to welcome foreign capital into their economies. Roughly speaking, the gain from switching to an open policy is proportional to the *square* of the difference between real interest rates at home and abroad. Foreign direct investment may well be particularly appealing for countries where that difference is big – and this will mean countries where GDP per head is very low. For those countries that have accumulated somewhat more capital, the benefit from going "open" may well be regarded as much less pressing.

Another factor that may distinguish countries' attitudes towards welcoming or restricting international capital flows is size, as captured, say, by population. The smaller the economy, the likelier its production is to be concentrated on a very narrow range of goods; the greater, therefore, is its likely dependence on and openness to trade. With larger population comes greater diversification. More specialized economies are also more vulnerable to shocks in particular markets. So their aggregate income will tend to be relatively more volatile. And they will be less able to arrange any form of internal redistribution to protect losers. A final consideration that could be important is that governments of large countries (measured say by area or population) may find restrictions on international capital mobility somewhat easier to enforce.

All this suggests two hypotheses: first, that receptivity to international capital mobility may be expected to decline as income per head rises from very low to somewhat higher levels; and second, that it may be negatively related to population. These hypotheses are tested below.

The introduction of risk takes us beyond the confines of the simple model with which we began. It also exposes the *insurance* motive for international capital mobility. Essentially, opportunities to lend or borrow overseas tend to divorce expenditure (and particularly consumption) from income at the aggregate level. Such transactions represent intertemporal trade; and, in many forms, they allow an element of trade across states, as well as dates. Consumption smoothing is always attractive if the utility function is increasing but concave.

But insurance is not just a matter of demand. Supply is no less important. It is the most advanced economies where borrowing from abroad is likely to be easiest and cheapest because lenders will typically regard it as relatively safe. Furthermore, residents of the richer economies are likely to have acquired more familiarity with financial markets and more confidence in them. They might also be more risk-averse (suggesting that h is not a parameter, but rather an elasticity that rises with consumption). And it is in the richer economies where efficiency gains from international capital movements may be better understood – and the advantages of capital *exports* (as well as imports) most apparent.

This suggests a third hypothesis: beyond some intermediate level, income per head should exert a *positive* effect on a country's willingness to adopt the "open" policy rather than the closed one. This hypothesis will also be tested empirically below. Taken in combination with the first hypothesis, it suggests that restrictions on capital imports and exports are likely to be most stringent in middle-income countries. We shall therefore be searching for any evidence of a hump in the curve linking capital account restrictions to income per head.

2.2 Some inhibitions about opening the capital account

Is it, though, a clear case of capital mobility being universally advantageous, and certain countries suffering from governments that fail to appreciate this? We should in fact shrink from such a statement, because it is exaggerated.[5] Its validity is guaranteed on certain definitions and under certain conditions. But it fails to generalize beyond them. There could be groups in the population for which the short-term effects of switching from a closed to an open policy could well be adverse. Equilibrium real wage rates in capital-exporting countries stand to fall as a result. (And if and where they are sticky, we must expect unemployment to result.) Another source of income undermined by the open policy is profits earned by residents in capital-importing countries. In the absence of compensation (through higher wages or some transfer mechanism) they, too, will suffer. In addition, there are potentially disagreeable consequences for (and from) exchange rates and/or the evolution of monetary aggregates, stemming from large and reversible short-term capital flows.

Then there are arguments based on externalities, taxation at the margin, monopoly or other distortions, which remind us that free trade may be inferior to restricted trade or even autarky, if these distortions cannot be removed directly. These arguments are most familiar in the context of intratemporal trade in goods, but they apply with equal force to international trade with an intertemporal or insurance dimension.

Most worrying of all, perhaps, is the thought that one country may have a higher real rate of interest than another *in the steady state*. Residents of the first might, for example, have greater impatience (a higher discount rate on utility, β) than those in the second. Without some additional refinement to our model, this will imply that if the two countries adopt open policies, the first community will go deeper and deeper into debt vis-à-vis the second, and carry on mortgaging its future consumption with no limit. It was Lucas (1992) that first exposed this problem in the context of different individuals in a closed economy; but its application to different economies is immediate and telling. There are devices that can prevent this, however, one of them is to introduce the notion that utility depends not just on consumption, but also (positively) on net assets, too. This assumption can easily make for steady states where consumption, capital, wealth and both domestic and national output are all tied down in the steady state (see Sinclair (2004) for a detailed model that explores this idea).

For example, we might postulate that the maximand for agents is

$$\Phi = \int_0^\infty \{\exp(-\beta t)[\ell nc(t) + \theta \ell na(t)] + \lambda(t)[f(k(t)) + r^*(a(t) - k(t))$$
$$- \dot{a}(t) - c(t)]\}dt.$$

Here, r^* is a given real interest rate prevailing in the rest of the world; a, c, k and $f(k)$ denote assets, consumption, capital and gross domestic product; taxation, depreciation, technical progress and population growth are set to zero; and $\dot{a}(t)$ stands for asset accumulation. The rate of impatience is β, and θ represents the strength of preference for net assets. If domestic agents are free to choose paths for their choice variables to maximize Φ, starting off at initial values of $k(0) = a(0)$, they will immediately set capital where $f'(k) = r^*$. That will fix capital, output and real wages (the excess of output over capital income). In the end, they will approach a steady state where the ratio of a to real wages settles down at $\theta/[\beta - r^*(1 + \theta)]$. In the steady state, the ratio of consumption to a will equal $(\beta - r^*)/\theta$. In this steady state, domestic residents may be net claimants or net debtors against the rest of the world (and which they are will depend on how β and θ compare with the same parameters elsewhere).

Even in a model of this kind, though, the domestic authorities in a country trying to decide whether to open the capital account of its balance of payments may well not know what the domestic residents' values of impatience and asset-preference really are. They may fear that β is high and that θ is low, resulting in a long-term net-debtor status for the country as a whole if borrowing and lending on international capital markets is allowed.

They may also fear that residents may try to escape domestic income tax by salting assets away abroad (and either failing to declare this to the home tax authority, or, whether legally or illegally, paying tax to foreign tax collectors only). If domestic financial markets have not developed far, there is also the likelihood that sudden access to overseas credit, for people hitherto credit-constrained, may prompt them to borrow heavily abroad, possibly with long-term consequences that both they and their government will regret. Yet a further argument for caution could be that domestic investors, who are likely to be ill-informed, may invest in foreign ventures that prove unprofitable. And if the country deems itself to be a likely net investor overseas, there is the worry, already noted, that a reduction in the domestic capital stock will place downward pressure on equilibrium real wages rates – and on employment if real wages rates are sticky. On the other hand, if it anticipates that foreign capital will come in, the government's implicit social welfare function could place a high value on domestic profit income, which an inflow of capital is almost certain to reduce.

2.3 Seignorage issues

A final concern could be seignorage. Restrictions on capital flows may not be powerful enough to deter domestic residents from holding foreign exchange, but their removal will surely encourage them to augment these if the country's exchange rate is thought likely to depreciate. Opportunities to substitute foreign for domestic currency may well limit seignorage sharply. Opportunities to substitute foreign for domestic bonds will similarly make it very much harder for the authorities to engage in policies of financial repression (unwise, by normal criteria, though these are).

Consider this example. Suppose that government debt takes two forms: bonds, b, that bear a real rate of interest of r, and currency, m, on which the nominal rate of interest is zero. Government sets r, and also the rate of inflation, π. Government also sets a real rate of return, R, on loans for investment by the private sector. For simplicity, there is no income taxation, and no default. International capital movements are banned. Total public sector income, in the steady state, equals

$$S = \pi m - rb + Rk$$

where k is the stock of capital accumulated by the private sector. Currency, and to a limited extent bonds, offer the advantage of saving labour time, $1 - s$, with $s(t) = \delta(m(t)^{-1} + \eta[m(t) + b(t)]^{-1})$. Here the parameter η is positive, reflecting the idea that bonds also offer some liquidity services, although money is more valuable in this respect. The production function per agent (all of whom are identical) equals $Tk(t)^{1/3}(1 - s(t))^{2/3}$. The private sector's problem is to choose paths for consumption ($c(t)$), capital ($k(t)$), currency ($m(t)$) and bonds ($b(t)$), to maximize

$$\Psi = \int_0^\infty \{\exp(-\beta t)u(c(t)) + \lambda(t)[Tk(t)^{1/3}(1-s(t))^{2/3} - S(t) - \dot{m}(t) - \dot{b}(t) - c(t)]\}dt$$

subject to the above functional form for shopping time, $s(t)$.

In the steady state, currency holdings equal $\sqrt{[2\delta x/3(r+\pi)]}$, and bond holdings equal $\sqrt{[2\eta\delta x/3(\beta-r)]}$ minus currency, where $x = T^{1/3}(3R)^{-1/2}$. Suppose now that the government aims to maximize $S + \theta c$. Here, θ represents the relative importance that the government places on private consumption. So the more anxious government is to defend seignorage, the lower θ will be. What does this assumption imply?

If $\eta = 4/27$ and $\theta = 1/3$, for example, the rate of inflation will be set at β, and the real rate on bonds at $3\beta/4$. If θ, the government's preference weight on consumption, were lower, inflation would be higher, and the real bond rate lower. So there is some (mild) financial repression, attributable to the government's concern to keep down the total cost of servicing its obligations. On a more sinister note, the parameter θ may reflect the extent to which the government is motivated by altruism as opposed to corruption. Kleptocratic administrations will set a low value on θ; perhaps even a zero one. The only argument for a kleptocrat giving θ any positive value at all would be that it reflected a "participation" constraint on the part of the citizens: if consumption is squeezed too low, the risks of emigration (and death, or coups) could build up to unacceptable levels.

Opening the economy to free international capital movements would transform the picture: government bonds would now have to yield (something close to) the world real rate of interest, and the implied rise in real bond rates would bite into the seignorage from currency, by raising its opportunity cost. In all likelihood, S would fall. These observations suggest that restrictions on international capital movements may well, in practice, display a positive link with the rate of inflation. A strong desire to protect seignorage revenue from the erosion that a policy of openness on the capital account should bring may well lead a government to eschew that policy. This hypothesis is explored below.

2.4 Further points

So far we have presented the choice of controls on capital exports and imports as a binary one: countries need to choose between an open door policy or a policy of prohibition. Reality is more complex. There are in practice *degrees* of restriction. Capital exports and imports can be taxed, and the rates of tax can be high or very low. Some kinds of flows may be permitted freely, while others require approval. Domestic residents may face tighter restrictions than foreigners. The optimal rates of tax on each and any of these flows may well lie somewhere between zero and prohibition, and not at one of the edges. Using the analogy of optimal taxes on imports and exports, we can argue that they *must* be zero for an altruistic, well-informed government with the power to remove any market distortions at source and no power to influence world prices. But they will be positive if the country can influence the terms on which it borrows or lends abroad (and bigger, the greater this influence is). They will also be positive, in the government's eye, if that government "sells" forms of protection in return for political support (as in Grossman and Helpman (1994)), and the corruption-seignorage issue touched on in the previous section is in a sense an extreme instance of this.

3 The empirical evidence

3.1 Data sources

For our empirical work, we obtained annual data from different sources. For a measure of capital transaction restriction, we follow the example of Quinn (1997) and using a scoring method based on the summary tables reported in the Annual Report on Exchange Arrangements and Exchange Restrictions[6] (AREAER) from 1970 to 2001. This is explained in section 3.2 below following Quinn (1997). We use the UN dataset for individual countries' GDP, and for other monetary and financial data International Financial Statistics (IFS), which, like AREAER, is published by the IMF.

3.2 Defining the restrictions

Following Quinn (1997) we construct an index based on the summary table reported in AREAER, for the years 1970–2001. For each country, we assign one point for each of the following categories for which a restriction exists:

(i)   Separate (exchange) rate(s) for some or all capital transactions and/or some or all invisibles.
(ii)   Import (exchange) rate(s) different from export rate(s).
(iii) More than one (exchange) rate for imports.
(iv)   More than one (exchange) rate for exports.
(v)   Prescription of currency.
(vi)   Bilateral payments arrangements with members.
(vii) Bilateral payments arrangements with non-members.
(viii) There are restrictions on payments in respect of current transactions.
(ix)   There are restrictions on payments in respect of capital transactions.
(x)   Import surcharges.
(xi)   Advance import deposits.
(xii) A requirement to surrender export proceeds.

We do not use any weighting, as we do not know the relative effects that different categories may have, and should therefore make the Laplacean assumption – in the absence of other information – that each is (potentially) of equal importance. The listing remained consistent throughout the period 1970–1996, although the countries that feature in these tables have changed. For the first time in 1997 and thereafter, a new classification was introduced. This distinguished in greater detail those restrictions or controls that bore upon capital transactions from those on current transactions. The measure for this later period was revised and converted into this old measure. This is discussed further below.

Examination of the above list reveals that the summary tables refer more to current than to capital transaction restrictions. However, we would argue that this is superficial and that many of these restrictions are actually for capital control purposes. The distinction between current and capital transactions on the balance of payments is in practice rather blurred, and restrictions relating to either are often hard to enforce. Capital flows can be disguised as trade flows by adjustments to invoicing for goods. Estimates of trade between different national divisions of international companies can only rely on reports of those companies themselves, which they will clearly have some incentive to distort when restrictions are in place. Expected inflation contaminates nominal interest payments on loans, a flow on the current account of the balance of payments, which will incorporate an element of real capital repayment that ought to belong on the capital account. Similarly, risk premia reflected in interest or dividend payments are there to balance ex-ante probabilities of losses of capital. Opportunities to reclassify, or engage in swaps, may in practice stretch the limits to convertibility on one type of transaction, or with one class of counterparty. So what look like restrictions on one account of the balance of payments have repercussions on the other. Furthermore, evidence (reviewed, for example, in Sinclair and Shu (2001); see also Cardoso and Goldfajn (1998), Johnston and Ryan (1994) and Reinhart and Smith (2002)) that controls have greatest effect when first applied suggest that companies tend to learn how to bypass them.

We present, in Figure 13.1 below, the frequency distribution of the scoring from the AREAER summary report for years 1996–2001. We selected the scoring for these years because the two types of restrictions (current and capital) were more clearly differentiated. As can be seen, countries with a high score for current transactions tend to also have high score for capital restrictions.

Beginning in 1996 and thereafter, the categorization in the ARERAR summary tables was changed. The list of current and capital restrictions became more differentiated. In all there were 23 new categories of restrictions, 8 such categories were current transaction restrictions and 13 were capital transaction restrictions. These are listed below:

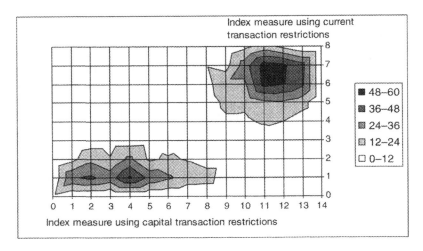

Figure 13.1 Frequency graph – countries' measured control on current transactions versus restriction on capital transactions for the years 1996–2001.

Exchange rate structure
(i)   Dual
(ii)   Multiple
(iii)   Arrangements for payments and receipts
(iv)   Bilateral payments arrangements
(v)   Payments arrears
(vi)   Payments for Invisible Transactions and Current Transfers

Proceeds from exports
(vii)   Repatriation requirements
(viii)   Surrender requirements

Proceeds from invisible transactions
(ix)   Repatriation requirements
(x)   Surrender requirements

Capital Transactions
(xi)   On capital market securities
(xii)   On money market instruments
(xiii)   On collective investment securities
(xiv)   Controls on derivatives and other instruments
(xv)   Commercial credits
(xvi)   Financial credits
(xvii)   Guarantees, sureties and financial backup facilities
(xviii)   Controls on direct investment

(xix)   Controls on liquidation of direct investment
(xx)   Controls on real estate transactions
(xxi)   Controls on personal capital transactions
(xxii) Provisions specific to commercial banks and other credit institutions
(xxiii) Provisions specific to institutional investors

The main difference between the new categorization and the old is that more categories under capital restrictions were added. We constructed two series, the first a scoring for current transaction restrictions (items (i) to (x) in this new list) and a separate second one for capital transaction restrictions (items (xi) to (xxiii)). Each category attracts a scoring of one (except for items (vii) and (viii), to which we gave a score of one half because the two categories were combined as one category under the old categorization). The frequency graph of the two scoring series in Figure 13.1 reveals that countries with high current restriction tend to also have high capital restriction scores.

In order to convert the new scoring into the old scoring scheme, we use the summary tables for year 1996. For this year, summary tables were available in the old and the new formats. We constructed the scoring in the old and compared this to a scoring that consists of items (i) to (x) in the listing above. We chose these ten items for the new scoring because these most closely resemble that of the old index.

Figure 13.2 presents the frequency graph of the old index versus the new index for the one year they share, 1996. The maximum value possible under the new index is 8 (this is because (i) and (ii) are alternatives, and (vii) and (viii) each get a weight of one half) and 11 under the old index (not 12, because (ix) is dropped).

As can be seen there is a near linear relationship between the old and new scoring. To transform the new scoring into to a comparable scale to the old scoring, we use an OLS regression to obtain a linear best fit. The fitted equation was imposed with no constant, on the grounds that there were many countries with no transaction restriction (a score of zero) in both the old and new measure. We found that the equation that best fit the data was:

$$y = 0.664x, \ R^2 = 0.2833$$

	Coefficients	Standard error	t-stat	P-value
X	0.664031	0.035625	18.63931	7.64E-42

Here, y is the new score and x is the old score. The value of the coefficient on x is rather close to what one might expect (8/11), simply on the basis

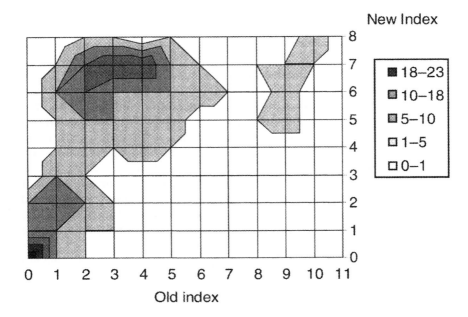

Figure 13.2 Old and new capital transactions indices compared for 1996.

that the maximum number of restrictions fell from 11 to 8. We therefore converted the new "current restriction" measure into its old format equivalent at the rate of 0.664, rounded to the nearest integer, to obtain a complete capital control measure for the entire period. For the period 1985–2000 we display descriptive statistics about the capital controls in Table 13.1.

While the scaling described gives sensible figures for the countries with light or intermediate levels of restriction, it becomes problematic for

Table 13.1 Capital control data for groups of countries: 1985–2000

	Transition	OECD	Latin America and the Caribbean	Asia	Africa	Group
Mean	5.2	0.9	4.5	3.9	4.2	3.7
Median	4	0	4	3.5	4	3
Maximum	11	6	11	10	10	11
Minimum	1	0	0	0	0	0
Standard deviation	2.9	1.4	2.9	2.7	1.8	2.8
Number of countries	16	21	18	14	40	176

some highly restrictive countries. In particular we see from Figure 13.2 that there is a small group of countries that have high restrictions under both the old index and the new. The countries in this group are: Angola, Azerbaijan, Belarus, Colombia, Ecuador, Iran, Kazakhstan, Kenya, Guinea-Bissau, Romania, Sudan, Syria, Turkmenistan, the Ukraine and Egypt.

3.3 Trends over time

What has been happening to the level of restrictions over time? The two percentile graphs in Figure 13.3 a reveal a declining trend in the 1990s. During the 1970s and 1980s, there is relatively little overall movement, apart from a tendency towards liberalization on the part of countries with

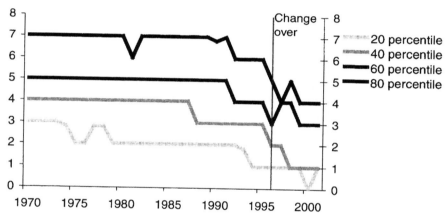

Figure 13.3 Double-decile graphs of capital restriction index (excluding the maximum value); data from 1970.

Note

The above graph uses only those countries that report from 1985 onwards. These are: Afghanistan, the Netherlands Antilles, Argentina, Antigua, Australia, Austria, Burundi, Belgium, Benin, Bourkina Fasso, Bangladesh, Bahrain, the Bahamas, Belize, Bolivia, Brazil, Barbados, Bhutan, Botswana, Canada, Chile, China, the Ivory Coast, Cameroon, Congo (Brazzaville), Colombia, Comoros, the Cape Verde Islands, Costa Rica, Cyprus, Germany, Djibouti, Dominica, Denmark, the Dominican Republic, Algeria, Ecuador, Egypt, Spain, Ethiopia, Finland, Fiji, France, Gabon, Great Britain, Ghana, Guinea, Gambia, Guinea-Bissao, Guinea Equitorial, Greece, Grenada, Guatamala, Guyana, Hong Kong, Honduras, Haiti, Hungary, Indonesia, India, Ireland, Iran, Iraq, Iceland, Israel, Italy, Jamaica, Jordan, Japan, Kenya, St Kitts-Nevis, South Korea, Kuwait, Laos, Lebanon, Liberia, Libya, St Lucia, Sri Lanka, Lesotho, Morocco, Madagascar, the Maldives, Mexico, Mali, Malta, Myanmar, Mozambique, Mauretania, Mauritius, Malawi, Malaysia, Niger, Nigeria, Nicaragua, the Netherlands, Norway, Nepal, New Zealand, Oman, Pakistan, Panama, Peru, the Philippines, Papua New Guinea, Portugal, Paraguay, Qatar, Romania, Rwanda, Saudi Arabia, Sudan, Senegal, Singapore, Slovenia, the Solomons, Somalia, Sao Tomas e Principe, Surinam, Sweden, Switzerland, the Seychelles, Syria, Chad, Togo, Thailand, Trinidad and Tobago, Tunisia, Turkey, Uganda, Uruguay, the USA, St Vincent, Venezuela, Vietnam, Vanuatu, Western Samoa, Yugoslavia, South Africa, Zambia and Zimbabwe.

light restrictions. In the early 1990s, there is more pronounced movement in the liberalization direction.

Turning to the data for a sample of various countries, we can see from Figure 13.4 that the OECD countries have all but eliminated restrictions by the end of the period, and that a sharp downward trend is evident for transition countries. Restrictions in both the Asian and Latin American and Caribbean countries selected have also been falling. The results for Africa (not shown), on the other hand, display quite a good deal of movement for individual countries, with no discernible overall trend.[7]

Over a longer data span, however, capital account and convertibility restrictions appear to be no lower today than they were at the beginning of the twentieth century, a point emphasized by Bordo *et al.* (1999). The exigencies of financing problems during and immediately after the First World War, and the great recession of the early 1930s, led many countries to adopt, retain and then tighten restrictions. With many countries embroiled (and not a few destroyed) in the turmoil of the Second World War, the financial difficulties and political changes that succeeded it kept controls in place for many years. It was really only in the late 1950s and 1960s that many of the advanced countries started to remove them. And the advent of independence of former colonies in post-war decades, in a climate where liberal economic doctrines had fallen out of favour, meant that much of the Third World was to retain and even strengthen capital controls, too. There are a few early signs of a trend away from these controls in the 1970s and 1980s outside the OECD area, but the greatest changes, together with the transition from communism, were not to come until the 1990s.

3.4 A test of our hypotheses

In section 2, we argued that the richest and the poorest countries would be likeliest to impose light restrictions on international capital movements, while countries in an intermediate position should impose greater restrictions. We also surmised that population should have a positive effect on the extent of a country's controls, and that the rate of inflation could well do so too. What does the evidence tell us?

We regressed each country's average restriction score (S) observed in the period 1985–2000 on the 1985 level of its GDP per head in US dollars (G), its average inflation rate (I) and its average population (P) in these years. There were 144 observations here. The regression was by ordinary least squares.

Population and the logarithm of inflation both had very significant positive influences upon the level of restrictions. As far as GDP per head is concerned, a humped relationship was apparent: restrictions were lowest when income per head was either high or low in 1985, and larger at intermediate values. The initial positive effect of real income on restrictions is

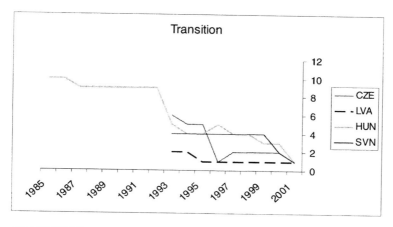

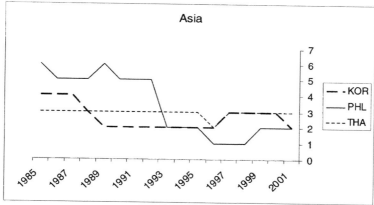

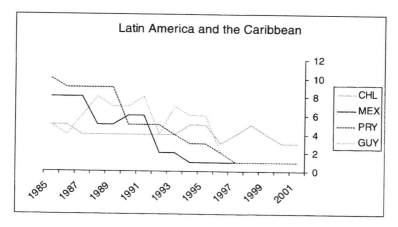

Figure 13.4 A sample of various different countries' capital restriction measures.   *continued*

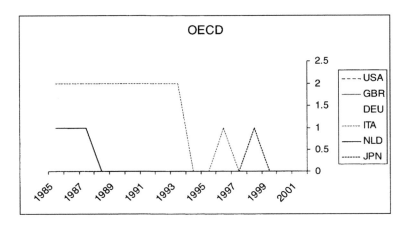

Figure 13.4 continued

Note
USA, GBR and DEU are flat at zero throughout.

significant at the 2.5 per cent level, and the negative one which dominates higher up, at 99 per cent. All else equal, restrictions tended to be lower in OECD countries than elsewhere: the dummy on these Group 1 countries was significant at the 10 per cent level.

So the three hypotheses with which this chapter began receive corroboration from our results. Diagnostics and full details for this regression are presented in the appendix.

Appendix

The details of the regression of 144 countries' average capital controls on various influences suggested by our theoretical discussion in section 2 are presented here. GDPCAP-USD8500 denotes the value of real GDP per head measured in 1985 US dollars. The first regressor is the square of the reciprocal of the log of this variable, calculated as a period average for the country in question. The second regressor is its log. Next in the list comes 1985 population in millions, and after that, the logarithm of average inflation measured by the consumer price index, and finally a dummy for OECD countries as of 1985, which is unitary for these and zero for others.

Dependent variable: CAP_RES8500
Method: Least squares

Included observations: 144
Excluded observations: 40 after adjusting endpoints
White heteroskedasticity-consistent standard errors and covariance

Variable	Coefficient	Std. error	t-statistic	Prob.
C	15.09	4.10	3.68	0.00
1/LOG(GDPCAP_USD8500)^2	−154.10	67.06	−2.30	0.02
LOG(GDPCAP_USD8500)	−1.25	0.37	−3.39	0.00
POP8500/1000000	0.002	0.00	4.68	0.00
LOG(INF85_00)	0.48	0.08	5.89	0.00
GRP_DUM1	−0.75	0.42	−1.78	0.08

R^2	0.51	Mean dependent var	3.56
Adjusted R^2	0.49	S.D. dependent var	2.23
S.E. of regression	1.59	Akaike info criterion	3.80
Sum squared resid	348.16	Schwarz criterion	3.93
Log likelihood	−267.89	F-statistic	28.67
Durbin–Watson stat	1.90	Prob(F-statistic)	0.00

Notes

1 Such as Lane and Milesi-Ferretti (2001) and Lane's contribution to this book.
2 It was Lucas (1990) who first raised this question; see Alfaro *et al.* (2003) for an empirical investigation.
3 See, for example, Obstfeld (1998) and Sinclair and Shu (2001).
4 We shall assume here that *y* is everywhere increasing and concave in *k* in the production function, that utility depends on consumption alone, displaying a positive and diminishing marginal utility of consumption, and that agents optimize over an infinite horizon.
5 Sinclair and Shu (2001) provide a recent review of the arguments for and against restrictions on capital movements in greater detail.
6 Various issues 1970–2001.
7 Figures available from the authors on request.

References

Alfaro, L., Kalemzi-Ozcan, S. and Volosoyvych, V. (2003), "Why doesn't capital flow from rich countries to poor countries? An empirical investigation", University of Houston, mimeo.
Bordo, M.D., Eichengreen, B. and Irwin, D.A. (1999), "Is globalization today really different than globalization a hundred years ago?", NBER Working Paper no. 7195.
Cardozo, E. and Goldfajn, I. (1998), "Capital flows to Brazil: the endogeneity of capital controls", IMF Working Paper no. 97/115.
Grossman, G.M. and Helpman, E. (1994), "Protection for sale", *American Economic Review*, 84: 833–850.
Johnston, J.B. and Ryan, C. (1994), "The impacts of capital movements on the private accounts of countries' balance of payments: empirical estimates and policy implications", IMF Working Paper no. 94/78.
Lane, P. and Milesi-Ferretti, G.M. (2001), "The external wealth of nations:

measures of foreign assets and liabilities for industrial and developing countries", *Journal of International Economics*, 55: 263–294.

Lucas, R.E. (1990), "Why doesn't capital flow from rich to poor countries?", *American Economic Review*, 80: 92–96.

Lucas, R.E. (1992), "On efficiency and distribution", *Economic Journal*, 102: 233–247.

Obstfeld, M. (1998), "The global capital market: Benefactor or menace?", *Journal of Economic Perspectives*, 12: 9–30.

Quinn, D. (1997), "The correlates of changes in international financial regulations", *American Political Science Review*, 91: 531–551.

Reinhart, C.M. and Smith, R.T. (2002), "Temporary controls on capital flows", *Journal of International Economics*, 57: 327–351.

Sinclair, P. (2004), "On creditors and debtors, and their rates of interest and exchange", University of Birmingham, mimeo.

Sinclair, P. and Shu Chang (2001), "International capital movements and the international dimension to financial crises", in Brealey, R.A., Goodhart, C., Healey, J. *et al.* (eds), *Financial Stability and Central Banks: A Global Perspective*, London: Routledge.

14 An empirical analysis of the "impossible trinity"

An East Asian perspective*

*Izumi Takagawa***

1 Introduction

A number of policy makers are faced with the dilemma of the three components – free capital mobility, exchange rate stability, and independent monetary policy. The macroeconomic models to deal with these conflicting problems were elaborated in the early 1960s by Robert Mundell (1963) and Marcus J. Fleming (1962). In the Mundell–Fleming conceptual framework, these three policy objectives cannot be achieved simultaneously. For instance, if a country deems it necessary to liberalise its capital market and stabilise the exchange rate, then monetary policy becomes useless to influence its economy. Alternatively, if a country desires to maintain free capital movements and pursue an independent monetary policy, it has to forego exchange rate stability. These situations where only two of three components are feasible are known as the so-called "impossible trinity."[1]

Whereas this classical theory has been widely believed to hold for the small open economies, some economists have pointed out that pre-crisis East Asian economies are exempt from the "impossible trinity." Reisen (1993) mentions that some countries in East Asia have had great success in achieving all three components of the trinity. His statement can be better understood by describing the economic situation which East Asian economies are confronted with prior to the Asian financial crisis.

East Asia had experienced high economic growth for a decade from the mid-1980s, which was sometimes called the "Asian miracle." This exceptionally high growth had come about partly due to massive capital inflows to this region as a whole that promoted a dramatic increase in investment. High growth attracted further capital inflows, which contributed to sharply improved income per capita. According to "the impossible trinity" theorem, the policy choice during periods of capital inflow surges is either exchange rate stability or independent monetary policy. In the pre-crisis period, however, it had been fairly evident that most East Asian currencies maintained *de facto* pegs against the US dollar and their interest rates remain at high levels, compared with those of industrial countries. This pre-crisis evidence in East Asia seems to violate the "impossible trinity."

The main purpose of this chapter is to investigate empirically whether the three elements of free capital movements, exchange rate stability, and independent monetary policy, had been mutually compatible as actually observed before the financial turmoil in Asia. The empirical analysis on the "impossible trinity" has been very limited although nearly forty years has passed since the Mundell–Fleming model was developed. As far as we know, Rose (1996) is the only available paper treating with the "impossible trinity" empirically. He employs a monetary model of exchange rate, allowing two different variants of the model: one with flexible prices and the other with sticky prices. This chapter is based mainly on his methodology, but the models are partially modified by allowing for the distinction between traded and non-traded goods. Whereas Rose's (1996) data set deals with the twenty-two OECD countries, we exploit a panel data for seven selective East Asian countries: Hong Kong, Indonesia, Malaysia, the Philippines, Singapore, South Korea, and Thailand.[2] Our empirical finding points to strong evidence that free capital mobility, exchange rate stability, and independent monetary policy are mutually compatible prior to the Asian financial crisis when our data set is applied. However, estimation results considering the effects of policy regime changes after the crisis show that the simultaneous achievement of the three goals becomes impossible and seem to support the validity of the "impossible trinity."

The remainder of the chapter is organised as follows. Section 2 provides brief overviews of the East Asian economies before the Asian financial crisis in terms of capital flows, exchange rate, and monetary policy. Section 3 presents theoretical framework and methodology used for our empirical analysis. Section 4 provides estimation results after discussing measurement issues related to capital mobility. Section 5 concludes with a summary of empirical findings.

2 Overview of pre-crisis East Asian economies: a perspective from the "impossible trinity"

This section describes pre-crisis East Asian experiences in the lights of capital flows, exchange rate, and monetary policy which are three elements of the trinity. At first, stylised facts regarding the nature of capital inflows in the region will be reviewed, which will be followed by a discussion of how monetary authorities had reacted in an environment of increasing capital inflows.

2.1 Capital flows

East Asia had experienced an unprecedented surge of capital inflows from the end of the 1980s through to early 1997. The massive capital inflows to this region had stimulated investments, resulting in prominent high economic growth.

Figure 14.1 plots the balance of payments in selective East Asian countries since 1990 onwards and disaggregates net capital flows into foreign direct investment, portfolio investment, and other investment. Each set of data is scaled by nominal GDP to facilitate comparison across economies. Among the seven countries, Malaysia, Thailand, and the Philippines are those of the largest recipients of capital flows in the 1990s. At their respective peaks, capital flows as a percentage of GDP exceeded 15 per cent in Malaysia, 13 per cent in both Thailand and the Philippines. Singapore is

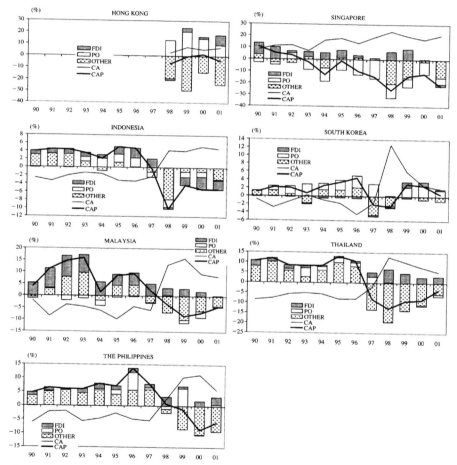

Figure 14.1 Balance of payments in selective East Asian countries (in per cent of GDP) (source: IMF, *International Financial Statistics*, Annual data).

Notes
1 All data are expressed as "net" and are scaled by nominal GDP.
2 FDI = foreign direct investment, PO = portfolio investment, OTHER = other investment, CA = current account, CAP = capital account.

the only country, which has experienced consistent net capital outflows even before the Asian financial crisis.

Looking at the three types of capital flows ("foreign direct investment,"[3] "portfolio investment,"[4] and "other investment"[5]), these compositions are different across countries. Malaysia received relatively large "foreign direct investments," compared with the other two components. Prior to the emergence of the Asian financial crisis in 1997, South Korea and Thailand, which were the nations severely affected by the crisis, had received the most capital inflows as "portfolio investment" and "other investment." These investments are considered to be susceptible to reverse in a very short time. The risk of flow-reversal may increase the volatility in exchange rates, interest rates, or assets prices.

The massive capital inflows in East Asia can be attributed to both *internal* and *external* factors. The factors that are *internal* to the recipient countries included the economic policies which East Asian economies had adopted such as trade and capital market liberalisation, and exchange rate stability (discussed below). Moreover, improved macroeconomic fundamentals through lower inflation and reductions in public sector deficits attracted capital inflows.

Contrastingly, some factors that were *external* to the recipient countries are considered as the long trend of the Japanese *yen* appreciation, the declining trend of interest rates in the industrialised nations, a slowdown of economic activity in the capital-exporting countries. Concretely, the *yen* appreciation had shifted the Japanese investment towards lower-cost areas in East Asia. In addition, relatively higher interest rates, in East Asia, than that of the US and recession in the US in the early 1990s had played a significant role to attract the capital inflows.

2.2 Exchange rate

Given a growing openness of the capital account, most monetary authorities had pursued exchange rate stability as a means of pegging the domestic currency to the US dollar with an extremely large weight.

Figure 14.2 depicts movements of nominal exchange rates of selective East Asian currencies vis-à-vis the US dollar in the 1990s. Until July 1997, exchange rate behaviour in these countries seems to be stable, but it dramatically changed after this period. According to the official IMF classification, exchange rate regimes in Hong Kong, Indonesia, Malaysia, Singapore, and South Korea were categorised as the *managed floating system* in the 1990s prior to the crisis. The exchange rate arrangement of the Philippines is classified as an *independent floating system* whereas that of Thailand is categorised as a *peg system as currency composites*. Broadly speaking, the monetary authorities in East Asian countries rarely adopted a *pure* floating prior to the crisis: they either fix, fix within a band, or intervene from time to time (thus, dirty float). The policy pursuing exchange

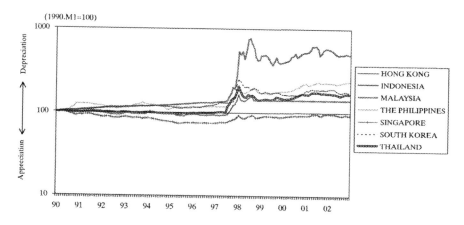

Figure 14.2 Nominal exchange rates of East Asian currencies against the US dollar (source: IMF, *International Financial Statistics*, Monthly data).

Notes
1 Nominal exchange rates are plotted in logarithm form.
2 Base year is January 1990 which is set as 100.

rate stability is widely thought to enhance macroeconomic stability, contributing to lower inflation. Central banks in East Asia had been afraid of the disadvantage arising from a *pure* float because massive capital inflows may induce appreciation of domestic currencies, which in turn may damage export sectors in the economy.

2.3 Monetary policy

One of the indicators of the conduct of independent monetary policy is to see whether interest rates in East Asia do not follow the cycle of US interest rate. Figure 14.3 plots the short-term interest rates in East Asian economies with the US in 1990 onwards. Prior to the Asian financial crisis, movements of East Asian interest rates had not followed that of the US interest rate except for Hong Kong. In most East Asian countries, domestic interest rates are higher than the US rate and the differences between them are persistent, even widening at times.

From a theoretical aspect, however, the problem may arise from inconsistency between free capital mobility, exchange rate stability, and independent monetary policy. Consider a country desiring to stabilise the exchange rate and keeping domestic interest rate relatively higher than the US rate. Given a growing openness of the capital account, investors can move their capital to the location where its interest rate is higher (all else equal). The monetary authorities faced appreciation of the domestic

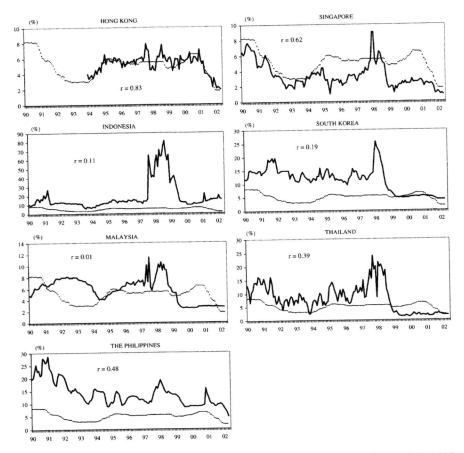

Figure 14.3 Nominal interest rates in selective East Asian countries and the US
(source: IMF, *International Financial Statistics*, Monthly data).

Notes
1 "Monthly market rates" are used in Hong Kong, Malaysia, South Korea and Thailand;
  "Call money rate" for Indonesia; "Treasury bill rate" for the Philippines; "Three month
  interbank rate" for Singapore; "Federal funds rate" for the US.
2 A solid line indicates short-term interest rate of each country while the dotted line represents that of the US.
3 "r" is the cross-correlation between two variables.

currency resulting from the surge of capital inflows. Then, it has to buy the
foreign currency that is flowing into the country. As a result, money supply
will increase and domestic interest rate will fall due to a rapid monetary
expansion.

Yet, judging from the East Asian experiences, the mechanism above
did not seem to work because their interest rates had remained high

before the Asian crisis. The question is "How did East Asian countries cope with these policy conflicts?" Reisen (1993) discusses that the Asian evidence clearly establishes "sterilised intervention" as an effective instrument to target both monetary base and exchange rates without recourse to capital controls. In fact, "sterilised intervention" has been well known as the most common policy response among pre-crisis East Asian countries such as Indonesia, Malaysia, the Philippines, South Korea, and Thailand in reaction to capital inflow surges.

"Sterilised intervention" is defined as the operation through which a rise in the net foreign assets is offset by a decrease in the net domestic assets. If the monetary authorities choose to sterilise, it is possible to limit increase in monetary growth despite a surge of capital inflows under the fixed exchange rate regime.[6] Thus, most East Asian countries could maintain domestic interest rates higher than the US rate via "sterilised intervention," as seen in Figure 14.3.[7]

3 Theoretical framework and methodology

The empirical analysis on the "impossible trinity" has been very limited so far. Rose (1996) is the only available known to the author that treats the "impossible trinity" empirically. He conducts the empirical analysis of the "impossible trinity" by employing the monetary approach to exchange rate determination, allowing two different variants of the model: one with flexible prices and the other with sticky prices. Based on his methodology, we modify these models by allowing for the distinction between traded and non-traded goods. In this section, we outline the theoretical underpinnings of our approach, which will be followed by the discussion of empirical strategy.

3.1 Flexible-price monetary model

The flexible-price monetary model was first developed by Frenkel (1976), which assumes that purchasing power parity (PPP) holds continuously. Whereas PPP implies that there exist only traded goods, our modified model allows for the distinction between traded and non-traded goods. The PPP in the logarithmic transformation takes the following form:

$$s_t = p_t^T - p_t^{T*} \tag{1}$$

where s denotes the nominal exchange rate measured in the domestic price of a unit of foreign exchange, p^T, p^{T*} are domestic and foreign price of traded goods, respectively. Then, let the aggregate price levels for both domestic and foreign countries be given as the weighted averages of the prices of traded goods and the prices of non-traded goods such that

$$p_t = \gamma p_t^N + (1 - \gamma)p_t^T, \ p_t^* = \gamma p_t^{N*} + (1 - \gamma)p_t^{T*} \tag{2}$$

where γ is the share of non-traded goods in the aggregate price level.[8]

A conventional way of deriving a monetary model of exchange rate starts with a structural money market equilibrium condition, expressed in logarithmic form as

$$m_t - p_t = \alpha y_t - \beta i_t + \mu_t \tag{3}$$

where m is the quantity of money demanded which is equal to exogenous money supply in the money market equilibrium, p denotes the price level, y denotes the real income, i denotes the nominal interest rate (in levels, not logarithms), and μ denotes a stationary shock to money demand. The parameters α and β are the income elasticity and the interest rate semi-elasticity of money demand, respectively. For simplicity, we assume that the same equation holds for the foreign country, allowing that domestic and foreign elasticities are equal. Combining equations above, the final equation of the monetary model of exchange rate can be obtained as

$$s_t = (m_t - m_t^*) - \alpha(y_t - y_t^*) + \beta(i_t - i_t^*) + \gamma(q_t - q_t^*) - (\mu_t - \mu_t^*) \tag{4}$$

where $q = p^T - p^N$ denotes the relative price between traded goods and non-traded goods. For simplicity, equation (4) can be written as

$$s_t = FUND_t^F \tag{5}$$

where $FUND_t^F \equiv (m_t - m_t^*) - \alpha(y_t - y_t^*) + \beta(i_t - i_t^*) + \gamma(q_t - q_t^*) - (\mu_t - \mu_t^*)$.

The term, $FUND$ measures the deviation of monetary fundamentals between domestic and foreign countries, that is, the monetary independence.

3.2 Sticky-price monetary model

The model described above imposes an assumption that PPP holds continuously and prices are perfectly flexible in both the short and long-run. In reality, however, prices seem to be sticky. In fact, empirical evidence shows that there are significant deviations from the PPP exchange rate in the short run. Based on this shortcoming of the flexible-price model, the sticky-price monetary model, which was first elaborated by Dornbusch (1976), relaxes the postulation of short-run PPP although the assumption that PPP holds in the long run is maintained. His model represents a major advance on the flexible-price monetary model, but it does not explicitly take into account "expectations formation mechanism." Frankel (1979) develops the model which combines the insights of Dournbusch's (1976) sticky-price monetary model with the inflationary expectation elements.

The sticky-price monetary model postulates that the expected change in exchange rate is composed of both a deviation of the current rate from the long-run equilibrium rate and the expected inflation differentials in traded goods.

$$\Delta s_{t+1}^e = -\theta(s_t - \bar{s}_t) + (\Delta p_{t+1}^{eT} - \Delta p_{t+1}^{e*T}) \tag{6}$$

where Δs_{t+1}^e is the expected change in the domestic exchange rate and θ is the rate of reversion of the current exchange rate to its long-run equilibrium value, $\bar{s}_t$. Δp_{t+1}^{eT} and Δp_{t+1}^{e*T} are the expected inflation rates of traded goods in domestic and foreign countries, respectively. Equation (6) indicates that in the short run, the spot exchange rate, s, is expected to drift to its long-run equilibrium value of $\bar{s}_t$ at a rate θ. In the long run, the expected change in domestic exchange rate is equal to the difference of the expected inflation rate of domestic and foreign traded goods. By combining equation (6) and the uncovered interest parity condition $(\Delta s_{t+1}^e = i_t - i_t^*)$, we obtain,

$$s_t - \bar{s}_t = -\frac{1}{\theta}[(i_t - i_t^*) - (\Delta p_{t+1}^{eT} - \Delta p_{t+1}^{e*T})] \tag{7}$$

Equation (7) shows that nominal interest rate differentials are equal to the differences of expected rate of inflation in traded goods in the long run. In order to derive the short-run sticky-price monetary model, we first define the long-run sticky-price model by substituting $i_t - i_t^* = \Delta p_{t+1}^{eT} - \Delta p_{t+1}^{e*T}$ into equation (4).

$$\bar{s}_t = (m_t - m_t^*) - \alpha(y_t - y_t^*) + \beta(\Delta p_{t+1}^{eT} - \Delta p_{t+1}^{e*T}) + \gamma(q_t - q_t^*) - (\mu_t - \mu_t^*) \tag{8}$$

Then, we obtain the solution for the short-run sticky-price model by combining equations (7) and (8) as follows:

$$s_t = (m_t - m_t^*) - \alpha(y_t - y_t^*) - \frac{1}{\theta}(i_t - i_t^*) + \left(\beta + \frac{1}{\theta}\right)(\Delta p_{t+1}^{eT} - \Delta p_{t+1}^{e*T})$$
$$+ \gamma(q_t - q_t^*) - (\mu_t - \mu_t^*) \tag{9}$$

Again, for simplicity, equation (9) can be written as

$$s_t = FUND_t^S \tag{10}$$

where $FUND_t^S \equiv (m_t - m_t^*) - \alpha(y_t - y_t^*) - \frac{1}{\theta}(i_t - i_t^*) + (\beta + \frac{1}{\theta})(\Delta p_{t+1}^{eT} - \Delta p_{t+1}^{e*T})$
$+ \gamma(q_t - q_t^*) - (\mu_t - \mu_t^*)$

3.3 Empirical strategy

We exploit a panel data covering seven East Asian countries: Hong Kong, Indonesia, Malaysia, the Philippines, Singapore, South Korea, and Thailand to examine whether free capital mobility, exchange rate stability, and independent monetary policy had been mutually compatible before the Asian financial crisis. In order to test this hypothesis by using our data set, it is necessary to modify the flexible- and sticky-price monetary models obtained above.

Following Rose's (1996) transformation of equations, we take the first differences of equations (5) and (10), then by moving from first to second moments.

$$\sigma(\Delta s)_t = \sigma(\Delta FUND^j)_t \tag{11}$$

where $j = F, S$ for the flexible and sticky-price types of models, respectively. The main purpose of this chapter is to test quantitatively whether the three elements of the trinity are mutually compatible in pre-crisis East Asia. To do this, two variables are augmented to equation (11); one is the capital mobility index (CAP) measuring the degree of capital movements, and the other is an interactive term ($CAP^*[\sigma(\Delta FUND^j)]$) measuring the interaction between capital mobility and (the volatility of) monetary independence although these additional regressors are not implied by economic theory. These two regressors can capture the impacts that the degree of capital mobility has on exchange rate volatility. The final estimating equation will be:

$$\sigma(\Delta s)_{it} = \Sigma_i C_i + \delta_1 [\sigma(\Delta FUND^j)]_{it} + \delta_2 CAP_{it} + \delta_3 \{CAP_{it}^*[\sigma(\Delta FUND^j)]_{it}\} + \epsilon_{it} \tag{12}$$

where subscript, i and t represent each country and time period, respectively. The left-hand side of equation (12) indicates conditional exchange rate volatility that is calculated as non-overlapping *annual* standard deviations of the first difference of the *quarterly* natural logarithm of the nominal exchange rate against the US dollar. On the right-hand side, $\Sigma_i C_i$ are country-specific fixed effects, letting the intercepts differ, but restricting the slope coefficients and the variances to be the same across countries. $\sigma(\Delta FUND^j)$ is defined as the conditional volatility of monetary fundamentals which is calculated in the same way as the exchange rate volatility. CAP is an index which measures the degree of capital mobility, taking a value of one if capital is perfectly mobile and a value of zero if capital is completely immobile.

The most important term of equation (12) is $CAP^*[\sigma(\Delta FUND^j)]$ which represents the compatibility with capital mobility and the volatility of monetary fundamentals. A positive value for δ_3 indicates that higher (less) volatility in monetary fundamentals leads to an increase (decrease) in the volatility of exchange rate, given the extent of capital mobility. Hence, we expect a positive sign for δ_3 if the "impossible trinity" holds. On the other hand, a negative sign for δ_3 would show that higher volatility in monetary fundamentals tends to less volatility of exchange rate, given the extent of capital mobility. As mentioned above, there was strong evidence that three components of trinity had been mutually compatible in pre-crisis East Asian economies. Therefore, we foresee the negative value of δ_3 in equation (12) when the pre-crisis data are applied.

To proceed, we need to define some parameter values, that is, α, β, γ for both flexible- and sticky-price models and $1/\theta$ only for the latter. We have used relatively uncontroversial values taken from the existing literature. The reason why we calibrate the parameters in monetary models relates to data availability difficulties for some East Asian economies. Rather than employing unstable parameter values, we believe that calibrated parameters carry reasonable values. For α and β, we follow Rose's (1996) values taken from his previous literature.[9] He set the income elasticity of money demand, α, to be one while he chose two alternative values, 0.1 and 0.5 for the interest elasticity, β. The term of relative price differentials, γ, is included to allow for the distinction between traded and non-traded goods which is not included in Rose's (1996) type of specification. This coefficient represents the share of non-traded goods in the price level. We choose 0.5 and 0.8 as two alternative measures of γ.

Empirical analysis also requires the parameter value for $1/\theta$ for sticky-price monetary model. Chinn (1998) estimates the same equation as equation (12) using Johansen co-integration techniques for five East Asian countries: Indonesia, Singapore, South Korea, Taiwan, and Thailand. His estimates of the coefficients of interest rate differential and expected inflation rate differentials vary considerably across countries.[10] We follow the value of -1.4 for the parameter on interest rate differentials, $-1/\theta$, which was obtained as the parameter for Taiwan in Chinn's (1998) analysis. In this case, the rate of reversion of the price level to the long-run value, θ, is approximately 0.7 which seems to be a reasonable value. We choose 1.5 and 1.9 as the parameter on expected inflation differentials, $\beta + 1/\theta$, since β is set to be 0.1 and 0.5 above.

In addition, we assume that the expected rates of inflation in domestic and foreign traded goods, Δp_{t+1}^{eT} and Δp_{t+1}^{e*T}, are equal to those in aggregate price, Δp_{t+1}^{e} and Δp_{t+1}^{e*}, for simplicity. Last terms of equations (4) and (9) represent disturbances, $(\mu_t - \mu_t^*)$. For simplicity, we set the $(\mu_t - \mu_t^*)$ term equal to its expected value of zero as seen in Rose's (1996) assumption.[11]

4 Empirical evidence

In this section, we first explain our data set. Next, we proceed to discuss measurement issues on capital mobility and then define four indices of capital mobility employed in our empirical analysis. Third, we present the pre-crisis estimation results of equation (12) for both flexible- and sticky-price models and assess whether the co-existence of free capital mobility, exchange rate stability, and independent monetary policy are possible. The rest of this section examines whether a number of changes in the design and conduct of both exchange rate and monetary policies resulting from the Asian financial crisis will affect the pre-crisis results obtained.

4.1 Data description

The macroeconomic data used in this chapter come mostly from the IMF's *International Financial Statistics* (IFS), supplemented by the CEIC database. As for the capital mobility index, the data are taken from the IMF's *Annual Report on Exchange Arrangements and Exchange Restrictions* (hereafter, AREAER). The seven East Asian economies under our consideration are Hong Kong, Indonesia, Malaysia, the Philippines, Singapore, South Korea, and Thailand. The United States, which is considered the most influential country for Asian economies, is chosen as the home country.

The raw macroeconomic data are at the quarterly frequency and the data set covers the period from 1977 onwards. Starting and ending periods of sample differ among countries due to their data availability, thus an unbalanced panel is employed to estimate equation (12). Our data set includes nominal exchange rate, money supply, real income, nominal interest rate, relative price, expected rate of inflation, and capital mobility indices. More details in the source and definition of data is given in Appendix A. Capital control indices used in our analysis are defined in the following sub-section.

Moreover, two variables used in equation (12), $\sigma(\Delta s_t)$ and $\sigma(\Delta FUND_t^j)$ are defined in second moments. As explained above, they are calculated as non-overlapping *annual* standard deviations of the first difference of the *quarterly* natural logarithm of the nominal exchange rate against the US dollar. It is widely known that most macroeconomic data becomes stationary with finite second-moments. Both the Augmented Dickey–Fuller (ADF) test and the Phillips–Perron (PP) test were conducted to check for stationarity of both variables. Our results confirm that they are all stationary.

4.2 Measures of capital controls

Measuring the degree of capital mobility is notoriously difficult and challenging since it is subject to considerable debate. Various measures of capital mobility experimented in the previous literature are introduced in Box 14.1.

Box 14.1 Measurement issues on capital controls

Pioneering work to assess the degree of capital mobility is by Feldstein and Horioka (1980) who investigated the correlation between savings and investment. They argue that with perfect capital mobility, the savings and investment should be uncorrelated in a specific country. Using the data from 1960 to 1974 for 16 OECD countries, they found that savings and investment ratios were highly positively correlated. Their result seems to be inconsistent with the reality in the process of increasing mobility of capital. Therefore, this paradox is called the "Feldstein and Horioka puzzle." This puzzle has been replicated in a number of subsequent studies using different samples and different empirical techniques (see, for example, Frankel (1991), Montiel (1994)).

Others have used alternative measures such as onshore–offshore interest rate differentials, the size of the black market exchange rate premium and deviations from covered interest rate parity (see Giavazzi and Pagano (1988), Dooley and Isard (1980), Ito (1983)).

Many economists try to build indices on capital account liberalisation based on the data published by the IMF in its *Annual Report on Exchange Arrangements and Exchange Restrictions* (AREAER). Alesina *et al.* (1994) is probably the first work to employ a concept of capital controls defined in AREAER. The important shortcomings based on the IMF's indices are that they do not take into account different intensities of capital restrictions and do not distinguish which types of restriction are imposed. Montiel and Reinhart (1999) have constructed an index on the intensity of capital control by combining the IMF's AREAER and country-specific information. Quinn (1997) has attempted to construct an indicator using the narrative information contained in the IMF's AREAER.

Moreover, other studies have focused on controls of international sales and purchases of equities in recent years. For instance, Edison and Warnock (2001) construct a measure that is based on restrictions of foreign ownership of domestic equities, using the ratio of the market capitalisation of the country's Global index to the Investable index that is compiled by the International Finance Corporation (IFC) in their Emerging Market Database that is now maintained by Standard and Poor's.

We define capital mobility indices used in our empirical analysis. Four different indices are considered as measures of degree of capital mobility. We label them *CAP*1 to *CAP*4. All indices are based on the AREAER. This report, which has been issued since 1950, provides a description of the exchange rate system and capital restrictions in each IMF member country. Since the 1967 issue, the AREAER has included a summary table that lists whether each country had various restrictions on exchange rates and payments for capital transactions. The data presented in this table is used to construct dummy variables, taking the value of one when a restriction is in place for a given year in a given country, and zero otherwise.[12] We define four capital mobility indices used in our analysis below.

*CAP*1 is partly based on Glick and Hutchison's (2000) measure. Starting with the 1997 AREAER, the category "Restrictions on payments for capital transaction," used in the former classification is broken into eleven separate categories that can make it easier to distinguish between controls on capital inflows and outflows.[13] These changes in categorisation create problems for researchers seeking to create long time series for capital account liberalisation. In order to connect two different categories of data, we follow Glick and Hutchison's (2000) method in which they define the capital account to be restricted if five or more of the AREAER subcategories of capital account restrictions *and* "Financial credit" is one of the categories restricted. Using this *CAP1* allows to expand the sample period even after the Asian financial crisis.

*CAP*2 is constructed by the simple average of two dummy variables for "Restrictions on payments for capital transaction" and "Separate exchange rates for some or all capital transactions and/or all invisibles" in the AREAER categories. This measure of capital controls is followed by Loungani *et al.* (2000). Yet, this enables us to estimate equations until the period 1996 just before the format for new categories of AREAER has started.

We follow Bartolini and Drazen's (1997) choices of categories on capital controls for creating the index of *CAP*3. They take up three dummy variables, each taking a value of one when a country was classified in the survey as "Restricting payments for capital restrictions," "Multiple exchange rates," or "Restricting repatriation of export proceeds" in a given year, respectively. We add up over countries and then normalise by the number of categories (three) for each country. This index takes a value of one if all three types of restriction are in place and a value of zero if no such restriction is imposed.

*CAP*4 is a measure created by using eleven categories in the old classification.[14] We sum up eleven dummy variables for each country for a given year and then normalise by the number of dummy variables, taking a value of one if all restrictions are imposed and a value of zero if no such restriction is imposed.

An important point is that all capital mobility indices explained above, take a value between one and zero, with the strongest restriction on capital at a value of one. To make it easy to interpret the coefficient δ_3 in equation (12), however, we reverse the measures of these indices, with one representing perfect capital mobility and with zero meaning complete capital immobility. Figure 14.4 plots four types of capital mobility indices.

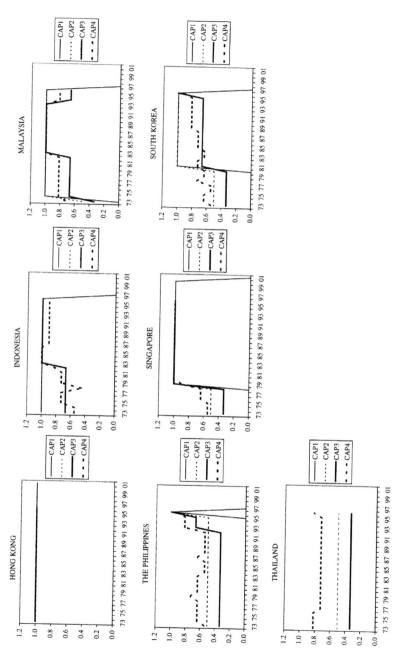

Figure 14.4 Various measures of capital mobility (source: IMF, *Annual Report on Exchange Arrangements and Exchange Restrictions* (AREAER), Annual data).

Note
All capital mobility indices take a value between one and zero, meaning less restriction on capital towards a value of one and stronger restriction on capital towards a value of zero.

4.3 Estimation results

Estimated results of equation (12) are reported in Table 14.1 (for flexible-price monetary model) and Table 14.2 (for sticky-price monetary model). All estimation periods cover 1977 to 1996, just before the Asian financial crisis.

Flexible-price monetary models when the indices from $CAP1$ and $CAP4$ are used, show that the coefficients of $\sigma(\Delta FUND_t^f)$, δ_1, indicating the divergence of monetary fundamentals between the US and local country, are of the expected positive sign and moderately significant, irrespective of the values of β and γ. The terms of capital mobility, δ_2, are never significant. Moreover, the interaction terms between capital mobility and monetary fundamentals, δ_3, that are added to examine whether the effect of capital mobility on exchange rate volatility depends on the volatility of monetary fundamentals, indicate that they are negative and significant in most cases. Their t-values are between -0.7 and -2.4, depending both on the particular measure of capital mobility used and on the scenario of β, γ adopted. This interactive term tends to be more significant when the interest rate semi-elasticity, β, is 0.5 than 0.1.

The important shortcoming of flexible-price monetary model is that its assumption contradicts the key assumption underlying the Mundell–Fleming open-economy model. The former assumes that PPP holds continuously whereas the latter postulates that the price level is fixed. It seems to be more appropriate to look at sticky-price monetary models in the context of the Mundell–Fleming framework.

Table 14.2 shows the estimation results of sticky-price monetary model as an alternative methodology. As seen in flexible-price monetary models, the coefficients on $\sigma(\Delta FUND_t^s)$, δ_1 are always positive and significant. Thus, the rise in the divergence of monetary fundamentals between the US and local country tends to increase the volatility of exchange rate, which is consistent with economic theory. As for the effect of capital mobility on exchange rate, the coefficients on $CAP1$ and $CAP2$ are positive and moderately significant, irrespective of the values of $\beta + 1/\theta$ and γ. The most important term in our analysis, δ_3, remains negative and significant and is more negatively significant when the coefficient on the expected inflation rate differentials, $\beta + 1/\theta$, is set to be 1.9. Furthermore, the coefficients, δ_3 tend to be more significant when sticky-price monetary model is used.

To sum up, estimation results obtained from two alternative methodologies show strong evidence of a negative relationship between exchange rate volatility and the interactive term, indicating the mutual compatibility of free capital mobility, exchange rate stability, and independent monetary policy.[15] They appear to support the argument that pre-crisis East Asian countries had experienced as explained in section 2. In other words, our finding may imply that East Asian economies had violated the so-called "impossible trinity" before the currency crisis occurred in this region.

Table 14.1 Estimation results of flexible-price monetary model

	β=0.1							β=0.5						
	γ=0.5			γ=0.8				γ=0.5			γ=0.8		
	Coefficient	t-value	Adj R²	Coefficient	t-value	Adj R²		Coefficient	t-value	Adj R²	Coefficient	t-value	Adj R²
$FUND^F$	0.177	1.957	0.180	0.152	1.879	0.210		0.191	2.120	0.187	0.164	2.041	0.216
CAP1	0.003	0.337		0.001	0.118			0.004	0.408		0.002	0.178	
$CAP1*FUND^F$	−0.172	−1.657		−0.140	−1.496			−0.187	−1.805		−0.152	−1.638	
$FUND^F$	0.349	1.858	0.180	0.292	1.733	0.210		0.378	2.018	0.187	0.316	1.889	0.216
CAP2	0.007	0.337		0.002	0.118			0.008	0.408		0.003	0.178	
$CAP2*FUND^F$	−0.345	−1.657		−0.280	−1.496			−0.373	−1.805		−0.304	−1.638	
$FUND^F$	0.260	2.135	0.200	0.220	1.985	0.210		0.274	2.267	0.208	0.232	2.116	0.215
CAP3	−0.002	−0.121		−0.005	−0.359			−0.001	−0.070		−0.004	−0.314	
$CAP3*FUND^F$	−0.298	−2.266		−0.242	−1.949			−0.313	−2.405		−0.254	−2.075	
$FUND^F$	0.264	1.008	0.239	0.245	1.109	0.276		0.322	1.242	0.228	0.290	1.336	0.266
CAP4	−0.022	−0.842		−0.023	−0.965			−0.018	−0.679		−0.020	−0.834	
$CAP4*FUND^F$	−0.234	−0.723		−0.211	−0.799			−0.312	−0.974		−0.270	−1.043	

Notes
1 All estimation periods are from 1977 to 1996. 2 β: Interest semi-elasticity of money demand. γ: Relative price elasticity of money demand.

	β=0.1							β=0.5						
	γ=0.5			γ=0.8				γ=0.5			γ=0.8		
	Coefficient	t-value	Adj R²	Coefficient	t-value	Adj R²		Coefficient	t-value	Adj R²	Coefficient	t-value	Adj R²
$FUND^F$	0.113	0.908	0.549	0.127	1.110	0.566		0.115	0.922	0.546	0.129	1.125	0.564
CAP1	−0.069	−5.588		−0.067	−5.642			−0.069	−5.535		−0.067	−5.594	
$CAP1*FUND^F$	0.087	0.548		0.054	0.367			0.079	0.497		0.046	0.315	

Note
Estimation periods are from 1977 to 2000.

Table 14.2 Estimation results of sticky-price monetary model

| | β+1/θ=1.5 | | | | | | β+1/θ=1.9 | | | | | |
| | γ=0.5 | | | γ=0.8 | | | γ=0.5 | | | γ=0.8 | | |
	Coefficient	t-value	Adj R²	Coefficient	t-value	Adj R²	Coefficient	t-value	Adj R²	Coefficient	t-value	Adj R²
$FUND^s$	0.330	4.447	0.307	0.282	4.011	0.314	0.314	4.805	0.334	0.278	4.412	0.342
CAP1	0.013	1.585		0.007	0.873		0.013	1.677		0.009	1.113	
$CAP1*FUND^s$	-0.287	-3.595		-0.206	-2.537		-0.275	-3.890		-0.215	-3.057	
$FUND^s$	0.617	4.076	0.307	0.487	3.333	0.314	0.589	4.414	0.334	0.493	3.797	0.342
CAP2	0.013	1.585		0.015	0.873		0.027	1.677		0.018	1.113	
$CAP2*FUND^s$	-0.573	-3.595		-0.411	-2.537		-0.551	-3.890		-0.430	-3.057	
$FUND^s$	0.417	4.087	0.276	0.355	3.620	0.271	0.400	4.365	0.310	0.349	3.924	0.311
CAP3	0.012	0.848		0.006	0.461		0.013	0.937		0.008	0.571	
$CAP3*FUND^s$	-0.401	-3.599		-0.325	-2.859		-0.372	-3.788		-0.304	-3.046	
$FUND^s$	0.538	3.190	0.305	0.404	2.312	0.324	0.542	3.630	0.342	0.447	3.007	0.360
CAP4	-0.001	-0.040		-0.012	-0.551		-0.003	-0.169		-0.005	-0.240	
$CAP4*FUND^s$	-0.494	-2.717		-0.316	-1.544		-0.503	-3.127		-0.377	-2.287	

Notes
1 All estimation periods are from 1977 to 1996. 2 β: Interest semi-elasticity of money demand. γ: Relative price elasticity of money demand. θ: Rate of reversion of current exchange rate to its long-run value.

| | β+1/θ=1.5 | | | | | | β+1/θ=1.9 | | | | | |
| | γ=0.5 | | | γ=0.8 | | | γ=0.5 | | | γ=0.8 | | |
	Coefficient	t-value	Adj R²	Coefficient	t-value	Adj R²	Coefficient	t-value	Adj R²	Coefficient	t-value	Adj R²
$FUND^s$	0.159	1.453	0.534	0.162	1.525	0.540	0.155	1.450	0.510	0.158	1.504	0.515
CAP1	-0.060	-4.985		-0.060	-4.976		-0.058	-4.714		-0.058	-4.705	
$CAP1*FUND^s$	-0.047	-0.370		-0.054	-0.441		-0.074	-0.619		-0.078	-0.660	

Note
Estimation periods are from 1977 to 2000.

4.4 Analysis after the crisis

We investigate whether policy regime changes resulting from the Asian financial crisis will alter the pre-crisis results obtained above.

Since the currency crisis that erupted in Thailand in July 1997 which subsequently spread to other newly-industrialised Asian economies, a number of these Asian central banks have sought to formulate new policy objectives. Below, we succinctly overview the post-crisis East Asia in terms of three elements of the trinity – capital flows, exchange rate, and monetary policy.

Capital inflows, which had been the driving force of economic growth since the mid-1980s, abruptly turned into capital outflows during the crisis. As Figure 14.1 indicates, post-crisis, our selected countries have all experienced considerable capital outflows of "other investment." This means that they had depended heavily on short-term funds such as bank loans to finance current account deficits. There is increasing recognition that excess build-up of short-term debt triggered the crisis. Once the crisis had started, Thailand and Indonesia imposed the restrictions on capital outflows. Moreover, the Philippines took a number of successive measures to tighten certain capital controls from mid-1997.[16] The Malaysian authority imposed a number of administrative capital control measures in September 1998 to contain the outflow of capital by eliminating the offshore *ringgit* market and to stabilise short-term capital inflows.[17]

In retrospect, the Asian crisis has represented a watershed in exchange rate and monetary policy making. Broadly speaking, the policy goal in this region has changed from *exchange rate stability* towards *price stability*.

Looking at the exchange rate behaviour at each country level (Figure 14.2), the Indonesian *rupiah*, the South Korean *won*, the Philippine *peso*, and the Thai *baht* moved from hard pegs towards greater floating exchange rate post-crisis. On the other hand, the Hong Kong *dollar* and the Malaysia *ringgit* are cases where fix-rate or quasi-fixed-rate regimes were retained or even adopted after the crisis.[18] Singapore has retained a multi-currency peg (the currency basket) with unannounced and adjustable bands to stabilise the effective exchange rate.

Countries which abandoned exchange rate stability needed to establish an alternative nominal anchor to retain credibility. Indeed, the move towards the flexible exchange rate has enabled the monetary authorities to regain an increased degree of autonomy in the management of monetary policy. Against this background, inflation targeting such as those adopted in several industrial countries since the early 1990s are likely to receive increasing attention as an appropriate goals of monetary policy. Thailand, South Korea, and Indonesia among nations severely affected by the crisis have moved towards the inflation targeting as a means of price stability. The Bank of Korea has adopted explicit inflation targeting with the support of the IMF since September 1998. Indonesia announced its intention to move to inflation targeting in 2000, but has yet to implement this. In Thailand, where the crisis initially occurred, its central bank has adopted an inflation targeting policy in May 2000 as the main framework for the conduct and implementation of monetary policy, with an increasing emphasis, however, on avoiding exchange rate instability after 2001.

We now move to investigate how the policy regime changes resulting from the Asian financial crisis will affect our pre-crisis results that free capital mobility, exchange rate stability, and independent monetary policy are mutually compatible. Unfortunately, the data after the crisis is very limited, and which does not allow any stability tests. In order to test the above hypothesis, we extend the sample period up to 2000 and examine how the coefficients, δ_3, in equation (12), change. Among our four available capital mobility indices, $CAP1$, defined by Glick and Hutchison (2000), is the only index which enables us to expand the sample period of estimation until 2000.

The bottom tables of Tables 14.1 and 14.2 show the estimation results for flexible- and sticky-price monetary models, respectively. The noteworthy point in common between two alternative models is that the coefficient of $CAP1*[\sigma(\Delta FUND^j)]$ becomes insignificant when we extend the period to the end of 2000. These results lead us to the conclusion that there is a structural change of policy regimes in East Asia before and after the crisis and that the simultaneous achievement of three goals – free capital mobility, exchange rate stability, and independent monetary policy – becomes impossible after the crisis.

5 Conclusion

In this chapter, we have empirically investigated the policy trade-off of free capital mobility, exchange rate stability, and independent monetary policy in East Asia. According to the Mundell–Fleming model, these three goals cannot be achieved at the same time. Although the "impossible trinity" proposition is widely taken for granted, our finding, however, shows strong evidence that they had been mutually feasible prior to the Asian financial crisis. The results appear to be plausible considering the economic situation that the pre-crisis East Asia had experienced. On the other hand, our results considering the effects of policy regime changes after the crisis support a structural change of policy regimes and suggest that the simultaneous achievement of three goals becomes impossible. What do our results imply?

One possible interpretation is that the co-existence of free capital mobility, exchange rate stability, and independent monetary policy is possible in the short run, but not in the long run. Most East Asia countries had left some scope for independent monetary policy through a sterilised intervention. As Kwack (2001) argues,[19] however, such a sterilised intervention is not sustainable over the long time. As a result, East Asian countries severely affected by the crisis have to abandon exchange rate stability while retaining capital account openness and independent monetary policy. What happened during the Asian currency crisis seems to support the validity of the "impossible trinity."

As with many econometric investigations, on the other hand, the results should be interpreted with some caution, given the shortcomings of methodology used and the special difficulty associated with measuring capital mobility. First, our analytical technique appears to be disputable in the sense that PPP is valid in the short-run Mundell–Fleming model. Whereas flexible-price monetary model of exchange rate is built on the assumption that PPP holds continuously, sticky-price model postulates that prices are sluggish in the short run, but PPP holds in the long run. These models contradict the assumption of the Mundell–Fleming model. Apart from Rose's (1996) methodology, however, there is no alternative method to test the "impossible trinity" due to the lack of empirical research in this area. Second, our results depend on assumed values for parameters taken from the previous literatures. Although we choose reasonable values for them, they are not country-specific and different calibrations might lead to different conclusions. Third, as discussed above, measurement of capital mobility is a very controversial issue. There is no definitive and fully satisfactory measure on capital mobility although a number of literatures have attempted to measure true capital mobility. Despite its disadvantage of our models, we believe that our empirical analysis can provide useful insights as to the relationship between capital account freedom, exchange rate stability, and independent monetary policy.

East Asia has been truly facing the problems of policy balances because of the need for more capital to develop their economies, stability of exchange rate to promote exports, as well as monetary independence for domestic macroeconomic stabilisation. While the appropriate monetary regime choice for a country depends on its development stage and underlying circumstance, the experience from the Asian financial crisis appears to give an important lesson to monetary policy makers in small open economies about the mutual incompatibility to maintain an open capital account, exchange rate stability, and independent monetary policy.

Appendix: Source and definition of data

Data	Source	Definition
Exchange rate	IFS (line rf)	Period averages of nominal exchange rate in US dollar/national currency unit, quarterly basis.
Money supply	IFS (line 34)	Narrow money (M1), quarterly basis. Natural logarithm of money indices expressed on the base 1995 = 100.
Real income	CEIC	Real GDP index, quarterly basis. Real GDP index is based on the real GDP data and expressed on the base 1995 = 100.
Nominal interest rate	IFS (line 60b)	Short-term money market rate, quarterly basis. For the Philippines, *Treasury bill rate* is used (line 60c). Nominal interest rates are divided by 100.
Relative price	IFS (WPI: line 63) (CPI: line 64)	WPI for traded goods and CPI for non-traded goods (both are on quarterly basis, 1995 = 100). Relative prices between traded and non-traded goods are defined as natural logarithm of (WPI/CPI).
Expected inflation rate	IFS (line 64)	Estimate country-specific fitted linear regressions of the appropriate variable on an information set consisting of current and lagged values of prices, interest rates, real income, and money supply.
Capital mobility index	AREAER	Annual basis.
*CAP*1		Combines the old and new classifications of AREAER. Before 1996, "Restrictions on payments for capital transaction" is used in the former classification of AREAER. After 1997, defines the capital account to be restricted if five or more of the sub-categories of capital restrictions *and* "Financial credit" is one of the categories is restricted.
*CAP*2		Constructed by the simple average of two dummy variables for "Restrictions on payments for capital transaction" and "Separate exchange rates for some or all capital transactions and/or all invisibles."
*CAP*3		Adds up three dummy variables for "Restricting payments for capital restrictions," "Multiple exchange rates," and "Restricting repatriation of export proceeds" and then normalised by the number of categories (three) for each country in a given year.
*CAP*4		Constructed by the simple average of restrictions on eleven sub-categories in the capital account (see endnote 14).

Notes

* This paper was presented to the Conference on International Capital Movements, held at the Centre for Central Banking Studies, Bank of England, 30 August 2002.
** The author is highly indebted to Professor Peter Sinclair, Christoph Thoenissen, and Dan Huynh for their invaluable comments, support, and technical guidance, workshop participants for very helpful suggestions, and all CCBS staff for their generous assistance. Any remaining errors are solely the author's, as are the opinions expressed, which should be ascribed neither to Bank of Japan nor to Research and Statistics Department.
1 Several authors express the same reality in different ways: "unholy trinity," "the impossible theorem," "the inconsistent trinity," "the incompatible trinity," "open-economy trilemma," among others.
2 China and Taiwan should be included, but they are not because of limited data availability.
3 "Foreign direct investment" includes equity capital, reinvested earnings, other capital, and financial derivatives associated with various intercompany transactions between affiliated enterprises.
4 "Portfolio investment" includes transactions with nonresidents in financial securities of any maturity such as corporate securities, bonds, notes, and money market instruments.
5 "Other investment" covers transactions in currency and deposits, loans, and trade credits.
6 See Frankel (1994) for detailed analysis.
7 It is well known that "sterilised intervention" is not sustainable over the long period. Kwack (2001) argues that sterilisation substitutes foreign exchange reserve assets with low rates of interest for domestic assets with high rates of interest rates. Thus, when sterilisation is undertaken, it creates a financing burden, which is called the cost of sterilisation or quasi-fiscal cost of sterilisation.
8 This assumes a Cobb–Douglas utility for a representative consumer.
9 See Flood and Rose (1995).
10 Chinn's (1998) estimation results show that coefficients on interest rates are statistically significant for Indonesia (-0.343), Singapore (-11.921), and Taiwan (-1.417). The coefficient on it for Taiwan is statistically significant even at the 1 per cent significance level.
11 Rose (1996) also used the alternative technique to estimate the residual term, $(\mu_t - \mu_t^*)$. He directly estimated it from the money demand equation.
12 An important limitation of this IMF-based index is that they do not allow one to measure the intensity of capital restrictions and to differentiate across types of restrictions. It is however, difficult to find such data that are internationally comparable across developing countries for a sufficiently long period of time. With these caveats in mind, the IMF's dummy variable based measure can be seen as a proxy for the intensity of controls to some extent.
13 The eleven categories under capital restrictions in new classification are controls on: (1) Capital market securities, (2) Money market instruments, (3) Collective investment securities, (4) Derivatives and other instruments, (5) Commercial credits, (6) Financial credits, (7) Guarantees, sureties, and financial backup facilities, (8) Direct investment, (9) Liquidation of direct investment, (10) Real estate transactions, and (11) Personal capital movements.
14 The eleven categories in old classification are: (1) Special rate(s) for some or all capital transactions and/or some or all invisibles, (2) Import rate(s) different from export rate(s), (3) More than one rate for imports, (4) More than one rate

for exports, (5) Restrictions exist on payments in respect of current transactions, (6) Restrictions exist on payments in respect of capital transactions, (7) Bilateral payments arrangements with members, (8) Bilateral payments arrangements with nonmembers, (9) Import surcharges, (10) Advance import deposits, and (11) Surrender of export proceeds required.

15 The possible reason to reach the same conclusion despite using two different models is that the calibrated value for the reversion rate, θ in equation (6) may be large. This means that the reversion rate is so high that the expected exchange rate quickly returns to its long-run value.

16 See IMF (1999) Chapter 6 in detail.

17 See IMF (2000) in detail.

18 Hong Kong has employed a currency board system that commits to a fixed link since 1983 to the US dollar. Bank Negara Malaysia adopted a fixed exchange rate regime since September 1998.

19 Kwach (2001) discusses that the longer the sterilisation operation continues the higher the cost. The high cost makes it difficult for sterilisation policy to last over a long period.

References

Alesina, Alberto, Grilli, Vittorio and Milesi-Ferretti, Gian Maria (1994), "The political economy of capital controls," in Leidermand, Leonardo and Razin, Assaf (eds), *Capital Mobility: The Impact on Consumption, Investment, and Growth*, Cambridge: Cambridge University Press, pp. 289–328.

Bartolini, L. and Drazen, Allan (1997), "When liberal policies reflect external shocks: What do we learn?," *Journal of International Economics*, 42: 249–273.

Chinn, M.D. (1998), "On the won and other East Asian currencies," NBER Working Paper no. 6671.

Dooley, Michael P. and Isard, Peter (1980), "Capital controls, political risk, and deviations from interest-rate parity," *Journal of Political Economy*, 88: 370–384.

Dornbusch, R. (1976), "Expectations and exchange rate dynamics," *Journal of Political Economy*, 84: 1161–1176.

Edison Hali and Warnock, Frank (2001), "A simple measure of the intensity of capital controls," International Monetary Fund Working Paper no. WP/01/180.

Feldstein Martin and Charles, Horioka (1980), "Domestic saving and international capital flows," *Economic Journal*, 90: 314–329.

Fleming, J.M. (1962), "Domestic financial policies under fixed and under flexible exchange rates," *International Monetary Fund Staff Papers*, 9: 369–380.

Flood, R.A. and Rose, A.K. (1995), "Fixing exchange rates," *Journal of Monetary Economics*, 36: 3–37.

Frankel, J.A. (1976), "A monetary approach to the exchange rate: doctrinal aspects and empirical evidence," *Scandinavian Journal of Economics*, 78: 169–191.

Frankel, Jeffery A. (1979), "On the mark: a theory of floating exchange rates based on real interest rate differentials," *American Economic Review*, 69: 610–622.

Frankel, Jeffrey A. (1991), "Quantifying international capital mobility in the 1980s," in Bernheim, D. and Shoven, J. (eds), *National Saving Economic Performance*, Chicago: University of Chicago Press, pp. 227–260.

Frankel, Jeffrey A. (1994), "Sterilization of money inflows: Difficult (Calvo) or easy (Reisen)?", International Monetary Fund Working Paper no. WP/94/159.

Giavazzi, Francesco and Pagano, Marco (1988), "Capital controls and the European monetary system," in Fair, Donald E. and de Boissieu, Cristian (eds), *International Monetary and Financial Integration*, Dordrecht: Martinus Nijhoff, pp. 261–289.

Glick, R. and Hutchison, M. (2000), "Stopping 'hot money' or signaling bad policy? Capital controls and the onset of currency crises," Economic Policy Research Unit Working Paper no. 00-14, University of Copenhagen.

International Monetary Fund (1999), "Capital account liberalization in selected Asian crisis countries," in *Exchange Rate Arrangements and Currency Convertibility: Developments and Issues* (Section VII), World Economic and Financial Surveys, Washington: IMF, chapter 6.

International Monetary Fund (2000), *Capital Controls: Country Experiences with Their Use and Liberalization*, Occasional Paper no. 190, Washington: IMF.

Ito, Takatoshi (1983), "Capital controls and covered interest parity," NBER Working Paper no. 1187.

Kwack, S.Y. (2001), "An empirical assessment of monetary policy responses to capital inflows in Asia before the financial crisis," *International Economic Journal*, 15: 95–113.

Loungani, Prakash, Razin, Assaf and Chi-Wa Yuen (2000), "Capital mobility and the output-inflation tradeoff," International Monetary Fund Working Paper no. WP/00/87.

Montiel, Peter J. (1994), "Capital mobility in developing countries: some measurement issues and empirical estimates," *The World Bank Economic Review*, 8(3): 311–350.

Montiel, Peter and Reinhart, Carmen (1999), "Do capital controls and macroeconomic policies influence the volume and composition of capital flows? Evidence from the 1990s," *Journal of International Money and Finance*, 18: 619–635.

Mundell, R. (1963), "Capital mobility and stabilization policy under fixed and flexible exchange rates," *Canadian Journal of Economics and Political Science*, 29: 459–468.

Quinn, Dennis (1997), "The correlates of changes in international financial regulations," *American Political Science Review*, 91: 531–551.

Reisen, H. (1993), "The impossible trinity in South-East Asia," *International Economic Insights*, Washington DC: Institute for International Economics, pp. 21–23.

Rose, A.K. (1996), "Explaining exchange rate volatility: an empirical analysis of "the holy trinity" of monetary independence, fixed exchange rates, and capital mobility," *Journal of International Money and Finance*, 15: 925–945.

15 Sterilized intervention and monetary control

The case of Korea

*Byung Han Seo**

1 Introduction

In the late 1980s, a large volume of capital began to flow into developing countries. This phenomenon can be attributed to both foreign (or push) and domestic (or pull) factors (Calvo *et al.* 1993, 1994; Montiel and Reinhart 1999). International capital flows, of course, have both advantages and disadvantages (Calvo *et al.* 1993; Isard 1995; Montiel 1998; Reinhart and Reinhart 1998; Sinclair and Shu 2001). As disadvantageous aspects particularly evident to the central bank, large foreign capital inflows may bring about a rapid monetary expansion leading to an excessive rise in aggregate demand and inflationary pressures. Allowing exchange rate to appreciate in response to the higher demand for the currency of the recipient countries created by the capital inflows can adversely affect their international competitiveness widening current account deficits. Capital inflows may also increase the vulnerability of the recipient economy to a large and sudden reversal in capital flows. The Mexican peso crisis of 1994–95 and the Asian financial crisis of 1997 highlighted the point that large capital inflows to developing countries can create problems as well as benefits.

In contrast to other Asian countries, Korea experienced significant trade balance surpluses and net capital outflows during the period of 1986–89 peaking at about 6 percent of GDP in 1987, followed by net capital inflows beginning in 1990. The volume of cumulative capital inflows until 1995 amounted to about 10 percent of GDP. Confronted with such large current balance surpluses and capital inflow surges, the Korean monetary authorities actively implemented sterilized foreign exchange interventions through open market operations (OMOs), increases in reserve requirements, and other various measures, as most countries have commonly done, in an effort to balance longer-term monetary control and short-term exchange rate stability. As the main instrument for OMOs, they have used the central bank's interest-bearing bonds called "monetary stabilization bonds" (MSBs) that are directly backed by printing money rather than government bonds that are primarily backed by legal taxation. Attempting to insulate the monetary base from foreign exchange market interventions, the Bank of Korea (BOK) has incurred high "quasi-fiscal costs" from buying low-yielding foreign assets and selling high-yielding short-term MSBs with maturities of 3 months to 1 year. Such opportunity costs may give rise to differences in the dynamics of foreign exchange interventions, sterilization, and monetary controls relative to those of the countries in which government bonds are used as the principal tools of OMOs.

The extent to which a central bank sterilizes the effect of foreign exchange intervention on the monetary base can vary with many factors. Among those are capital mobility, different types and nature of disturbances underlying movements in exchange rate, business cycle, fiscal flexibility, and private agents' asset demand behavior (Calvo 1991; Frankel 1994; Kletzer and Spiegel 1996; Glick and Hutchison 2000). There is little scope for sterilization as financial markets are increasingly globalized and in turn capital mobility or substitutability between foreign and domestic assets becomes greater and greater. Although sterilized intervention remains feasible to some degree, its effectiveness depends on the way it is implemented. Furthermore, monetary policy will be independent of exchange rate policies only if foreign exchange interventions are completely sterilized in the long run. The fact that the degree of short-term sterilization is high has no significant implications for monetary control, while it can reduce the initial impact of intervention on the monetary base and distribute its effect more smoothly over time.

This chapter presents an empirical analysis of the relationship between foreign exchange market intervention and monetary controls in Korea over the managed floating exchange rate period 1981–2001. The study investigates how the Korean monetary authorities intervened in the foreign exchange market in response to exchange rate movements, and the extent to which such exchange rate policies might have influenced the monetary base and money supply or interest rates. The rest of the chapter is organized as follows. Section 2 sets out balance of payments and central bank balance sheet identities as well as monetary policy reaction functions and reviews the theoretical predictions of the possible linkages between foreign exchange interventions, sterilization, and monetary controls. Section 3.1 reviews some stylized facts about movements in the exchange rate of the Korean won against the US dollar, official foreign reserves, and related variables during the period 1981–2001. Section 3.2 and 3.3 present econometric analyses of the behavior of foreign exchange intervention and sterilization respectively. Section 4 concludes with some implications of empirical findings for monetary policy.

2 Relationship between foreign exchange intervention, sterilization, and monetary control

In order to address possible linkages between exchange rate policies and monetary controls, it would be helpful to start from the identities of balance of payments and central bank's balance sheet as well as central bank's policy reaction functions of foreign exchange intervention and sterilization.

$$CA_t + KA_t = \Delta FA_t \tag{1}$$

$$\Delta H_t = \Delta FA_t + \Delta DC_t \tag{2}$$

$$\Delta FA_t = -(\rho_M + \rho_B)\Delta S_t \tag{3}$$

$$\Delta DC_t = \rho_B \Delta S_t + \gamma_D U_t \tag{4}$$

where Δ is a first difference operator. The balance of payments identity (equation (1)) states that the sum of the current account (CA) and the capital account (KA) balances during a period equals the change in the (net) foreign assets (FA). The simplified flow identity of the central bank balance sheet (equation (2)) also states that the change in monetary base or high-powered money (H) during the period equals the sum of changes in foreign assets (FA) and domestic credit (DC) of the central bank.

It is then assumed that the central bank adjusts holdings of foreign assets and domestic assets in response to movements in exchange rate and other exogenous factors. The foreign exchange intervention equation (3) represents the central bank's response of foreign assets to changes in exchange rate (S). The parameter $\rho_M + \rho_B$ measures the intensity of the central bank's intervention actions against changes in exchange rate. It is assumed $\rho_M + \rho_B > 0$ indicating that such actions involve "leaning against the wind" in the direction of dampening exchange rate fluctuations. Furthermore, the parameter ρ_B measures the extent to which the central bank sterilizes unwanted changes in the monetary base resulting from foreign exchange market intervention by offsetting changes in domestic credit. The domestic credit reaction function or sterilization equation (4) represents the central bank's adjustment of domestic credit in association with foreign exchange interventions and other exogenous variable changes (U). The exogenous factors other than the exchange rate, such as shocks to income and price, may affect a target level of domestic credit component of the monetary base and $\gamma_D > 0$ indicates a desire by the central bank to accumulate domestic assets.

Consider an economy in which, at the prevailing exchange rate, the current account is balanced ($CA_t = 0$) and there is a tendency for inflow of foreign currency ($KA_t > 0$). Holders of foreign currency will put pressure on the exchange rate to appreciate ($\Delta S < 0$) as they seek to convert their foreign currency into domestic assets. On the one hand, if the central bank of the capital recipient country does not intervene in the foreign exchange market ($\rho_M = \rho_B = 0$), the exchange rate will appreciate freely to the point where it is unprofitable for capital to flow in. Balance of payments is then in equilibrium ($CA_t = 0$, $KA_t = 0$, and $\Delta FA_t = 0$) and in turn the monetary base growth is independent of external conditions. If the central bank, on the other hand, wishes to prevent its currency appreciation, it will intervene in the foreign exchange market by purchasing foreign exchange resulting in an increase in the holding of foreign assets or official foreign exchange reserves ($\Delta FA_t > 0$). Therefore, changes in the foreign assets of the central bank reflect the balance of payments conditions of a country as well as exchange rate policies.

If the central bank purchases foreign exchange in response to (perceived) currency appreciation, equations (2), (3), and (4) suggest that the central bank has three options with respect to domestic monetary control. First, it may accommodate (not sterilize) the increase in foreign assets by allowing the monetary base to increase by the same amount ($\rho_B = 0$; $\Delta FA_t = \Delta H_t > 0$) if it has a target for the exchange rate. Second, it may sterilize (not monetize) the increase in foreign assets to leave the monetary base unchanged by reducing domestic credit ($\rho_M = 0$; $\Delta FA_t = -\Delta DC_t$, $\Delta H_t = 0$) if it has a monetary growth target for the period. Finally, it can also choose some combination of accommodation and sterilization. Such a combination policy can be characterized by both ρ_M and ρ_B greater than zero.

Many central banks of developing as well as developed countries have commonly attempted to prevent changes in official foreign reserves from affecting the monetary base by implementing offsetting changes in domestic credit particularly at the initial stage of capital inflows or trade balance surpluses. For example, there are voluminous studies discussing the wisdom of sterilization policy in the US, Germany, and Japan (Herring and Marston 1977; Obstfeld 1983; Rogoff 1984; von Hagen 1989; Takagi 1991; Hetzel 1996; Glick and Hutchison 1994, 2000). Latin American and East Asian countries responded to a large increase in foreign assets by sterilizing the expansionary effect on the growth of monetary aggregates in the late 1980s and in the early 1990s (Calvo 1991; Calvo *et al.* 1996; Montiel and Reinhart 1999; Takagi and Esaka 2001). Sterilization can also work the other way. In 1994, the Mexican central bank offset monetary contraction due to declining foreign reserves by increasing domestic credit (World Bank 1997).

The extent to which sterilization of intervention is possible and, in a broad sense, the ability to insulate domestic monetary policy objective from external shocks by simultaneously targeting some monetary aggregate or domestic interest rate and nominal exchange rate, depends importantly on the degree of capital mobility and many other factors.[1] As is well known in the literature on "Impossible Trinity," there is little scope for sterilization if capital mobility is high. Even if sterilization remains possible, the conditions necessary for sterilization intervention to be effective imply that its effectiveness may depend on how it is attempted.[2] For example, sterilization by raising reserve requirements is likely to be less effective than sterilization through open market bond sales (Spiegel 1995; Montiel 1996; Reinhart and Reinhart 1998).[3]

If sterilization of intervention is feasible to some extent, it would be desirable whenever the prices of domestic assets need to be insulated from transitory shocks to portfolio preferences perhaps due to domestic nominal shocks such as an exogenous decrease in money supply by the central bank or external financial shocks such as a fall in the world interest rate. Sterilization would also be beneficial if the central bank seeks to accommodate gradually a permanent shift in portfolio preferences into domestic assets from foreign assets in response to market reforms or a decrease in the attractiveness of assets abroad. By contrast, domestic real shocks, such as productivity shocks, exogenous export boom, and exogenous increase in domestic spending, do not call for sterilized intervention because the asset price adjustments caused by such shocks are likely to be stabilizing without impairing international competitiveness. In the case of the increase in demand for money, on the other hand, it is better not to sterilize but rather to accommodate the money that private agents want to hold. Such accommodations are not likely to endanger price stability. In general, a program of stabilization and liberalization might cause investors to increase their demand for both domestic money and domestic bonds, and then the capital inflow should be partially sterilized by supplying both assets for which they are desired.[4]

Furthermore, sterilization may carry high "quasi-fiscal costs" which stem from interest rate differentials between government or central bank bonds and foreign exchange reserve assets. This is particularly true for the government of which claimed intentions not to devalue or default on debts are not fully credible on the basis of "permanent money," resulting in high domestic interest rates which reflect expected inflation or depreciation in the future (Calvo 1991; Calvo *et al.* 1993; Frankel and Okongwu 1996; Kletzer and Spiegel 1996). The extent of quasi-fiscal costs may play an important role in determining the degree of sterilization or the timing of the abandonment of a sterilization program since bond-financed sterilization may not be sustainable in the long run.[5] If optimal monetary policy is subject to an inter-temporal budget constraint of the central bank or the consolidated government sector, then the central bank with too large quasi-fiscal costs will rationally adjust the degree of sterilization by allowing either the exchange rate to appreciate or its money supply to rise. The solvency condition implies that the degree of sterilization will be less the higher the opportunity cost of sterilization, the larger the outstanding stock of public debt, and the larger official reserves for a given stock of base money (Kletzer and Spiegel 1996). Consequently, the use of sterilized intervention without impairing the government's solvency requires fiscal flexibility. A country that lacks such flexibility may be tempted to sterilize through changes in reserve requirements and other distortionary direct control measures despite the likelihood that they will result in imperfect insulation because the fiscal implications of doing so are less adverse than those of open market operations.

As discussed above, exchange rate management requires intervention in the foreign exchange market, on the one hand, by buying and selling foreign assets leading to a change in the monetary base. Domestic monetary policy, on the other hand, is conducted primarily by controlling the growth rate of the monetary base consistent with the natural rate of output under price stability. In order to assess how exchange rate policies affect domestic monetary control, therefore, one must know the extent to which foreign exchange intervention affects the growth of the monetary base. Sterilization of foreign exchange intervention requires offsetting purchases or sales of domestic assets such that the monetary base remains unchanged. Only if foreign exchange interventions are completely sterilized, will monetary policy be independent of exchange rate policies. Otherwise, monetary policy cannot be independent of foreign exchange market interventions.

Short-term sterilization can reduce the immediate impact of intervention on the monetary base and distribute its effect more smoothly over time. The transitory nature of foreign exchange interventions may not seriously endanger monetary control even if they are not sterilized in the short term. Different transitory interventions may offset each other neutralizing their individual effects on the monetary base. Such offsetting interventions can occur over time if, in the absence of interventions, the exchange rate is subject to purely transitory, random fluctuations of mean zero, while the underlying fundamental exchange rate is constant. If the central bank decides to moderate exchange rate fluctuations by intervening in the foreign exchange market, the resulting interventions would produce purely transitory changes in foreign reserves that average out to zero over time. Such transitory foreign exchange interventions contribute little to the growth of the monetary base over time even without sterilization, while they increase the variability of monetary base growth (von Hagen 1989).

Long-term sterilization can make the growth of the monetary base independent of the consequences of exchange rate policies. Therefore, the degree of long-term sterilization is a more relevant issue to the possible conflict between exchange rate policies and monetary controls. The strong negative correlations between contemporaneous or short-lagged changes in domestic credit and the foreign reserves only suggest a high degree of short-term sterilization (Obstfeld 1983; Glick and Hutchison 2000). Even if the degree of short-term sterilization is high, foreign exchange market intervention can result in accelerations or decelerations in the monetary base over time. The transitory changes in the source side of the monetary base are reversed during subsequent periods. In this regards, it is crucial to make the distinction between short- and long-term sterilization in addressing how foreign exchange market interventions affect monetary controls.

3 Empirical analysis

3.1 Overview of movements in exchange rate and monetary variables

During the last two decades before the outbreak of the financial and currency crisis in late 1997, the monetary policy regime in Korea can best be characterized as monetary targeting with a US dollar exchange rate constraint. The Korean monetary authorities switched from a fixed exchange rate against the US dollar to a more flexible multi-currency basket peg in February 1980 and then to a managed floating system called a "market average exchange rate" (MAR) in March 1990. Under the MAR system, the Korean won–US dollar rate was determined on the basis of a weighed average of inter-bank rates of won–dollar spot transactions in the previous day. The exchange rate each day was allowed to move within a band against this rate. The band was adjusted gradually with wider margins over time. Eventually, the monetary authorities were left to abandon managed floating officially and to adopt independently floating exchange rate regime after the crisis. Although exchange rate policies have allowed more flexibility in currency movements over time, the Korean economy appears to have been very susceptible to domestic as well as external shocks that contributed to balance of payments disequilibria and complicated efforts at monetary controls.

For domestic policies, credit of BOK consisted predominantly of policy-directed loans that support the government's industrial policy. The discount window credit was rationed with the discount rates kept well below money market rates regardless of the current money market conditions, and thus could hardly be reconciled with the objective of price stability. Furthermore, the BOK's portfolio of open market paper – government securities and treasury bills – made up only a very small fraction of its assets. Against this background, BOK relied on the issue and redemption of its own interest-bearing bonds called "monetary stabilization bonds" (MSBs) as the most important instrument to control monetary conditions with repurchase agreements for temporary liquidity management. The stock of MSBs tended to increase rapidly particularly after the financial crisis, amounting to approximately three times the monetary base in 2001 as shown in Table 15.1.

Figure 15.1 shows quarterly growth rates of the Korean won value of the US dollar exchange rate (S) and won-denominated net foreign assets (NFA) or US dollar-denominated foreign exchange (IR) held by the Korean monetary authorities. Positive values of changes in the exchange rate indicate a rise in the won value of the dollar and a depreciation of the won.[6] Movements in the exchange rate and net foreign assets are negatively correlated during most periods in the sample. The coefficient of correlation between growth rates of S and NFA is −0.57 for the entire period,

Table 15.1 Main sources of the monetary base (end of year, billions of won)

Year	H	NFA		DC		MSBs	
1981	2,802	987	(0.35)	5,708	(2.04)	1,934	(0.69)
1985	4,319	1,075	(0.25)	11,836	(2.74)	8,418	(1.95)
1990	13,811	10,701	(0.77)	22,360	(1.62)	18,403	(1.33)
1995	29,306	25,267	(0.86)	30,597	(1.04)	29,598	(1.01)
1996	25,723	27,851	(1.08)	26,983	(1.05)	29,068	(1.13)
1997	22,519	10,236	(0.45)	70,374	(3.13)	26,701	(1.19)
1998	20,703	42,478	(2.05)	52,431	(2.53)	53,580	(2.59)
1999	28,487	76,564	(2.69)	34,755	(1.22)	61,389	(2.15)
2000	28,238	112,403	(3.98)	22,547	(0.80)	79,142	(2.80)
2001	32,827	136,183	(4.15)	19,232	(0.59)	93,120	(2.84)

Notes

H, currency in circulation + reserve deposits; NFA, foreign assets − foreign liabilities; DC, claims on central government, official entities, and deposit money banks; MSBs, monetary stabilization bonds issued. The numbers in parentheses denote the ratios to monetary base (H).

and −0.71 for the period after the introduction of market average exchange rate system in 1990. A depreciation (appreciation) of the won tends to be accompanied by decreases (increases) in foreign exchange reserves. This suggests that the Korean monetary authorities have generally bought (sold) foreign exchange reserves when the exchange rate appreciated (depreciated) in an effort to dampen exchange rate fluctuations. However, it should be noted that, if S and NFA are expressed in level terms rather than in percent changes, the relationship is not evident. They are positively correlated with correlation coefficient of 0.70 for the entire period although negatively correlated with the coefficient of −0.62 for the period before the first quarter of 1990. The fact indicates that the two variables in level appear to be non-stationary exhibiting trends and thus simple correlation between the two time series would not be informative.

Particularly significant increases in the stock of foreign reserves were observed following the periods of sustained appreciation during 1986–89 as well as of sharp appreciation episode after the crisis. The Japanese yen appreciated sharply following the Plaza Accord in September 1985, and the Korean economy began to recover from recessions during the first half of the 1980s. Against this background, Korea experienced a large magnitude of trade balance surpluses and the won began to appreciate steadily from late 1985. Until the middle of 1989, the exchange rate appreciated from 890 to 670 won per dollar. The Korean monetary authorities actively purchased dollars and simultaneously implemented offsetting changes in net domestic credit in response to the pressure of current balance surpluses or the appreciating won. Consequently, foreign exchange reserves grew rapidly from about 2.6 billion dollars in the first quarter of 1986 to

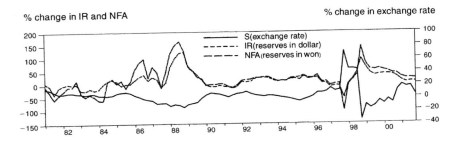

% change in IR and NFA

% change in exchange rate

Figure 15.1 Movements of the nominal Korean won/US dollar exchange rate and foreign exchange reserves.

Note
Percent change of CPI over four quarters. Exchange rate in won/dollar; positive values imply a won depreciation.

17.0 billion dollars in the third quarter of 1989. This intervention was accompanied by high growth in the monetary base and relatively low interest rates. As shown in Figure 15.2, the monetary base growth began to accelerate sharply from 1987 and peaked at higher than 40 percent in the middle of 1988. Figure 15.3 also shows that both three-years-maturity-corporate bonds rate (CBR) and overnight-call-money interest rate (CR) fell more or less and remained stable throughout most of the period. In contrast, both M1 and M2 growth rates remained steady at their trends at around 13 percent and 19 percent respectively. Inflation of consumer price index (P) was also maintained at a relatively low level during most of this period, while it began to accelerate from 1990.

Likewise, the stock of foreign reserves declined significantly following periods of sustained depreciation during the early 1980s as well as sharp depreciation around the onset of the financial crisis. During the period 1996–97, the won depreciated by more than 110 percent against the dollar

% change

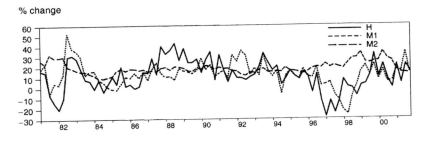

Figure 15.2 Movements of monetary base (H), M1 and M2.

Note
Percent change of CPI over four quarters.

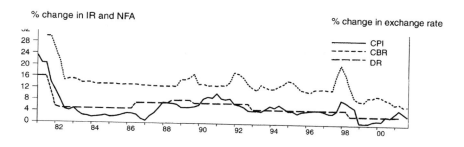

Figure 15.3 Movements of inflation and interest rates.

Note
Percent change of CPI over four quarters and annual interest rate of corporate bonds (CBR) and discount rate (DR).

and substantial foreign exchange market dollar sales to support the won led to a sharp drop in foreign reserves from around 36 billion dollars to around 20 billion dollars. This intervention was accompanied by the highest negative growth rates of both monetary base and M1, −28 percent in the first quarter of 1987 and −26 percent in the second quarter of 1988 each, which reflect the partially sterilized intervention operations. In addition, call money interest rate also rose sharply to 25 percent in the first half of 1998. However, M2 growth rates again remained steady at its trend. These stylized facts suggest that there is a link between fast (slow) monetary growth during the periods of steady or sharp appreciation (depreciation) and unsterilized foreign exchange market interventions, but not necessarily a linkage between M2 growth and foreign exchange rate and reserve changes.

As can be seen in Figure 15.2, movements in H, M1, and M2 growth exhibit similar secular trends although the contemporaneous correlations between the two series are low or even negative. It is noteworthy that M2 growth is most stable and also negatively correlated with the growth of H and M1. For the entire period, the coefficients of variation for H, M1, and M2 growth are 1.30, 0.97 and 0.29 respectively. The correlation coefficients of H and M2 growth and M1 and M2 growth are −0.21 and −0.19 respectively, although that of H and M1 growth is 0.52. These results may reflect the fact that M2 was the aggregate variable that BOK targeted for most of the sample period before adopting an inflation targeting framework in April 1998. In order to achieve the annual target growth rate of M2, BOK employed various direct monetary control measures such as credit controls, changes in reserve requirements, and moral suasion. The direct monetary control measures were taken largely because there were insufficient instruments based on market principles for indirect monetary control.

In addition, Table 15.1 reports the main components of BOK's balance sheet. Relative to movements in the monetary base (H), movements in NFA, domestic credit (DC) and MSBs exhibit substantial variability particularly around the financial crisis period. However, the trend of comovements among these monetary variables is observable over the sample period. This suggests a shift over time in either the desire or ability of BOK to completely sterilize the effects of its foreign exchange intervention and consequent movements in net foreign assets and monetary base.

The econometric study below uses monthly data over the managed exchange period 1981:1–2001:12. The starting point is chosen allowing for the transition from a fixed exchange rate as well as the turbulent international debt crisis in the late 1970s and the early 1980s. The sample period is somewhat arbitrarily divided into two sub-periods corresponding to periods before and after 1990:4, when a more flexible market average exchange rate system was adopted. The split of the sample period may be desirable for either reflecting a possible structural shift or focusing on the more recent developments. The variables considered in the econometric analysis were all found to be stationary in the log first difference form except for interest rates in the percent level difference form. The cointegration tests based on Johansen's maximum likelihood procedure also failed to reject the hypothesis of no cointegrating relationships among the log levels of industrial production (y), consumer price index (P), net foreign assets (NFA), net domestic assets (NDA), and other monetary variables. Based on the time-series properties of the variables,[7] we specify the econometric model of intervention and sterilization in the log first difference form. We also use a vector error correction modeling (VECM) strategy for specifying a set of simultaneous equations, which allows us to evaluate single equation reduced-form effects of a monetary policy reaction function such as sterilization equation without explicitly modeling the structural linkages in the system.

3.2 Behavior of foreign exchange intervention

The preliminary examination of the data indicates some linkages of foreign exchange intervention with monetary growth over the managed floating exchange rate period. To explore if there is any systematic relationship between foreign exchange intervention by the Korean monetary authorities and movements in the nominal exchange rate, we specify the conventional foreign exchange intervention function that relates the magnitude of intervention to the change in exchange rate (Hutchison 1984; Takagi 1991; Glick and Hutchison 1994).

$$NFAG_t = C + \beta SG_t + \rho NFAG_{t-1} + e_t \tag{5}$$

where C is a constant; NFAG is the monthly (log) percent change in net foreign assets which can be interpreted as a measure of the amount of intervention during the month; SG is the monthly (log) percent change in the exchange rate with an increase defined as a depreciation of the won against the dollar; and e_t is a random variable that represents other changes. The inclusion of a constant term and the lagged dependent variable can reflect the response of foreign exchange reserves to factors other than foreign exchange intervention. For example, the inclusion of the lagged dependent variable can be justified by the partial adjustment of foreign official reserves to the desired level for a country's demand for international liquidity.

Estimating equation (5) by ordinary least squares (OLS) is subject to simultaneity bias if intervention affects the level of exchange rate contemporaneously. However, there is a broad consensus that sterilized intervention does not significantly change the exchange rate (Rogoff 1984; Obstfeld 1988; Edison 1993). As can be seen in the next section, net monthly intervention was almost fully sterilized contemporaneously during the sample period. Therefore, it can be assumed that the effect of intervention on the exchange rate is of second-order importance.[8]

Table 15.2 reports the estimation results for equation (5) including a time trend, 11 seasonal dummies, and a crisis dummy that has a value of 1

Table 15.2 Response of net foreign assets to exchange rate changes

	1981:01–2001:12	1981:01–1990:03	1990:04–2001:12
Regression coefficients			
Constant	−0.02 (−0.69)	−0.04 (−0.15)	−0.01 (−0.29)
Exchange rate changes	−1.80 (−6.48)**	−4.51 (−1.86)*	−1.67 (−14.78)**
Lagged dependent variable	0.01 (0.25)	−0.05 (−0.53)	0.06 (1.12)
Summary statistics			
R^2 (adj. R^2)	0.21 (0.16)	0.16 (0.05)	0.70 (0.67)
SEE	0.15	0.21	0.66
D-W	2.01	2.02	1.83
LM(2)	0.49 (0.62)	0.63 (0.54)	0.74 (0.48)
Exchange rate changes			
Depreciation (β_1)	−1.57 (−4.69)**	−4.31 (−0.86)	−1.48 (−11.01)**
Appreciation (β_2)	−2.50 (−3.85)**	−4.61 (−1.09)	−2.32 (−8.37)**
	F-statistics under the restriction $\beta_1 = \beta_2$		
	1.42 (0.23)	0.00 (0.96)	6.48 (0.01)

Notes
All equations include a time trend and 11 seasonal dummy terms. Dependent variables are expressed as the logarithmic changes in the monthly net foreign assets. The exchange rate variables are expressed as the logarithmic changes in the monthly exchange rate of the Korean won against the US dollar; and increase in the value is defined to be a depreciation of the won. The numbers in parentheses are t-statistics.
**(*) indicates that the statistics is significant at the 1 (10) percent level. LM(2) refers to the General Lagrange multiplier (χ^2) statistic for second-order serial correlation in residuals. The numbers in parentheses for F-statistics denote the marginal significance levels of F-test against complete sterilization.

after 1998:01 and a value of 0 otherwise. The time trend and dummy terms are not reported. The estimated coefficient of exchange rate variable is significantly negative as expected, indicating that the Korean monetary authorities tended to buy (sell) foreign exchange when the won appreciates (depreciates). This is consistent with the intervention policy of "leaning against the wind" to moderate exchange rate fluctuations. On average, the monetary authorities respond to a 1 percent appreciation of the won by increasing official foreign reserves by around 1.8 percent. The lagged dependent variable is not significantly different from zero, indicating that the longer-term intervention response is similar to that of the initial impact effects.[9]

In order to examine if the exchange rate regime shift of 1990 had any significant effect on the response of intervention to exchange rate movements, we re-estimate equation (5) by splitting the sample period into two sub-periods 1981:01–1990:03 and 1990:04–2001:12.[10] As reported in the third and fourth columns in Table 15.2, the coefficients of exchange rate are negative and significant in both sub-samples. However, the extent of intervention in the latter period is smaller than roughly one third of the former period. The smaller scale of intervention presumably reflects the fact that the Korean monetary authorities respond more flexibly to movements in the exchange rate after adopting a market average exchange rate system. The adjusted R^2 statistics also increases by more than four times in the latter period, indicating that a much larger portion of changes in foreign reserves is explained by the model.

Furthermore, we re-estimate equation (5) with separate variables for SG when the won was appreciating and when it was depreciating in order to examine if the monetary authorities were symmetric with respect to depreciation and appreciation. The depreciation variable is created by multiplying SG by a dummy variable that has a value of 1 when SG is positive and a value of 0 otherwise; the appreciation variable is created analogously with a dummy variable that has a value of 1 when SG is negative and a value of 0 otherwise. As reported in the lower panel of Table 15.2, the coefficient of the appreciation variable is higher than that of the depreciation variable, while both coefficients are not significant for the former period. For the latter period, the hypothesis of the same coefficients in both appreciation and depreciation variables can be rejected at the 1 percent level.

The regression results suggest that the Korean monetary authorities tended to intervene more heavily in response to appreciation than to depreciation with the tendency more pronounced in the latter period. Greater resistance to appreciation than to depreciation may reflect the efforts that they pursued to maintain international competitiveness and also accumulated the stock of foreign reserves to improve the resilience of the economy to unanticipated shocks. This stance of intervention policy toward foreign exchange purchase against appreciation might be incompatible with monetary control, due to potentially excessive monetary stimuli associated with the trend accumulation of foreign reserves. It is in sharp contrast with the findings of Takagi (1991) and Glick and Hutchison (1994) that the Japanese monetary authorities tended to intervene more actively in response to depreciation than to appreciation placing more weight on the price stability.

3.3 Behavior of sterilization

As discussed in the previous section, an activist foreign exchange intervention does not necessarily impede a central bank's ability to control either monetary aggregates or domestic interest rates. The central bank may sterilize most of the effects of official foreign reserve changes on monetary aggregates by systematically adjusting the level of domestic credit. To investigate how the degree of sterilization of foreign exchange intervention by BOK varies over time and across episodes of won depreciation and appreciation, this section employs a single equation approach and a simultaneous equation time series model as well.

3.3.1 Single equation approach

Following the standard sterilization equation in the literature (Obstfeld 1983; von Hagen 1989; Glick and Hutchison 1994), it is assumed that BOK adjusts domestic credit changes in response to current and lagged foreign exchange interventions as well as lagged domestic credit changes.

$$\text{NDAG}_t = C + \sum_{j=0}^{m} \beta_j \, \text{NFAG}_{t-j} + \sum_{j=1}^{n} \rho_j \text{NDAG}_{t-j} + u_t \tag{6}$$

where C is a constant; NFAG and NDAG denote the monthly (log) percent changes in net foreign assets and net domestic assets respectively; and u_t is a random error term. Net domestic assets (NDA) are constructed as the ratio of the monetary base to net foreign assets of the monetary authorities, and hence NDAG is the difference between the log percent changes in the monetary base and net foreign assets. The constant term and lagged dependent variables are included to capture either the partial adjustment or the reaction of the central bank to past developments in net domestic assets.

The lag pattern of the individual β_j coefficients shows how sterilization of a given intervention is distributed over the current and following months, while the sum of the individual coefficients $\Sigma \beta_j$ measures the medium-term degree of sterilization. In addition, the long-term multiplier response of net domestic assets to changes in foreign assets is given by $\sum_{j=0}^{m} \beta_j / \left(1 - \sum_{j=1}^{m} \rho_j\right)$. If β_0 is less than 1 in absolute value, intervention is partially sterilized in the current month, resulting in an initial effect on the monetary base. Whether foreign exchange market interventions are completely sterilized in the long run depends on the lagged pattern of interventions.

Preliminary estimates of equation (6) with 11 seasonal dummies and a crisis dummy of 1 after 1998:01 were run to select the appropriate lag lengths for the regressors. Considering the significance of individual coefficients, the magnitude of R^2, and Akaike information and Schwarz criterions, the preferred specification has $m = n = 2$ lags for both net foreign assets and lagged dependent variables. Table 15.3 summarizes the estimation results for the entire sample period and two sub-periods divided at 1990:04 as in the intervention regression.

The upper panel of Table 15.3(a) indicates that the coefficients of β_j are negative and highly significant as anticipated for the whole sample as well as two sub-samples, and the regressions also explain monthly changes in the net domestic assets fairly well.[11] Of particular interest is the sum of

Table 15.3 Response of net domestic assets to net foreign asset changes

(a)	1981:01–2001:12	1981:01–1990:03	1990:04–2001.12
Regression coefficients			
Constant	0.13 (9.50)**	0.17 (7.44)**	0.10 (5.96)**
$NFAG_t$	−0.94 (−38.92)**	−0.95 (−31.36)**	−0.94 (−19.15)**
$NFAG_{t-1}$	−0.40 (−6.13)**	−0.40 (−3.88)**	−0.49 (−5.11)**
$NFAG_{t-2}$	−0.09 (−1.38)	−0.06 (−0.59)	−0.14 (−1.42)
$NDAG_{t-1}$	−0.38 (−5.83)**	−0.40 (−3.86)**	−0.36 (−4.11)**
$NDAG_{t-2}$	−0.11 (−1.65)	−0.05 (−0.53)	−0.18 (−2.11)
Summary statistics			
R^2 (adj. R^2)	0.89 (0.89)	0.93 (0.92)	0.86 (0.84)
SEE	0.06	0.06	0.05
D-W	2.02	1.99	2.00
LM(2)	0.60	0.63	0.30

F-statistics for contemporaneous sterilization		
7.26 (0.01)	2.69 (0.10)	1.39 (0.24)
F-statistics for medium-term sterilization		
14.70 (0.00)	5.57 (0.02)	11.42 (0.00)
F-statistics for long-term sterilization		
2.40 (0.12)	0.73 (0.40)	0.07 (0.79)

Notes
All equations include a time trend and 11 seasonal dummy terms. Dependent variables are expressed as the logarithmic changes in the monthly net domestic assets measure. The exchange rate variables are expressed as the logarithmic changes in the monthly exchange rate of the Korean won against the US dollar; and increase in the value is defined to be a depreciation of the won. The numbers in parentheses are t-statistics.
** indicates that the statistics is significant at the 1 percent. LM(2) refers to the General Lagrange multiplier (χ^2) statistic for second-order serial correlation in residuals. The numbers in parentheses for F-statistics denote the Marginal significance levels of F-test against complete sterilization.

(b)	*1981:01–2001:12*	*1981:01–1990:03*	*1990:04–2001.12*
Depreciation			
Contemporaneous response (c_1)	−0.94	−0.96	−0.86
Medium-run response (m_1)	−1.52	−1.62	−1.46
Long-run response (l_1)	0.97	1.00	1.07
Appreciation			
Contemporaneous response (c_2)	−0.92	−0.92	−1.03
Medium-term response (m_2)	−1.37	−1.43	−1.54
Long-term response (l_2)	0.93	0.91	1.07
	F-statistics under the restriction		
$c_1 = c_2$	0.10 (0.76)	0.51 (0.48)	2.69 (0.10)
$m_1 = m_2$	0.71 (0.40)	0.65 (0.42)	0.06 (0.80)
$l_1 = l_2$	1.01 (0.32)	2.19 (0.14)	0.78 (0.38)

Note
The numbers in parentheses for F-statistics denote the marginal significance levels of F-test against complete sterilization.

coefficients on the lagged dependent variables is significantly negative with the absolute values less than 1. This fact implies that the initial changes in domestic assets in response to intervention can be reversed over the subsequent months with the oscillating effects of the sterilization successively smaller over time. As reported in the lower panel of Table 15.3(b), the contemporaneous coefficient on NFAG of −0.94 is significantly different from −1 at the conventional level, indicating that foreign exchange intervention is under-sterilized in the current month although almost fully sterilized. By contrast, the null hypothesis of $\Sigma\beta_j = -1$ against the alternative hypothesis of $\Sigma\beta_j > |1|$ can be rejected with high confidence, indicating that foreign exchange intervention is over-sterilized in the medium term. That is, the net domestic assets change more than one-for-one in response to changes in the net foreign assets. However, the hypothesis of $\Sigma(1 - \rho_j)^{-1}\beta_j = -1$ cannot be rejected. Thus in the long run, net foreign asset changes are completely sterilized by equal and offsetting changes in net domestic assets, leaving the monetary base unchanged. This "yo-yo swing" pattern of sterilization tends to increase the volatility of the monetary base and other monetary aggregates growth, while it presumably reflects the uncertainty about the nature of exchange rate movements and interventions.

These results are in contrast with the finding of von Hagen (1989) that the foreign exchange interventions in Germany of the period of 1979–88 were fully sterilized in the short term, but not fully sterilized in the long term. They are also in contrast with the study of Glick and Hutchison (1994) that the foreign exchange interventions in Japan over the period

1973–90 were not fully sterilized in the short term and in the long term as well.

In order to examine whether there is asymmetry in the sterilization response across the periods of won depreciation and appreciation, we also re-estimate equation (6) with separate variables for contemporaneous and lagged net foreign asset variables as well as lagged dependent variables when the won is depreciating and when it is appreciating. The estimated coefficients of sterilization are reported in Table 15.3(b). For the full sample period, the tests fail to reject the hypothesis that the contemporaneous, medium- and long-term degree of sterilization are the same irrespective of whether the won is depreciating or appreciating. For the latter period, the contemporaneous sterilization coefficient is -0.86 for intervention when the won is depreciating and -1.03 when it is appreciating. The hypothesis that the coefficients are the same can be rejected at the 10 percent level. The medium- and long-term degrees of sterilization also appear to be higher during the intervention episodes associated with appreciation than during those associated with depreciation although the differences are not statistically significant. This is in contrast to the tendency for the former period to be a higher degree of sterilization during depreciation periods. These estimates suggest that BOK tended to attempt more actively to sterilize the effects of foreign exchange intervention on the monetary base when they were likely to be expansionary.

3.3.2 Simultaneous equation approach

The sterilization coefficient estimates discussed above are derived from the single domestic asset equation (6) – the policy reaction function. They represent a partial equilibrium impact of central bank foreign asset changes on central bank domestic asset changes in the context of a broader, simultaneously determined system of the macroeconomy. The full reduced-form effect of foreign asset changes on domestic assets depends not only on the policy response itself but also on feedback effects of the private sector in response to intervention and sterilization operations. Such ultimate effects of intervention on monetary controls are not adequately captured by the policy reaction function estimates alone. Therefore, it is desirable to estimate reduced-form effects of intervention on monetary controls from a broader simultaneous equation system.

In this regard, we employ a vector error correction model (VECM) approach following Glick and Hutchison (1994, 2000). The approach can describe the full reduced-form effects of a change in net foreign assets on net domestic assets, while controlling for the short-term dynamic interactions of these and other variables in the system.

$$\Delta Y_t = \Gamma_1 \Delta Y_{t-1} + \ldots + \Gamma_{k-1} \Delta Y_{t-k+1} + \alpha(\beta' Y_{t-1}) + \phi D + C + \epsilon_t \qquad (7)$$

where Y is a four-endogenous variable vector which consists of industrial production (y), consumer price level (P), NFA, and NDA (or other monetary variable H, M1, M2, CR, and CBR); all variables except for interest rates CR and CBR in percent levels are specified in the log levels; $\beta'Y$ denotes the vector of error-correction terms; α is the parameter vector indicating the speed of adjustment to a long-term equilibrium; $\Gamma_1 \ldots \Gamma_{k-1}$ are parameter vectors reflecting short-term dynamics; D is a vector of 11 seasonal dummy variables and crisis dummy after 1998:01; C is a vector of constants; and ϵ is a vector of random error terms. Industrial production and consumer price are included in the model to control for other factors that may influence the timing and magnitude of NDA response to changes in NFA. The model reflects a cointegrating (long-term equilibrium) relationship among the variables in Y. Such a long-term relationship implies that the variables tend to move together over longer time or policy reaction functions and other structural features of the economy linking those variables are stable.

We estimate the model with a single error-correction term over the period 1990:04–2001:12 to focus on the recent developments. The lag-length (k) of the VECM model is set at 2 on the basis of the lag specification criterions of Akaike information and Schwarz criterion.[12] The model is identified by orthogonalizing the variance–covariance matrix of the composite errors to the four equations using the Choleski decomposition. The causal ordering y, P, NFA, NDA (or H, M1, M2, CR, CBR) is used in performing the decomposition. Consequently, shocks to NFA and NDA are assumed not to influence either y or P within the current month. Shocks to NFA, perhaps due to an exogenous foreign capital inflow, the focus of our concern is assumed to influence NDA contemporaneously, but to influence y and P with a one-month lag.

As reported in Table 15.4, contemporaneous correlation of residuals in y and P is relatively small, suggesting that the estimation results are not sensitive to the ordering assumed for these variables. However, there is a strong negative contemporaneous correlation (−0.83) of residuals in NFA and NDA. One possible interpretation of this high correlation is that exogenous shocks to NFA lead to offsetting contemporaneous changes in NDA reflecting sterilized intervention by the BOK.

The causal ordering adopted here is consistent with such an interpretation. An alternative interpretation of the correlation is that changes in

Table 15.4 Contemporaneous correlation of residuals

	y	*P*	*NFA*	*NDA*
y	1			
P	0.007	1		
NFA	0.006	−0.483	1	
NDA	0.046	0.389	−0.835	1

NDA lead to changes in the exchange rate that a policy authority seeks to avoid through intervention. For example, persistent budget surpluses in Singapore tend to drain liquidity and the Monetary Authority of Singapore (MAS) injects enough liquidity through intervention in foreign exchange markets to achieve its exchange rate target (Moreno and Spiegel 1997). Given the high correlation between NFA and NDA, adopting such an interpretation to identify the model by reversing the causal ordering may affect the results.

Table 15.5(a) presents the dynamic responses of NDA and H to Choleski one-standard innovation in NFA.[13] The estimates indicate that an increase in NFA is sterilized by about 96 percent in the current month and sterilized by about 104 percent in the next month. These estimation results are consistent with the contemporaneous under-sterilization and medium-term over-sterilization partial equilibrium estimates derived from the single policy reaction function in Table 15.3. However, the degree of sterilization declines over time to around 65 percent after 9 months. The results are inconsistent with the long-term complete sterilization from the partial equilibrium estimates. The different estimates of the long-term degree of sterilization between a single equation and VECM approaches suggest that the feedback effects of private sector and central bank adjustments to intervention and sterilization operations become more important over time. The effect of initial sterilization operations may be offset not only by private sector portfolio adjustment but also by higher quasi-fiscal costs of sterilization or the redemption of MSBs due. This explanation is compatible with the study of Seo (1996) that both the growth of MSBs and inflation tend to move together in the long term.

Table 15.5(b) presents the dynamic responses of M1, M2, CR, and CBR to Choleski one-standard innovation in NFA. In the case of M1, the degree of sterilization declines over time similarly to the case of the monetary base. By contrast, M2 is little affected in the short term as well as in the long term. Furthermore, interest rates of CR and CBR fall significantly instead of rising in response to shocks in net foreign assets. Effective sterilization under imperfect substitutability of foreign and domestic assets tends to raise the level of domestic interest rates. Domestic interest rates must rise so as to induce the market participants to hold the greater amount of domestic assets willingly or so as to clear the money market, given the restricted money supply.[14]

Furthermore, we can assess the relative importance of net foreign assets on monetary aggregates and interest rates by measuring the contribution of innovations in NFA to the variance of forecast error of those variables.[15] The contribution of NFA to NDA (or H) tends to decrease (or increase) with the length of the forecast horizon. The higher impact of NFA on NDA and the lower impact of NFA on H in the short term and vice versa in the long term reflect efforts to sterilize become less effective over time. The impact of NFA shocks on M1, CR, and CBR

Table 15.5 Impulse responses to Choleski one-standard innovations in NFA

(a) *y, P, NFA, NDA(or H) model*

Months ahead	NFA	NDA	H
1	0.0742	−0.0673	0.0069
2	0.0685	−0.0715	−0.0030
3	0.0719	−0.0645	0.0074
4	0.0556	−0.0508	0.0048
5	0.0461	−0.0405	0.0057
6	0.0365	−0.0296	0.0069
9	0.0263	−0.0178	0.0085
12	0.0283	−0.0200	0.0083
18	0.0300	−0.0218	0.0081
24	0.0297	−0.0216	0.0082
30	0.0298	−0.0216	0.0081
36	0.0298	−0.0216	0.0081

(b)

Months ahead	y, P, NFA, M1 model		y, P, NFA, M2 model		y, P, NFA, CR model		y, P, NFA, CBR model	
	NFA	M1	NFA	M2	NFA	CR	NFA	CBR
1	0.0748	0.0118	0.0770	−0.0013	0.0850	−0.4564	0.0836	−0.6535
2	0.0714	0.0084	0.0806	0.0011	0.0887	−1.0356	0.0866	−0.9814
3	0.0797	0.0060	0.0878	−0.0005	0.0985	−1.1910	0.0957	−0.8923
4	0.0690	0.0113	0.0884	0.0000	0.0906	−1.3454	0.0869	−0.8920
5	0.0595	0.0124	0.0842	0.0011	0.0833	−1.4028	0.0749	−0.8866
6	0.0502	0.0139	0.0800	0.0011	0.0760	−1.4111	0.0658	−0.9002
9	0.0414	0.0145	0.0733	0.0003	0.0677	−1.3728	0.0572	−0.9518
12	0.0437	0.0139	0.0702	0.0000	0.0678	−1.3611	0.0579	−0.9731
18	0.0445	0.0139	0.0692	−0.0002	0.0682	−1.3629	0.0573	−0.9759
24	0.0444	0.0139	0.0692	−0.0002	0.0682	−1.3628	0.0573	−0.9765
30	0.0444	0.0139	0.0692	−0.0002	0.0682	−1.3628	0.0573	−0.9765
36	0.0444	0.0139	0.0692	−0.0002	0.0682	−1.3628	0.0573	−0.9765

also increase with the forecast horizon. But M2 responds little to fluctuations in NFA regardless of the forecast horizon. These variance decomposition results may accord with the results that the effects of foreign exchange intervention were nearly fully sterilized in the short term, but not fully sterilized in the long term, and that the official target M2 was almost completely insulated from intervention in the foreign exchange market.

4 Conclusion

During the last two decades, the Bank of Korea implemented relatively active sterilized interventions first by selling and buying its own interest-bearing bonds to insulate the monetary base from exchange rate policies and then by taking a wide range of measures to limit the effect of capital flows on the growth of monetary aggregates. The empirical analysis suggests that foreign exchange interventions were almost completely sterilized in the short term but not in the long term, and thus had a significant effect on the monetary base growth. This difference between short- and long-term sterilization of foreign exchange interventions sheds some light on how sterilized interventions affect exchange rates. If the market participants understand that sterilization is complete only in the short term, while incomplete in the long term, such interventions would change their expectations about the money supply growth in the future, and this change in expectations would affect exchange rate even if the interventions were fully sterilized initially. That is, sterilized interventions give a signal about future central bank behavior.[16]

The empirical results also suggest that sterilization of foreign exchange interventions was successful for controlling the official intermediate target M2 growth only but not effective for controlling overall monetary aggregates or domestic interest rates. One possible explanation for the result is that sterilization measures in the broad sense such as changes in reserve requirements, credit controls, and moral suasion, rather than sterilization measure in the narrow sense or the conventional form of sterilized intervention exchanging domestic and foreign securities in an open market transaction, may be effective against the banking sector under relatively strict regulations but result in disintermediation particularly in an economy where there is a large non-bank sector. This disintermediation interpretation is consistent with the analysis of Spiegel (1995) and is also not incompatible with Goodhart's law.[17]

Notes

* The author would like to thank Peter Sinclair, Christoph Thoenissen, Dan Huynh, and Richhild Moessner, the discussant, participants at the Centre for Central Banking Studies Bank of England *International Capital Movements* conference, and anonymous referees for helpful comments and suggestions. He is also grateful to Bank of England and the Bank of Korea that provided the opportunity to work for *International Capital Movements* research project at the centre. Needless to say, the author alone assumes responsibility for any remaining errors. The views expressed here are solely those of the author and do not represent those of the Bank of Korea or the Bank of England.
1 Glick and Hutchison (2000) develop a model of foreign exchange intervention and sterilization dynamics when there are adjustment costs to changing private portfolios, and show that the degree of sterilization depends upon the speed of adjustment of assets to their long-term equilibrium, private agent's asset

demand behavior, central bank's policy strategy for intervention as well as the nature of the underlying disturbance.

2 Sterilization is most effective when domestic interest-bearing assets are close substitutes among themselves but are poor substitutes for foreign assets. For details, see Frankel (1994) and World Bank (1997).

3 Spiegel develops an open economy version of the Bernanke–Blinder (1987) model predicting that sterilization through increase in reserve requirements will have limited impact if viable financial alternatives to the banking sector exist. He shows that Korea with the largest non-bank financial sector, experiencing the greatest degree of disintermediation and real exchange rate appreciation among the seven developing Asian nations, had the least success in stemming the impact of capital inflow surges despite its intervention through both open market operations and increased reserve requirements.

4 In practice, it is almost impossible to credibly reduce the expected rate of money growth, while simultaneously increasing the level of the money supply. Under these circumstances, it may be best to simply allow the money flow in through the balance of payments (Calvo 1991; Frankel 1994).

5 This public finance approach to optimal monetary policy originally comes from "Unpleasant Monetarist Arithmetic" of Sargent and Wallace (1981).

6 The won-denominated net foreign assets are constructed as the difference between foreign assets of monetary authorities, from *IFS*, line 11, and foreign liabilities of monetary authorities, from *IFS*, line 16c. Since NFA of the monetary authorities balance sheet are measured at constant exchange rates, they do not distinguish between changes in international reserves due to intervention and changes due to other sources. However, this does not pose a serious problem in discussing intervention and sterilization. The US dollar-denominated value of foreign exchange is obtained from *IFS*, line 1d. *d*, which is independent of exchange rate changes. Since there is a high correlation (0.92) between NFA and IR growth for the entire sample period, the analysis below is focused on NFA.

7 Stationary and cointegration test results are omitted and available from the author upon request.

8 The use of two stage least squares (2SLS) is made difficult by the well-known empirical observation that short-term exchange rate behavior is closely approximated by a random walk process; it is thus almost impossible to structurally model exchange rate determination or to use lagged changes in the exchange rate as an instrumental variable (Takagi 1991). Preliminary results based on 2SLS in which three lags each of the Federal Funds rate, the corporate bonds rate, the logarithmic changes in the CPI and the exchange rate were used as the instruments indicated that the sign of the coefficient of SG remains the same but that statistical significance and the R^2 deteriorate sharply relative to the OLS results.

9 Equation (5) was also estimated using the dollar-denominated foreign exchange (IR) from *IFS*, line 1d. *d* as an alternative measure of intervention which is unaffected by changes in the exchange rate and the estimation results were not qualitatively different from those for the won-denominated net foreign assets (NFA).

10 When estimated equation (5) with separate SG variables corresponding to the periods before and after 1990:04 by creating dummy variables for the coefficient of SG in the two sub-periods, F-statistics (p-value) was 3.17 (0.07) under the hypothesis of the same coefficients of SG in two sub-periods.

11 One potential econometric problem with estimating equation (6) by OLS arises from the possible simultaneity of NFAG and NDAG, if the change in reserves

valued at a constant exchange rate is correlated with the disturbance to net domestic assets in the presence of a systematic foreign exchange intervention. Preliminary estimation results based on 2SLS in which three lags each of the Federal Reserve funds rate, the corporate bonds rate, the logarithmic changes in the CPI, industrial production, and the exchange rate were used as the instruments were not qualitatively different from the OLS results.

12 Including or omitting more or less lags did not change significantly the estimation results.

13 Preliminary estimation results by reversing the causal ordering between NFA and NDA were not qualitatively different from the impulse response and variance decomposition results obtained by the ordering adopted here.

14 Takagi and Esaka (2000) argue as follows: In either case, a rise in foreign assets would be prevented from increasing the volume of monetary aggregates at least one to one, and the resulting rise in interest rate differentials favoring the domestic assets would promote additional capital inflows, given flexible but stable nominal exchange rates. Of course, no additional capital inflows would result if the market participants correctly perceived that the higher interest rates only reflected the higher risk premium of domestic assets and the non-zero probability of currency depreciation. However, Furman and Stiglitz (1998) document that many market participants tried to exploit the interest rate differentials between US dollar denominated and East Asian currency denominated assets by taking unhedged short-term positions for supposed financial gains, believing that the markets were imperfect.

15 The results of the forecast error variance decomposition are not reported but are available from the author upon request.

16 This is the expectations argument of sterilized interventions by Mussa (1981).

17 Goodhart' law (1984) refers to the phenomenon that "any observed statistical regularity will tend to collapse once pressure is placed upon it for control purposes."

References

Bernanke, B.A. and Blinder, Alan S. (1987), "Credit, money and aggregate demand," *American Economic Review*, 78(2): 108–151.

Calvo, Guillermo (1991), "The perils of sterilization," *IMF Staff Papers*, 38: 921–926.

Calvo, Guillermo, Leiderman, Leonardo and Reinhart, Carmen M. (1993), "Capital inflows and real exchange rate appreciation in Latin America: the role of external factors," *IMF Staff Papers*, 40(1): 108–151.

Calvo, Guillermo, Leiderman, Leonardo and Reinhart, Carmen M. (1994), "The capital inflows problem: concepts and issues," *Contemporary Economic Policy*, 12: 54–66.

Calvo, Guillermo, Leiderman, Leonardo and Reinhart, Carmen M. (1996),"Inflows of capital to developing countries in the 1990s: causes and effects," *Journal of Economic Perspective*, 10(2): 123–139.

Edison, H.J. (1993), "The effectiveness of central-bank intervention: a survey of the literature after 1982," *Special Papers in International Economics, No. 18*, Princeton: Princeton University Press.

Frankel, J.A. (1994), "Sterilization of money inflows: Difficult (Calvo) or easy (Reisen)?,"IMF Working Paper no. WP/94/159.

Frankel, Jeffrey and Okongwu, Chudozie (1996), "Liberalized portfolio capital inflows in emerging markets: sterilization, expectations, and the incompleteness of interest rate convergence," *International Journal of Finance and Economics*, 7 (March): 1–23.

Furman, J. and Stiglitz, J. (1998), "Economic crises: evidence and insights from East Asia," *Brookings Papers on Economic Activity*, 2: 1–135.

Glick, Reuven and Hutchison, Michael (1994), "Monetary policy, intervention, and exchange rates in Japan," Federal Reserve Bank of San Francisco, Center for Pacific Basin Monetary and Economic Studies Working Paper no. PB93-07.

Glick, Reuven and Hutchison, Michael (2000), "Foreign reserve and money dynamics with asset portfolio adjustment: international evidence," *Journal of International Financial Markets, Institutions and Money*, 10: 229–247.

Goodhart, C.A. (1984), *Monetary Theory and Practice: The UK Experience*, London: Macmillan.

Herring, R. and Marston, R. (1977), "Sterilization policy: the trade-off between monetary autonomy and control over foreign exchange reserves," *European Economic Review*, 10: 225–243.

Hetzel, Robert L. (1996), "Sterilized foreign exchange intervention: the Fed Debate in the 1960s," *Federal Reserve Bank of Richmond Economic Quarterly*, 82/2.

Hutchinson, M.M. (1984), "Official Japanese intervention in foreign exchange markets: Leaning against the wind?," *Economics Letters*, 15: 115–120.

Isard, Peter (1995), *Exchange Rate Economics*, Cambridge: Cambridge University Press.

Kletzer, Kenneth M. and Spiegel, Mark M. (1996), "Speculative capital inflows and exchange rate targeting in the Pacific Basin: theory and evidence," Center for Pacific Basin Monetary and Economic Studies, Federal Reserve Bank of San Francisco, Working Paper no. PB96-05.

Montiel, Peter (1996), "Policy responses to surges in capital inflows: issues and lessons," in Calvo, Guillermo, Goldstein, Morris and Hochreiter, Eduard (eds), *Private Capital Flow to Emerging Markets after the Mexican Crisis*, Washington, DC: Institute for International Economics.

Montiel, P. (1998), "The capital inflow problem," Washington DC: World Bank Institute Working Paper no. 37135.

Montiel, P. and Reinhart, C.M. (1999), "Do capital controls and macroeconomic policies influence the volume and composition of capital flows? Evidence from the 1990s," *Journal of International Money and Finance*, 18, 619–635.

Moreno, Ramon and Spiegel, Mark M. (1997), "Are Asian economies exempt from the 'impossible trinity?': Evidence from Singapore," Center for Pacific Basin Monetary and Economic Studies, Federal Reserve Bank of San Francisco, Working Paper no. PB97-01.

Mussa, Michael (1981), *The Role of Official Intervention*, Washington DC: Group of Thirty.

Obstfeld, M. (1983), "Exchange rates, inflation and the sterilization problem: Germany 1975–1981," *European Economic Review*, 21: 161–189.

Obstfeld, M. (1988), "The effectiveness of foreign exchange intervention, recent experience: 1985–1988," NBER Working Paper no. 2796.

Reinhart, Carmen and Reinhart, V. (1998), "Some lessons for policymakers who deal with the mixed blessing of capital inflows," in Kahler, M. (ed.), *Capital Flows and Financial Crises*, New York: Council on Foreign Relations.

Rogoff, Kenneth (1984), "On the effects of sterilized intervention: an analysis of weekly data," *Journal of Monetary Economics*, 14 (September): 133–150.

Sargent, Thomas and Wallace, Neil (1981), "Some unpleasant monetarist arithmetic," *FRB Minneapolis Quarterly Review*, 5(3).

Seo, Byung Han (1996), "Inflation and government budget constraint in Korea," Federal Reserve Bank of San Francisco, Center for Pacific Basin Monetary and Economic Studies Working Paper no. PB96-03.

Sinclair, P. and Shu, C. (2001), "International capital movements and the international dimension to financial crises," in Brealey, R., Clarke, A., Goodhart, C. *et al.* (eds), *Financial Stability and Central Banks*, Routledge, 187–220.

Spiegel, Mark (1995), "Sterilization of capital inflows through the banking sector: evidence from Asia," *Federal Reserve Bank of San Francisco Economic Review*, 3: 17–34.

Takagi, Shinji (1991) "Foreign exchange market intervention and domestic monetary control in Japan, 1973–1989," *Japan and the World Economy*, 3: 147–180.

Takagi, Shinji and Esaka, Taro (2001), "Sterilization and the capital inflow problem in East Asia, 1987–97," in Ito, Takaatoshi and Kruger, Anne O. (eds) *Regional and Global Capital Flows: Macroeconomic Causes and Consequences*, Chicago: University of Chicago Press.

von Hagen, Jurgen (1989), "Monetary targeting with exchange rate constraints: the Bundesbank in the 1980's," *Federal Reserve Bank of St. Louis Review* (September): 53–69.

World Bank (1997), "Private capital flows to developing countries: the road to financial integration," A World Bank Policy Research Report, Oxford University Press.

16 Intervention in the foreign exchange market in a model with noise traders

Paul De Grauwe and Marianna Grimaldi*

1 Introduction

The "Washington consensus" of the 1990s about the desirable features of the international economic order included the view that countries allowing open goods and capital markets would have no other choice than to move to a pure floating exchange rate regime or else to enter into a monetary union. In this view intermediate regimes characterized by management of the exchange rate should be avoided because they are inherently unstable and sooner or later lead to a crisis. This consensus was reached mainly as a result of the collapse of fixed exchange rate regimes during the 1990s, first in Europe when the EMS disintegrated during 1992–93 and later in South-East Asia during 1997–98. This view was also given intellectual respectability by the development of theoretical models of exchange crises. In these models, rational agents trigger the collapse of the fixed exchange rate when the authorities fail to discipline monetary and fiscal policies to the rigours imposed by the markets, or worse when these rational agents create the crisis by the very fact that they predict it to happen.

Despite the power of this analysis many countries have refused to follow the prescriptions of the "Washington consensus", and have continued to manage their exchange rate, out of "fear of floating" (see Calvo and Reinhart 2000). In Asia in particular we observe that after the crises of 1997–98 many countries have gradually narrowed the size of the exchange rate fluctuations by active management of the exchange market (McKinnon and Schnabl 2002). There are several reasons for this creeping return to pegged exchange rates. First, in the case of Asia, the dollar maintains its dominating position as an invoicing currency despite the increasing intra-Asian trade. As a result, pegging to the dollar allows these countries to stabilize their exchange rates among themselves. A failure to do so carries the risk of "beggar-thy-neighbour" devaluations. Second, there is what Eichengreen and Hausmann (1999) have called the "original sin": because of underdeveloped capital markets, Asian countries lack the ability to borrow in their own currency. This also makes it difficult for stabilizing speculation to operate. As a result, there are few if any private market makers. Free float would under those circumstances lead to excessive volatility. Intervention in the foreign exchange market is seen as a way to stabilize the market (McKinnon an Schnabl 2002).

The academic models of the exchange rates have been based on the rational expectations paradigm, in which agents know the true distribution of the shocks in the fundamentals of the exchange rate. With this knowledge they force the exchange rate to reflect these fundamentals at each point in time. In such a world there is very little the authorities can do to influence the exchange rate without changing the current or future fundamentals. Sterilized intervention, i.e. intervention that keeps the current fundamentals unchanged is mostly futile, except if it is seen as a signal of a future change of (policy induced) fundamentals (see Dominguez and Frankel 1993). In this view only non-sterilized intervention can be effective.[1]

Despite this analysis, many central banks like those in Asia, that actively manage their exchange rates, overwhelmingly use sterilized interventions. Thus not only is there a strong desire to peg, but in addition, central banks use intervention policies that academic models predict to be relatively ineffective. One way to react to this official stubbornness is to shrug our academic shoulders and to predict that these attempts at managing the exchange markets will prove to be futile. Another way is to analyse our own models critically. There may be something in the foreign exchange markets not captured by our models that leads the monetary authorities to use sterilized interventions and to have more success than predicted.

In this chapter we present a model of the foreign exchange markets in which heterogeneous agents hold different beliefs about the future exchange rate. These agents are not rational in the sense given to this notion in mainstream models. Instead they use limited information sets to make forecasts. Rationality comes in the model in that these agents evaluate the profitability of these forecasting rules and decide ex post whether or not to switch to the more profitable one. The interaction of these heterogeneous agents leads to a rich dynamics in which the exchange rate is dissociated (disconnected) from its fundamentals most of the time, and in which periods of tranquillity and turbulence alternate in unpredictable fashion. We will analyse the rationale for sterilized intervention in the context of such a model. We will show that sterilized intervention has the capacity to change the nature of the dynamics of such a market.

2 The effectiveness of sterilized intervention: a brief review of the literature

While the consensus about the effectiveness of non-sterilized intervention has always been strong, the same cannot be said about the effectiveness of sterilized intervention.

Two major channels have been identified through which sterilized intervention can potentially affect the exchange rate, i.e. the portfolio balance channel (PBC) and the signalling channel (see Sarno and Taylor 2001, for a brief but exhaustive survey). According to the PBC, sterilized intervention can affect the exchange rate because it changes the investors' portfolio composition. However, the effect of the intervention will occur only if there is some degree of imperfect substitutability of the assets held in the portfolio (see Branson 1983) and/or Ricardian equivalence does not hold (Barro 1974). In a world of increasing capital mobility and perfect substitutability among domestic and foreign assets the importance of this channel will tend to be reduced. In the limit when foreign and domestic assets are perfect substitutes, sterilized intervention will not affect the exchange rate, anymore.

Sterilized intervention can still be effective under perfect substitutability through the signalling channel (Mussa 1981; Dominguez and Frankel 1993). The idea is that economic agents consider the exchange rate intervention as a signal about the future monetary policy. In other words, they interpret this intervention to lead to future changes in fundamentals. It is important to stress here that the implicit presumption is that the central bank backs up intervention with a subsequent change in the monetary policy as expected by the agents. If this is not the case, the central bank loses its credibility and future intervention will be unsuccessful. This leads to considering a possible drawback of the signalling channel. If the central bank has a weak reputation or a low credibility, then the signalling might fail or even give rise to a "perverse" reaction from the market. But such a drawback can be mitigated by the practise of coordinated intervention, i.e. two or more central banks intervene in the market simultaneously in support of the same currency. In the case of coordinated intervention, the effectiveness of intervention increases since the agents are willing to follow a multiple consistent signal rather than a single signal (see Dominguez and Frankel 1993). The coordination channel can be seen as representing a third channel through which the central bank can affect the exchange rate.

A closely related strand of literature addresses the issue of the existence of a link between profitability of technical trading rules and central bank intervention in the foreign exchange market.[2] This literature investigates whether simple trading rules have some predictive power and whether the forecastibility of the exchange rate is influenced by central bank interventions. The general results are that the exchange rate predictability is dramatically reduced when intervention periods are excluded from the analysis (see Le Baron 1996, 1999). However, such a link between predictability of exchange rates and profitability of technical trading rules has been found to be weak or non existent by other researchers (see Neely and Weller 2001). According to the latter, the predictability of the exchange rate is mainly due to the existence of trends in the exchange rate that intervention tends to reverse. It is important to note that these studies do not consider intervention acting as a signal of future monetary policy. Thus they do not take into account that if the signalling channel works, intervention policies can affect the exchange rate because these policies carry information that current and past exchange rates do not have.

3 The model

In this section we develop a simple non-linear model of the exchange rate. We assume agents of different types i depending on their beliefs about the future exchange rate. Each agent can invest in two assets, a domestic and a foreign one. The agent's utility function can be represented by the following equation:

$$U(W_{t+1}^i) = E_t(W_{t+1}^i) - \frac{1}{2}\mu V^i(W_{t+1}^i) \tag{1}$$

where W_{t+1}^i is the wealth of agent of type i at time $t+1$, E_t is the expectation operator, μ is the coefficient of risk aversion and $V^i(W_{t+1}^i)$ represents the conditional variance of wealth of agent i. The wealth is specified as follows:

$$W_{t+1}^i = (1+r^*)s_{t+1}d_t^i + (1+r)(W_t^i - s_t d_t^i) \tag{2}$$

where r and r^* are respectively the domestic and the foreign interest rates, s_{t+1} is the exchange rate at time $t+1$, $d_{i,t}$ represents the holdings of the foreign assets by agent of type i at time t. Thus, the first term on the right-hand side of equation (2) represents the value of the foreign portfolio in domestic currency at time $t+1$ while the second term represents the value of the domestic portfolio at time $t+1$.

Substituting equation (2) in (1) and maximizing the utility with respect to $d_{i,t}$ allows us to derive the optimal holding of foreign assets by agents of type i:

$$d_{i,t} = \frac{(1+r^*)E_t^i(s_{t+1}) - (1+r)s_t}{\mu \sigma_{i,t}^2} \tag{3}$$

The market demand for foreign assets at time t is the sum of the individual demands, i.e.:

$$\sum_{i=1}^{N} n_{i,t}d_{i,t} = D_t \tag{4}$$

where $n_{i,t}$ is the number of agents of type i.

Market equilibrium implies that the market demand is equal to the market supply X_t. The latter increases (declines) when the current account is positive (negative) and when the monetary authorities sell (buy) foreign assets. We assume here that X_t is exogenous. (When we introduce interventions this variable will become endogenous.) Thus,

$$X_t = D_t \tag{5}$$

Substituting the optimal holdings into the market demand and then into the market equilibrium equation and solving for the exchange rate s_t yields the equilibrium exchange rate:

$$s_t = \left(\frac{1+r^*}{1+r}\right) \frac{1}{\left(\sum\limits_{i=1}^{N} \frac{n_{i,t}}{\sigma_{i,t}^2}\right)} \left[\sum\limits_{i=1}^{N} n_{i,t} \frac{E_t^i(s_{t+1})}{\sigma_{i,t}^2} - \mu \frac{X_t}{1+r}\right] \tag{6}$$

In order to model the expectations formation we assume that there are two types of agents: chartists and fundamentalists. As a result equation (6) specializes to:

$$s_t = \left(\frac{1+r^*}{1+r}\right) \frac{1}{\left(\frac{n_{f,t}}{\sigma_{f,t}^2} + \frac{n_{c,t}}{\sigma_{c,t}^2}\right)} \left[n_{f,t} \frac{E_t^f(s_{t+1})}{\sigma_{f,t}^2} + n_{c,t} \frac{E_t^c(s_{t+1})}{\sigma_{c,t}^2} - \mu \frac{X_t}{1+r}\right] \tag{7}$$

Thus the exchange rate is determined by the expectations of fundamentalists and chartists about the future exchange rate. These forecasts are weighted by their respective variances.

We now specify how fundamentalists and chartists form their expectations of the future exchange rate. Then we will specify how they take into account the risk as measured by the variances.

The fundamentalists base their forecast on a comparison between the market and the fundamental exchange rate, i.e. they forecast the market rate to return to the fundamental rate in the future. In this sense they use a negative feedback rule that introduces a mean reverting dynamics in the exchange rate. The speed with which the market exchange rate returns to the fundamental is assumed to be determined by the speed of adjustment in the goods market. Thus, the forecasting rule for the fundamentalists is:

$$E_t^f(\Delta s_{t+1}) = -\psi_t(s_t - s_t^*) \tag{8}$$

where s_t^* is the fundamental exchange rate at time t, which is assumed to follow a random walk.

The parameter ψ_t is determined by the speed of adjustment in the goods market. There is a large body of empirical evidence indicating that the speed of adjustment in the goods market follows a non-linear dynamics, i.e. the speed with which prices adjust towards equilibrium depends positively on the size of the deviation of the exchange rate from its fundamental value (misalignment) (Kilian and Taylor 2001; Taylor *et al.* 2001; Michael *et al.* 1997). We will assume that the fundamentalists take into account this non-linear adjustment process in making their forecasts. We specify ψ_t as follows:

$$\psi_t = \theta |s_t - s_t^*| \tag{9}$$

The economics behind this non-linear specification is that in order to profit from arbitrage opportunities in the goods market, some fixed investment must be made, e.g. trucks must be bought, planes chartered, etc. These investments become profitable with sufficiently large deviations from the fundamental exchange rate. Note that we do not model the goods market explicitly but we assume that in order to form their expectations about the exchange rate, the fundamentalists take into account the dynamics of the goods market and the speed of adjustment of goods prices.

The chartists forecast the future exchange rate by extrapolating past exchange rate movements. Their forecasting rule can be specified as:

$$E_t^c(\Delta s_{t+1}) = \beta \sum_{i=0}^{T} \alpha_i \Delta s_{t-i} \tag{10}$$

Thus, the chartists compute a moving average of the past exchange rate changes and they extrapolate this into the future exchange rate change. The degree of extrapolation is given by the parameter β. Note that in contrast to the fundamentalists they do not take into account information concerning the fundamental exchange rate. In this sense they can be considered to be pure noise traders.

Our choice to introduce chartists' rules of forecasting is based on empirical evidence. The evidence that chartism is used widely to make forecasts is overwhelming (see Cheung and Chinn 1989; Taylor and Allen 1992). Therefore, we give a prominent role to chartists in our model. It remains important, however, to check if the model is internally consistent. In particular, the chartists' forecasting rule must be shown to be profitable within the confines of the model. If these rules turn out to be unprofitable, they will not continue to be used. We return to this issue when we let the number of chartists be determined by the profitability of the chartists' forecasting rule.

We now analyse how fundamentalists and chartists evaluate the risk. The latter is measured by the variance terms in equation (7), which we define as the weighted average of the squared (one period ahead) forecasting errors made by chartists and fundamentalists, respectively. Thus,

$$\sigma_{i,t} = \sum_{k=1}^{\infty} \gamma_k [E_{t-k}^i(s_{t-k+1}) - s_{t-k+1}]^2 \tag{11}$$

where γ_k are geometrically declining weights.

However fundamentalists and chartists perceive the risk in a different way. In particular the fundamentalists are assumed to take into account the deviation of the exchange rate from the fundamental in addition to the forecasting error. We will call the deviation of the market exchange rate from fundamentals, the misalignment. Thus the fundamentalists' risk term can be written as:

$$\sigma_{f,t} = \frac{\sum_{k=1}^{T} \gamma_k [E_{t-k}^f(s_{t-k+1}) - s_{t-k+1}]^2}{(s_{t-1} - s_{t-1}^*)^2} \tag{12}$$

where $(s_{t-1} - s_{t-1}^*)$ is the misalignment.

The logic behind this specification is that the fundamentalists consider the fundamental exchange rate as a benchmark. The larger is the misalignment the less the fundamentalists will attach importance to the short-term volatility as measured by the one-period ahead forecasting error. Put differently, the larger is the deviation of the exchange rate from its fundamental, the more confident the fundamentalists are about the probability of a return towards the fundamental rate. As a result, they perceive the risk of using a fundamentalist forecasting rule to decline when the misalignment increases. In contrast the chartists do not take into account the misalignment.

We now specify the dynamics that governs the number of chartists and fundamentalists, namely n_{ct} and n_{ft}. In order to do so, we describe how the number of chartists and fundamentalists change from period $t-1$ to period t:

$$n_t^c = n_{t-1}^c + n_{t-1}^f p_t^{fc} - n_{t-1}^c p_t^{cf} \tag{13}$$

$$n_{f,t} = n_{f,t-1} + n_{c,t-1} p_t^{cf} - n_{f,t-1} p_t^{fc} \tag{14}$$

where $n_{c,t}$ and $n_{f,t}$ are the number of chartists and fundamentalists in period t; p_t^{cf} represents the fraction of the chartists who decide to become fundamentalists in period t, and p_t^{fc} is the fraction of the fundamentalists who decide to become chartists in period t.

These fractions are assumed to be a function of the relative utilities of chartism and fundamentalism. These utilities depend on the profitability of the forecasting rules and the risk associated with their use. The fractions are specified as follows:[3]

$$p_t^{fc} = s \frac{exp(U_{c,t-1})}{exp(U_{c,t-1}) + exp(U_{f,t-1})} \tag{15}$$

$$p_t^{cf} = s \frac{exp(U_{f,t-1})}{exp(U_{c,t-1}) + exp(U_{f,t-1})} \tag{16}$$

where $U_{c,t-1}$ and $U_{f,t-1}$ are the utility functions of the chartists and fundamentalists in period $t-1$. The parameter ς measures the sensitivity of the decision to switch with respect to the relative profits adjusted for the risk. Thus this parameter can be interpreted as a measure of the degree of inertia in the decision of switching. A low ς implies a high degree of inertia. Note also that $0 < \varsigma < 1$. Equations (15) and (16) can be interpreted as follows. When the utility associated with using chartist information increases relative to the utility of using fundamentalist information the agents tend to switch from fundamentalism to chartism and vice versa. Taking into account the specification of the utility function (equation (1)), we can rewrite equations (15) and (16) as follows:

$$p_t^{fc} = \varsigma \frac{exp(\pi_{c,t-1} - \mu\sigma_{c,t-1}^2)}{exp(\pi_{c,t-1} - \mu\sigma_{c,t-1}^2) + exp(\pi_{f,t-1} - \mu\sigma_{f,t-1}^2)} \tag{17}$$

$$p_t^{cf} = \varsigma \frac{exp(\pi_{f,t-1} - \mu\sigma_{f,t-1}^2)}{exp(\pi_{c,t-1} - \mu\sigma_{c,t-1}^2) + exp(\pi_{f,t-1} - \mu\sigma_{f,t-1}^2)} \tag{18}$$

Thus, the decision to switch depends on the relative profits adjusted for the risk. When the risk adjusted profits of chartist rules increase relative to the risk adjusted profits of fundamentalist rules, a certain fraction of fundamentalists decide to switch towards the use of chartist rules. Agents make a profit when they correctly forecast the direction of the exchange rate movements. They make a loss if they wrongly predict the direction of its movements. The profit (the loss) they make equals the one-period return of investing $1.

4 The model with transactions costs

There is an increasing body of theoretical literature stressing the importance of transactions costs as a source of non-linearity in the determination of the exchange rate (Dumas 1992; Sercu *et al.* 1995; Obstfeld and Rogoff 2000). The importance of transactions costs has also been confirmed empirically (Taylor *et al.* 2001; Kilian and Taylor 2001). Therefore, we develop a version of the previous model in which the transactions costs play a role.

We take the view that if transactions costs in the goods markets exist, the fundamentalists take this information into account. Therefore, if the exchange rate is within the transactions costs band the fundamentalists behave differently than if the exchange rate moves outside the transactions costs band.

Consider the first case, when the exchange rate deviations from the fundamental value are smaller than the transactions costs. In this case the fundamentalists know that arbitrage in the goods market does not apply. As a result, they expect the changes in the exchange rate to follow a white noise process. The best they can do is to forecast no change. More formally,

when $|s_t - s_t^*| < C$, then $E_t^f(\Delta s_{t+1}) = 0$.

In the second case, when the exchange rate deviation from its fundamental value is larger than the transactions costs C (assumed to be of the "iceberg" type), then the fundamentalists follow the same forecasting rule as in equation (8). More formally,

when $|s_t - s_t^*| > C$, holds, then equation (8) applies.

This formulation implies that when the exchange rate moves outside the transactions costs band, market inefficiencies other than transactions costs continue to play a role. As a result, these inefficiencies prevent the exchange rate from adjusting instantaneously. In our model these inefficiencies are captured by the fact that the speed of adjustment in the goods market is not infinite (equation (9)).

5 Solution of the model

In this section we investigate the properties of the solution of the model. We first study its deterministic solution. This will allow us to analyse the characteristics of the solution that are not clouded by exogenous noise. We use simulation techniques since the non-linearities do not allow for a simple analytical solution. We select "reasonable" values of the parameters, i.e. those that come close to empirically observed values.[4]

We first concentrate on the fixed-point solutions of the model. We find that for a relatively wide range of parameters the solution converges to a fixed point (a fixed-point attractor). However, there are many such fixed points (attractors) to which the solution converges depending on the initial conditions. We illustrate this feature in Figure 16.1 where we plot the fixed point solutions (attractors) as a function of the different initial conditions. On the horizontal axis we set out the different initial conditions. These are initial shocks to the deterministic system. The vertical axis shows the solution corresponding to these different initial conditions. Note the complex pattern of these fixed-point solutions, with many discontinuities. This has the implication that a small change in the initial condition can have a large effect on the solution. This feature lies at the heart of some of the results that are obtained with this model relating to the unpredictability of the effect of shocks in exogenous variables. We return to this phenomenon in section 6.

It is also interesting to point out the existence of critical points. These are often obtained close to the limits of the transactions cost band. A continuous line is then broken into a cluster of points. These have a fractal nature, in that they have an infinite self-replicating characteristic.

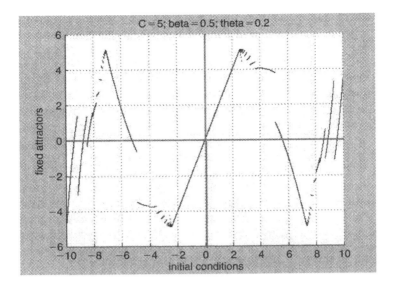

Figure 16.1 Attractors as a function of initial conditions.

6 Sensitivity analysis

In this section we perform a sensitivity analysis. We do this by showing diagrams that relate the solutions to different values of important parameters of the model. We concentrate on the extrapolation parameter used by the chartists, as this turns out to be a crucial parameter determining the nature of the solution.[5] Figure 16.2 shows an example of such a diagram. It is analogous to the so-called bifurcation diagram. On the vertical axis we set out different values of the extrapolation parameter. On the vertical axis we show the solutions for the exchange rate. This is the exchange rate obtained after 1000 periods, given an initial shock. We observe the following. For values of $\beta \leq 0.8$ we obtain a continuous line. This means that there is a unique fixed-point solution for each value of β. When β is approximately 0.8 we have a critical point where the continuous line breaks into a fractal pattern. We still have fixed-point solutions, though. The continuous line, however, is fractured in such a way that for each value of β only one solution is found. When β reaches a value of approximately 0.9, we enter the chaotic region. This is characterized by infinitely many solutions for each value of β. These points correspond to strange attractors within which the exchange rate then travels. Note that we do not obtain bifurcations in this model, like the Hoppf bifurcation. The transition to chaos is abrupt. We do find that increasing the value of β can lead us in and out of the chaotic region.[6]

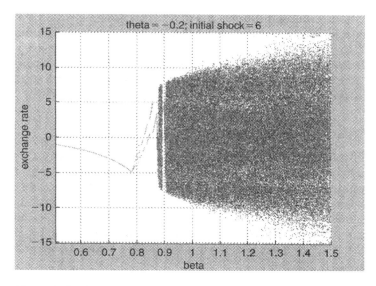

Figure 16.2 Bifurcation diagram: exchange rate as a function of β.

It is also important to analyse the dynamics of the weights of chartists and fundamentalists. We find that when the exchange rate converges towards a fixed-point attractor the weights of chartists and fundamentalists converge to 0.5. This can be explained as follows. When the exchange rates reach a fixed-point solution, chartists and fundamentalists expect no change anymore.[7] Therefore, they do not buy or sell, and thus make neither profits nor losses. As a result, the profit related selection rule of the model (see equations (17) and (18)) assures that they will be equally represented in the market.

Things are very different when the exchange rate follows a chaotic pattern. In this case the chartists and fundamentalists weights will show cyclical movement. In general the chartists' weight will tend to fluctuate around a value larger than 0.5 provided the chartist extrapolation is not too high. We come back to this feature in section 9 where we analyse the dynamics of the weights of chartists and fundamentalists in more detail.

The empirical evidence in favour of deterministic chaos is not very strong. Sometimes deterministic chaos has been detected in the data, but most often no such dynamics has been found (Granger 1994; Guillaume 1996; Schittenkopf *et al.* 2001). This suggests that we should restrict the analysis of the model to parameter configurations that do not produce deterministic chaos. Typically this implies restricting the extrapolation parameter used by chartists not to exceed 0.9. The borderline between fixed-point solutions and deterministic chaos remains interesting though. As we have seen, even with an extrapolation parameter between 0.9 and 1 different initial conditions lead to switches in and out of chaos, making it difficult to detect deterministic chaos from the data.[8]

In the next section we restrict the analysis of the model for parameter values that do not lead to deterministic chaos. We will show that in combination with stochastic shocks this model is capable of producing a complex dynamics that exhibits many of the features of chaotic dynamics despite the fact that the deterministic solutions of the model are fixed points.[9]

7 The stochastic version of the model

We now introduce stochastic disturbances to the model. In our model these disturbances affect the fundamental, which is assumed to be a random walk. In addition, as can be seen from equation (8), there is exogenous noise leading to forecast errors of chartists and fundamentalists. We simulate the model with a certain combination of parameter values that we refer to as the "standard case". This includes setting $c = 5$, $\beta = 0.5$ and $\theta = 0.2$. (Similar results are obtained for a wide range of parameter values.)

A first feature of the solution of the stochastic version of the model is the sensitivity to initial conditions. In order to show this, we first simulated the model with the "standard" parameter values and then we simulated the model with the same parameters setting but with a slightly different initial condition. In both cases we used identical stochastic disturbances. We show the time paths of the (market) exchange rate in Figure 16.3.

We observe that after a certain number of periods the two exchange

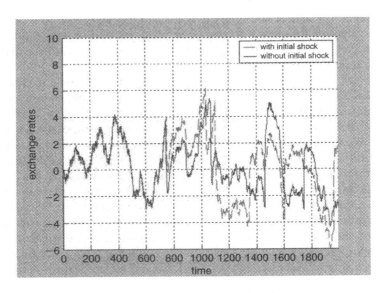

Figure 16.3 Sensitivity to initial conditions of exchange rate.

rates start following a different path. This result is related to the presence of many fixed-point attractors in the deterministic part of the model, which are themselves dependent on the initial conditions (see Figure 16.1, that shows how slight differences in initial conditions can lead to fixed-point attractors that are very far apart). As a result, the two exchange rates can substantially diverge because they are attracted by fixed points that are far away from each other. The nice aspect of this is that we obtain a result that is typical for chaotic systems, however, without chaos being present in the deterministic part of the model. The combination of exogenous noise and a multiplicity of fixed-point attractors creates chaos-like dynamics. As will be seen later, interventions in the foreign exchange markets have the capacity to alter this feature of the model.

A second feature of the model relates to the way shocks in the fundamental exchange rate are transmitted into the market exchange rate. In linear models a permanent shock in the fundamental has a predictable effect on the exchange rate, i.e. the coefficient that measures the effect of the shock in the fundamental on the exchange rate converges after some time to a fixed number. Things are very different in our non-linear model. We illustrate this by showing how a permanent increase in the fundamental is transmitted to the exchange rate. We assumed that the fundamental rate increases by 10, and we computed the effect on the exchange rate by taking the difference between the exchange rate with the shock and the exchange rate without the shock. In a linear model we would find that in the long run the exchange rate increases by 10. This is not the case in our model. We present the evidence in Figure 16.4 where we show the effect of the same permanent shock of 10 in the fundamental rate on the exchange rate. The simulations are done assuming exactly the same

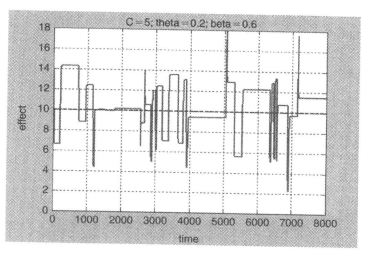

Figure 16.4 Effect on exchange rate of shock in fundemental.

stochastics in the scenario with than without the permanent shock in the fundamental exchange rate. Thus, there is no exogenous noise in the model that could blur the transmission process from the fundamental rate to the exchange rate.

The most striking feature of these results is that the effect of the permanent shock does not converge to a fixed number. In fact, it follows a complex pattern. Thus, in a non-linear world it is very difficult to predict what the effect will be of a given shock in the fundamental, even in the long term. Such predictions can only be made in a statistical sense, i.e. our model tells us that on average the effect of a shock of 10 in the fundamental will be to increase the exchange rate by 10. In any given period, however, the effect could deviate substantially from this average prediction.[10]

The importance of the initial conditions for the effect of a permanent shock in the fundamental can also be seen by the following experiment. We simulated the same permanent shock in the fundamental but applied it in two different time periods. In the first simulation we applied the shock in the first period; in the second simulation we applied it in the next period. The exogenous noise was identical in both simulations. Thus the only difference is in the timing of the shock. We show the results in Figure 16.5.

We observe that the small difference in timing changes the whole future history of the exchange rate. As a result, the effect of the shock measured at a particular point in time can be very different in both simulations. Thus history matters. The time at which the permanent shock occurs influences the effects of the shock.

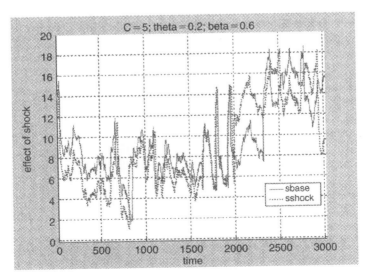

Figure 16.5 Effect of fundemental shock in different periods.

Our results help to explain why in the real world it appears so difficult to predict the effects of changes in the fundamental exchange rate on the market rate, and why these effects seem to be very different when applied in different periods. In fact this is probably one of the most intriguing empirical problems. Economists usually explain the difficulty of forecasting the effects of a particular change in one exogenous variable (for example, an expansion of the money stock) by invoking the *ceteris paribus* hypothesis, i.e. there are usually other exogenous variables changing unexpectedly, preventing us to isolate the effect of the first exogenous variable. In our model the uncertainty surrounding the effect of a disturbance in an exogenous variable is not due to the failure of the *ceteris paribus* hypothesis. No other exogenous variable is allowed to change. The fact is that the change in the exogenous variable occurs at a particular time, which is different from all other times. Initial conditions (history) matters to forecast the effect of shocks. Since each initial condition is unique, it becomes difficult to forecast the effect of a shock at any given point in time with precision.

Finally, it should be stressed that the uncertainty about the effect of a permanent shock in the fundamental only holds in a particular environment that is related to a low variance of the noise. In a later section we will analyse how different environments concerning the variance of shocks affect the results.

8 Empirical relevance of the model

In this section we analyse how well our model mimics the empirical anomalies and puzzles that have been uncovered by the flourishing empirical literature. The way we proceed is to calibrate the model in such a way that it best replicates the observed statistical properties of the exchange rate movements. One result of this calibration effort is that we reject the parameter sets that produce deterministic chaos, because when the latter occurs we fail to reproduce the observed statistical properties of exchange rate movements. Put differently, we find that chaotic dynamics does not provide for a good explanation of the empirical puzzles detected in the foreign exchange markets. This calibration effort can be considered as a way to "discipline" the model, whereby the discipline is provided by the observed statistical properties of the exchange rates that the model should replicate.

8.1 The disconnect puzzle

First and foremost, the empirical puzzle has been called the "disconnect" puzzle (see Obstfeld and Rogoff 2000), i.e. the exchange rate appears to be disconnected from its underlying fundamentals most of the time. It was first analysed by John Williamson (1985) who called it the "misalignment problem". This puzzle was also implicit in the celebrated Meese and Rogoff (1983) study documenting that there is no stable relationship between exchange rate movements and the news in the fundamental variables. Goodhart (1989) and Goodhart and Figliuoli (1991) found that most of the changes in the exchange rates occur when there is no observable news in the fundamental economic variables. This finding contradicted the theoretical models (based on the efficient market hypothesis), which imply that the exchange rate can only move when there is news in the fundamentals.

Our model is capable of mimicking this empirical regularity. In Figure 16.6 we show the market exchange rate and the fundamental rate for a combination of parameters that does not produce deterministic chaos. (Our results hold equally well for a large set of parameter values including those that produce deterministic chaos.)

We observe that the market rate can deviate from the fundamental value substantially and in a persistent way. Moreover, it appears that the exchange rate movements are often disconnected from the movements of the underlying fundamental. In fact, they often move in opposite directions.

We show the nature of the disconnect phenomenon in a more precise way by applying a cointegration analysis to the simulated exchange rate and its fundamental, using the same parameter values as in Figure 16.6 for a sample of 8000 periods. We found that there is a cointegration relationship between the exchange rate and its fundamental. Note that in our setting there is only one fundamental variable. This implies that no bias from omitted variables can occur.

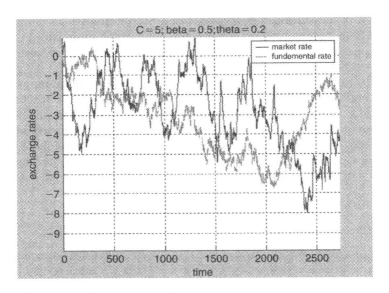

Figure 16.6 Market and fundemental exchange rate disconnect.

In the next step we specify an EC model in the following way:

$$\Delta s_t = \mu(s_{t-1} - \gamma s_{t-1}^*) + \sum_{i=1}^{n} \lambda_i \Delta s_{t-i} + \sum_{i=1}^{n} \phi_i \Delta s_{t-i}^* \qquad (19)$$

The first term on the right-hand side is the error correction term. The result of estimating this equation is presented in Table 16.1 where we have set $n = 4$.

We find that the error correction coefficient (μ) is very low. This suggests that the mean reversion towards the equilibrium exchange rate takes a very long time. In particular, only 0.5 per cent of the adjustment takes place each period. It should be noted that in the simulations we have assumed a speed of adjustment in the goods market equal to 0.2. This implies that in each period, the adjustment in the goods market is 20 per cent. Thus the nominal exchange rate is considerably slower to adjust towards its equilibrium than what is implied by the speed of adjustment in the goods market. This slow adjustment of the nominal exchange rate is due to the chartist extrapolation behaviour. This phenomenon has been observed in reality. Cheung *et al.* (2002) have recently discovered that most of the slow mean reversions of the real exchange rate is due to slow adjustment of the nominal exchange rate and not of the goods prices.

From Table 16.1, we also note that the changes in fundamentals have a small and insignificant impact on the change in exchange rate. In contrast, the past changes in the exchange rate play a significant role in explaining the change in exchange rate. These results are consistent with the empirical findings using VAR approach, which suggests that the exchange rate is driven by its own past (see De Boeck 2000).

Thus, our model generates an empirical regularity (the "disconnect" puzzle) that has also been observed in reality. We can summarize the features of this puzzle as follows. First, over the very long term the exchange rate and its fundamentals are cointegrated. However, the speed with which the exchange rate reverts to its equilibrium value is very slow. Second, in the short term the exchange rate and its fundamentals are "disconnected", i.e. they do not appear to be cointegrated. Our model closely mimics these empirical regularities.

Table 16.1 Parameter estimates of EC model (equation (19))

Error correction term		Δs_{t-i}				Δs_{t-i}^*			
μ	γ	λ_1	λ_2	λ_3	λ_4	φ_1	φ_2	φ_3	φ_4
−0.005	1.06	0.18	0.15	0.09	0.05	0.04	0.03	0.02	0.01
−6.4	11.3	16.4	13.1	7.06	4.3	2.2	1.6	1.3	1.06

This feature is important to analyse the effectiveness of intervention policies. It is precisely because the exchange rate is systematically disconnected from its fundamentals that foreign exchange market interventions of the sterilized type have the potential to affect the exchange rate. The scope for such interventions in the traditional rational expectations models is limited because these models predict that the exchange rate must always reflect its fundamentals.

8.2 The "excess volatility" puzzle

In this section we discuss another important empirical regularity, which has been called the "excess volatility" puzzle, i.e. the volatility of the exchange rate by far exceeds the volatility of the underlying economic variables. Baxter and Stockman (1989) and Flood and Rose (1995) found that while the movements from fixed to flexible exchange rates led to a dramatic increase in the volatility of the exchange rate no such increase could be detected in the volatility of the underlying economic variables. This contradicted the "news" models that predicted that the volatility of the exchange rate can only increase when the variability of the underlying fundamental variables increase.

In order to deal with this puzzle we compute the noise-to-signal ratio in the simulated exchange rate. We derive this noise to signal ratio as follows:

$$var(s) = var(f) + var(n) \qquad (20)$$

where $var(s)$ is the variance of the simulated exchange rate, $var(f)$ is the variance of the fundamental and $var(n)$ is the residual variance (noise) produced by the non-linear speculative dynamics which is uncorrelated with $var(f)$. Rewriting equation (20) we obtain

$$\frac{var(n)}{var(f)} = \frac{var(s)}{var(f)} - 1 \qquad (21)$$

The ratio $var(n)/var(f)$ can be interpreted as the noise-to-signal ratio. It gives a measure of how large the noise produced by the non-linear dynamics is with respect to the exogenous volatility of the fundamental exchange rate. We simulate this noise to signal ratio for different values of the extrapolation parameter beta (see Figure 16.7). In addition, since this ratio is sensitive to the time interval over which it is computed we checked how it changes depending on the length of the time interval. In particular, we expect that the noise-to-signal ratio is larger when it is computed on a short- than on a long-time horizon. We show the results in Figure 16.8.

First, we find that with increasing β the noise-to-signal ratio increases. This implies that when the chartists increase the degree with which they extrapolate the past exchange rate movements, the noise, i.e. the volatility

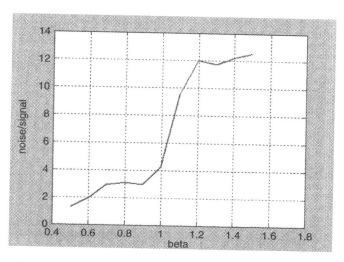

Figure 16.7 Noise-to-signal ratio as a function of β.

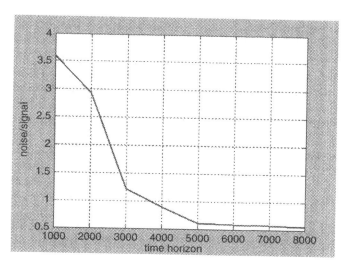

Figure 16.8 Noise-to-signal ratio as a function of the time interval.

in the exchange rate which is unrelated to fundamentals, increases. Thus, the signal about the fundamentals that we can extract from the exchange rate becomes more clouded when the chartists extrapolate more. Second, we find that when the time horizon increases the noise-to-signal ratio declines. This is so because over long time horizons most of the volatility of the exchange rate is due to the fundamentals' volatility and very little to the endogenous noise. In contrast, over short-time horizons the endogenous volatility is predominant and the signal that comes from the fundamentals is weak. This is consistent with the empirical finding concerning misalignments we discussed before.

One of the issues we will analyse when we incorporate foreign exchange market interventions into the model is whether these interventions are capable of reducing the noise-to-signal ratio, thereby making the exchange rate movements less sensitive to non-fundamentally driven noise.

8.3 Fat tails

It is well known that the exchange rate changes do not follow a normal distribution. Instead it has been observed that the distribution of exchange rate changes has more density around the mean than the normal and exhibits fatter tails than the normal (see de Vries 2001). This phenomenon was first discovered by Mandelbrot (1963) in commodity markets. Since then, fat tails and excess kurtosis have been discovered in many other asset markets including the exchange market. In particular, in the latter the returns have a kurtosis typically exceeding 3 and a measure of fat tails (Hill index) ranging between 2 and 5 (see Koedijk *et al.* 1992; Huisman *et al.* 2002). It implies that most of the time the exchange rate movements are relatively small but that occasionally periods of turbulence occur with relatively large exchange rate changes. However, it has also been detected that the kurtosis is reduced under time aggregation. This phenomenon has been observed for most exchange rates (Lux 1998; Calvet and Fisher 2002). We checked whether this is also the case with the simulated exchange rate changes in our model.

The model was simulated using normally distributed random disturbances (with mean = 0 and standard deviation = 1). We computed the kurtosis and the Hill index of the simulated exchange rate returns. We computed the Hill index for 4 different samples of 2000 observations. In addition, we considered three different cut-off points of the tails (2.5 per cent, 5 per cent, 10 per cent). We show the results of the kurtosis and of the Hill index in Table 16.2. We find that for a broad range of parameter values the kurtosis exceeds 3 and the Hill index indicates the presence of

Table 16.2 Median Hill index (4 samples 2000 observations)

Parameter values	Kurtosis	2.5% tail	5% tail	10% tail
c = 5, beta = 0.5, theta = 0.2	185.4	2.1	2.8	3.1
c = 5, beta = 0.7, theta = 0.2	66.7	1.7	1.6	1.9
c = 5, beta = 0.7, theta = 0.05	5.9	4.6	4.3	4.0
c = 5, beta = 0.5, theta = 0.1	48.8	2.9	3.4	3.4
c = 5, beta = 0.5, theta = 0.05	8.5	4.2	4.2	4.0

fat tails. Finally we check if the kurtosis of our simulated exchange rate returns declines under time aggregation. In order to do so, we chose different time aggregation periods and we computed the kurtosis of the time-aggregated exchange rate returns. We found that the kurtosis declines under time aggregation. In Table 16.3 we show the results for some sets of parameter values.[11] This suggests that the non-linear dynamics of the model transforms normally distributed noise in the exchange rate into exchange rate movements with tails that are significantly fatter than the normal distribution and with more density around the mean.

9 Is chartism evolutionarily stable?

An important issue is whether chartism survives in our model. Put differently, we ask the question under which conditions chartism is profitable such that it does not disappear. It should be noted that there is a broad literature that shows that technical analysis is used widely, also by large players (see Taylor and Allen 1992; Wei and Kim 1997).

We investigate this issue by analysing how chartism evolves under different conditions. In Figure 16.9 we show the share of chartists in the markets for increasing values of the extrapolation parameter β. We obtained the chartists weights by simulating the model over 10 000 periods and computing the weight of the last period. Our first finding is that chartism does not disappear, i.e. in all simulations, for many different parameters configurations, we find that the weight attached to chartists never goes to zero. Second, for a wide range of parameter values we find that the chartists' weight in the market fluctuates around a market share, which exceeds 50 per cent. Thus, in all our simulations of the model we find that chartist rules tend to dominate the fundamentalist rules. Third, as the extrapolation parameter β increases the weight of chartists first increases slightly. When β reaches a critical point around 0.9 (which is also the point where the dynamics switches into chaos), the market share of chartists jumps up to approximately 2/3. It then moves down to settle around 64 per cent. This suggests that as chartists become more aggressive in extrapolating past movements of the exchange rate, the chartist rule becomes more profitable attracting more agents to become chartists. Too

Table 16.3 Kurtosis under time-aggregation

Parameter values	1 period returns	5 periods returns	10 periods returns	25 periods returns
c = 5, theta = 0.2, beta = 1	7.1	4.5	4.0	2.2
c = 5, theta = 0.2, beta = 0.8	40.3	13.3	10.3	4.6
c = 5, theta = 0.2, beta = 0.5	182.9	37.9	24.2	9.9
c = 5, theta = 0.1, beta = 1	3.8	3.2	3.3	2.4
c = 5, theta = 0.3, beta = 1	8.9	4.9	3.6	2.2

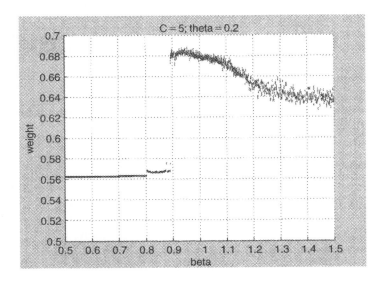

Figure 16.9 Chartists' weight as a function of β.

much extrapolation in turn reduces the relative profitability of chartism and reduces the market share of chartism. The latter results suggest that when chartists extrapolate too much the ensuing deviations from the fundamental exchange rate makes fundamentalist forecasting rules more profitable again.

A final step in the analysis consisted in analysing the question of how the profits of the chartists and the fundamentalists evolve when the shares of the chartists increase exogenously. In order to answer this question we simulated a different version of the model assuming that the shares of chartists vary exogenously from 0 to 0.9 (instead of being determined endogenously by relative profitability). We then computed the average profits of chartists' rules as the proportion of chartist's increases. We did the same for the fundamentalists profits. We show the results in Figures 16.10 and 16.11. The results are quite striking. As the weight of chartists increases the profits they make increases strongly. In fact the increase becomes exponential as the shares of the chartists in the market becomes very high. Conversely, the profitability of fundamentalists rules is very high when there are few chartists in the market, but drops precipituously as the chartists make inroads. This suggests that there is a self-fulfilling evolutionary dynamics present in the system which can be described as follows. When there are no chartists in the market, fundamentalist forecasting is very profitable. However, these fundamentalists' profits are very vulnerable to an invasion by chartists. An invasion by 10 per cent leads to a collapse of the fundamentalists' profits. From a market share of 20 per

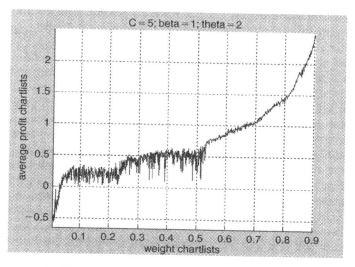

Figure 16.10 Average profits of chartists as a function of their weights.

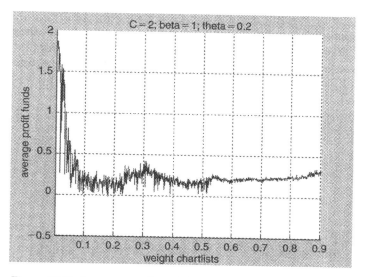

Figure 16.11 Average profits of fundamentalists as a function of chartists' weights.

cent on, the chartists' rule becomes more profitable than the fundamentalists' rule. As the chartists increase in numbers their profits tend to increase exponentially. The reason is that the increasing importance of chartists increases the noise in the exchange rate movements, making chartism more profitable. At the same time, the chartists have the effect of "creating smoke around the fundamentals", making fundamentalists' forecasting riskier. Another way to interpret this result is that chartism creates noisy information that becomes the source of profitable speculation. The more chartists there are the more such information is created and the more profitable chartists forecasting becomes. Thus, chartists create an informational environment which makes it rational to use chartists' rules.

Why does all this not lead to a corner solution, i.e. a situation in which chartism drives out all fundamentalists? The reason has to do with risk. When the weight of chartists increases in the market, so does volatility. We show this in Figure 16.12 where we present the exchange rate as a function of the weight of chartists. We observe that an increase in the chartists weight leads to a significant increase in volatility especially when the weight approaches 1. Thus, as the weight of chartists in the market increases both the profitability and risk of using chartist rules increase. The increasing risk is strong enough to prevent the chartists from completely driving out the fundamentalists and taking over the market.

10 The model with intervention

In this section we analyse how the exchange rate is determined when we introduce intervention by the monetary authorities in the foreign exchange rate market. From (7), it can be seen that the exchange rate is

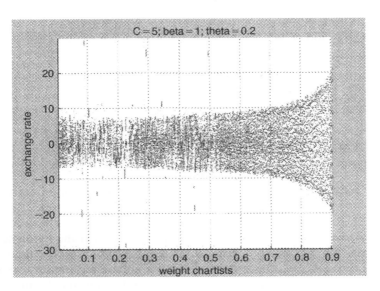

Figure 16.12 Exchange rate as a function of weight of chartists.

affected by the stock of net foreign assets X_t. Intervention affects the exchange rate through the changes in X_t. In particular, when the monetary authorities sell (buy) foreign exchange the stock of net foreign assets increases (decreases) thereby leading to a portfolio effect on the exchange rate. This creates the channel through which the authorities can affect the exchange rate. We model how the monetary authorities conduct this intervention. We start from the loss function of the authorities which we specify as follows:

$$L_t = (s_t - s_t^*)^2 + \omega(s_t - s_{t-1})^2 \tag{22}$$

The first term of equation (22) is the squared deviation of the exchange rate from its target level. We assume that the monetary authorities set the target equal to the fundamental rate. The second term represents the squared changes of the exchange rate, i.e. the volatility of the exchange rate. Thus, the monetary authorities also aim at minimizing the volatility of the exchange rate irrespective of the fundamental rate. The loss function therefore combines target intervention (first term) and "leaning against the wind" intervention (second term). The weight attached to the "leaning against the wind" intervention is given by ω. Since we consider only sterilized intervention, i.e. interventions that do not affect the fundamentals, the loss function does not include other possible targets that the authorities might pursue, for example, inflation and output targets.

We can write the effect of the intervention on the exchange rate as follows:

$$s_t - s_t^* = \varphi_t(inv_t) \tag{23}$$

where $inv_t = \Delta X_t$ is the amount of intervention. Thus the monetary authorities affect the exchange rate by manipulating X_t. When $inv_t > 0$ the monetary authorities sell foreign assets, when $inv_t < 0$ they buy. φ_t represents the effect of the interventions on the exchange rate and it is determined by the non-linear transmission dynamics of the model. From the previous section we know that this transmission process is highly uncertain. It is also time dependent, i.e. the non-linear nature of the model ensures that the same sale (purchase) of foreign exchange has a different effect on the exchange rate depending on the exact timing of the intervention. We return to this time dependent transmission effect later.

Substituting equation (23) into equation (22) and minimizing the loss function with respect to inv_t yields the optimal amount of intervention:

$$inv_t^{opt} = -\frac{1}{(1 + \omega)\varphi_t}(s_{t-1} - s_t^*) \tag{24}$$

Given the uncertainty surrounding the transmission φ_t we further assume that the authorities take a conservative view, in the sense that they gradually adjust their optimal intervention policies. We represent this as follows:

$$\Delta inv_t = -\lambda(inv_{t-1} - inv_t^{opt})$$ (25)

where $0 < \lambda < 1$ represents the speed with which they adjust their interventions to the optimal one.

Substituting equation (25) in equation (24) we obtain after rearranging:

$$\Delta X_t = (1 - \lambda)\Delta X_{t-1} - \lambda\left(\frac{1}{(1 + \omega)\varphi_t}\right)(s_{t-1} - s_t^*)$$ (26)

It can be easily seen that this expression implies that the authorities intervene in the foreign exchange rate market based on a weighted average of present and past deviations of the exchange rate from its fundamental value.[12]

We further assume that the fundamentalists take into account the optimal intervention rule of the authorities in their expectations. As a result, the fundamentalists' forecasting rule can be rewritten as:

$$E_t^f(\Delta s_{t+1}) = -\psi\lambda\left(\frac{1}{(1 + \omega)\varphi_t}\right)(s_{t-1} - s_t^*)(s_t - s_t^*)^2$$ (27)

This implies that the mean reverting process that the fundamentalists have in their forecasting rule is reinforced by the intervention.

Note that we continue to assume that the chartists use only the information about past exchange rates to forecast the future. The fact that the monetary authorities intervene in the market does not change this assumption. One could criticize this and argue that the information about intervention is readily available. This criticism, however, holds for almost all fundamental information. Most of the information about fundamentals is readily available. For example, data on inflation rates and output growth are published regularly and can be collected at (close to) zero cost. The reason why some agents decide not to use that information has to do with the fact that they do now know (or do not find it worthwhile to investigate) what the effect is of changes in these fundamental variables on the exchange rate. For the same reason they do not use information on intervention activity because they find it difficult to evaluate the effect of official interventions on the exchange rate. It will turn out, however, that intervention affects the behaviour of the chartists in an indirect way, i.e. it changes the time pattern of the exchange rate movements, and thus the information set used by chartists.

10.1 Results of the model with intervention

In this section we present the results of the model when the monetary authorities intervene in the market. In order to do so we set a value of $\omega = 2$, which implies that the authorities attach a relatively large weight to the volatility term in the loss function. We have also estimated φ_t by simulating the effect of changes in the net foreign assets on the exchange rate. We applied the same shock in X_t in 200 consecutive time periods. We show the distribution in Figure 16.13. We then computed the mean effect, which is equal to approximately 0.2 for a shock of 1 unit in X_t.

It is striking to find that the effects of the same shock in X_t but applied in different periods are so different. It is important to note that this feature is related to the sensitivity to initial conditions of the model. It implies that the transmission of the shock is time dependent and highly uncertain. This result suggests that occasional interventions are unlikely to be effective. An occasional purchase or sale by the authorities has very unpredictable effects on the exchange rate. If intervention is to have an effect, it should be systematic, following a rule that is well-known in the market. The next step in the analysis consists of simulating the model using the optimal intervention rule derived in the previous section and the mean transmission effect φ_t. In Figure 16.14 we present some results in the form of a bifurcation diagram that relates the equilibrium exchange rate to different values of β.

This figure should be compared with Figure 16.2 which presents the bifurcation diagram in a pure floating exchange rate regime. The comparison leads to the following conclusions. First, in the non-chaotic domain,

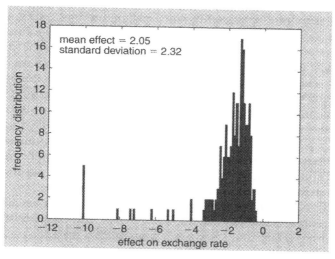

Figure 16.13 Frequency distribution of effect of an increase in net foreign assets on the exchange rate.

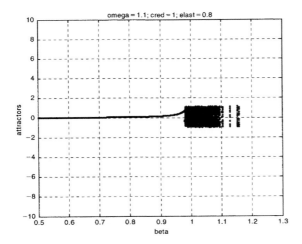

Figure 16.14 Bifurcation diagram with intervention.

i.e. for values of $\beta < 0.98$, the complexity of the solutions declines. More specifically, we observe that the fractured nature of the fixed-point solutions disappears. This also means that the sensitivity to initial conditions disappears. We show this in Figure 16.15 which presents the simulated exchange rates in the time domain. The two time series of the exchange rate only differ by a small initial shock of 0.1. Contrary to the floating exchange rate regime the slightly different initial conditions do not lead to divergent exchange rate movements when the authorities apply their optimal intervention rule.

Second, the chaotic domain is displaced to the right. In other words, intervention increases the range of parameters in which we obtain fixed point solutions. Third, in the chaotic domain the volatility of the exchange rate is dramatically reduced. Next we analysed how intervention affects the market structure, i.e. the share of fundamentalists and chartists in the market. We found that, as a result of intervention, the share of chartists in the market declines compared to the pure floating. We present this result in Figure 16.16 where we plotted the chartists' weight for different values of beta. Figure 16.16 should be compared with Figure 16.9 that represents the chartists' weight in a floating exchange rate environment.

These results suggest that by reducing the volatility of the exchange rate, foreign exchange market interventions reduce the profitability of the chartists' rule. Thus, the chartists' share in the market declines, which implies that the complexity of the exchange rate dynamics is also reduced.

A further result relates to the noise-to-signal ratio. As in the case of

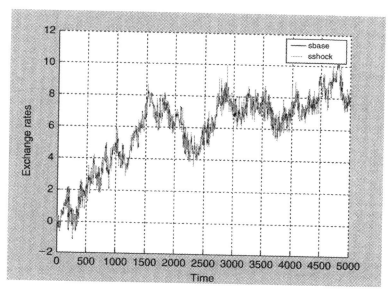

Figure 16.15 Sensitivity to initial conditions with intervention.

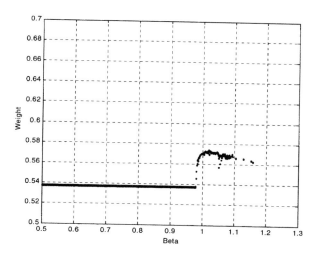

Figure 16.16 Chartists' weight for different values of the β with intervention.

pure floating we computed the noise-to-signal ratio when the authorities intervene in the foreign exchange market. Figure 16.17 shows the results and it should be compared with Figure 16.8. We observe that in both pure floating and intervention, the noise-to-signal ratio declines with the time horizon. However in the case of intervention the ratio drops dramatically.

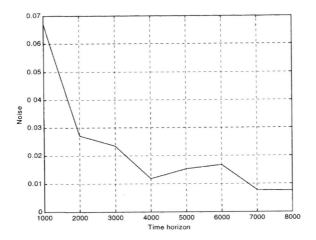

Figure 16.17 Noise-to-signal ratio with intervention.

This ratio now ranges between 0.07 and 0.01. The implication is that by intervening in the market the authorities are able to eliminate most of the noise produced by chartists.

From the previous analysis the following preliminary conclusion can be drawn. In a market where the interplay of chartists and fundamentalists creates a dynamic in which the exchange rate is disconnected from its fundamentals most of the time and in which the exchange rate movements are characterized by noise unrelated to fundamentals, there is scope for sterilized intervention in the foreign exchange markets. Thus even though the intervention does not affect the fundamentals it affects the structure of the market by making noise trading less profitable. In so doing, it strengthens the role of fundamentals and tightens the link between the exchange rate and the fundamentals. The condition for intervention to have these effects is that it should be systematic and performed according to a rule that the market (the fundamentalists) understands, whereby the target that the authorities pursue is common knowledge.

10.2 The effect of shocks in the fundamentals

Sterilized intervention, if successful, affects the structure of the foreign exchange market changing the composition of chartists and fundamentalists' forecasting activities. It also affects the structure of the economy in another way. In particular it affects the transmission mechanism of shocks in the fundamentals on the exchange rate. We show this by performing simulations whereby we introduce a permanent shock in the fundamental and analyse the effect on the exchange rate both in a situation of floating and of intervention. We show the results for a particular parameter configuration in Figures 16.18 and 16.19. The figures are constructed in the same way as Figure 16.5. The results are striking. In the case of floating we find the same result as the one discussed earlier, i.e. the shock in the fundamental has very unpredictable effects on the exchange rate (note that there is no stochastics in the model when this shock is performed). With

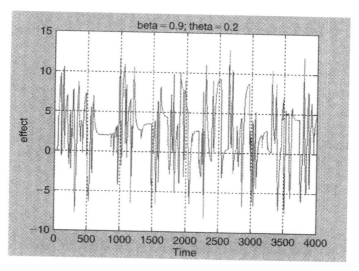

Figure 16.18 Effect of shock to fundamental exchange rate (floating regime).

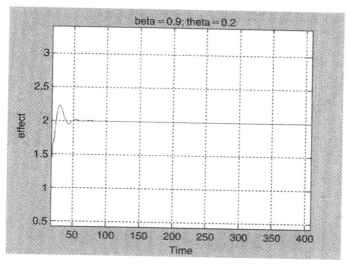

Figure 16.19 Effect of shock to fundamental exchange rate under intervention.

intervention we find that the same shock quickly leads to a perfectly predictable effect on the exchange rate. There is no complexity anymore. This result is related to the wider effect of intervention in that it reduces the chartist driven noise and the complex non-linearities that follow from the interaction of chartists and fundamentalists.

11 Is intervention sustainable?

An important issue relates to the sustainability of intervention policy. Put differently it is the question of whether the monetary authorities hold enough international reserves to use the kind of optimal intervention rules analysed in the previous sections. In order to analyse this issue we studied the behaviour of the stock of international reserves over time. We show an example in Figure 16.20, and we start with an initial stock of 1000. We did this for many other parameter configurations. A minimal condition for sustainability is that the stock of international reserves should be mean-reverting, i.e. the time series should not exhibit a unit root. If it does, we know that over time the stock of international reserves will be depleted or the country will own all the reserves of the world. We therefore performed an augmented Dickey–Fuller test on the simulated series of international reserves, with different numbers of lags. The results allow us to reject the hypothesis of a unit root.[13] This implies that there is a mean reverting process. Thus, the optimal intervention rule passes the necessary test of sustainability. This, of course, is not sufficient. It could still be that at some

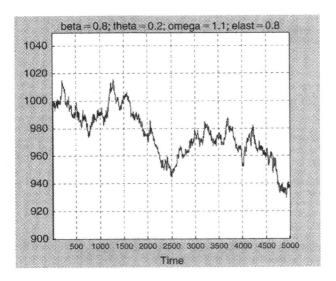

Figure 16.20 Stock of international reserves.

point the authorities face a constraint because the stock has dropped below a certain limit, even though this drop is temporary.

12 On the nature optimal intervention rules

In the previous section we showed that some (sterilized) intervention rules are capable of reducing the noise in the foreign exchange market and of keeping the exchange rate closer to its fundamental value than the free float regime does. In this section we analyse the nature of these successful rules further. We highlight two features of these rules. First, there should be some anchoring of the market's expectations. Second the rules should be applied gradually.

The importance of anchoring can be shown as follows. We analysed what would happen if the authorities would apply a pure "leaning against the wind" strategy. This means setting $\omega = 1$ in equation (22). In this case the authorities do not try to move the exchange rate towards its fundamental value, but are only concerned to reduce short-term volatility. We show a simulation result in Figure 16.21, in the form of a bifurcation diagram like Figure 16.14. It can be seen that this intervention rule does little to reduce the complexity of the exchange rate dynamics. Our interpretation is that a pure leaning against the wind strategy introduces a new time pattern of the exchange rates on which chartists can build their forecasting rules, thereby amplifying the actions of the monetary authorities. The mean reverting process is weakened compared to the intervention rules in which the authorities pursue a particular target for the exchange

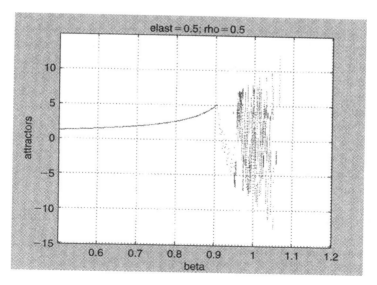

Figure 16.21 Bifurcation diagram (leaning against the wind intervention).

rate. Optimal intervention rules should also be applied in a gradual way. We experimented with intervention rules in which we eliminated gradualism by setting $\lambda = 1$ in equation (26). We found that such a rule quickly destabilizes the foreign exchange market. Thus, too much ambition by the monetary authorities aiming at quickly guiding the exchange rate to its fundamental rate should not be used, as it amplifies the volatility of the exchange rate compared to a free float regime.

13 Conclusion

In traditional exchange rate models in which the exchange rate always reflects present and future expected fundamentals, there is very little scope for interventions in the foreign exchange market. In these models interventions can be effective in only two cases. One is that the monetary authorities are willing to change their domestic policies thereby changing the time path of fundamentals. The second case is that the interventions signal a future change in policy. This analysis has greatly conditioned academic thinking on the subject leading to the view that sterilized interventions are an exercise in futility. The fact, however, is that most countries, which manage their exchange rates, use sterilized interventions and usually do not signal any future change of policy when they intervene in the market. Are these countries then acting foolishly?

We argued in this chapter that one needs more than a rational expectations, representative agents model to analyse interventions in the foreign exchange market. We developed a model with heterogeneity of beliefs about the future exchange rate. In such a model the exchange rate deviates from its fundamental rate most of the time. In addition, noise is created endogenously by the interaction of chartists (noise traders) and fundamentalists without any connection with the stochastic shocks in the fundamentals. Finally, in this model, periods of tranquillity and turbulence alternate unrelated to turbulence in the fundamentals. We showed that in the context of such a model, sterilized intervention can be quite effective in reducing the endogenous noise and in bringing the exchange rate closer to its fundamentals. This is achieved without this intervention signalling anything about the future fundamentals. The reason why this intervention can be quite effective is that it tends to reduce the noise generated by chartists' forecasting rules. As a result, it also reduces the profitability of chartists' forecasting rules and tends to drive out chartists from the market.

We also identified some conditions for this intervention to be effective. The first one is that it should be systematic. We found that occasional interventions do not work well, because the effect on the exchange rate of these occasional purchases and sales of foreign exchange are very unpredictable. Second, the authorities have to be transparent about the intervention rule they follow, in particular about the target exchange rate they pursue. This makes it possible for the fundamentalists to incorporate this rule in their expectations, thereby enhancing its effect. Third, pure leaning against the wind rules do not work well. The authorities need to pursue a target for the exchange rate. This has the effect of anchoring the expectations of the fundamentalists in the market, thereby increasing mean reversion in the exchange rate dynamics. Finally, the intervention rules should be applied gradually. When authorities intervene so as to bring the exchange rate too quickly towards its fundamental, they may actually destabilize the market.

There are several issues that were not solved in this chapter. The first has to do with the sustainability of the intervention rules analysed. We found that the stock of international reserves shows mean reversion when the authorities apply intervention. However, sufficiently large shocks may still lead to losses in international reserves that are large enough to make the interventions unsustainable. This possibility leads to the suggestion that these intervention rules would gain much in credibility when applied in a multilateral context.

A second unresolved problem has to do with the choice of the target exchange rate. We assumed that the authorities set the target exchange rate equal to the fundamental rate. Problems could arise if the authorities fail to select the right target exchange rate. We intend to pursue this matter in our future research.

Notes

* This chapter was prepared while the authors were visiting the Hong Kong Institute for Monetary Research during September 2002. The authors are grateful for the financial support and for the excellent research environment provided by the institute.
1 There are models (the portfolio balance models) that allow for the possibility of sterilized intervention to have an effect on the exchange rate. This comes from the fact that sterilized intervention changes the composition of portfolios and thus the risk premia. There is a consensus however that this effect is weak and cannot easily be exploited by the authorities (see Dominguez and Frankel 1993).
2 There is now a considerable amount of evidence to suggest that technical trading rules are profitable since they can earn significant excess returns in the foreign exchange market (see Taylor and Allen 1992; Neely and Weller 1999).
3 Such a specification is often found in discrete choice models (see, e.g. Brock and Hommes 1997, 1998).
4 In De Grauwe and Grimaldi (2002) we performed an extensive sensitivity analysis to check the robustness of the results.
5 In De Grauwe and Grimaldi (2002) we do a similar analysis varying other parameters.
6 Note that different initial conditions lead to different routes to the chaotic region.
7 Things are a little more complicated. When transactions costs are zero, we obtain non-zero fixed points. Since the fundamental exchange rate was

normalized at zero, this means that the market exchange rate is permanently different from the fundamental rate. Thus, in the steady state, the fundamentalists expect a constant appreciation (depreciation). However, because of the risk involved, fundamentalists do not act on this. The difference between the market rate and the fundamental rate can be considered to be a risk premium. Our model generates risk premia whose value depends on the initial conditions.

8 Note that this switching in and out of chaos depending on the initial conditions tends to disappear for sufficiently high values of β.

9 This result is similar to the one obtained by Malliaris and Stein (1999).

10 These results are maintained for different parameter configurations.

11 Another empirical regularity of the distribution of exchange returns is its symmetry. We computed the skewness, and we could not reject that the distribution is symmetric.

12 This can be seen by writing ΔX_{t-1} as a function of ΔX_{t-2} and $s_{t-1} - s_t^*$ as in equation (26) and then substituting. Repeating this procedure then leads to a weighted average of past misalignments.

13 ADF with a number of lags equal to three is -32.55. The autoregressive parameter on the stock of international reserves is 0.82.

References

Barro, R.J. (1974), "Are government bonds net wealth?", *Journal of Political Economy*, 82: 1095–1117.

Baxter, M. and Stockman, A. (1989), "Business cycles and the exchange rate regime: some international evidence", *Journal of Monetary Economics*, 23(May): 377–400.

Branson, W.H. (1983), "Macroeconomic determinants of real exchange risk", in Herring, R.J. (ed.), *Managing Foreign Exchange Risk*, Cambridge: Cambridge University Press.

Brock, W. and Hommes, C. (1997), "A rational route to randomness", *Econometrica*, 65: 1059–1095.

Brock, W. and Hommes, C. (1998), "Heterogeneous beliefs and routes to chaos in a simple asset pricing model", *Journal of Economic Dynamics and Control*, 22: 1235–1274.

Calvet, L. and Fisher, A. (2002), "Multifractality in asset returns: theory and evidence", *Review of Economics and Statistics*, 84: 381–406.

Calvo, G. and Reinhart, C. (2000), "Fear of floating", NBER Working Paper no. 7993, Cambridge, MA.

Cheung, Y. and Chinn, M. (1989), "Macroeconomic implications of beliefs and behaviour of foreign exchange traders", University of California, Santa Cruz, mimeo.

Cheung, Y., Lai, K. and Bergman, M. (2002), "Dissecting the PPP puzzle: the unconventional roles of nominal exchange rate and price adjustments", Paper presented at CES-Ifo Conference Munich 2002.

De Boeck, J. (2000), "The effect of macroeconomic 'news' on exchange rates: a structural VAR approach", University of Leuven, mimeo.

De Grauwe, P. and Grimaldi, M. (2002), "The exchange rate and its fundamentals: a chaotic perspective", CES-Ifo Discussion Paper no. 639.

de Vries, C. (2001), "Fat tails and the history of the guilder", *Tinbergen Magazine*, 4(Fall): 3–6.

Dominguez, K. and Frankel, J. (1993), "Does foreign exchange intervention matter: the portfolio effect", *American Economic Review*, 83(5): 1356–1369.

Dumas, B. (1992), "Dynamic equilibrium and the real exchange rate in a spatially separated world", *Review of Financial Studies*, 5(2): 153–180.

Eichengreen, B. and Hausmann, R. (1999), "Exchange rates and financial fragility", NBER Discussion Paper no. 7418, Cambridge, MA.

Flood, R. and Rose, A. (1995), "Fixing the exchange rate regime: a virtual quest for fundamentals", *Journal of Monetary Economics* 36(August): 3–37.

Goodhart, C. (1989), "News and the foreign exchange market", LSE Financial Markets Group Discussion Paper no. 71.

Goodhart, C. and Figliuoli, L. (1991), "Every minute counts in the foreign exchange markets", *Journal of International Money and Finance*, 10: 23–52.

Granger, C. (1994), "Is chaotic economic theory relevant for economists?", *Journal of International and Comparative Economics*, 3: 139–145.

Guillaume, D. (1996), "Chaos, randomness and order in the foreign exchange markets", PhD thesis, University of Leuven.

Huisman, R., Koedijk, K., Kool, C. and Palm, F. (2002), "The tail-fatness of FX returns reconsidered", *De Economist*, 150(3): 299–312.

Kilian, L. and Taylor, M. (2001), "Why is it so difficult to beat the random walk forecast of exchange rates?", University of Warwick, mimeo, p. 29.

Koedijk, K.G., Stork, P. and de Vries, C.G. (1992), "Foreign exchange regime differences viewed from the tails", *Journal of International Money and Finance*, 11: 462–473.

Le Baron, B. (1996), "Technical trading rule profitability and foreign exchange intervention", NBER Working Paper no. 5505.

Le Baron, B. (1999), "Technical trading rule profitability and foreign exchange intervention", *Journal of International Economics*, 49: 125–143.

Lux, T. (1998), "The socio-economic dynamics of speculative markets: interacting agents, chaos, and fat tails of return distributions", *Journal of Economic Behaviour and Organisation*, 33: 143–165.

Malliaris, A. and Stein, J. (1999), "Methodological issues in asset pricing: random walk or chaotic dynamics", *Journal of Banking and Finance*, 23: 1605–1635.

Mandelbrot, B. (1963), "The variation of certain speculative prices", *Journal of Business*, 394–416.

McKinnon, R. and Schnabl, G. (2002), "Synchronized business cycles in East Asia: fluctuations of the yen/dollar exchange rate and China's stabilizing role", IMES Discussion Paper Series no. 2002-E-13, Institute for Monetary and Economic Studies, Bank of Japan.

Meese, R. and Rogoff, K. (1983), "Empirical exchange rate models of the seventies: Do they fit out of sample?", *Journal of International Economics*, 14: 3–24.

Michael, P., Nobay, R. and Peel, A. (1997), "Transaction costs and non-linear adjustment in real exchange rates: an empirical investigation", *Journal of Political Economy*, 105(4): 862–879.

Mussa, M. (1981), "The role of official intervention", New York: Group of Thirty.

Neely, C.J. and Weller, P.A. (1999), "Technical trading rules in the European Monetary System", *Journal of International Money and Finance*, 18: 429–458.

Neely, C.J. and Weller, P.A. (2001), "Technical analysis and central bank intervention", *Journal of International Money and Finance*, 20: 949–970.

Obstfeld, M. and Rogoff, K. (2000), "The six major puzzles in international macro-economics: Is there a common cause?", NBER Working Paper no. 7777, July.

Sarno, L. and Taylor, M. (2001), "Official intervention in the foreign exchange market: Is it effective and if so, how does it work?", *Journal of Economic Literature*, 39(3): 839–869.

Schittenkopf, C., Dorffner, G. and Dockner, E. (2001), "On nonlinear, stochastic dynamics in economics and financial time series", *Studies in Nonlinear Dynamics and Econometrics*, 4(3): 101–121.

Sercu, P., Uppal, R. and Van Hulle, C. (1995), "The exchange rate in the presence of transaction costs: implications for tests of purchasing power parity", *Journal of Finance*, 50: 1309–1319.

Taylor, M. and Allen, H. (1992), "The use of technical analysis in the foreign exchange market", *Journal of International Money and Finance*, 11: 304–314.

Taylor, M., Peel, D. and Sarno, L. (2001), "Non-linear mean reversion in real exchange rates: towards a solution to the purchasing power parity puzzles", CEPR Discussion Paper no. 2658.

Wei, S.-J. and Kim, J. (1997), "The big players in the foreign exchange market: Do they trade on information or noise?", NBER Working Paper no. 6256.

Williamson, J. (1985), "The exchange rate system", *Policy Analyses in International Economics*, Washington, DC: Institute for International Economics.

17 Exchange rates, capital flows and policy

Some concluding observations

Rebecca Driver, Peter Sinclair and Christoph Thoenissen

Four main themes run through this volume. They are best posed as the questions:

- How much emphasis should be placed on the exchange rate when setting policy?
- What is the success, or otherwise, of different approaches to modelling exchange rates?
- What determines capital flows and their impact?
- What should policy makers do about monetary policy and capital flows?

These themes are linked. The choices of exchange rate, capital mobility and monetary policies cannot be fully independent of each other. Even a country pursuing an independent monetary policy, with no desire to intervene in the foreign exchange market, cannot afford to ignore exchange rate movements when setting monetary policy. This is because of their inflationary impact. The size and direction of the inflationary impact will clearly be influenced by the shock that has caused the exchange rate to move. An exchange rate change reflecting revised expectations of future productivity levels may have very different inflationary implications from those of a change due to a shift in consumer preferences for different goods, for example. Understanding why and how exchange rates move will therefore still be important. For a given shock, the extent of exchange rate movements will also be determined by the constraints placed on capital mobility, because of the links between exchange rates and capital flows. A decision to limit capital flows will implicitly be linked to the costs and benefits of such flows. This means that policy makers need to decide on their overall policy framework in a systematic way.

Let us start with the question of what role does the exchange rate play within the economy, as understanding this will partly determine the question of what policy should be. Most simple models depict the exchange rate as an equilibrating mechanism, which acts to reconcile demand and supply for different goods, factors of production and money across the world economy. Which of these factors is given prominence within the model varies depending on the framework chosen, but implicitly (if not always explicitly) equilibrium, means equilibrium in all these markets.

For example, consider nominal exchange rates, which are monetary variables. They represent the price of one country's currency in terms of another's. So both money demand and money supply are critically important. Money demand falls when local nominal interest rates go up. If A's authorities let its monetary aggregates rise persistently faster than B's, this should ultimately be registered one for one, all else equal, in a downward trend for A's nominal exchange rate against B. The long run levels of nominal exchange rates, like all other nominal variables, are inextricably linked to monetary policy (with direction of causation governed by the policy regime in force). A nominal interest rate differential between a pair of countries should eventually match the gap in their inflation rates and it is these inflation rates which link nominal and real exchange rates. However, monetary policy can exert very little, if any, influence on real variables (such as real exchange rates or output) in the long run, because nominal prices must sooner or later fully adjust to ensure real equilibrium occurs. Therefore the real exchange rates linked to a given nominal exchange rate will be determined elsewhere, by the demand for goods and factors of production that comes from the process of optimisation by households and firms. The chapter by Rebecca Driver and Peter West-away explores how different concepts of exchange rate equilibrium are linked in much greater detail.

One of the ways that equilibrium is achieved is through arbitrage. If prices differ across markets then arbitrage opportunities will occur, causing agents either to switch suppliers or to switch to alternatives. The evidence suggests that, at least within goods markets, arbitrage opportunities are not fully eliminated as the law of one price does not appear to hold. For example, Haskel and Wolf (2001) look at the prices of goods sold by a single retailer across different markets and shows that significant variation in relative prices occurs. This point is reinforced by Charles Engel, John Rogers and Shing-Yi Wang in this book, who use actual price data for different goods from multiple retailers in Canadian and US cities to show that prices are not equalised and that border effects are real and cannot fully be accounted for by distance or relative population sizes.

However, just because arbitrage in goods markets is not perfect, does not imply that some expenditure switching will not have occurred and the extent of these effects can have important implications for policy. The chapters by Ozge Senay and Alan Sutherland, and by Douglas Hostland and Lawrence Schembri both pick up on expenditure switching as an important mechanism for determining economic outcomes. For example Senay and Sutherland highlight the fact that the welfare implications of fixed versus floating exchange rate policies will depend on the degree of expenditure switching, with fixed regimes performing relatively well when expenditure switching is strong. Hostland and Schembri look at the sustainability of a country's debt and what determines its vulnerability to shocks. Most of the work by the IMF on sustainability has highlighted the import compression channel, whereby improvements in the trade balance are obtained by reducing aggregate demand. In contrast, Hostland and Schembri suggest that expenditure switching may also be important, with an increase in the degree of expenditure switching being associated with a reduction in concern about the sustainability of a given level of debt.

Of course regardless of whether changes in the exchange rate induce expenditure switching, it might still be the case that movements in the exchange rate itself are unconnected to macroeconomic fundamentals. Indeed, one of the problems facing exchange rate economists is their inability to forecast the exchange rate using macroeconomic variables. After over twenty years, the somewhat depressing result in Meese and Rogoff (1983), namely that exchange rate models based on macroeconomic fundamentals are unable to outperform a simple forecast of no change in the exchange rate, has gone mostly unchallenged. Two of the chapters in this book discuss factors in addition to macroeconomic variables, which may help explain exchange rates. They stem from two observations, first that market participants are heterogeneous and second that asset markets are risky. Market participants can never know what an asset price will be at any future date and their mean forecasts tend to vary between each other. Traders are heterogeneous in their information, objectives and behaviour. Yet we observe what looks like a market equilibrium, together with large, if volatile, volumes of trade in assets. This suggests risks matter: asset prices should be sensitive to the risks these traders perceive.

Paul de Grauwe and Marianna Grimaldi propose a model that highlights the importance of agent heterogeneity in determining exchange rates. They distinguish between two types of agent: short-term chartists, who do not look at macroeconomic fundamentals in their analysis of foreign exchange markets; and long-term fundamentalists who do. The proportions of these two types of agents within the foreign exchange market, and hence how closely exchange rates are related to fundamentals, will be determined by the relative profitability of their trading strategies.

Peter Smith, Steffen Sorensen and Mike Wickens explore the role of risk in the determination of exchange rates. Their contribution to this volume examines the implications of stochastic discount factor theory, which suggest that arbitrage opportunities should be eliminated within asset markets and that the price of risk should be equalised across markets. Their results suggest that asset markets are not fully integrated and that, for the UK at least, the risk premium in the foreign exchange market is more variable than the equity risk premium.

All this implies that, at least in the short term, the exchange rate may be acting as a source of noise, rather than a shock absorber. Duarte (2003) notes that the move from a floating to a fixed exchange rate regime leads to a dramatic reduction in the variability of the real exchange rate, but to no systematic change in the variability of other macroeconomic variables. In other words that the variability of the exchange rate under floating regimes does not appear to yield benefits in terms of a reduction in the variability of other variables. To put it another way, if exchange rates are noisy it is not because they are responding to macroeconomic news. This would also be compatible with the limited and very short-lived impact that the surprise component of macroeconomic announcements have on exchange rates; see, for example, Andersen *et al.* (2003) and Faust *et al.* (2003).

Part of the explanation for this may be pricing behaviour, namely the existence of local currency pricing. If producers have a degree of market power then they may be in a position to set different prices in different markets. Indeed the results in the chapter by Engel, Rogers and Wang suggests that this does indeed happen. As well as the price charged, producers also have a choice of which currency to set prices in: their own (often referred to as producer currency pricing), or the buyers' (so-called local currency pricing). This choice will be one of the key determinants of the transmission mechanism following exchange rate changes. In the case of producer currency pricing, exchange rate pass-through will be complete. In contrast, local currency pricing will act to reduce the degree of exchange rate pass-through, or the extent to which relative prices change following exchange rate changes. Consumers therefore may not observe any price signals, so that the degree of expenditure switching will be reduced. Instead exchange rate changes will influence consumers via a more indirect channel, namely the profitability of firms who will find the relative profitability of selling in different markets has changed. Clearly the choice of pricing policy is an important determinant of the transmission mechanism. Of the two chapters which explicitly consider firms' pricing rules, one, by Senay and Sutherland, uses producer currency pricing in its exploration of the importance of the expenditure switching channel, while the second, by Christoph Thoenissen, assumes local currency pricing. What determines firms' pricing policies is itself complex, as Bacchetta and van Wincoop (2004) show, and in reality different firms may be pursuing different pricing policies simultaneously. Which of these two pricing strategies dominates in practice is still an open question.

The extent to which exchange rates act simply as a source of noise will be one of the factors that will determine the optimal exchange rate policy. Of course there are many other influences as well. The chapters by Barry Eichengreen, by Senay and Sutherland and by Hostland and Schembri all consider some of the costs and benefits of choosing a fixed versus a floating regime. Eichengreen looks at how exchange rate movements under floating exchange rates may undermine the success of inflation targeters.

In contrast, Hostland and Schembri suggest that floating exchange rates may ease the constraints on policy makers, by improving the sustainability of a given level of external debt. Senay and Sutherland use explicit welfare analysis to show how key features of the economy, such as the degree of expenditure switching, may have a big influence on the relative benefits of fixed versus floating regimes.

In practice, such costs and benefits may well not be clear cut, often encouraging policy markers to attempt to keep a foot in both camps. One element of this is the 'fear of floating' discussed in Calvo and Reinhart (2002). The importance of such hedging behaviour in practice is discussed within this volume in the chapters by Rodrigo Caputo and Izumi Takagawa, among others. In some cases this hedging is very explicit: the cases discussed by Takagawa are those of countries who try both to peg their exchange rate at the same time as pursuing independent monetary policies. In other cases, such as the one examined by Caputo, it is more subtle.

Caputo analyses the evolution of monetary policy in Chile from the 1980s and charts how the central bank's reaction function evolved. In 1990, Chile became an explicit inflation targeter, but it was only in 1999 that it abandoned an explicit band for exchange rate movements. However, if anything, the use of interest rates to correct exchange rate misalignments became more aggressive following the move to floating exchange rates. The existence of an inflation target in Chile certainly does not imply official indifference to the value of the nominal exchange rate. Part of the explanation may be that the Chilean central bank's reaction function appears to be non-linear, with proportionately greater weight placed on larger real exchange rate deviations than smaller ones.

The broader question to which Chile's experience relates is whether inflation targets are appropriate – or even feasible – for developing countries or whether they should place more emphasis on exchange rates. Eichengreen poses this question head on: Can emerging countries' central banks target inflation successfully? The answer is that inflation targeting is not inherently impossible, but rendered harder for them, as a result of their greater openness, the extent of their (unhedged) dollar liabilities, and their relative lack of credibility. If the risks of serious adverse shocks, and the knock-on effects of exchange rate swings on balance sheets, are both large, a hard peg may well make more sense.

External liabilities, whether dollarised or not, form the central issue in the contribution by Hostland and Schembri. They ask what governs the *ex ante* sustainability of these external debts. The answer is that sustainability depends upon the economy's ability to adjust to adverse external shocks. This improves with increases in the extent of nominal exchange rate flexibility, trade openness, trade elasticities, exchange rate pass-through, the proportion of external debt in domestic currency and the degree to which monetary policy aims at steady low inflation. The chapter by Philip Lane looks at some additional features such as demographics and public debt which may account for some of the observed patterns in gross and net external asset positions. One key point that can reconcile Hostland and Schembri's conclusions on the desirability of floating exchange rates with Eichengreen's is that the level of external debt, particularly foreign currency denominated debt, is crucial. An open emerging economy can keep operating an inflation targeting regime with relatively free floating successfully, under suitable conditions, so long as these debts are low enough. Too much outside debt, public or private, will imperil any monetary policy regime that attempts to secure price stability.

Eichengreen notes that inflation targeting is difficult in emerging markets in part because of problems stemming from large swings in exchange rates. In practice, of course, an alternative policy of maintaining a fixed exchange rate is also not always easy. Two of the chapters in the book look at a particular case study, Argentina, to try and understand the causes of the collapse of the Argentine currency board. Kalin Hristov, looks to see whether the Argentine peso was very overvalued compared to medium-term fundamentals, using a method of calculating equilibrium exchange rates known as fundamental equilibrium exchange rates (or FEERs). Although Hristov finds some evidence of overvaluation, the level of overvaluation at the end of 2001 was by no means excessive and indeed was smaller than the estimated overvaluation for Estonia, a currency board that has survived. This suggests that Argentina's problems may have been more short term in nature, which would be compatible with the suggestion in the chapter by Driver and Westaway that the equilibrium exchange rate for a given point in time may differ depending on the time horizon of interest. If macroeconomic fundamentals themselves have not stabilised to their equilibrium level, then the exchange rate that will minimise the costs of being out of equilibrium will differ from the exchange rate that would reconcile supply and demand if all macroeconomic fundamentals had been at their equilibrium or trend levels.

The chapter by Paul Hallwood, Ian Marsh and Jörg Scheibe takes a different approach to assessing the causes of the collapse of Argentina's currency board. Instead of assessing the pressure on the exchange rate itself, Hallwood, Marsh and Scheibe look at the shocks hitting the Argentine economy, to see whether they differed significantly from those hitting the US. They find that, compared to the US, for much of the period from the mid-1990s Argentina experienced a series of large, positive permanent shocks (which can loosely be thought of as supply shocks). Within the FEER framework, such positive supply shocks would require a depreciation of the FEER relative to its original path to allow demand and supply to be reconciled, and permit the world market for Argentina's increased exports to clear. The results in Hristov are suggestive that this happened, as from the mid-1990s the rate of appreciation of the Argentine FEER slowed and indeed, for part of the period the FEER even depreciated. Although the cumulated differential of permanent shocks for Argentina and the US identified in Hallwood, Marsh and Scheibe remained positive even at the end of their sample period (2001Q4), this cumulated position had declined dramatically to almost zero in the last two quarters, following two large (greater than 2 per cent) negative permanent shocks in Argentina. This suggests that, contrary to the analysis in Hristov, it may have been medium-term factors that mattered. However, it is worth noting two things. First, the Argentine FEER calculated by Hristov appreciated sharply at the very end of the sample period, which would be compatible with a deteriorating supply potential. Second in contrast to Argentina's previous experience of large permanent shocks, the results in Hallwood, Marsh and Scheibe show that there were no offsetting temporary shocks. Indeed their analysis suggests that in 2001Q3 Argentina experienced an unusually large negative temporary shock as well as a large negative permanent shock. This suggests a way of reconciling the findings of Hristov and of Hallwood, Marsh and Scheibe.

An alternative episode of fixed, or at least pegged, exchange rates investigated in this book was that of several East Asian regimes in the 1990s. Unlike Argentina, however, which by adopting a currency board abandoned the possibility of an independent monetary policy, the East Asian regimes attempted to have both, while still allowing capital mobility, the so-called 'impossible trinity'. The chapter by Takagawa explores the experiences of seven East Asian countries: Hong Kong, Indonesia, Malaysia, Philippines, Singapore, South Korea and Thailand. The results suggest that before the 1997 crisis, these countries appeared to be able to attain the 'impossible trinity'. Sterilised intervention worked for a while, allowing independent monetary policy, fixed exchange rates and capital mobility to coexist in the period before the Asian crisis. However, ultimately this proved unsustainable, suggesting that the apparent success of East Asian economies in achieving the 'impossible trinity' may have been due to the benign nature of the shocks hitting the system before 1997.

The contribution by Byung Han Seo examines the South Korean experience and the role of sterilised intervention in greater detail, noting that monetary policy and exchange rate policy can only be completely independent if foreign exchange intervention is sterilised in the long run. His examination of the record of Korean monetary data reveals that official trading to limit the impact of reserve inflows on monetary aggregates achieved nearly 100 per cent sterilisation in the short term. However, the success of sterilisation in the long term appears much lower. Sterilised intervention triggered growing financial disintermediation, and created gaps between domestic and overseas interest rates.

National authorities intervene in foreign exchange markets for many reasons, not just to fix the exchange rate. Even clean-floating, inflation-targeting central banks, such as Australia's, will occasionally intervene to dampen volatility. De Grauwe and Grimaldi assess the role for official intervention to help reduce the level of noise in a market with heterogeneous agents. They argue that intervention can be effective. If it works, it does so by reducing the profitability, and hence the volume, of noise trading by the chartists. To work, intervention needs to be systematic, transparent, gradual and based upon deviations from long-term equilibrium as identified by the fundamentalists.

Ultimately, the success of intervention will depend on many things: Sarno and Taylor (2001) provide a general survey of the different channels and effectiveness of official exchange rate intervention. One factor influencing the success of intervention is the substitutability of assets, and hence the size of any portfolio effects coming from changes in relative asset stocks. The results in the chapter by Smith, Sorensen and Wickens in this volume suggest that risks are not equalised across markets. This means that different assets will not be perfect substitutes. The findings by Lane are also suggestive of a portfolio balance channel, with increased levels of external debt leading to rising interest rates. Limited substitutability of assets and the existence of portfolio effects in turn suggest that even sterilised intervention could potentially be effective. Yet even if assets are perfect substitutes, intervention may still have some impact through signalling. The signals that market participants extract from exchange rate intervention may in practice be quite complex. For example, Seo notes that if the ability of the central bank to sterilise intervention differs between the short and the long term then this divergence will contain information about future central bank behaviour that will influence agents' expectations.

One of the implications of intervention, whether sterilised or not, is that it works by changing countries' net foreign asset positions. Therefore, the alternative might be instead to limit capital mobility directly. There are many different ways to limit capital mobility and the exact choice of policy will determine both how successful it is at achieving its goals and minimising the associated costs, as well as the general macroeconomic consequences. For example, Forbes (2003) looks at a single episode of capital controls, the Chilean *encaje* which acted to limit capital inflows and was generally viewed as a success. The results in Forbes (2003) suggest that one of the consequences of the *encaje* was that access to capital became harder for small firms compared to large firms, in part because there were fewer options available for small firms to circumvent the controls. In an economy that is very reliant on small firms, such controls might therefore be unsuitable. This suggests that macroeconomic structure may be an important determinant of any decision to implement capital controls. This idea underlies much of the argument in the chapter by Dan Huynh and Peter Sinclair, which considers some of the macroeconomic features which are most often associated with capital controls from an historical perspective, as well as the rationale for the observed patterns.

Part of the decision about whether to limit capital flows will depend on both their causes and consequences. In addition to the chapters by Eichengreen and Hostland and Schembri, this theme is explored in depth in the contributions by Lane and Thoenissen, and touched upon by many others. There are profound differences between a world of financial autarky (capital accounts always balanced, with zero entries) and one where capital is internationally mobile.

When real interest rates are common across countries, in the long run it matters little for the capital stock whether governments permit international capital movements or not (setting aside the insurance gains from international portfolio diversification which are potentially very significant, if not fully exploited). However, if A has borrowed from B in the past, the cost of servicing these debts implies that A will run a trade surplus in the long run and B a deficit. With GNP below GDP in A (and the opposite in B), non-traded goods, if normal, should be a little cheaper against traded goods in A, and dearer in B. If the two countries are large, there is some tendency for the debtor country's terms of trade to be lower, and B's higher, than they would have been in the absence of cross-country claims. So this year's capital movements carry implications for real exchange rates later on. In other words, nonzero net foreign asset positions give rise to a transfer problem, and this is discussed in Lane's contribution to this book.

However, nonzero net foreign asset positions may have macroeconomic consequences which lead to asymmetric behaviour, over and above their implications for the long run terms of trade (the transfer problem). Kraay and Ventura (2000) discuss one such aspect, namely that the current account response to temporary shocks will be affected by existing portfolio allocations, assuming investment risk is high and diminishing returns are weak. Under these circumstances the marginal unit of wealth arising from a positive transitory shock will be allocated in line with existing portfolio choices rather than being invested solely in foreign assets as more traditional approaches suggest. Temporary shocks will therefore simply lead to portfolio growth, while permanent shocks will cause portfolio rebalancing.

The chapter by Thoenissen also explores asymmetries in the behaviour of the current account which depend on the sign of net foreign assets. Instead of focusing on differences in the impact of permanent and temporary shocks, Thoenissen examines the implications of shocks to preferences, monetary policy and productivity. He shows that for asymmetric shocks to monetary policy and productivity the correlation between the real exchange rate and the current account will depend crucially on the sign of net foreign assets. Only in the case of preference shocks is the sign of the correlation between the real exchange rate and the current account unaffected by the net foreign asset position. Clearly exchange rates and capital flows are linked in interesting and complex ways, which brings us full circle to the question with which this concluding chapter began: What determines exchange rates?

Life in an open economy is complicated, particularly for policy makers who need to think about how to treat exchange rates and capital flows.

Inevitably the answers will depend on a whole host of supplementary questions. For example if they seek to control the exchange rate directly, what are the costs of doing so and how effective are the instruments available to them? Will a policy of controlling the exchange rate prove sustainable and can they influence the likelihood that it will be? If, instead, they allow the exchange rate to float, how much attention should they pay to movements in the exchange rate? Will their exchange rate policy conflict with other policy goals? Is their understanding of the exchange rate good enough to provide useful guidance on what is causing it to move and therefore what the consequences will be? What will be the impact of capital flows and will changes in a country's holdings of gross and net foreign assets alter the structure of the economy and the optimal policy set up in important ways? Can they and should they limit capital mobility? The chapters within this book throw much light on these questions. However, given the diversity of the world economy, it should be no surprise that no simple one-size-fits-all answer emerges from this book. The hope is instead that it will have helped to illustrate some of the reasons why diversity is both inevitable and desirable, and to contribute towards a greater understanding of how an open economy really works in practice.

References

Andersen, T.G., Bollerslev, T., Diebold, F.X. and Vega, C. (2003), 'Micro effects of macro announcements: real time price discovery in foreign exchange', *American Economic Review*, 93: 38–62.

Bacchetta, P. and van Wincoop, E. (2004), 'A theory of the currency denomination of international trade', *Journal of International Economics*, forthcoming.

Calvo, G. and Reinhart, C. (2002), 'Fear of floating', *Quarterly Journal of Economics*, 177: 379–408.

Duarte, M. (2003), 'Why don't macroeconomic quantities respond to exchange rate variability?', *Journal of Monetary Economics*, 50: 889–913.

Faust, J., Rogers, J.H., Wang, S.-Y.B. and Wright, J.H. (2003), 'The high-frequency response of exchange rates and interest rates to macroeconomic announcements', Federal Reserve Board, International Finance Discussion Paper no. 784.

Forbes, K.J. (2003), 'One cost of the Chilean capital controls: increased financial constraints for smaller firms', NBER Working Paper, no. 9777.

Haskel, J. and Wolfe, H. (2001), 'The law of one price: a case study', *Scandinavian Journal of Economics*, 103: 545–558.

Kraay, A. and Ventura, J. (2000), 'Current accounts in debtor and creditor countries', *Quarterly Journal of Economics*, 115: 1137–1166.

Meese, R. and Rogoff, K. (1983), 'Empirical exchange rate models of the seventies: Do they fit out of sample?', *Journal of International Economics*, 14: 3–24.

Sarno, L. and Taylor, M.P. (2001), 'Official intervention in the foreign exchange market: Is it effective and, if so, how does it work?', *Journal of Economic Literature*, 39: 839–868.

Index

For Product Safety Concerns and Information please contact our EU
representative GPSR@taylorandfrancis.com Taylor & Francis Verlag GmbH,
Kaufingerstraße 24, 80331 München, Germany

Printed and bound by CPI Group (UK) Ltd, Croydon, CR0 4YY
08/05/2025
01864346-0001